A Witch's Printing Office

STORY
MOCHINCHI

ART
YASUHIRO MIYAMA

✦

ORIGINAL COVER DESIGN
SAVA DESIGN

COVER PAINTING
SIOKOJI

EDITOR IN CHARGE
KENTARO OGINO

EDITORIAL ASSISTANT
YUSUKE KATO

A WITCH'S PRINTING OFFICE

6

story **Mochinchi** *art* **Yasuhiro Miyama**

TRANSLATION: AMBER TAMOSAITIS
LETTERING: ERIN HICKMAN

MAHOTSUKAI NO INSATSUJO Vol. 6
©Mochinchi, Yasuhiro Miyama 2021
First published in Japan in 2021 by KADOKAWA CORPORATION, Tokyo.
English translation rights arranged with KADOKAWA CORPORATION, Tokyo
through Tuttle-Mori Agency, Inc., Tokyo.

Yen Press
150 West 30th Street, 19th Floor
New York, NY 10001

Visit us at yenpress.com
facebook.com/yenpress
twitter.com/yenpress
yenpress.tumblr.com
instagram.com/yenpress

First Yen Press Edition: June 2022
Edited by Yen Press Editorial: Carl Li
Designed by Yen Pess Design: Liz Parlett, Wendy Chan

Yen Press is an imprint of Yen Press, LLC.
The Yen Press name and logo are trademarks of Yen Press, LLC.

Library of Congress Control Number: 2019947774

ISBNs: 978-1-9753-4462-7 (paperback)
978-1-9753-4463-4 (ebook)

10 9 8 7 6 5 4 3 2 1

WOR

Printed in the United States of America

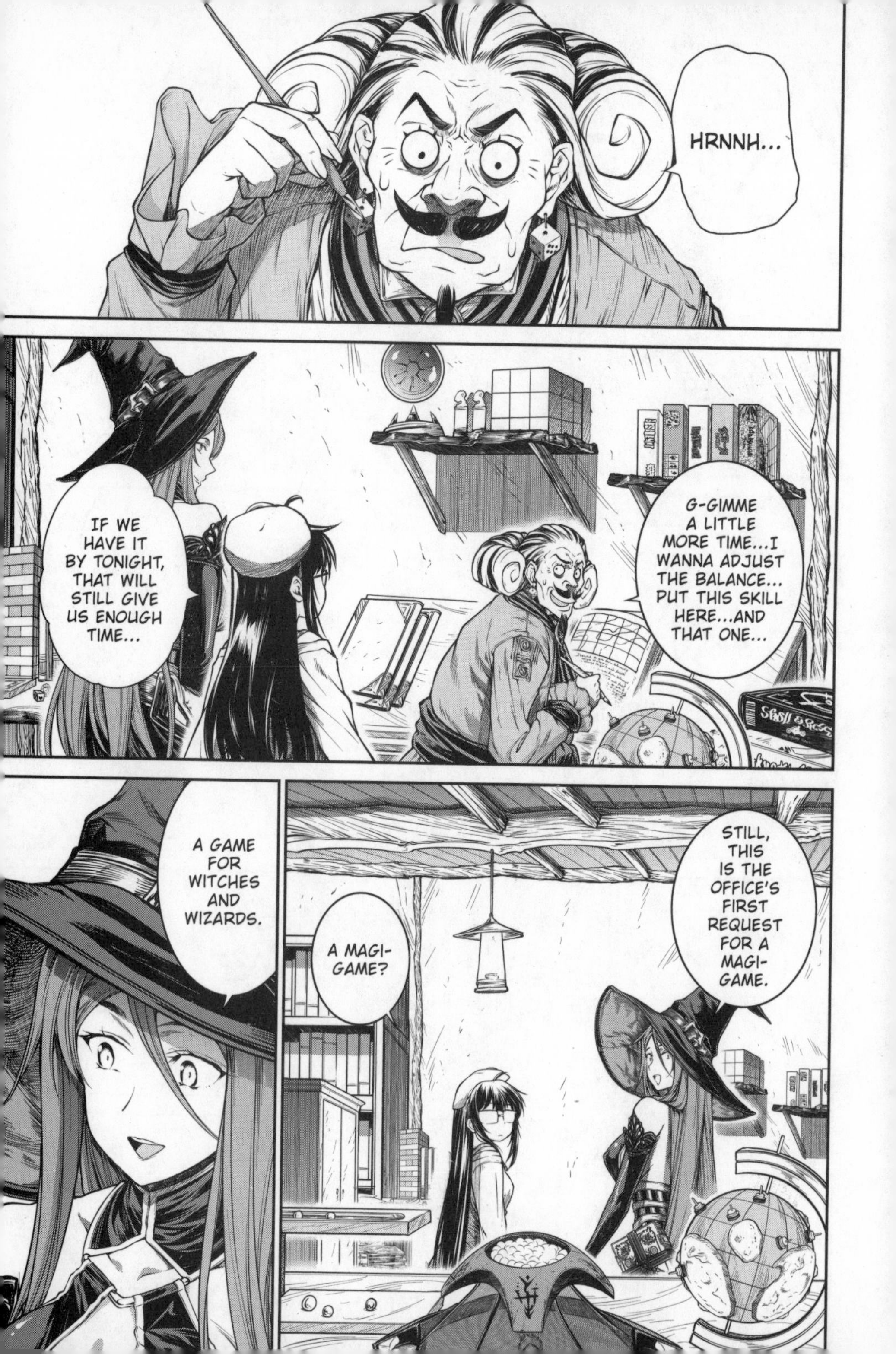
HRNNH...
G-GIMME A LITTLE MORE TIME...I WANNA ADJUST THE BALANCE... PUT THIS SKILL HERE...AND THAT ONE...
IF WE HAVE IT BY TONIGHT, THAT WILL STILL GIVE US ENOUGH TIME...
STILL, THIS IS THE OFFICE'S FIRST REQUEST FOR A MAGI-GAME.
A MAGI-GAME?
A GAME FOR WITCHES AND WIZARDS.

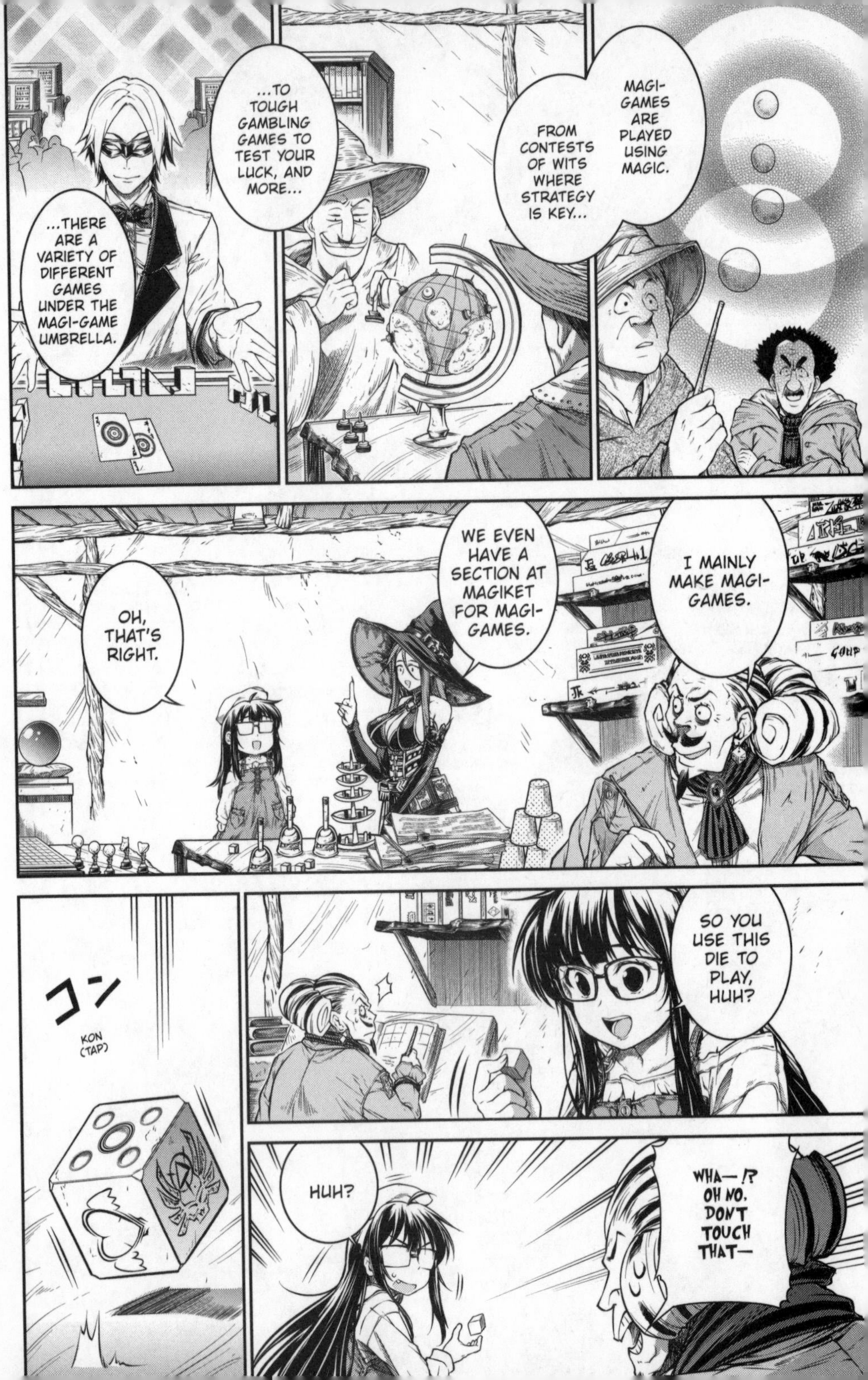
MAGI-GAMES ARE PLAYED USING MAGIC.
FROM CONTESTS OF WITS WHERE STRATEGY IS KEY...
...TO TOUGH GAMBLING GAMES TO TEST YOUR LUCK, AND MORE...
...THERE ARE A VARIETY OF DIFFERENT GAMES UNDER THE MAGI-GAME UMBRELLA.
I MAINLY MAKE MAGI-GAMES.
WE EVEN HAVE A SECTION AT MAGIKET FOR MAGI-GAMES.
OH, THAT'S RIGHT.
SO YOU USE THIS DIE TO PLAY, HUH?
WHA—!? OH NO. DON'T TOUCH THAT—
HUH?
コン
KON (TAP)

Chapter 32

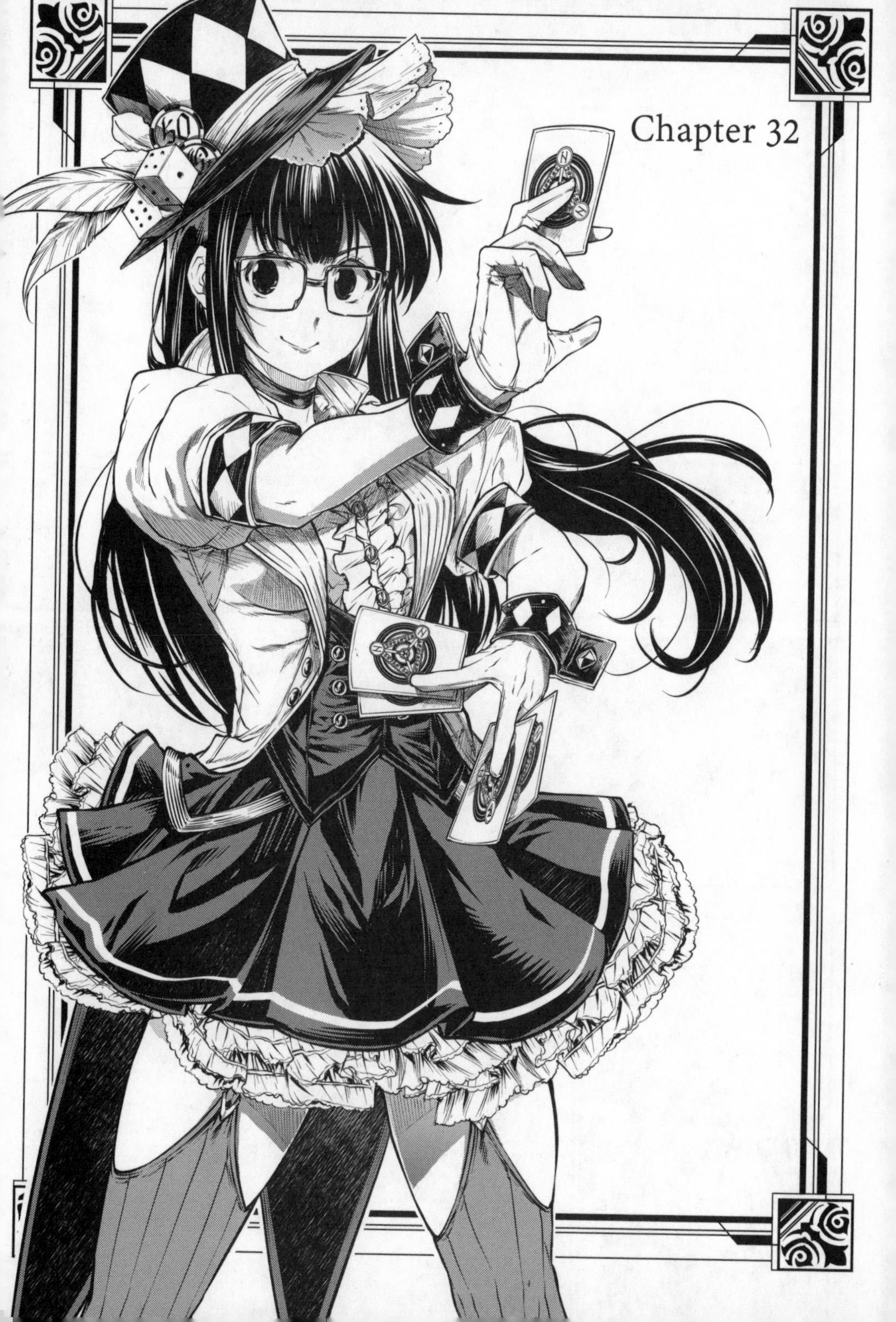

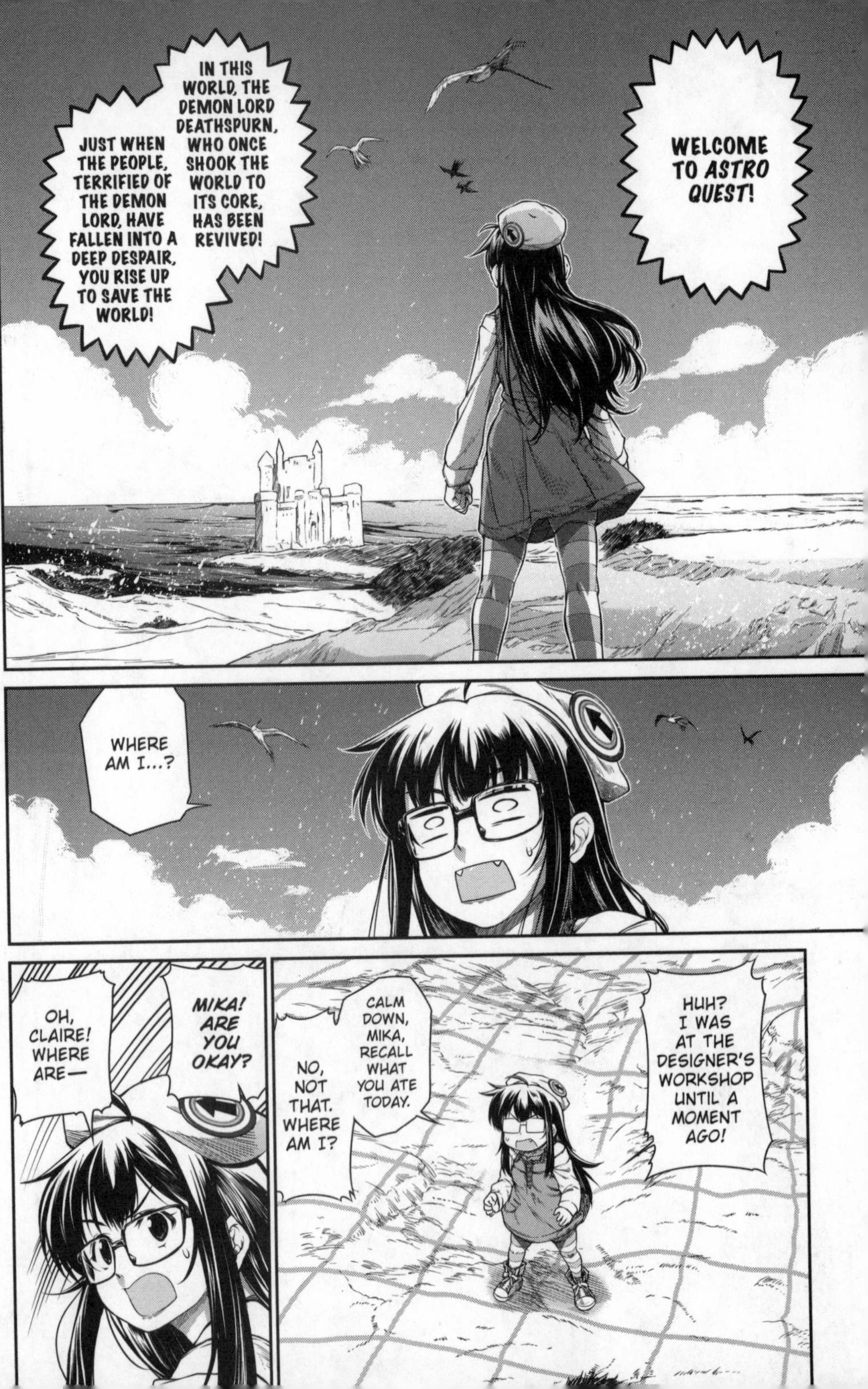
WELCOME TO *ASTRO QUEST!*
IN THIS WORLD, THE DEMON LORD DEATHSPURN, WHO ONCE SHOOK THE WORLD TO ITS CORE, HAS BEEN REVIVED!
JUST WHEN THE PEOPLE, TERRIFIED OF THE DEMON LORD, HAVE FALLEN INTO A DEEP DESPAIR, YOU RISE UP TO SAVE THE WORLD!
WHERE AM I...?
HUH? I WAS AT THE DESIGNER'S WORKSHOP UNTIL A MOMENT AGO!
CALM DOWN, MIKA, RECALL WHAT YOU ATE TODAY.
NO, NOT THAT. WHERE AM I?
MIKA! ARE YOU OKAY?
OH, CLAIRE! WHERE ARE—

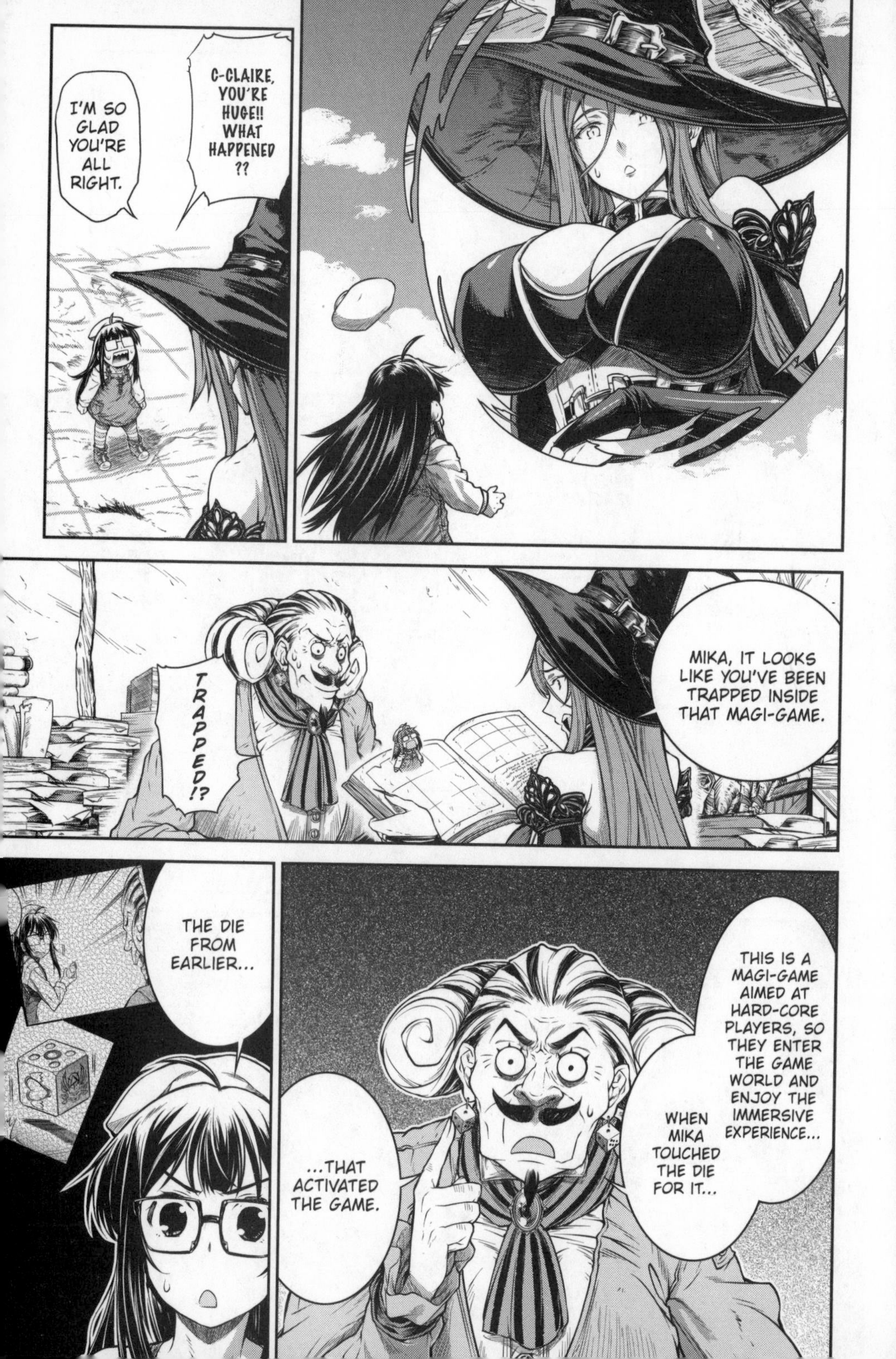
C-CLAIRE, YOU'RE HUGE!! WHAT HAPPENED ??
I'M SO GLAD YOU'RE ALL RIGHT.
MIKA, IT LOOKS LIKE YOU'VE BEEN TRAPPED INSIDE THAT MAGI-GAME.
TRAPPED!?
THIS IS A MAGI-GAME AIMED AT HARD-CORE PLAYERS, SO THEY ENTER THE GAME WORLD AND ENJOY THE IMMERSIVE EXPERIENCE...
WHEN MIKA TOUCHED THE DIE FOR IT...
...THAT ACTIVATED THE GAME.
THE DIE FROM EARLIER...

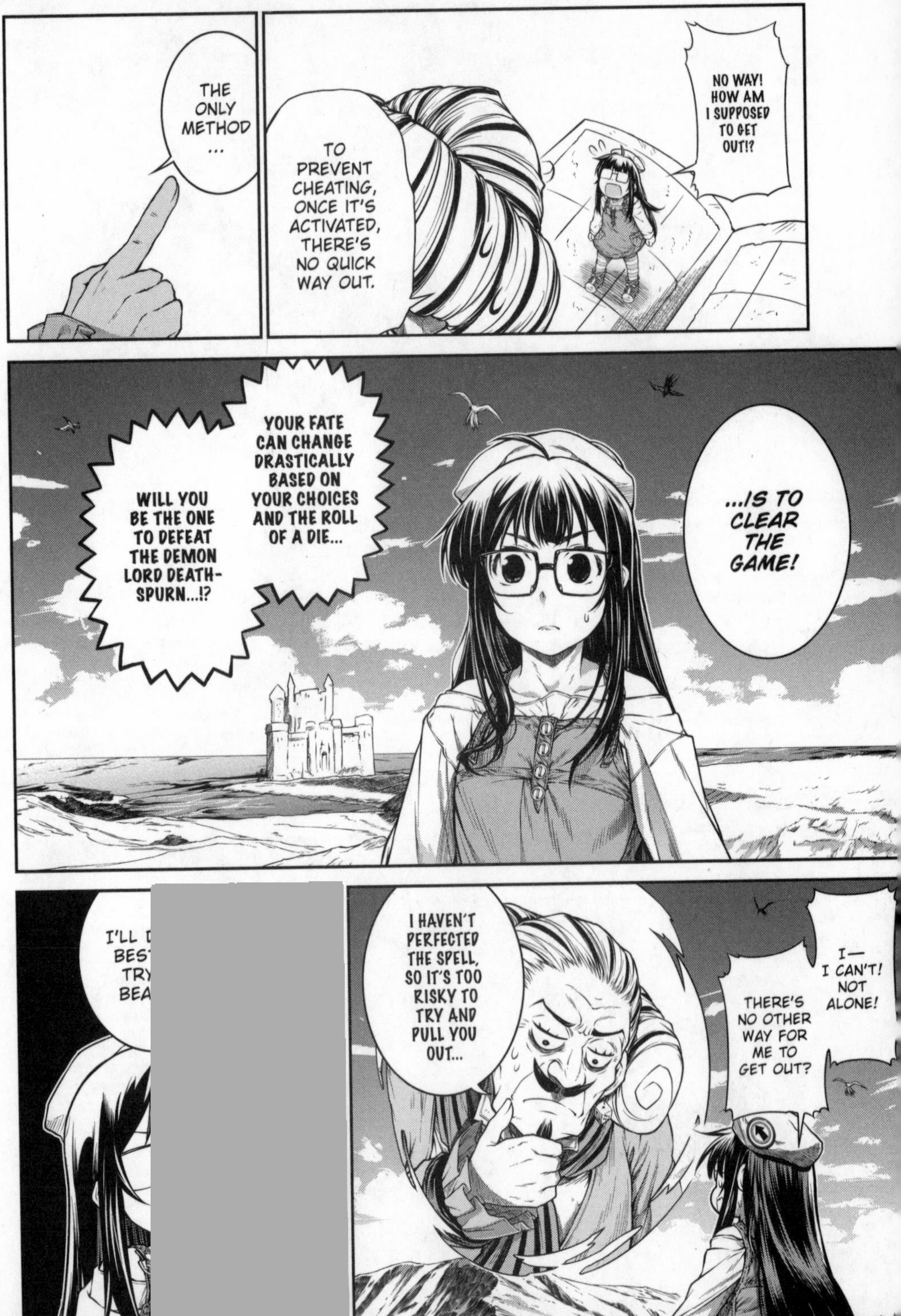
NO WAY! HOW AM I SUPPOSED TO GET OUT!?
TO PREVENT CHEATING, ONCE IT'S ACTIVATED, THERE'S NO QUICK WAY OUT.
THE ONLY METHOD ...
...IS TO CLEAR THE GAME!
YOUR FATE CAN CHANGE DRASTICALLY BASED ON YOUR CHOICES AND THE ROLL OF A DIE...
WILL YOU BE THE ONE TO DEFEAT THE DEMON LORD DEATH-SPURN...!?
I— I CAN'T! NOT ALONE!
THERE'S NO OTHER WAY FOR ME TO GET OUT?
I HAVEN'T PERFECTED THE SPELL, SO IT'S TOO RISKY TO TRY AND PULL YOU OUT...
I'LL D BEST TRY BEA

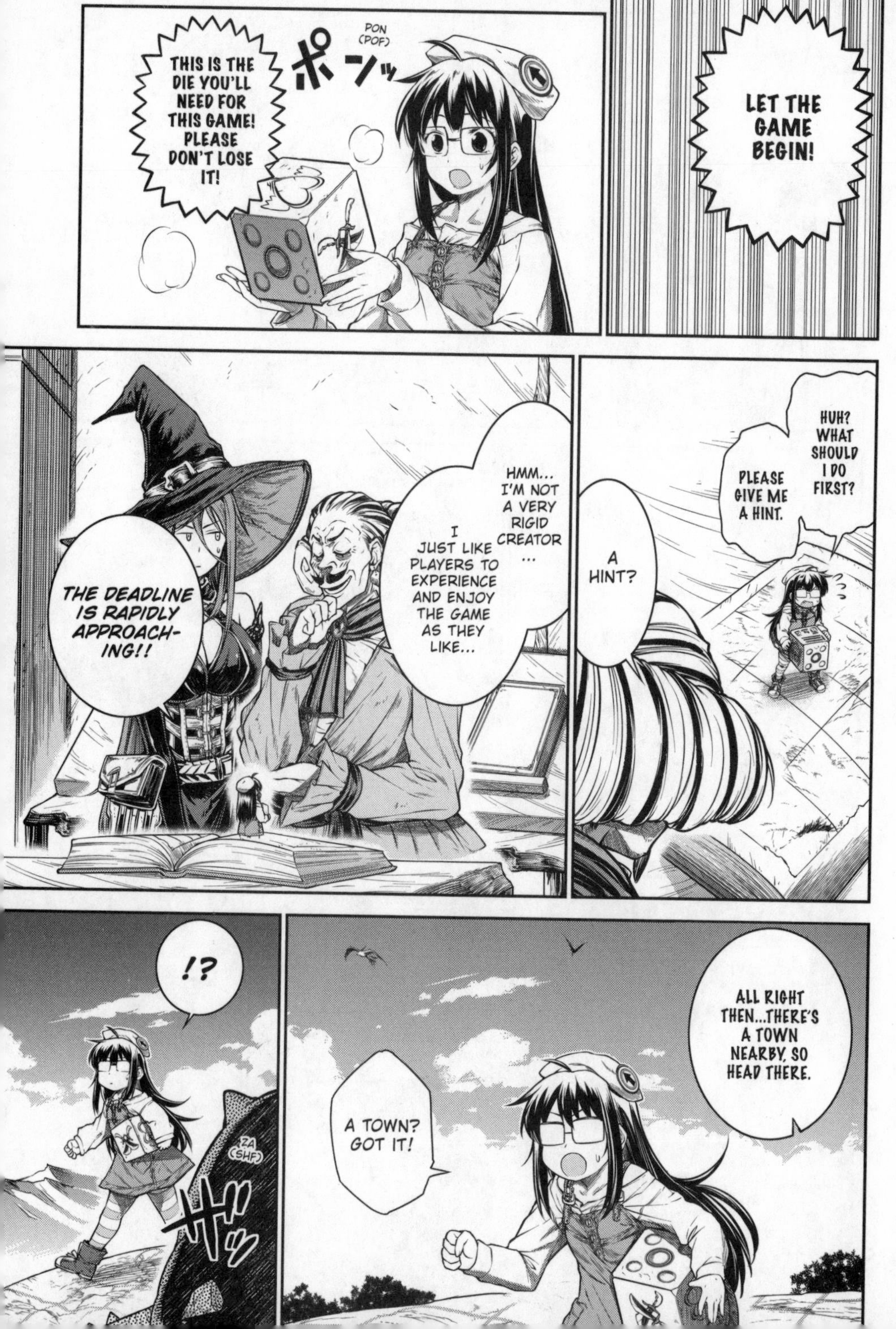
LET THE GAME BEGIN!
PON (POF)
ポンッ
THIS IS THE DIE YOU'LL NEED FOR THIS GAME! PLEASE DON'T LOSE IT!
HUH? WHAT SHOULD I DO FIRST?
PLEASE GIVE ME A HINT.
A HINT?
HMM... I'M NOT A VERY RIGID CREATOR ...
I JUST LIKE PLAYERS TO EXPERIENCE AND ENJOY THE GAME AS THEY LIKE...
THE DEADLINE IS RAPIDLY APPROACHING!!
ALL RIGHT THEN...THERE'S A TOWN NEARBY, SO HEAD THERE.
A TOWN? GOT IT!
!?
ZA (SHF)
ザッ

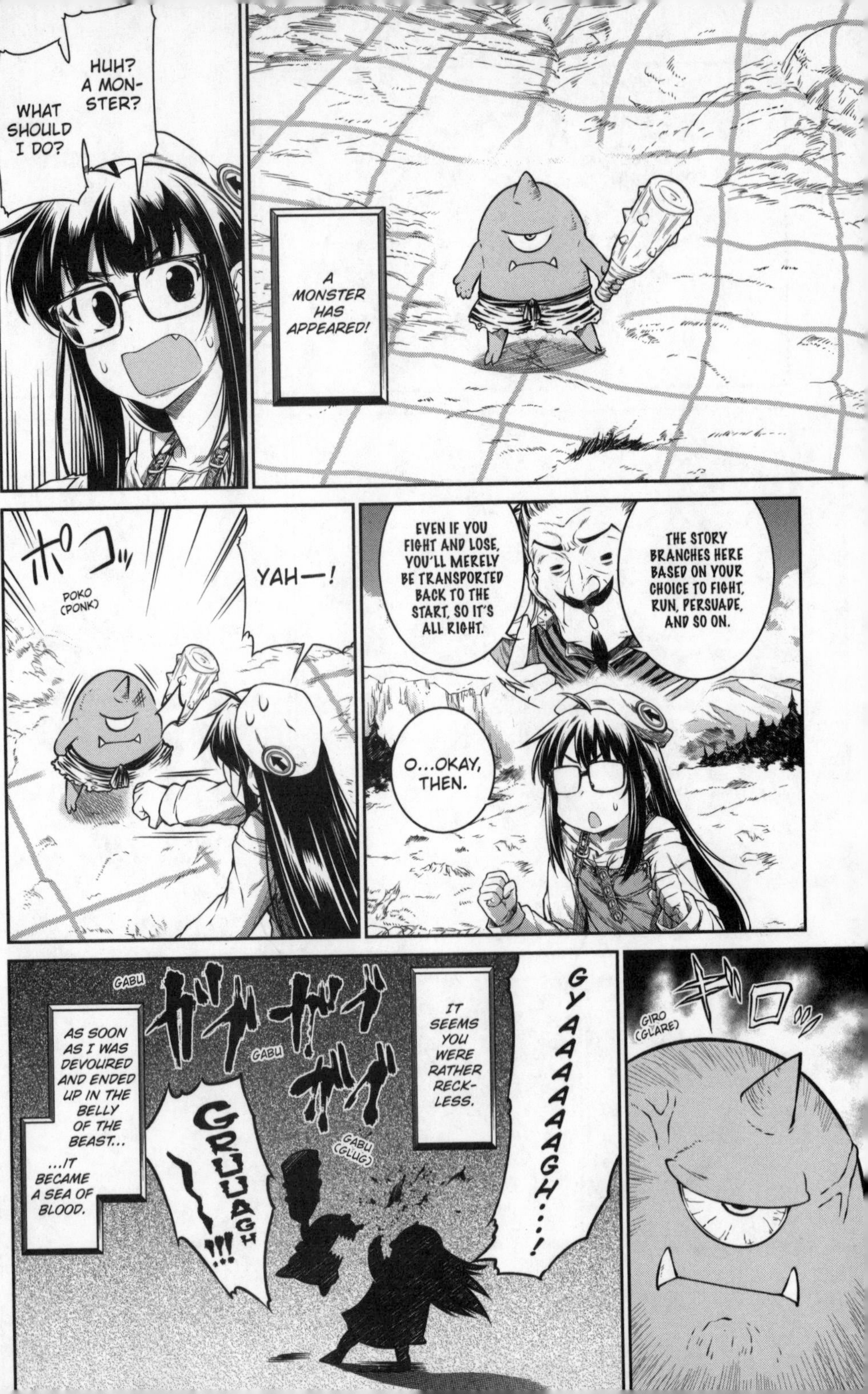
A MONSTER HAS APPEARED!
HUH? A MON-STER?
WHAT SHOULD I DO?
THE STORY BRANCHES HERE BASED ON YOUR CHOICE TO FIGHT, RUN, PERSUADE, AND SO ON.
EVEN IF YOU FIGHT AND LOSE, YOU'LL MERELY BE TRANSPORTED BACK TO THE START, SO IT'S ALL RIGHT.
O...OKAY, THEN.
YAH—!
ポコッ
POKO (PONK)
ギロッ
GIRO (GLARE)
GYAAAAAAAGH...!
IT SEEMS YOU WERE RATHER RECK-LESS.
ガブ ガブ ガブ
GABU
GABU
GABU (GLUG)
GRUUAGH—!!!
AS SOON AS I WAS DEVOURED AND ENDED UP IN THE BELLY OF THE BEAST...
...IT BECAME A SEA OF BLOOD.

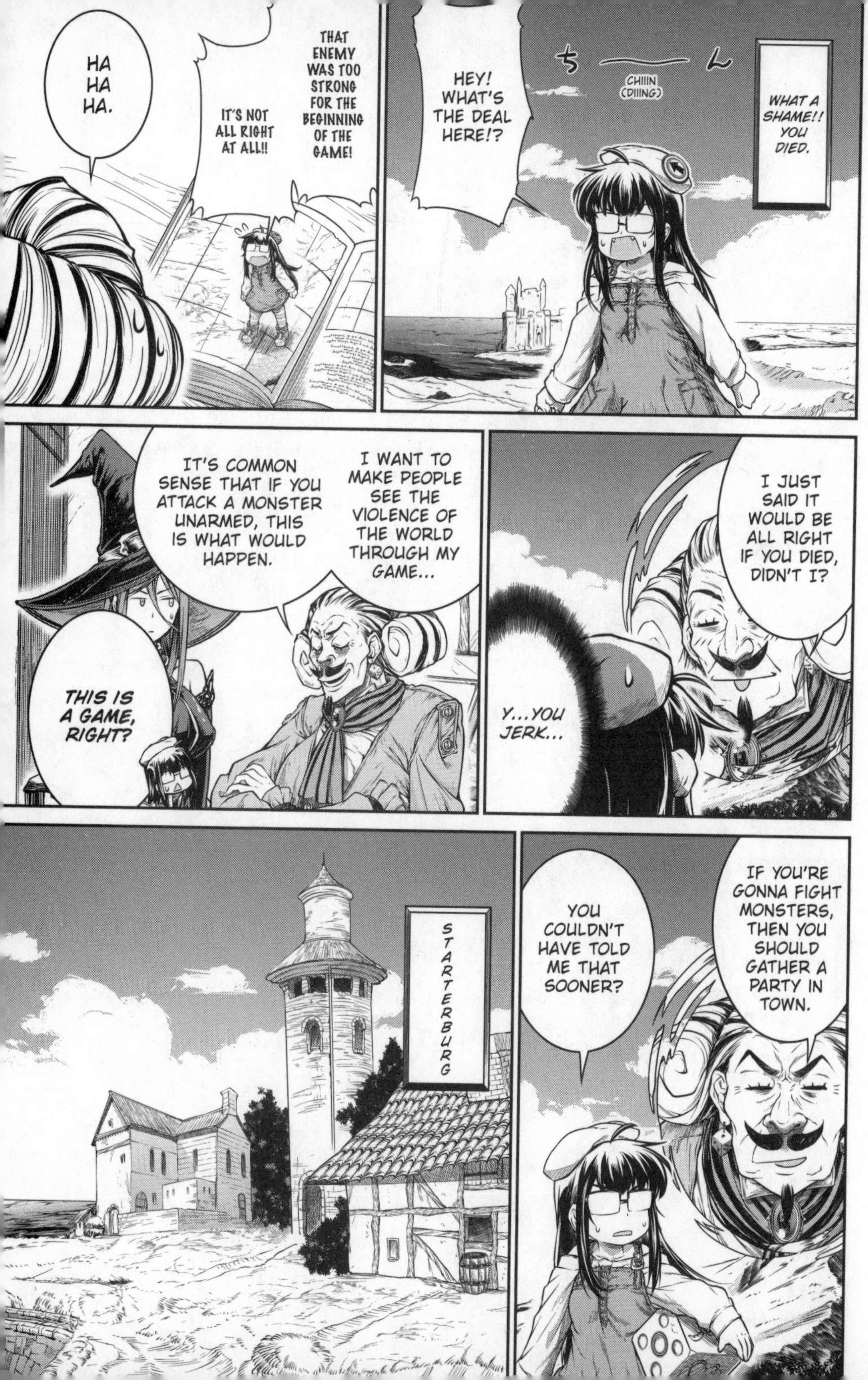
ち——ん
CHIIN (DIIING)
WHAT A SHAME!! YOU DIED.
HEY! WHAT'S THE DEAL HERE!?
THAT ENEMY WAS TOO STRONG FOR THE BEGINNING OF THE GAME!
IT'S NOT ALL RIGHT AT ALL!!
HA HA HA.
I JUST SAID IT WOULD BE ALL RIGHT IF YOU DIED, DIDN'T I?
Y...YOU JERK...
IT'S COMMON SENSE THAT IF YOU ATTACK A MONSTER UNARMED, THIS IS WHAT WOULD HAPPEN.
I WANT TO MAKE PEOPLE SEE THE VIOLENCE OF THE WORLD THROUGH MY GAME...
THIS IS A GAME, RIGHT?
IF YOU'RE GONNA FIGHT MONSTERS, THEN YOU SHOULD GATHER A PARTY IN TOWN.
YOU COULDN'T HAVE TOLD ME THAT SOONER?
STARTERBURG

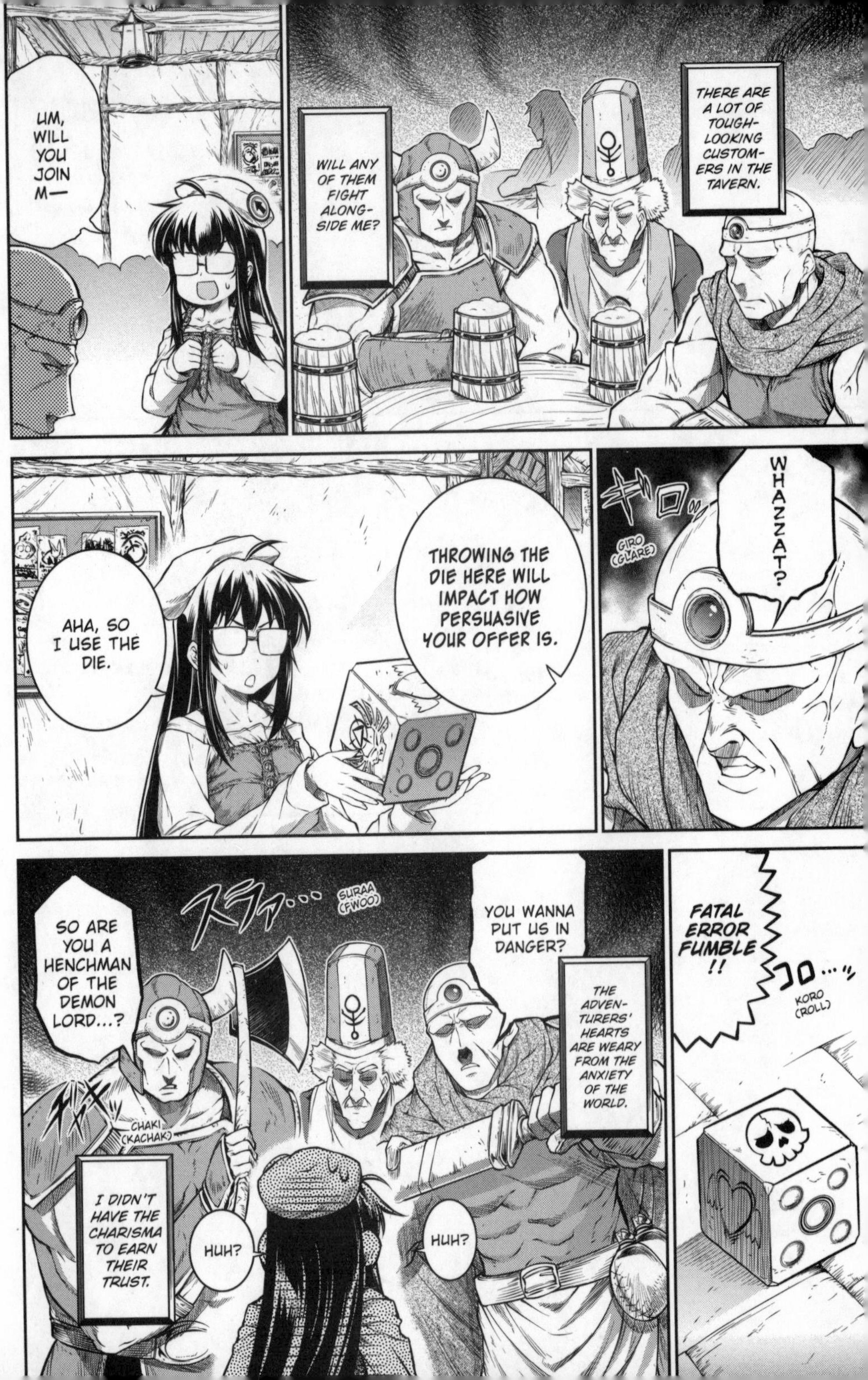

THERE ARE A LOT OF TOUGH-LOOKING CUSTOMERS IN THE TAVERN.
WILL ANY OF THEM FIGHT ALONGSIDE ME?
UM, WILL YOU JOIN M—
GIRO (GLARE)
WHAZZAT?
THROWING THE DIE HERE WILL IMPACT HOW PERSUASIVE YOUR OFFER IS.
AHA, SO I USE THE DIE.
FATAL ERROR FUMBLE!!
KORO (ROLL)
YOU WANNA PUT US IN DANGER?
SURAA (FWOO)
SO ARE YOU A HENCHMAN OF THE DEMON LORD...?
THE ADVENTURERS' HEARTS ARE WEARY FROM THE ANXIETY OF THE WORLD.
CHAKI (KACHAK)
HUH?
HUH?
I DIDN'T HAVE THE CHARISMA TO EARN THEIR TRUST.

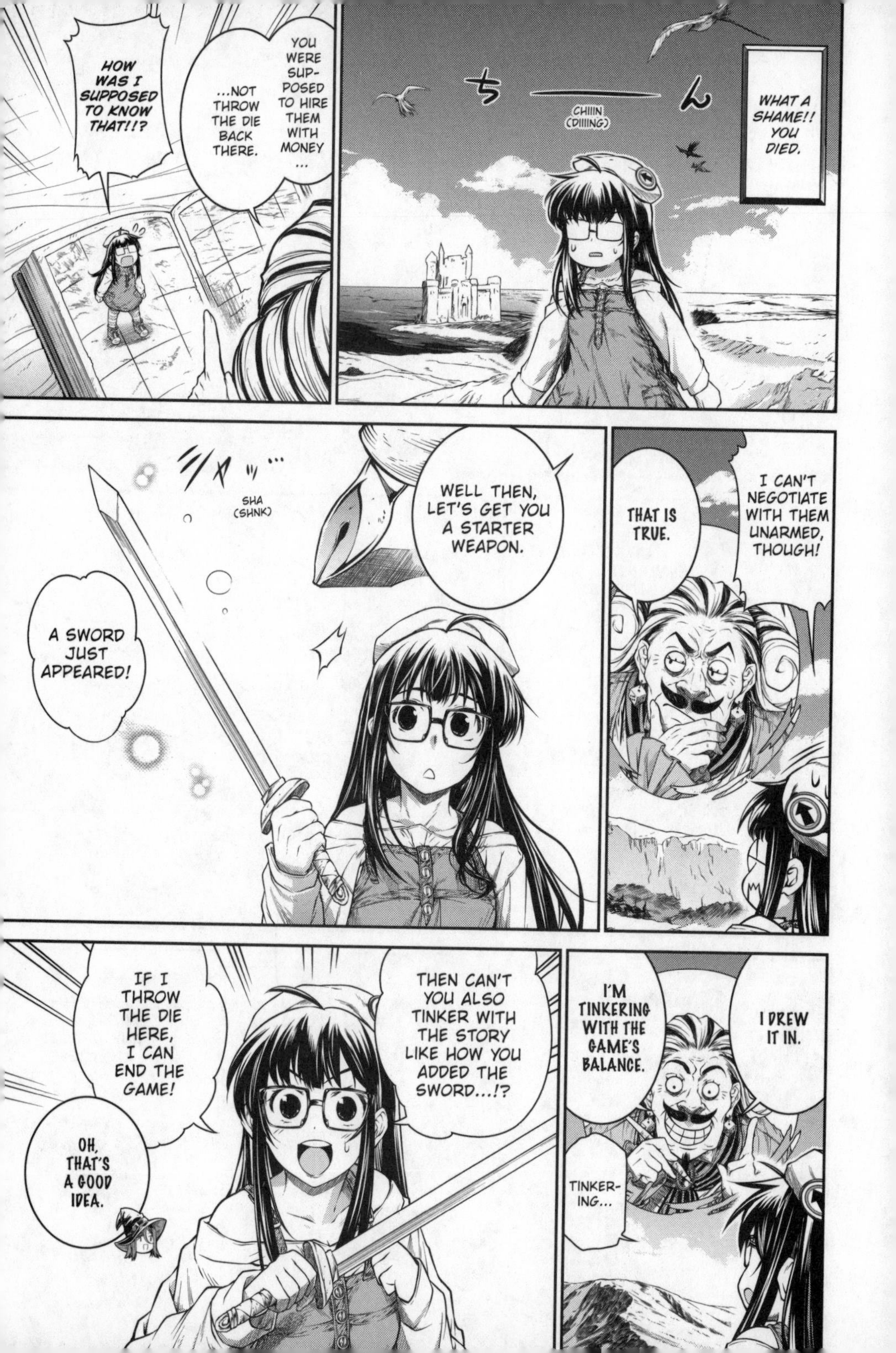
WHAT A SHAME!! YOU DIED.
ちーーーん
CHIIIN (DIIIING)
YOU WERE SUPPOSED TO HIRE THEM WITH MONEY...
...NOT THROW THE DIE BACK THERE.
HOW WAS I SUPPOSED TO KNOW THAT!!?
I CAN'T NEGOTIATE WITH THEM UNARMED, THOUGH!
THAT IS TRUE.
WELL THEN, LET'S GET YOU A STARTER WEAPON.
シャッ…
SHA (SHNK)
A SWORD JUST APPEARED!
I DREW IT IN.
I'M TINKERING WITH THE GAME'S BALANCE.
TINKERING...
THEN CAN'T YOU ALSO TINKER WITH THE STORY LIKE HOW YOU ADDED THE SWORD...!?
IF I THROW THE DIE HERE, I CAN END THE GAME!
OH, THAT'S A GOOD IDEA.

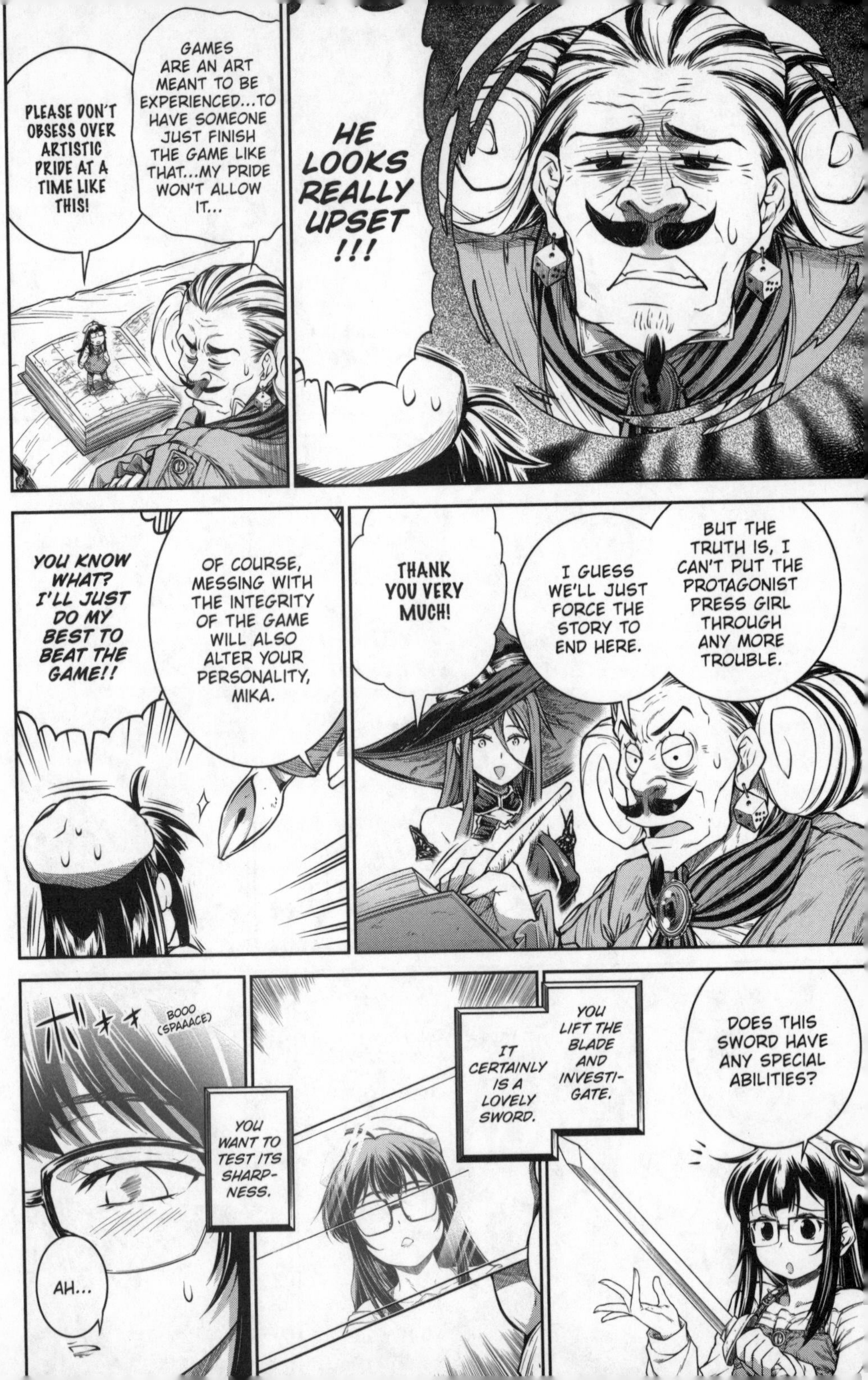
HE LOOKS REALLY UPSET!!!
GAMES ARE AN ART MEANT TO BE EXPERIENCED...TO HAVE SOMEONE JUST FINISH THE GAME LIKE THAT...MY PRIDE WON'T ALLOW IT...
PLEASE DON'T OBSESS OVER ARTISTIC PRIDE AT A TIME LIKE THIS!
BUT THE TRUTH IS, I CAN'T PUT THE PROTAGONIST PRESS GIRL THROUGH ANY MORE TROUBLE.
I GUESS WE'LL JUST FORCE THE STORY TO END HERE.
THANK YOU VERY MUCH!
OF COURSE, MESSING WITH THE INTEGRITY OF THE GAME WILL ALSO ALTER YOUR PERSONALITY, MIKA.
YOU KNOW WHAT? I'LL JUST DO MY BEST TO BEAT THE GAME!!
DOES THIS SWORD HAVE ANY SPECIAL ABILITIES?
YOU LIFT THE BLADE AND INVESTIGATE.
IT CERTAINLY IS A LOVELY SWORD.
YOU WANT TO TEST ITS SHARPNESS.
ボォォ
BOOO (SPAAACE)
AH...

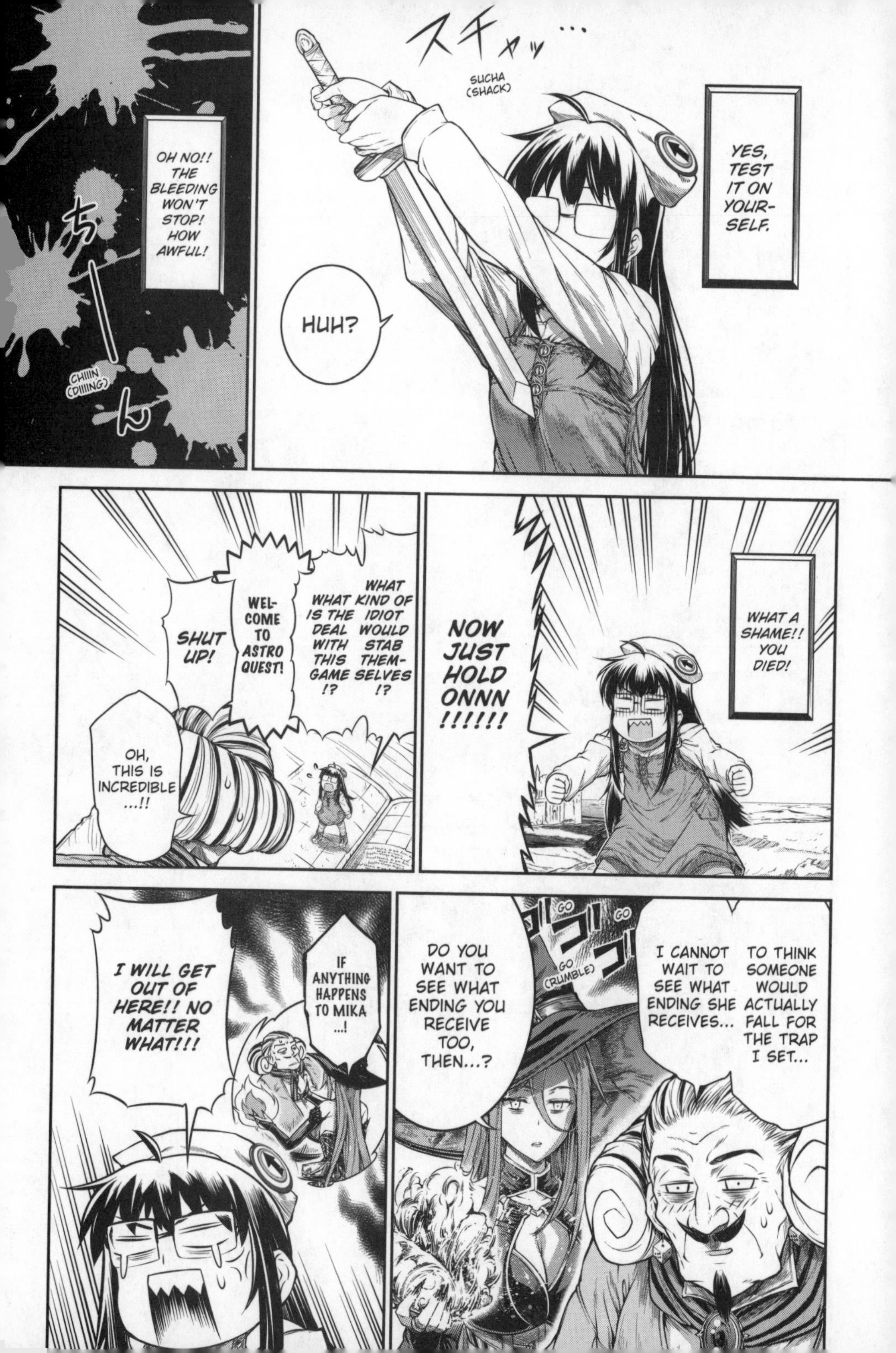
スチャッ…
SUCHA (SHACK)
YES, TEST IT ON YOURSELF.
HUH?
OH NO!! THE BLEEDING WON'T STOP! HOW AWFUL!
ち—ん
CHIIIN (DIIIING)
WHAT A SHAME!! YOU DIED!
NOW JUST HOLD ONNN!!!!!!
WHAT KIND OF IDIOT WOULD STAB THEMSELVES!?
WHAT IS THE DEAL WITH THIS GAME!?
WELCOME TO ASTRO QUEST!
SHUT UP!
OH, THIS IS INCREDIBLE...!!
TO THINK SOMEONE WOULD ACTUALLY FALL FOR THE TRAP I SET...
I CANNOT WAIT TO SEE WHAT ENDING SHE RECEIVES...
ゴゴゴ
GO GO GO (RUMBLE)
DO YOU WANT TO SEE WHAT ENDING YOU RECEIVE TOO, THEN...?
IF ANYTHING HAPPENS TO MIKA...!
I WILL GET OUT OF HERE!! NO MATTER WHAT!!!

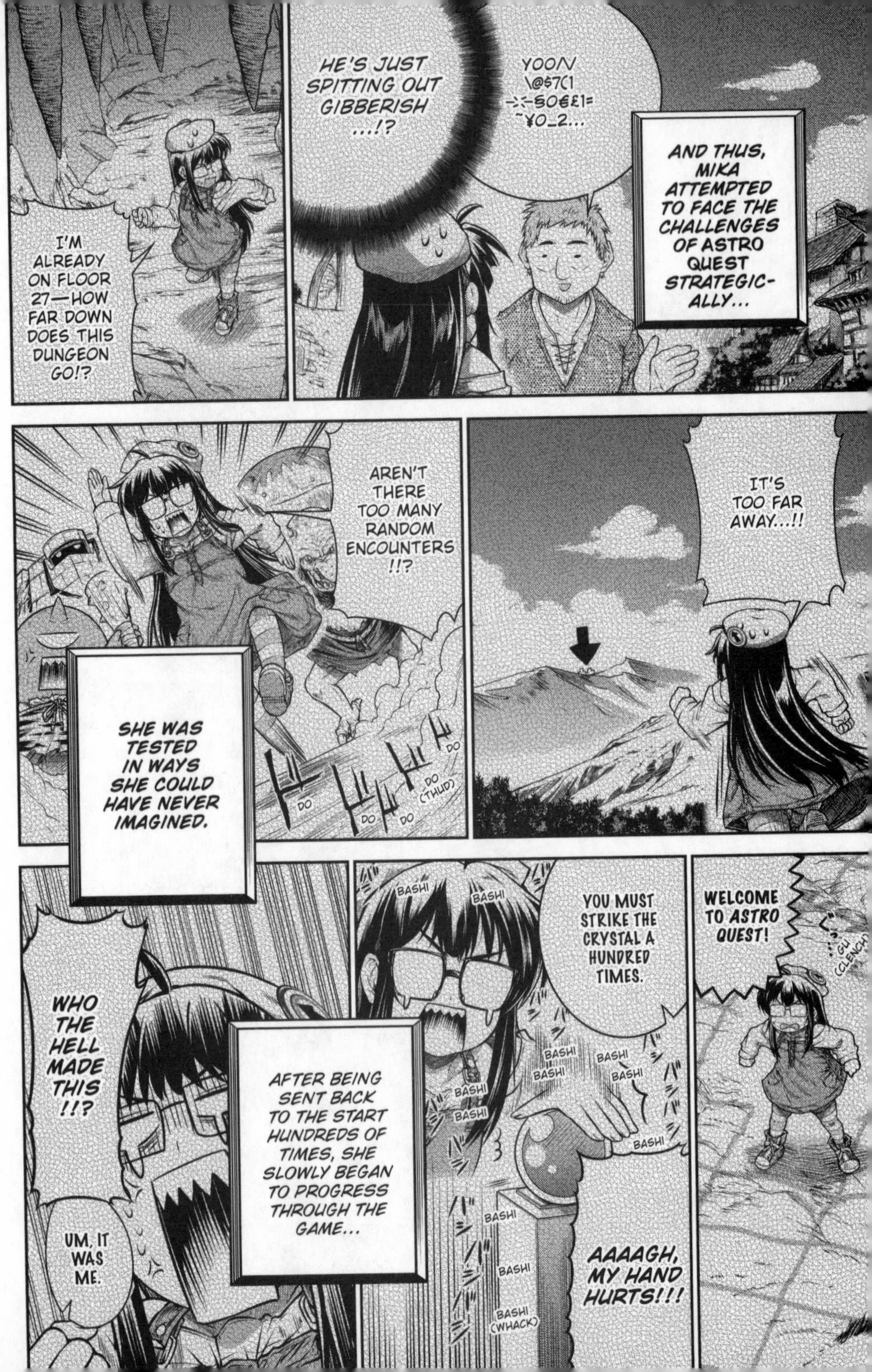

YOON/\ \@$7(1 -:-§0€£1= ~¥0_2...
HE'S JUST SPITTING OUT GIBBERISH ...!?
AND THUS, MIKA ATTEMPTED TO FACE THE CHALLENGES OF ASTRO QUEST STRATEGICALLY...
I'M ALREADY ON FLOOR 27—HOW FAR DOWN DOES THIS DUNGEON GO!?
IT'S TOO FAR AWAY...!!
AREN'T THERE TOO MANY RANDOM ENCOUNTERS !!?
DO DO (THUD)
DO DO DO
SHE WAS TESTED IN WAYS SHE COULD HAVE NEVER IMAGINED.
WELCOME TO ASTRO QUEST!
GU (CLENCH)
YOU MUST STRIKE THE CRYSTAL A HUNDRED TIMES.
BASHI BASHI
BASHI BASHI BASHI BASHI BASHI BASHI BASHI
AAAAGH, MY HAND HURTS!!!
BASHI BASHI BASHI (WHACK)
AFTER BEING SENT BACK TO THE START HUNDREDS OF TIMES, SHE SLOWLY BEGAN TO PROGRESS THROUGH THE GAME...
WHO THE HELL MADE THIS !!?
UM, IT WAS ME.

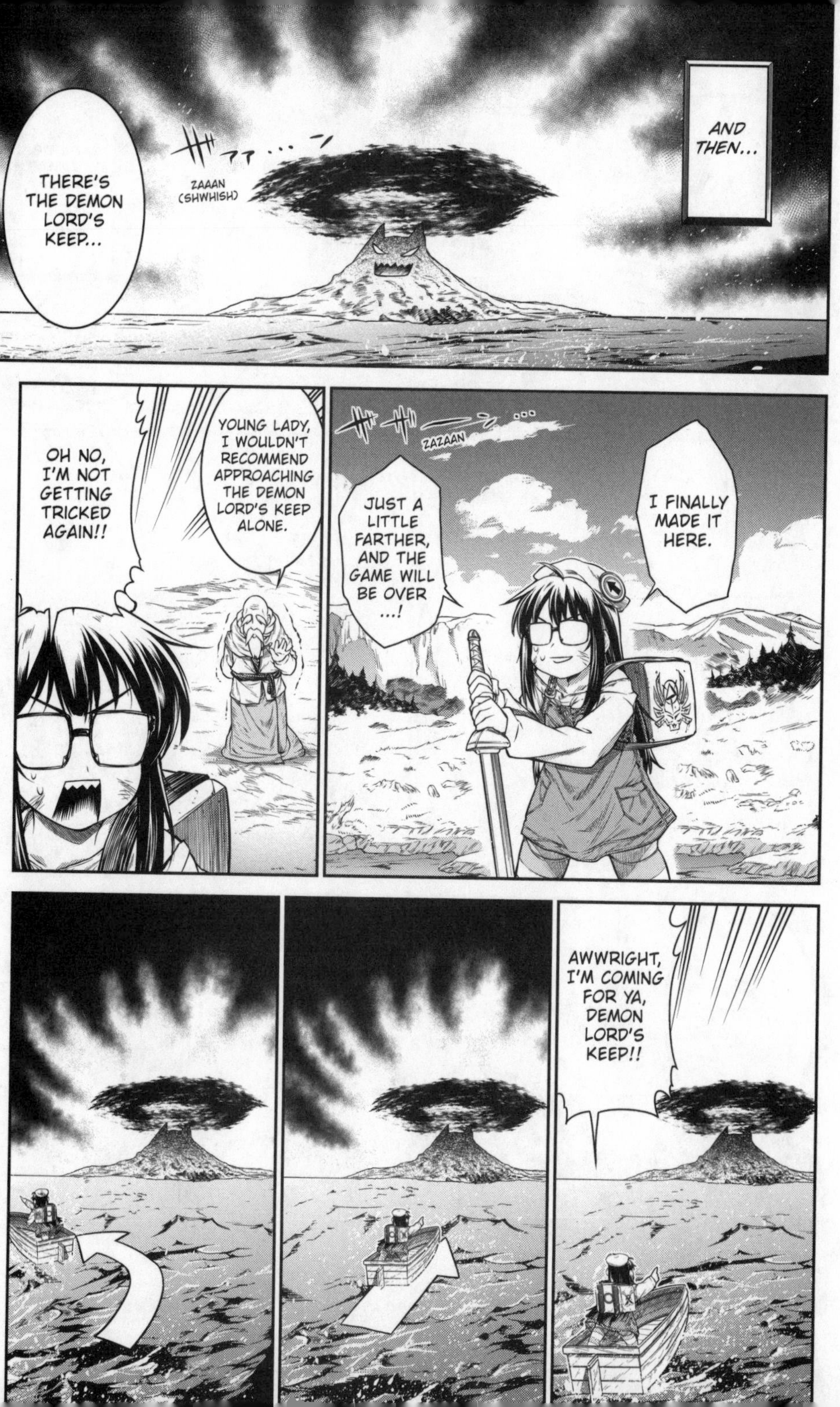
AND THEN...
ZAAAN (SHWHISH)
THERE'S THE DEMON LORD'S KEEP...
I FINALLY MADE IT HERE.
ZAZAAN
JUST A LITTLE FARTHER, AND THE GAME WILL BE OVER...!
YOUNG LADY, I WOULDN'T RECOMMEND APPROACHING THE DEMON LORD'S KEEP ALONE.
OH NO, I'M NOT GETTING TRICKED AGAIN!!
AWWRIGHT, I'M COMING FOR YA, DEMON LORD'S KEEP!!

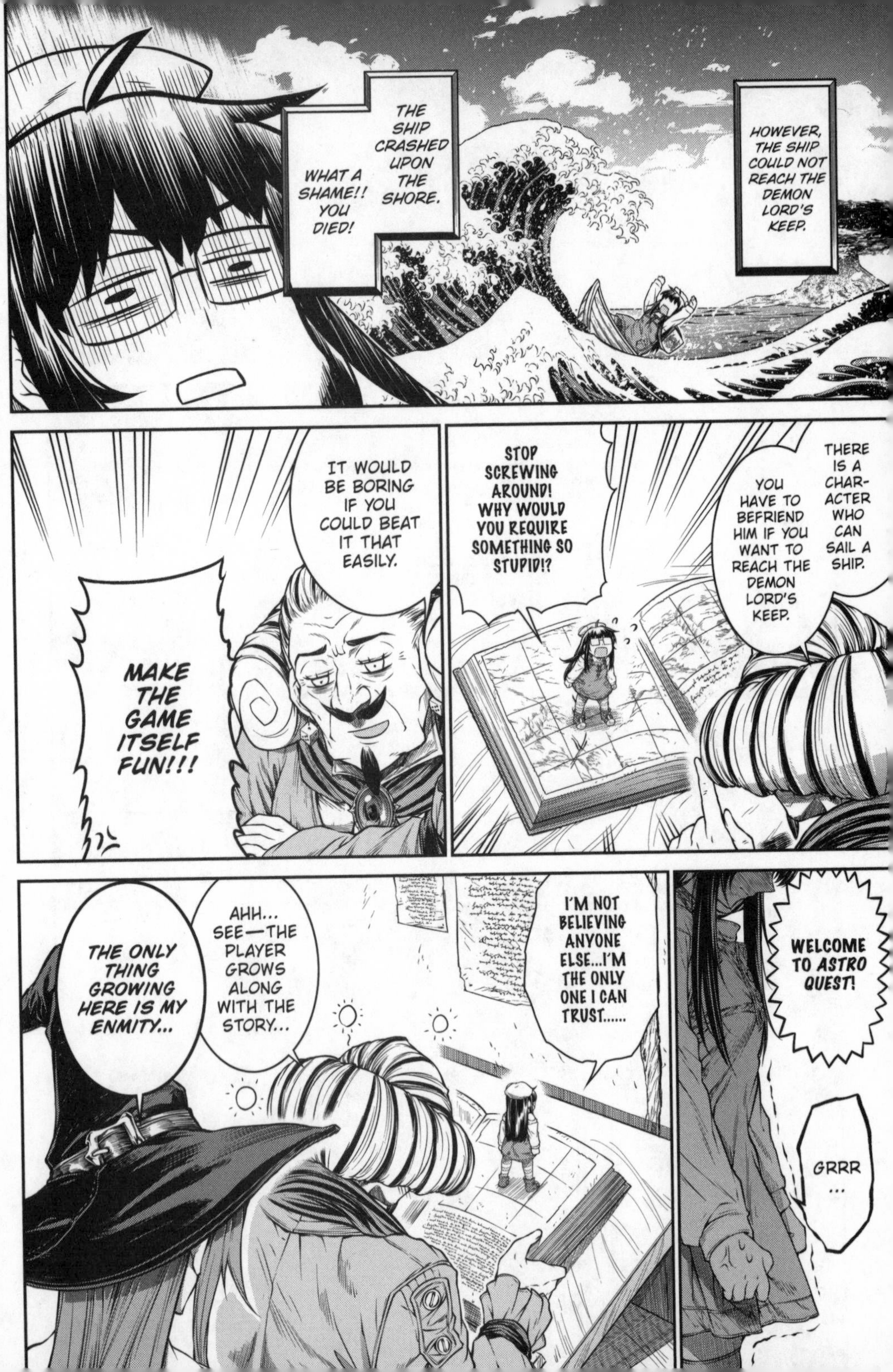
HOWEVER, THE SHIP COULD NOT REACH THE DEMON LORD'S KEEP.
THE SHIP CRASHED UPON THE SHORE.
WHAT A SHAME!! YOU DIED!
THERE IS A CHARACTER WHO CAN SAIL A SHIP.
YOU HAVE TO BEFRIEND HIM IF YOU WANT TO REACH THE DEMON LORD'S KEEP.
STOP SCREWING AROUND! WHY WOULD YOU REQUIRE SOMETHING SO STUPID!?
IT WOULD BE BORING IF YOU COULD BEAT IT THAT EASILY.
MAKE THE GAME ITSELF FUN!!!
WELCOME TO ASTRO QUEST!
GRRR...
I'M NOT BELIEVING ANYONE ELSE...I'M THE ONLY ONE I CAN TRUST......
AHH... SEE—THE PLAYER GROWS ALONG WITH THE STORY...
THE ONLY THING GROWING HERE IS MY ENMITY...

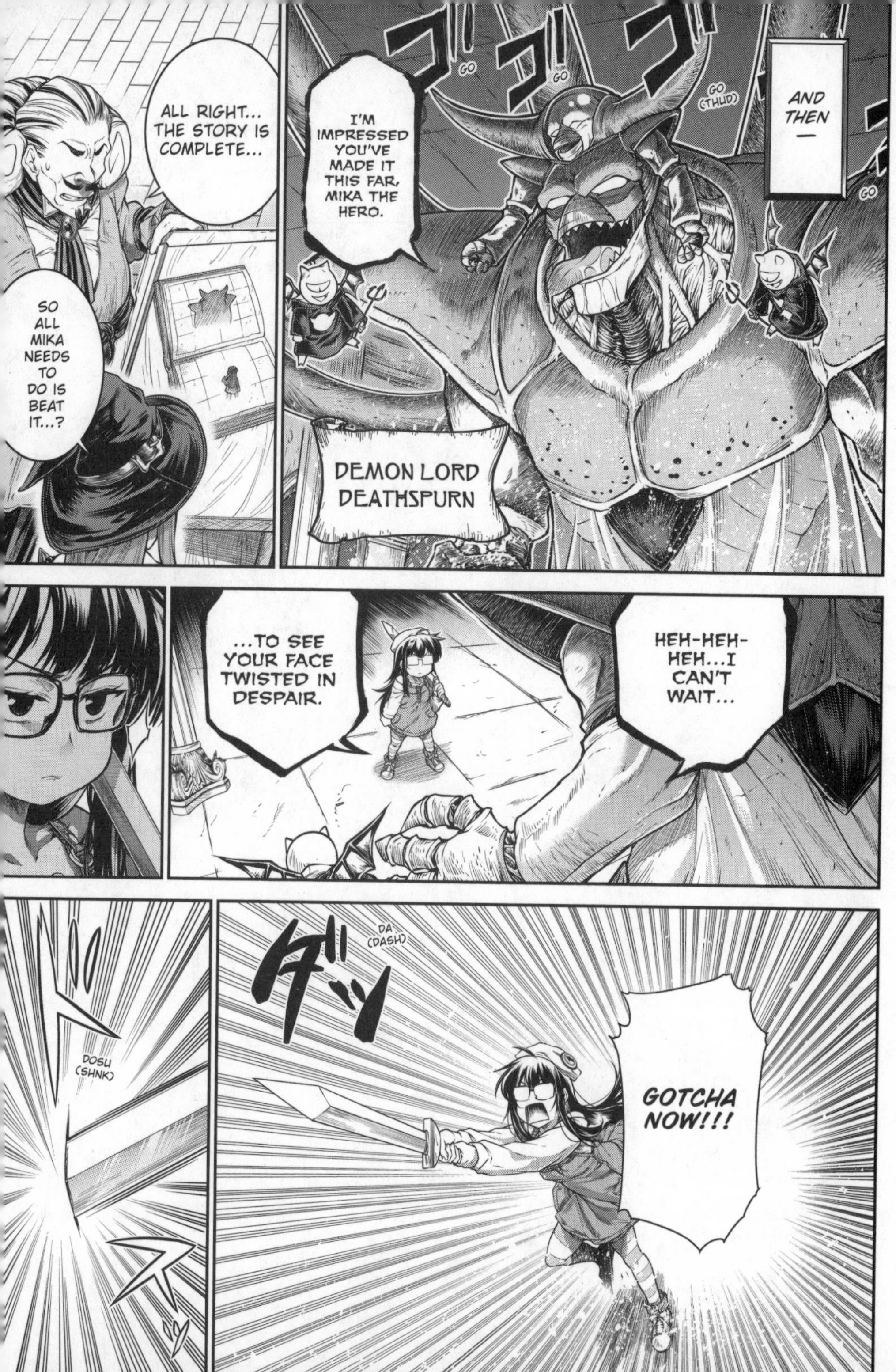
AND THEN —
GO
GO (THUD)
GO
GO
I'M IMPRESSED YOU'VE MADE IT THIS FAR, MIKA THE HERO.
DEMON LORD DEATHSPURN
ALL RIGHT... THE STORY IS COMPLETE...
SO ALL MIKA NEEDS TO DO IS BEAT IT...?
HEH-HEH-HEH...I CAN'T WAIT...
...TO SEE YOUR FACE TWISTED IN DESPAIR.
DA (DASH)
GOTCHA NOW!!!
DOSU (SHNK)

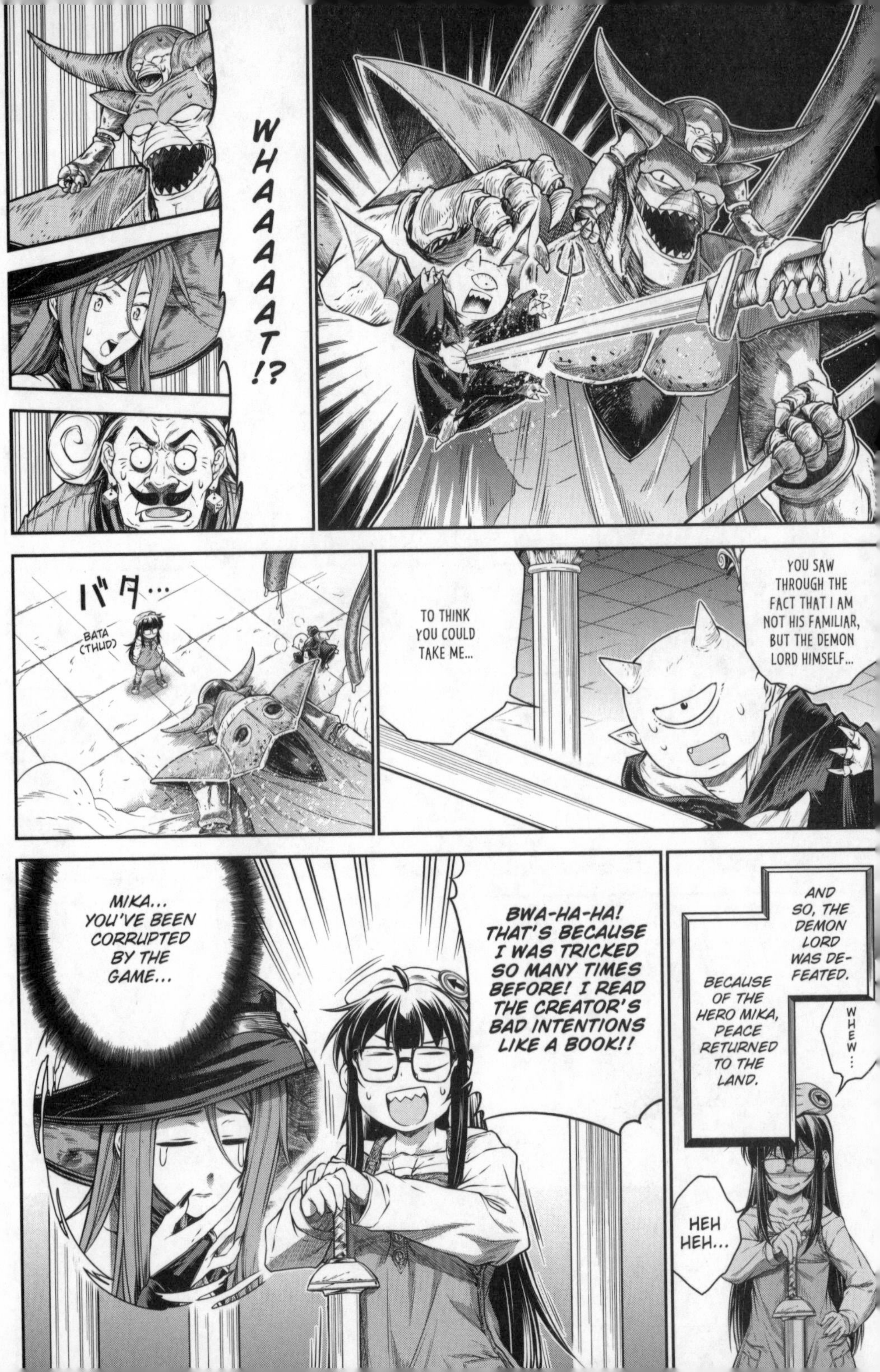
WHAAAAAAAT!?
YOU SAW THROUGH THE FACT THAT I AM NOT HIS FAMILIAR, BUT THE DEMON LORD HIMSELF...
TO THINK YOU COULD TAKE ME...
バタ…
BATA (THUD)
AND SO, THE DEMON LORD WAS DE-FEATED.
BECAUSE OF THE HERO MIKA, PEACE RETURNED TO THE LAND.
WHEW...
HEH HEH...
BWA-HA-HA! THAT'S BECAUSE I WAS TRICKED SO MANY TIMES BEFORE! I READ THE CREATOR'S BAD INTENTIONS LIKE A BOOK!!
MIKA... YOU'VE BEEN CORRUPTED BY THE GAME...

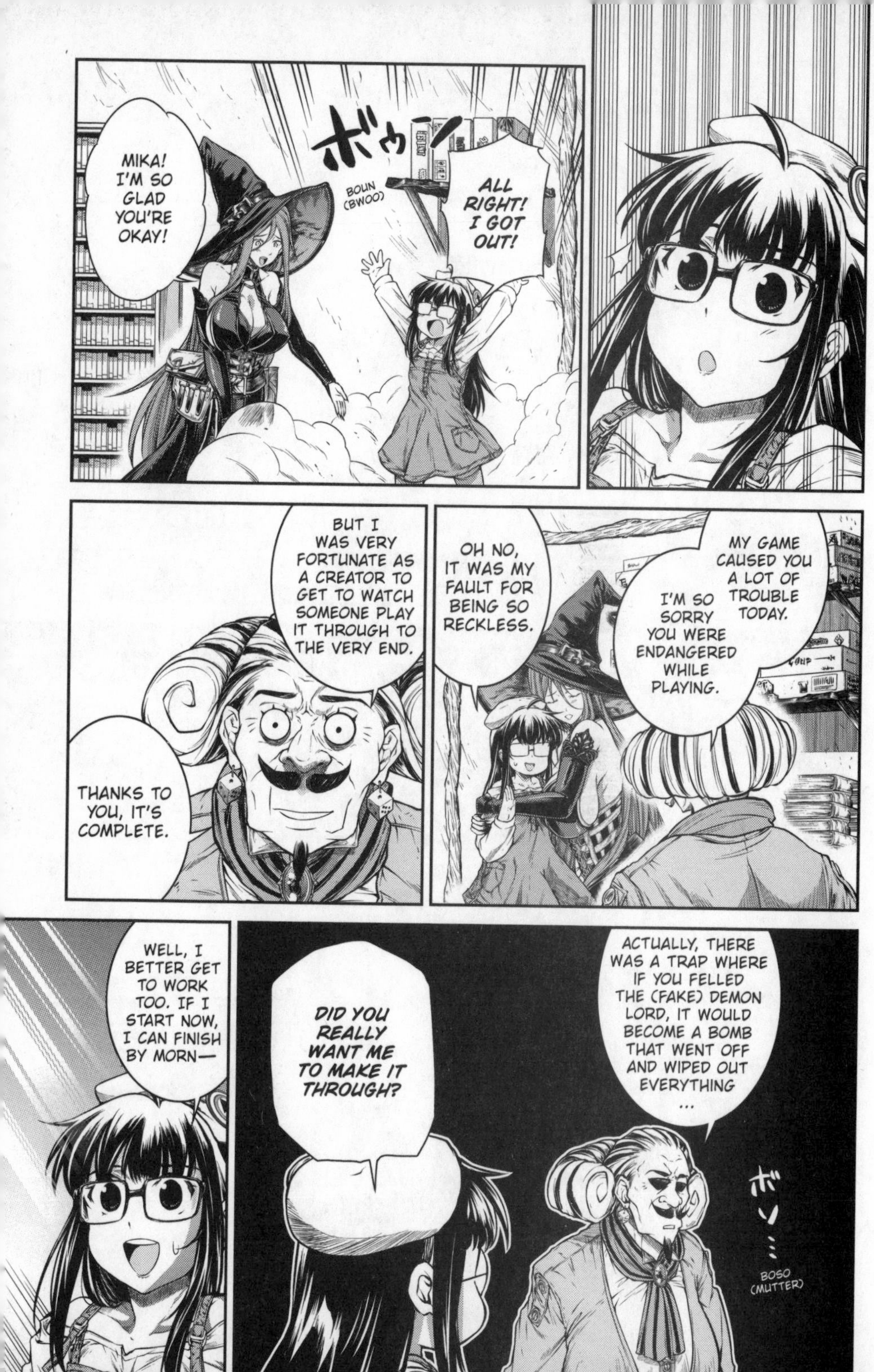

ボゥーノ
BOUN (BWOO)
ALL RIGHT! I GOT OUT!
MIKA! I'M SO GLAD YOU'RE OKAY!
MY GAME CAUSED YOU A LOT OF TROUBLE TODAY.
I'M SO SORRY YOU WERE ENDANGERED WHILE PLAYING.
OH NO, IT WAS MY FAULT FOR BEING SO RECKLESS.
BUT I WAS VERY FORTUNATE AS A CREATOR TO GET TO WATCH SOMEONE PLAY IT THROUGH TO THE VERY END.
THANKS TO YOU, IT'S COMPLETE.
ACTUALLY, THERE WAS A TRAP WHERE IF YOU FELLED THE (FAKE) DEMON LORD, IT WOULD BECOME A BOMB THAT WENT OFF AND WIPED OUT EVERYTHING ...
ボソ
BOSO (MUTTER)
DID YOU REALLY WANT ME TO MAKE IT THROUGH?
WELL, I BETTER GET TO WORK TOO. IF I START NOW, I CAN FINISH BY MORN—

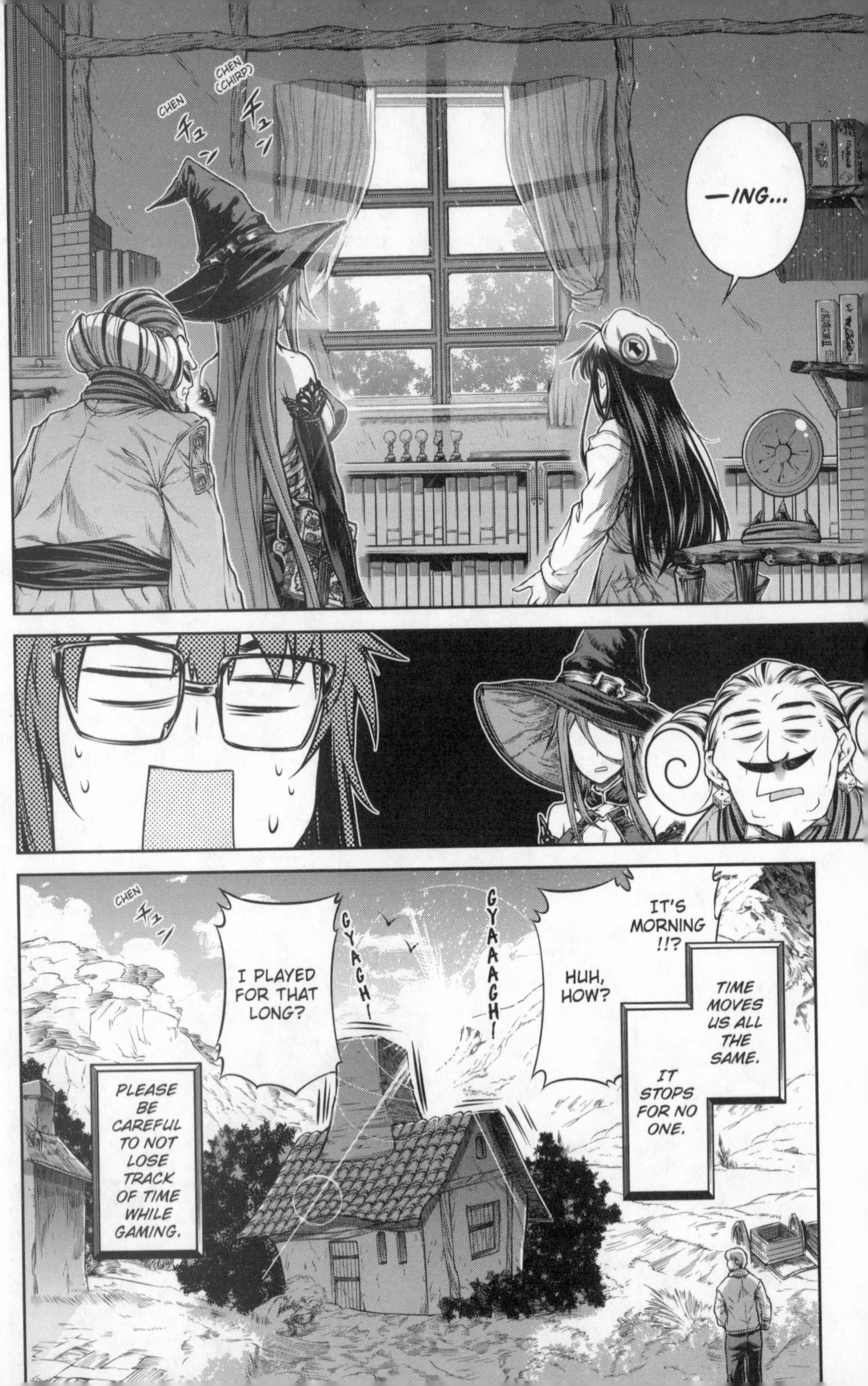
—ING...
CHEN (CHIRP)
CHEN
IT'S MORNING !!?
TIME MOVES US ALL THE SAME.
IT STOPS FOR NO ONE.
HUH, HOW?
GYAAAGH!
GYAGH!
I PLAYED FOR THAT LONG?
CHEN
PLEASE BE CAREFUL TO NOT LOSE TRACK OF TIME WHILE GAMING.

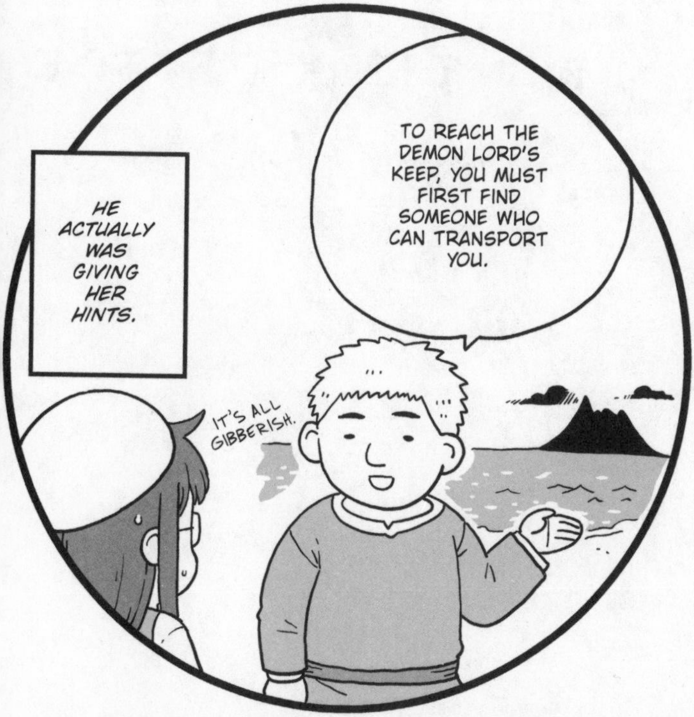
TO REACH THE DEMON LORD'S KEEP, YOU MUST FIRST FIND SOMEONE WHO CAN TRANSPORT YOU.
HE ACTUALLY WAS GIVING HER HINTS.
IT'S ALL GIBBERISH.

A WITCH'S PRINTING OFFICE

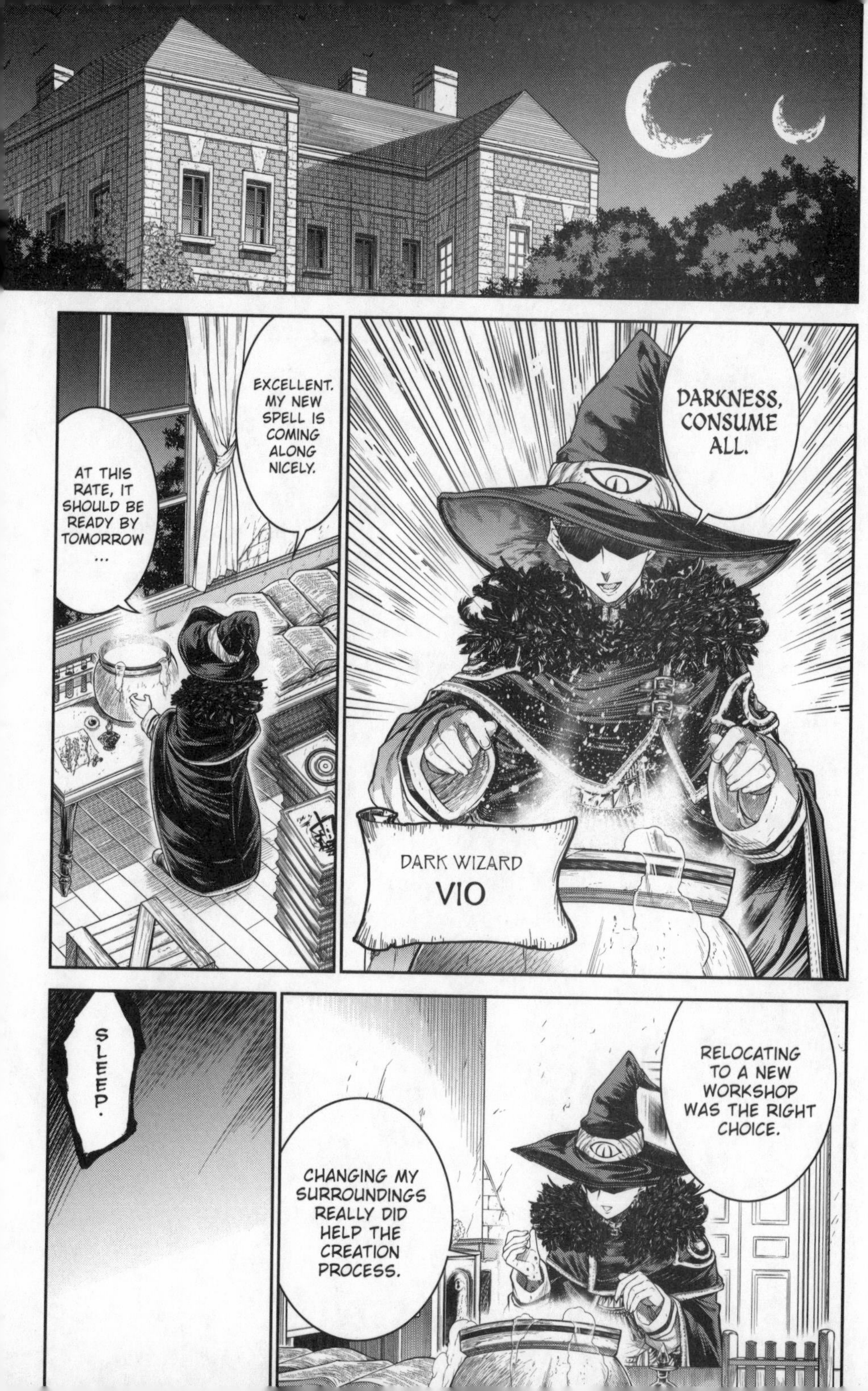
DARKNESS, CONSUME ALL.
DARK WIZARD VIO
EXCELLENT. MY NEW SPELL IS COMING ALONG NICELY.
AT THIS RATE, IT SHOULD BE READY BY TOMORROW...
RELOCATING TO A NEW WORKSHOP WAS THE RIGHT CHOICE.
CHANGING MY SURROUNDINGS REALLY DID HELP THE CREATION PROCESS.
SLEEP.

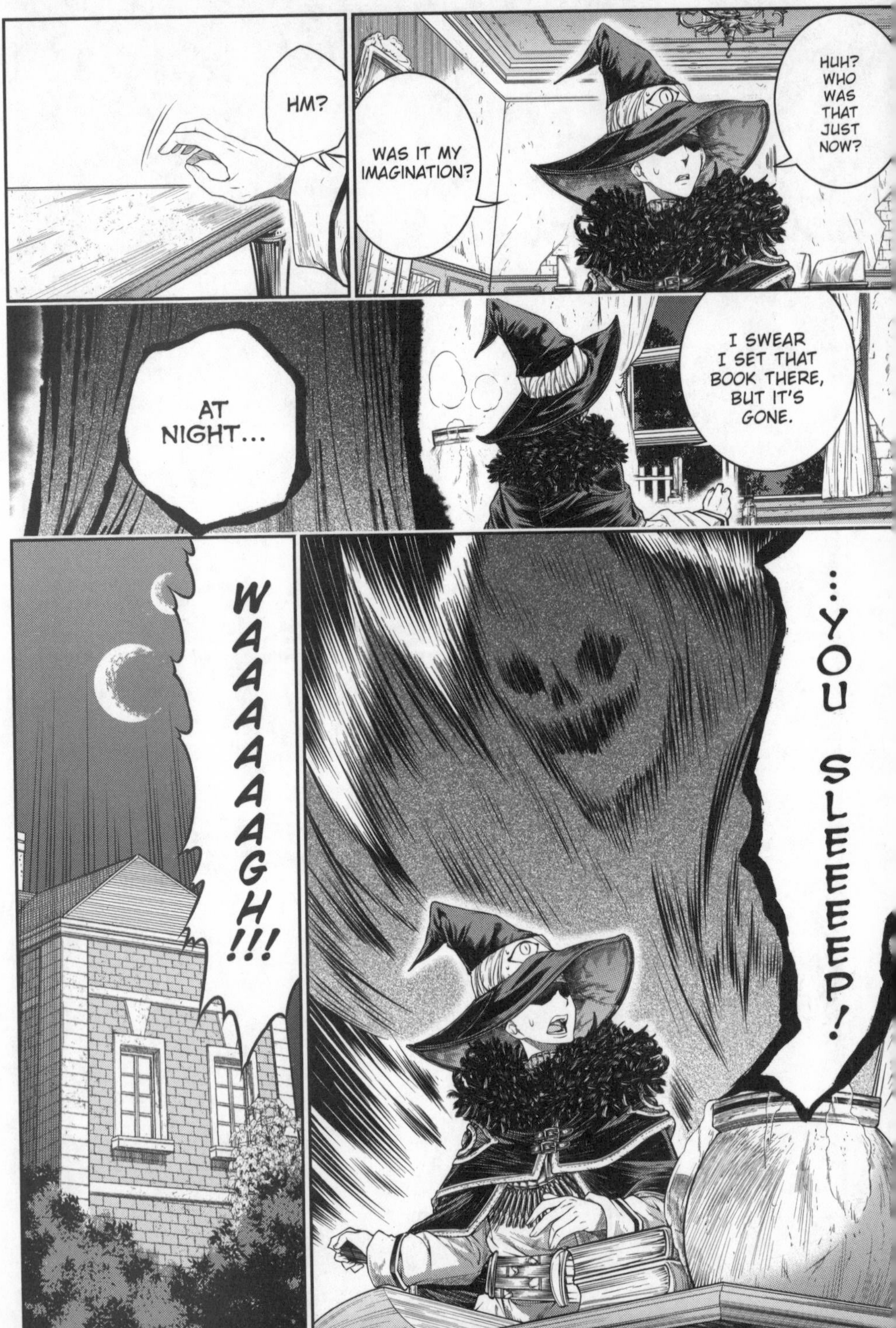
HUH? WHO WAS THAT JUST NOW?
WAS IT MY IMAGINATION?
HM?
I SWEAR I SET THAT BOOK THERE, BUT IT'S GONE.
AT NIGHT...
...YOU SLEEEEP!
WAAAAAAAGH!!!

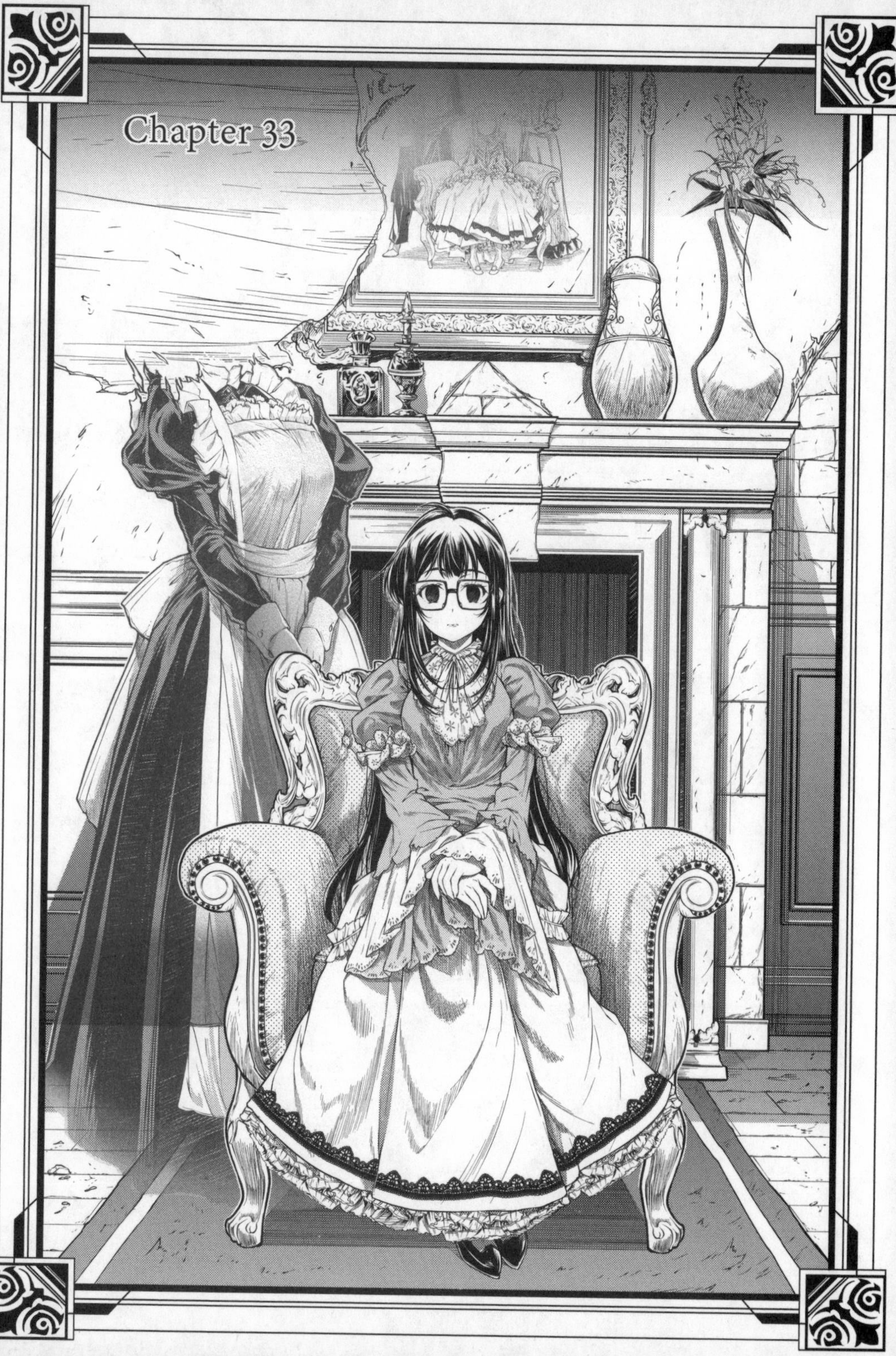
Chapter 33

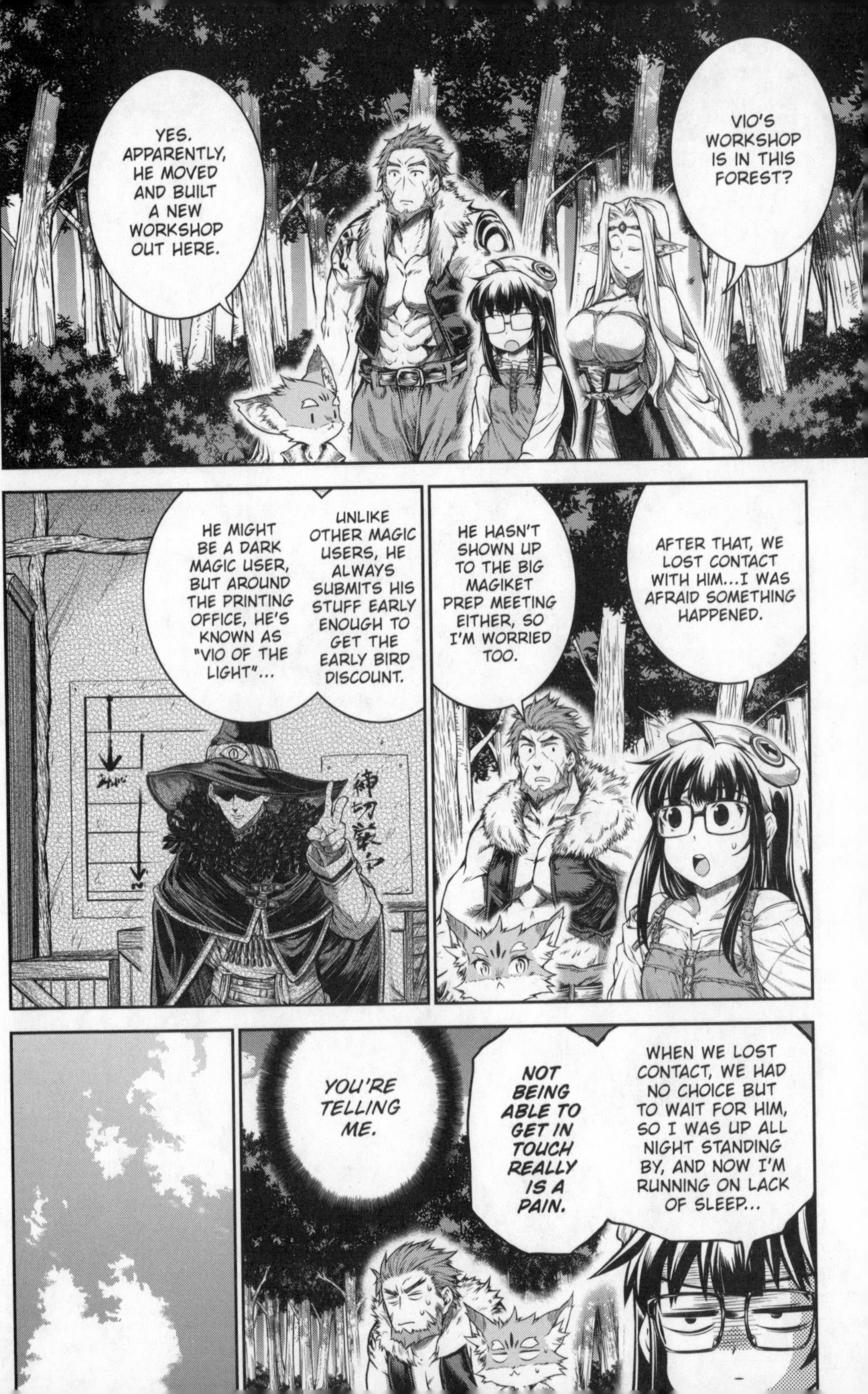
VIO'S WORKSHOP IS IN THIS FOREST?
YES. APPARENTLY, HE MOVED AND BUILT A NEW WORKSHOP OUT HERE.
AFTER THAT, WE LOST CONTACT WITH HIM...I WAS AFRAID SOMETHING HAPPENED.
HE HASN'T SHOWN UP TO THE BIG MAGIKET PREP MEETING EITHER, SO I'M WORRIED TOO.
UNLIKE OTHER MAGIC USERS, HE ALWAYS SUBMITS HIS STUFF EARLY ENOUGH TO GET THE EARLY BIRD DISCOUNT.
HE MIGHT BE A DARK MAGIC USER, BUT AROUND THE PRINTING OFFICE, HE'S KNOWN AS "VIO OF THE LIGHT"...
締切厳守
WHEN WE LOST CONTACT, WE HAD NO CHOICE BUT TO WAIT FOR HIM, SO I WAS UP ALL NIGHT STANDING BY, AND NOW I'M RUNNING ON LACK OF SLEEP...
NOT BEING ABLE TO GET IN TOUCH REALLY IS A PAIN.
YOU'RE TELLING ME.

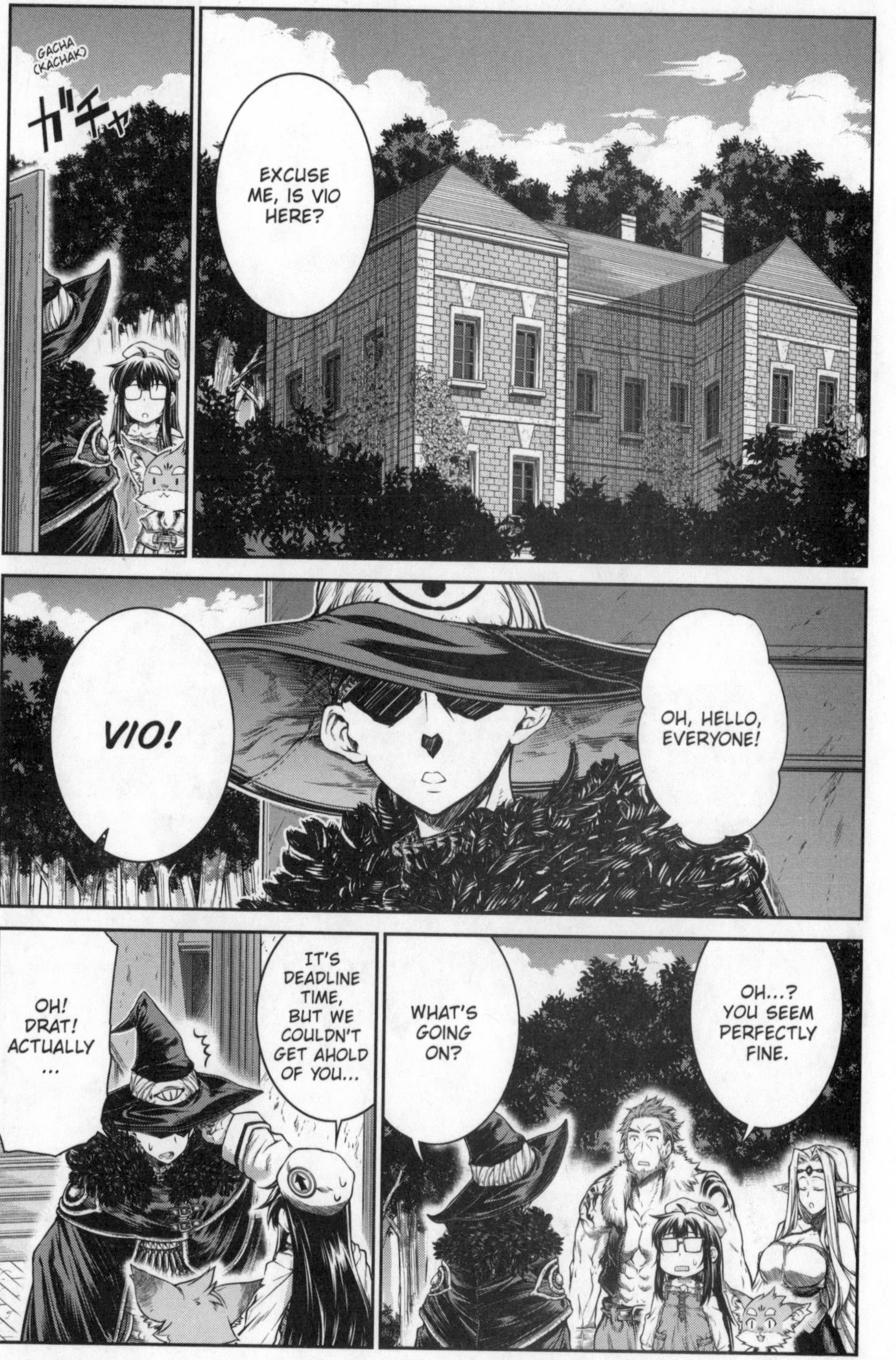
EXCUSE ME, IS VIO HERE?
ガチャ
GACHA (KACHAK)
VIO!
OH, HELLO, EVERYONE!
OH...? YOU SEEM PERFECTLY FINE.
WHAT'S GOING ON?
IT'S DEADLINE TIME, BUT WE COULDN'T GET AHOLD OF YOU...
OH! DRAT! ACTUALLY ...

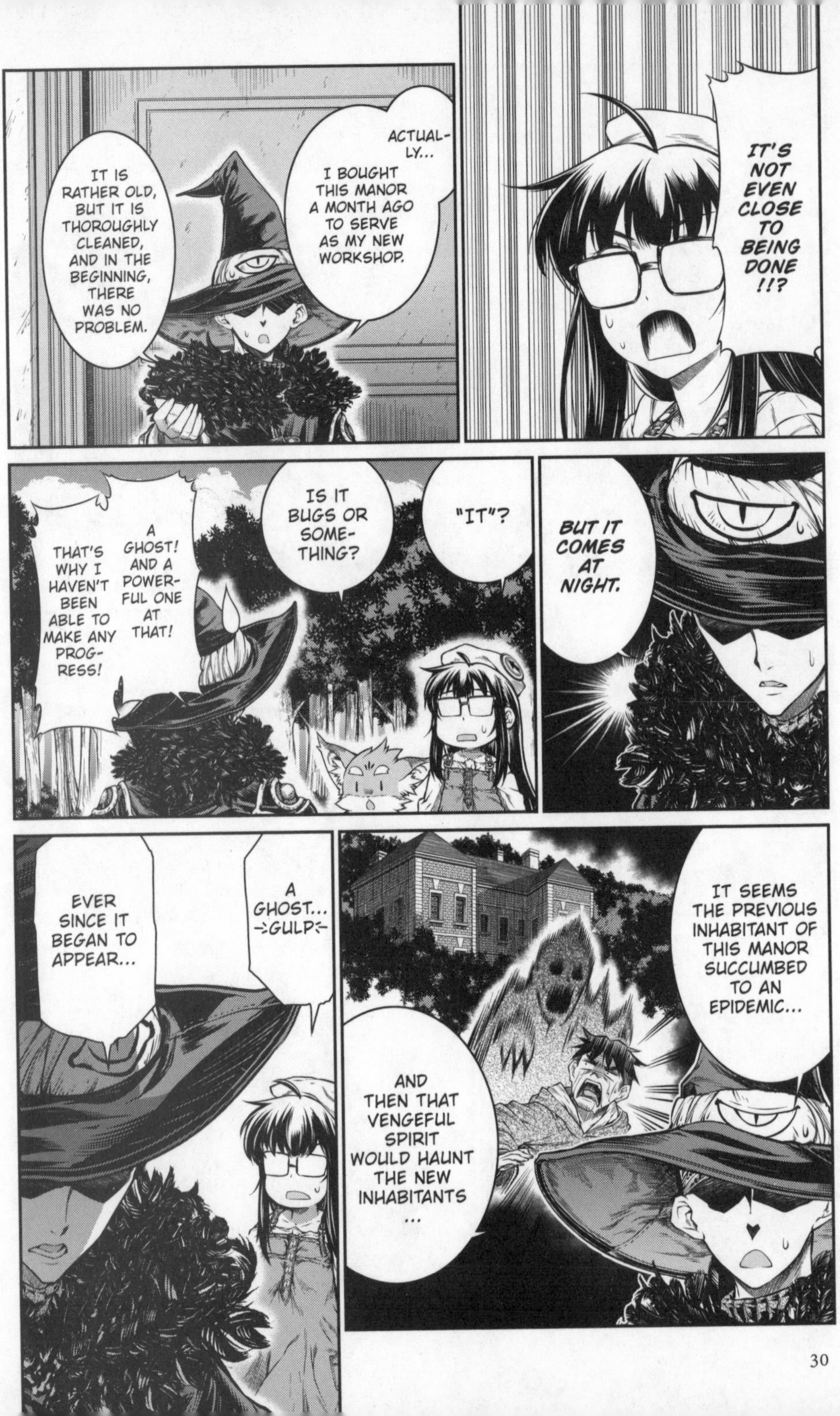
IT'S NOT EVEN CLOSE TO BEING DONE !!?
ACTUALLY... I BOUGHT THIS MANOR A MONTH AGO TO SERVE AS MY NEW WORKSHOP.
IT IS RATHER OLD, BUT IT IS THOROUGHLY CLEANED, AND IN THE BEGINNING, THERE WAS NO PROBLEM.
BUT IT COMES AT NIGHT.
"IT"?
IS IT BUGS OR SOMETHING?
A GHOST! AND A POWERFUL ONE AT THAT!
THAT'S WHY I HAVEN'T BEEN ABLE TO MAKE ANY PROGRESS!
IT SEEMS THE PREVIOUS INHABITANT OF THIS MANOR SUCCUMBED TO AN EPIDEMIC...
AND THEN THAT VENGEFUL SPIRIT WOULD HAUNT THE NEW INHABITANTS ...
A GHOST... GULP
EVER SINCE IT BEGAN TO APPEAR...

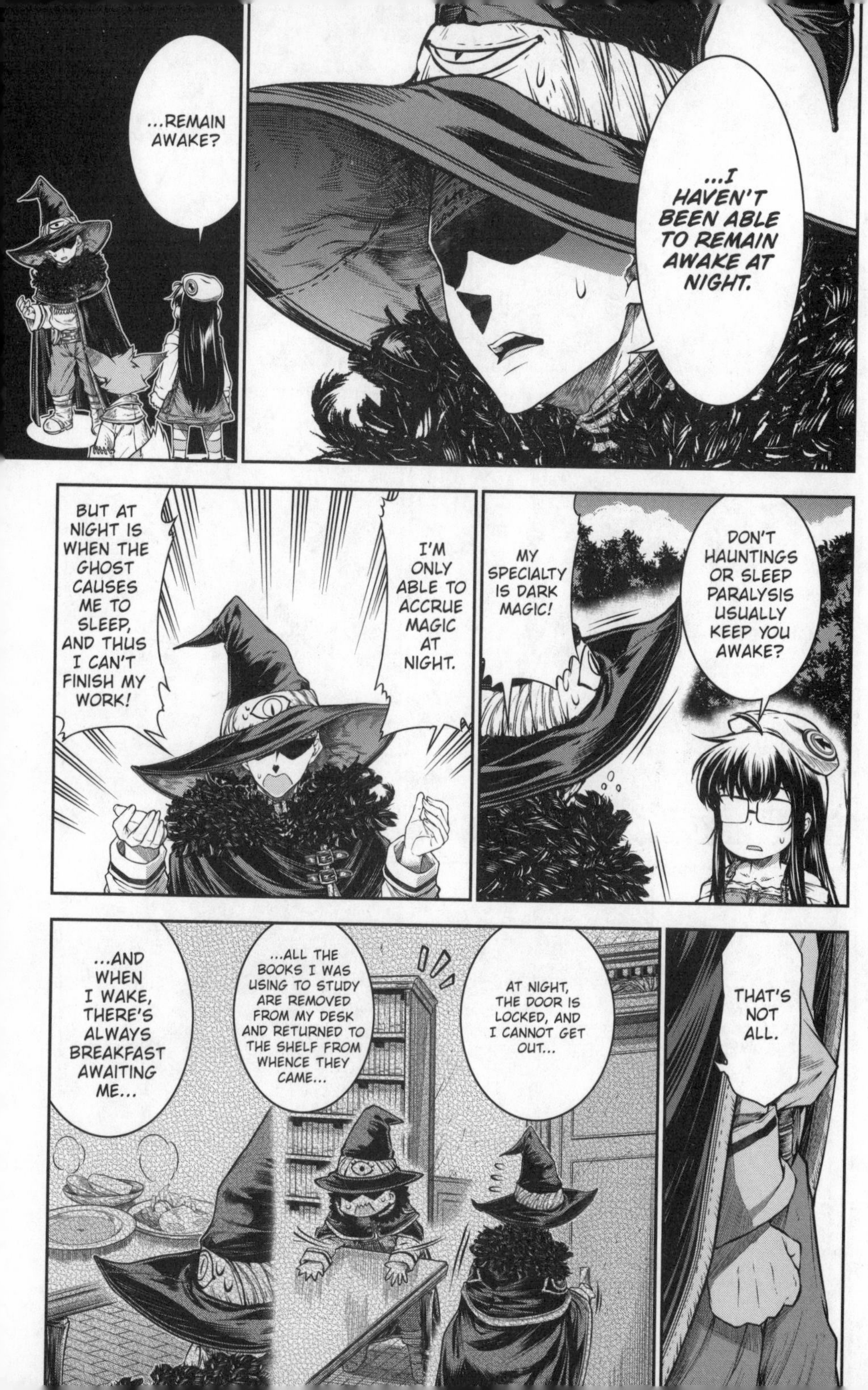
...I HAVEN'T BEEN ABLE TO REMAIN AWAKE AT NIGHT.
...REMAIN AWAKE?
DON'T HAUNTINGS OR SLEEP PARALYSIS USUALLY KEEP YOU AWAKE?
MY SPECIALTY IS DARK MAGIC!
I'M ONLY ABLE TO ACCRUE MAGIC AT NIGHT.
BUT AT NIGHT IS WHEN THE GHOST CAUSES ME TO SLEEP, AND THUS I CAN'T FINISH MY WORK!
THAT'S NOT ALL.
AT NIGHT, THE DOOR IS LOCKED, AND I CANNOT GET OUT...
...ALL THE BOOKS I WAS USING TO STUDY ARE REMOVED FROM MY DESK AND RETURNED TO THE SHELF FROM WHENCE THEY CAME...
...AND WHEN I WAKE, THERE'S ALWAYS BREAKFAST AWAITING ME...

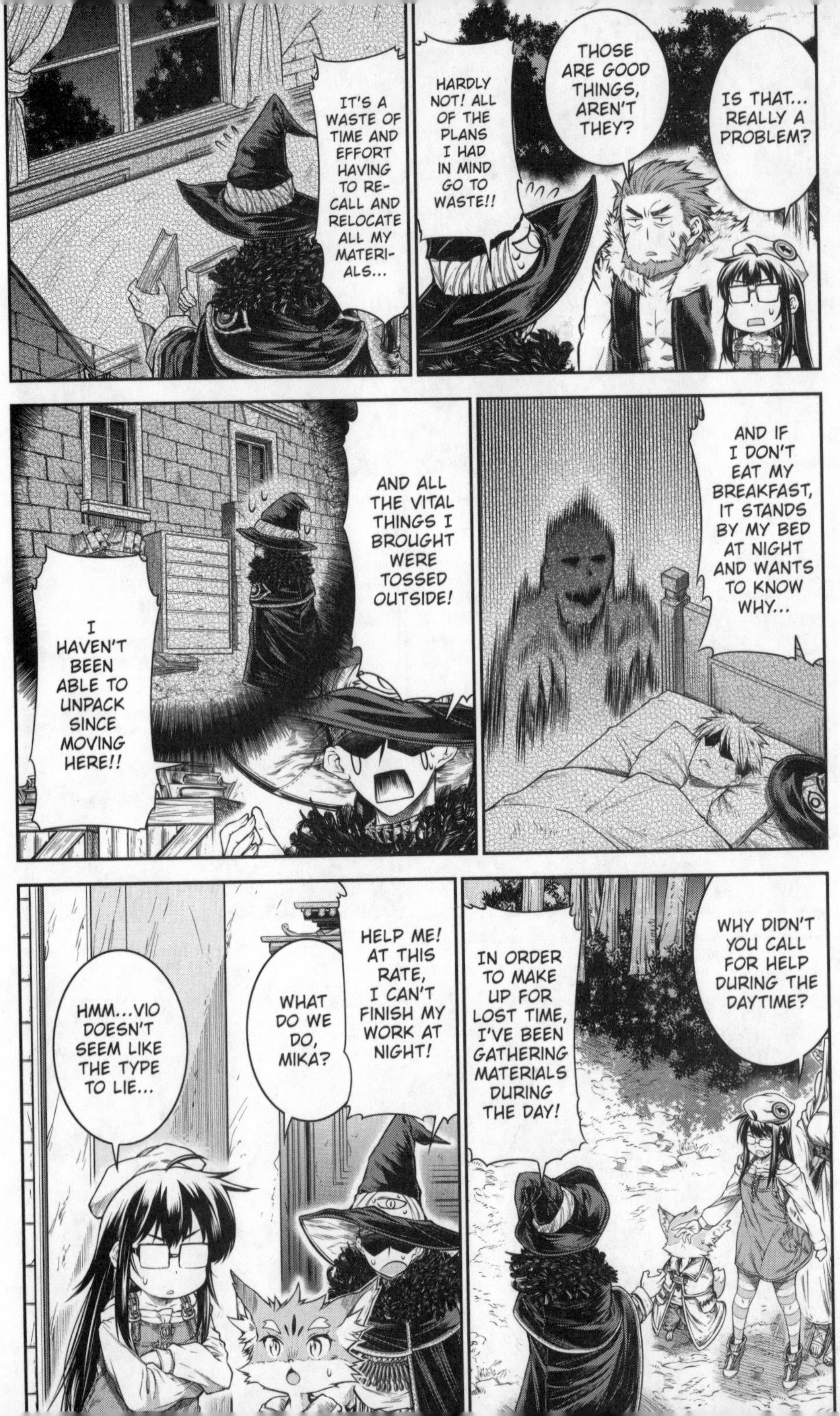
IS THAT... REALLY A PROBLEM?
THOSE ARE GOOD THINGS, AREN'T THEY?
HARDLY NOT! ALL OF THE PLANS I HAD IN MIND GO TO WASTE!!
IT'S A WASTE OF TIME AND EFFORT HAVING TO RE-CALL AND RELOCATE ALL MY MATERI-ALS...
AND IF I DON'T EAT MY BREAKFAST, IT STANDS BY MY BED AT NIGHT AND WANTS TO KNOW WHY...
AND ALL THE VITAL THINGS I BROUGHT WERE TOSSED OUTSIDE!
I HAVEN'T BEEN ABLE TO UNPACK SINCE MOVING HERE!!
WHY DIDN'T YOU CALL FOR HELP DURING THE DAYTIME?
IN ORDER TO MAKE UP FOR LOST TIME, I'VE BEEN GATHERING MATERIALS DURING THE DAY!
HELP ME! AT THIS RATE, I CAN'T FINISH MY WORK AT NIGHT!
WHAT DO WE DO, MIKA?
HMM...VIO DOESN'T SEEM LIKE THE TYPE TO LIE...

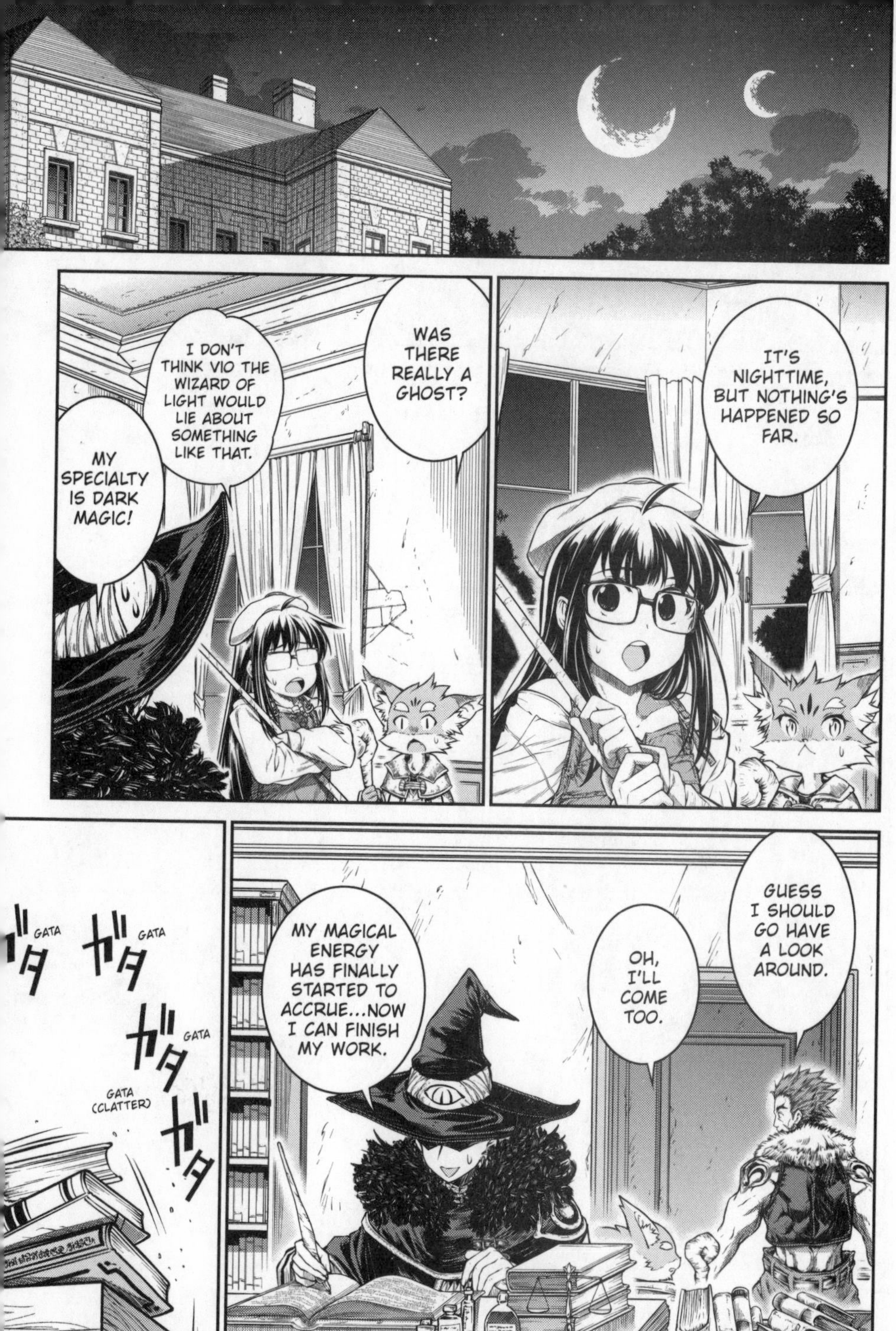
IT'S NIGHTTIME, BUT NOTHING'S HAPPENED SO FAR.
WAS THERE REALLY A GHOST?
I DON'T THINK VIO THE WIZARD OF LIGHT WOULD LIE ABOUT SOMETHING LIKE THAT.
MY SPECIALTY IS DARK MAGIC!
GUESS I SHOULD GO HAVE A LOOK AROUND.
OH, I'LL COME TOO.
MY MAGICAL ENERGY HAS FINALLY STARTED TO ACCRUE...NOW I CAN FINISH MY WORK.
ガタ GATA
ガタ GATA
ガタ GATA
ガタ GATA (CLATTER)

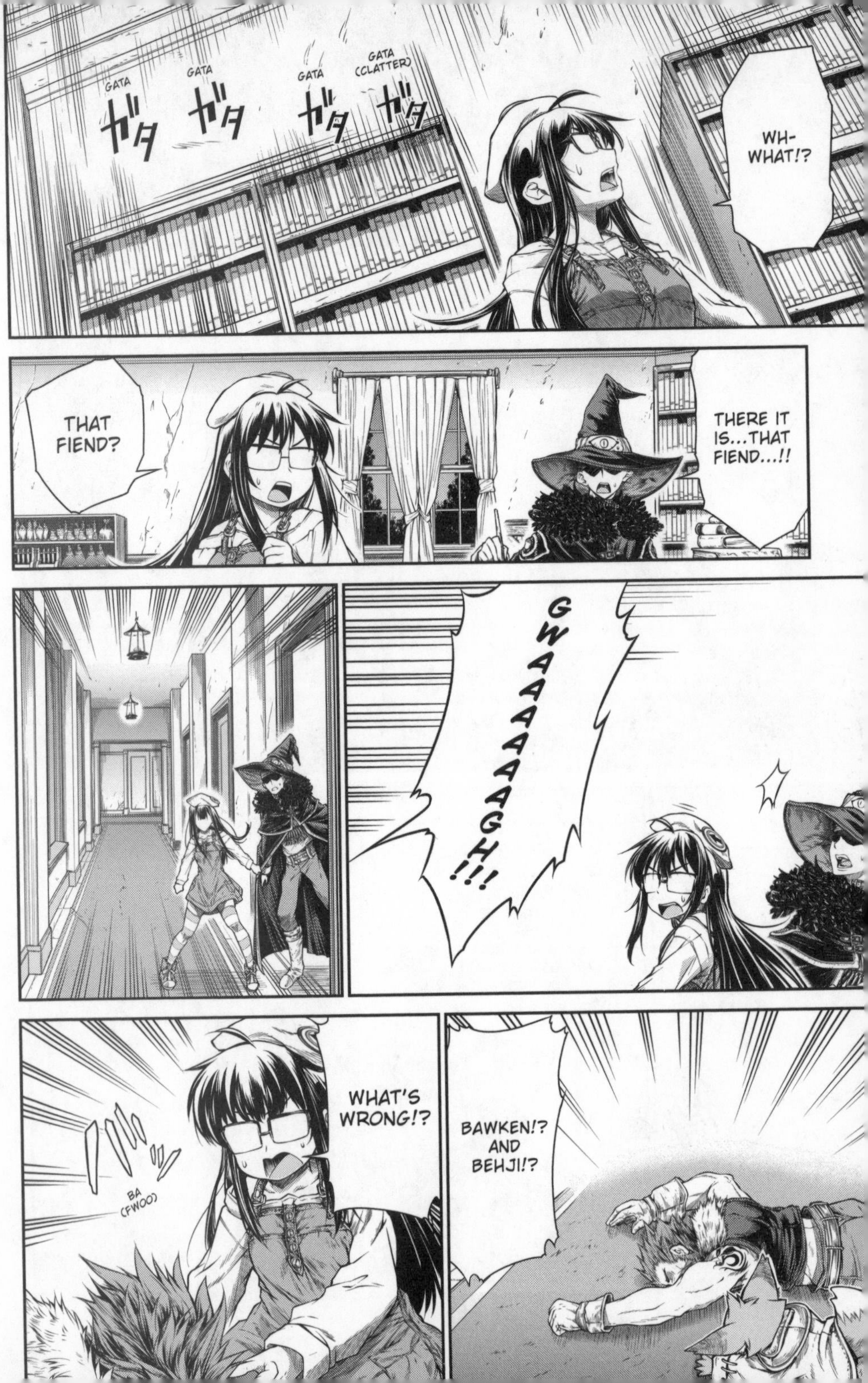
GATA (CLATTER)
GATA
GATA
GATA
WH-WHAT!?
THERE IT IS...THAT FIEND...!!
THAT FIEND?
GWAAAAAAAAGH!!!
BAWKEN!? AND BEHJI!?
WHAT'S WRONG!?
BA (FWOO)

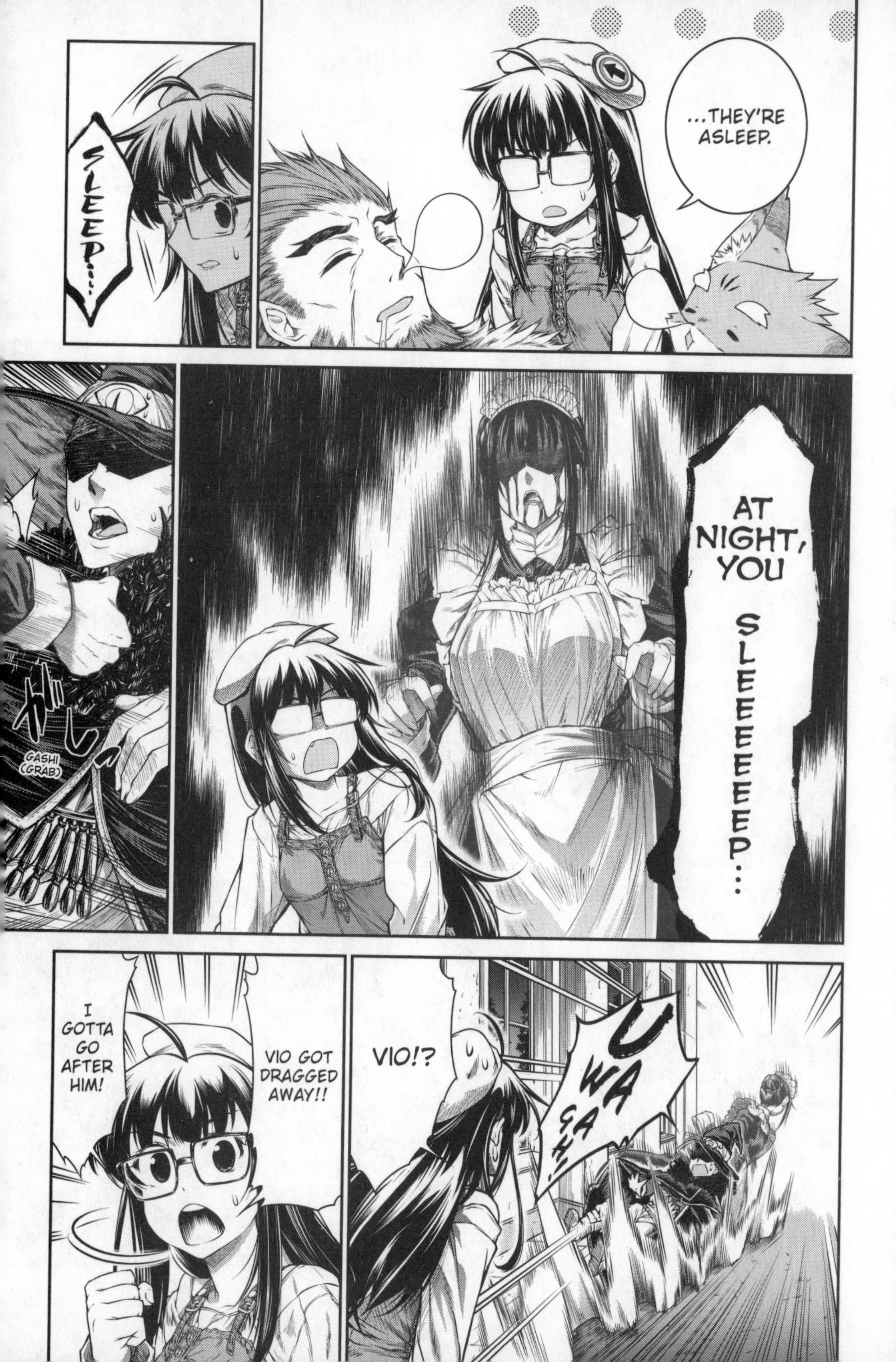
...THEY'RE ASLEEP.
SLEEP...
AT NIGHT, YOU SLEEEEEEP...
がし
GASHI (GRAB)
UWAGAH!
VIO!?
VIO GOT DRAGGED AWAY!!
I GOTTA GO AFTER HIM!

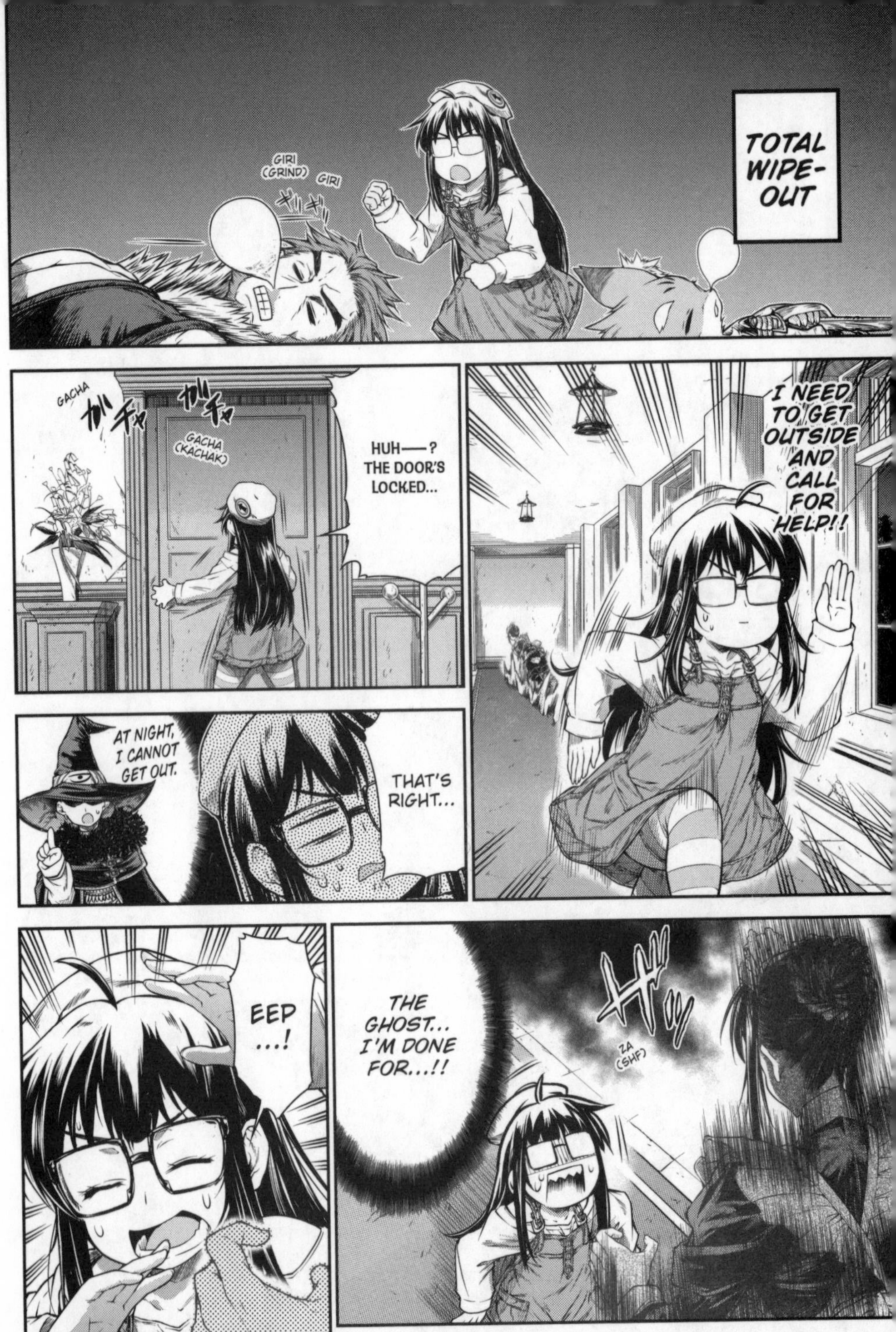
TOTAL WIPE-OUT
GIRI (GRIND) GIRI
I NEED TO GET OUTSIDE AND CALL FOR HELP!!
GACHA (KACHAK)
GACHA
HUH—? THE DOOR'S LOCKED...
AT NIGHT, I CANNOT GET OUT.
THAT'S RIGHT...
ZA (SHF)
THE GHOST... I'M DONE FOR...!!
EEP ...!

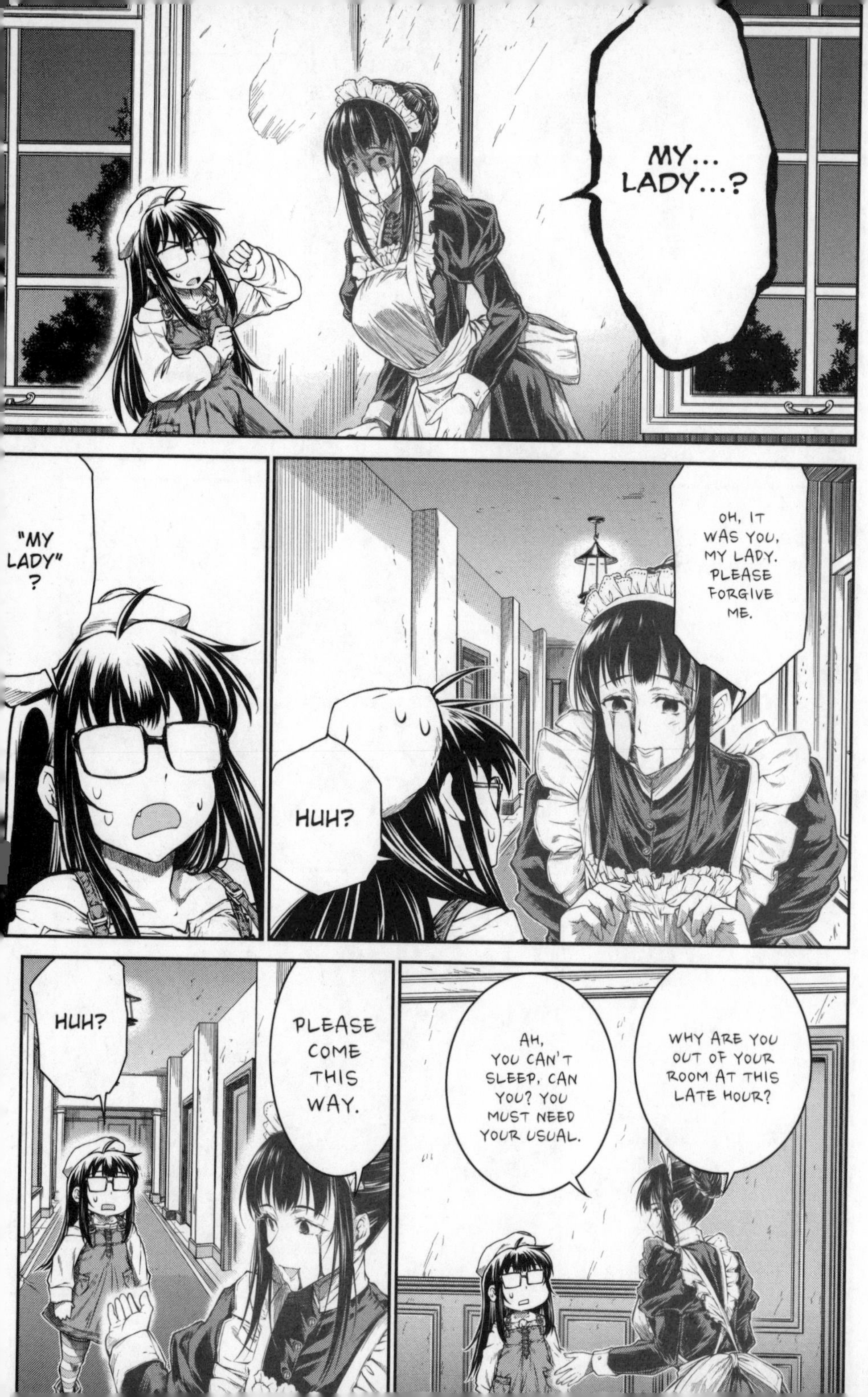
MY... LADY...?
OH, IT WAS YOU, MY LADY. PLEASE FORGIVE ME.
HUH?
"MY LADY"?
WHY ARE YOU OUT OF YOUR ROOM AT THIS LATE HOUR?
AH, YOU CAN'T SLEEP, CAN YOU? YOU MUST NEED YOUR USUAL.
PLEASE COME THIS WAY.
HUH?

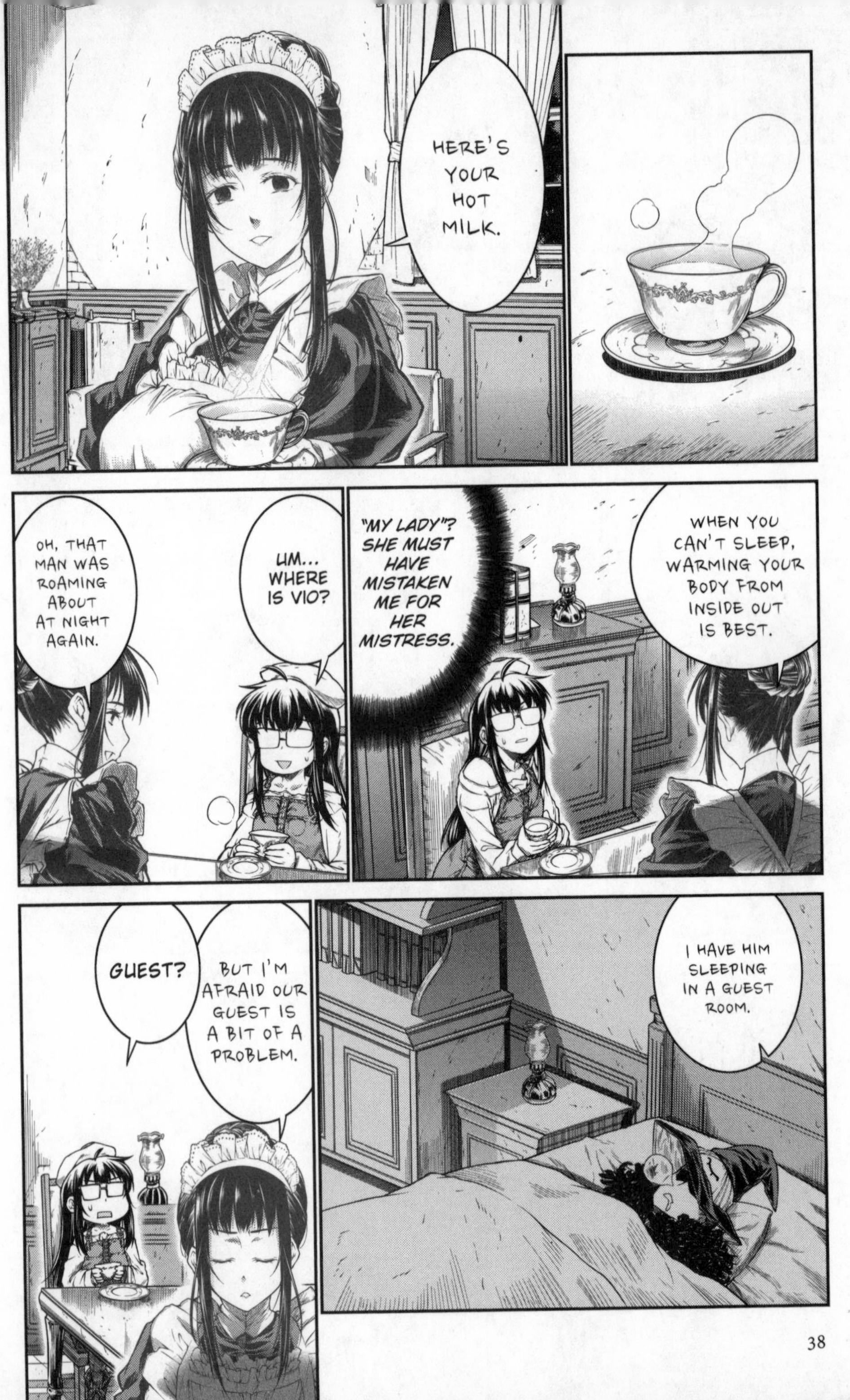
HERE'S YOUR HOT MILK.
WHEN YOU CAN'T SLEEP, WARMING YOUR BODY FROM INSIDE OUT IS BEST.
"MY LADY"? SHE MUST HAVE MISTAKEN ME FOR HER MISTRESS.
UM... WHERE IS VIO?
OH, THAT MAN WAS ROAMING ABOUT AT NIGHT AGAIN.
I HAVE HIM SLEEPING IN A GUEST ROOM.
BUT I'M AFRAID OUR GUEST IS A BIT OF A PROBLEM.
GUEST?

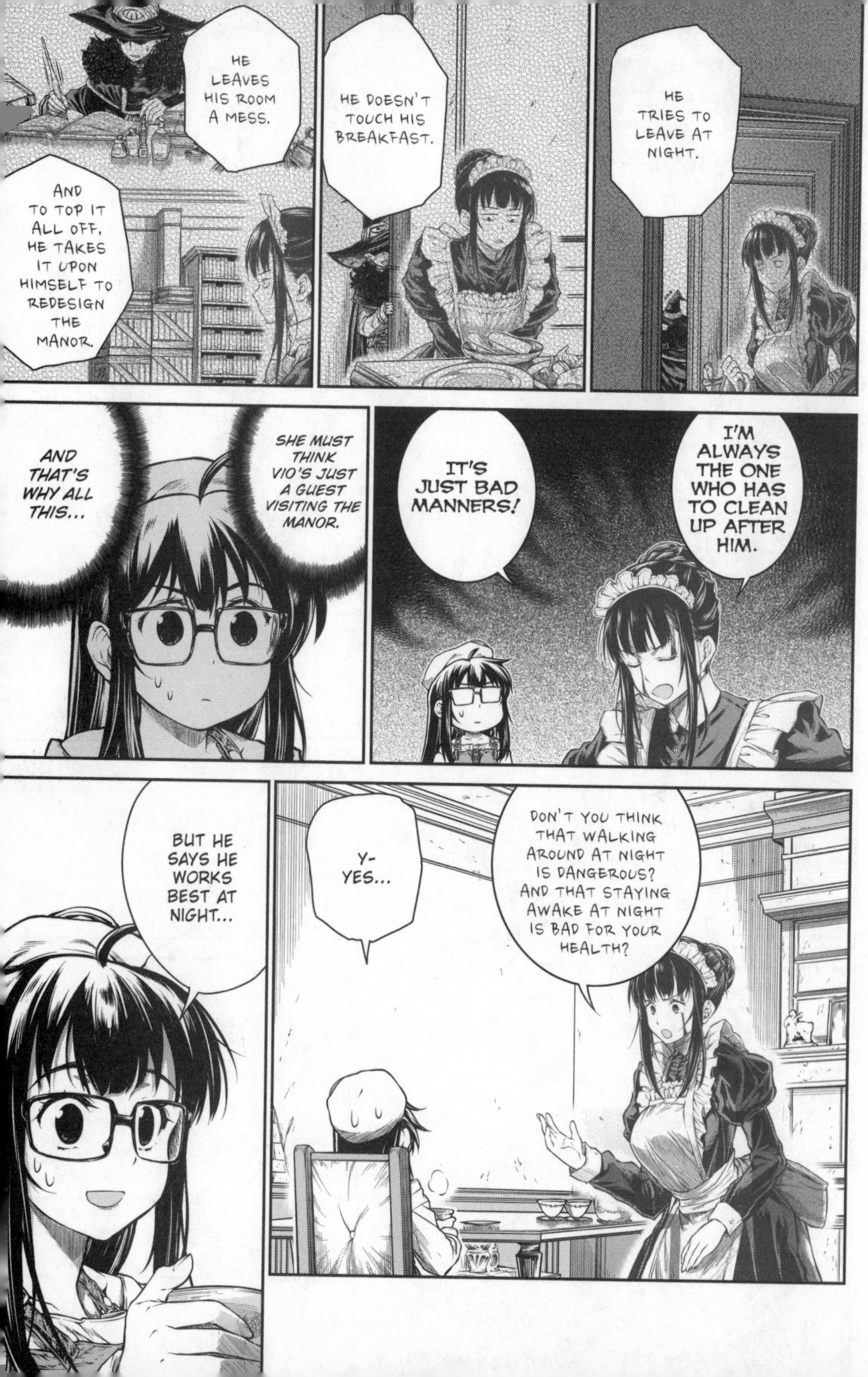
HE TRIES TO LEAVE AT NIGHT.
HE DOESN'T TOUCH HIS BREAKFAST.
HE LEAVES HIS ROOM A MESS.
AND TO TOP IT ALL OFF, HE TAKES IT UPON HIMSELF TO REDESIGN THE MANOR.
I'M ALWAYS THE ONE WHO HAS TO CLEAN UP AFTER HIM.
IT'S JUST BAD MANNERS!
SHE MUST THINK VIO'S JUST A GUEST VISITING THE MANOR.
AND THAT'S WHY ALL THIS...
DON'T YOU THINK THAT WALKING AROUND AT NIGHT IS DANGEROUS? AND THAT STAYING AWAKE AT NIGHT IS BAD FOR YOUR HEALTH?
Y- YES...
BUT HE SAYS HE WORKS BEST AT NIGHT...

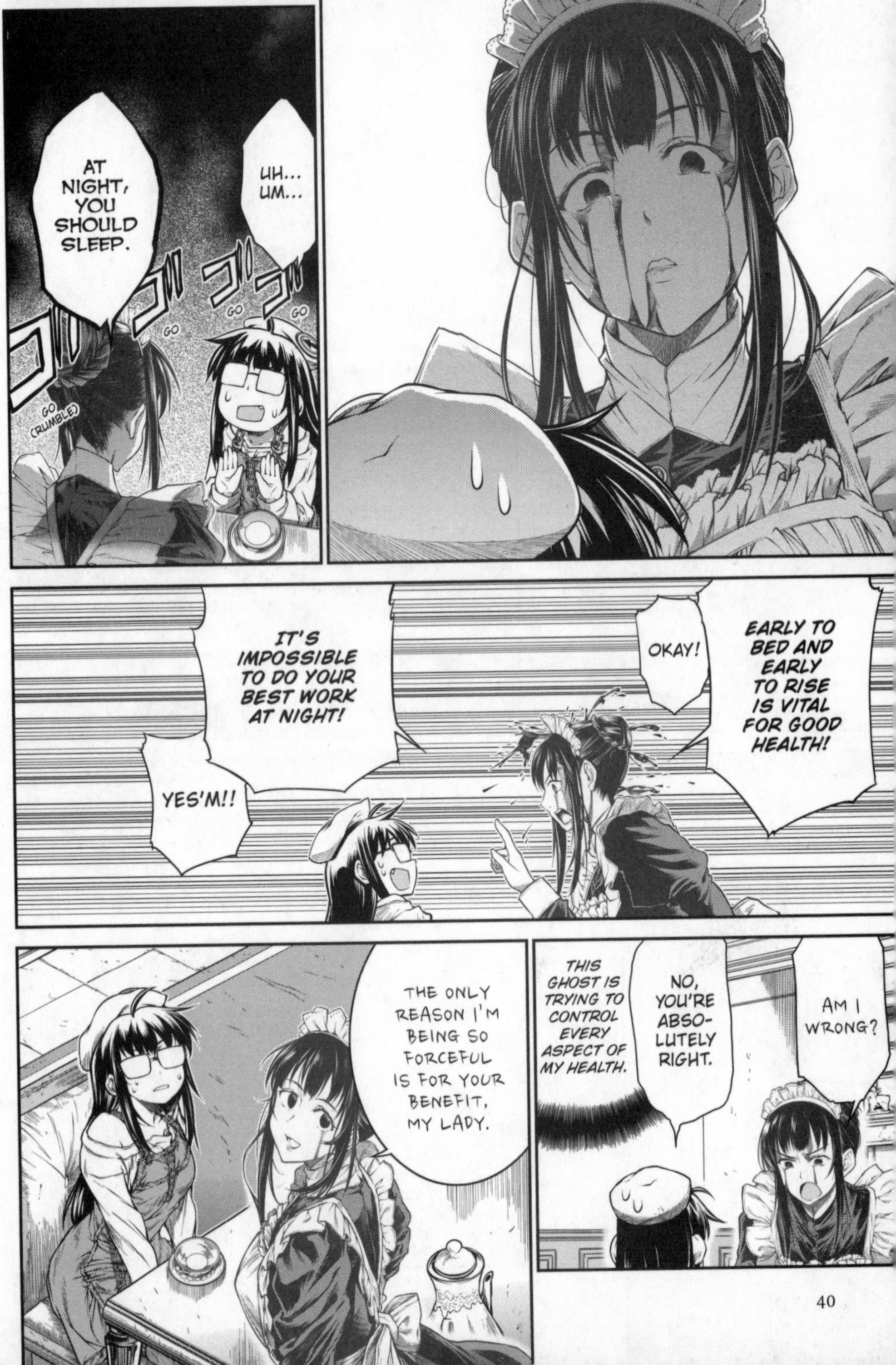
UH... UM...
AT NIGHT, YOU SHOULD SLEEP.
GO GO GO GO (RUMBLE)
EARLY TO BED AND EARLY TO RISE IS VITAL FOR GOOD HEALTH!
OKAY!
IT'S IMPOSSIBLE TO DO YOUR BEST WORK AT NIGHT!
YES'M!!
AM I WRONG?
NO, YOU'RE ABSO-LUTELY RIGHT.
THIS GHOST IS TRYING TO CONTROL EVERY ASPECT OF MY HEALTH.
THE ONLY REASON I'M BEING SO FORCEFUL IS FOR YOUR BENEFIT, MY LADY.

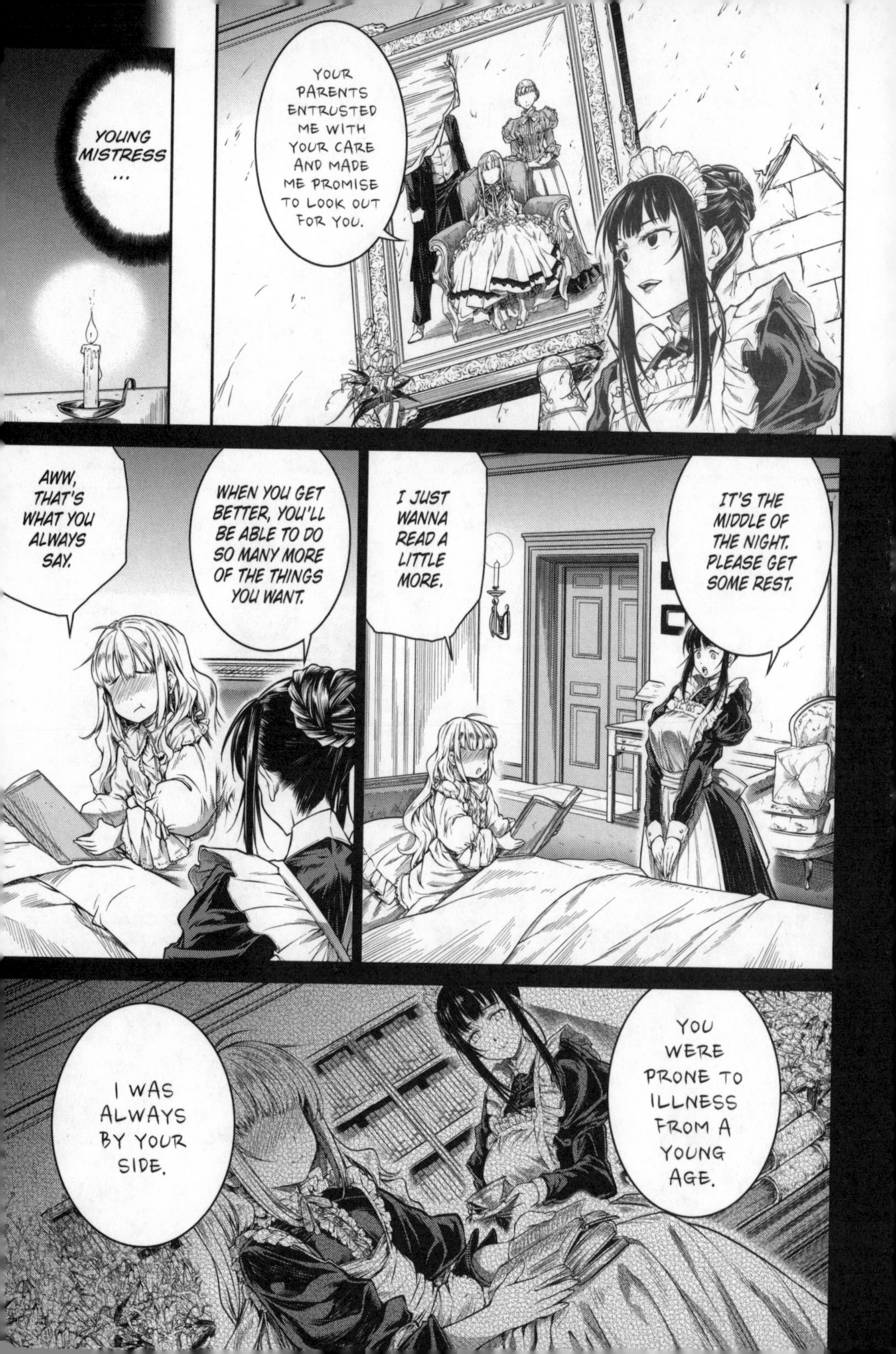
YOUR PARENTS ENTRUSTED ME WITH YOUR CARE AND MADE ME PROMISE TO LOOK OUT FOR YOU.
YOUNG MISTRESS ...
IT'S THE MIDDLE OF THE NIGHT. PLEASE GET SOME REST.
I JUST WANNA READ A LITTLE MORE.
WHEN YOU GET BETTER, YOU'LL BE ABLE TO DO SO MANY MORE OF THE THINGS YOU WANT.
AWW, THAT'S WHAT YOU ALWAYS SAY.
YOU WERE PRONE TO ILLNESS FROM A YOUNG AGE.
I WAS ALWAYS BY YOUR SIDE.

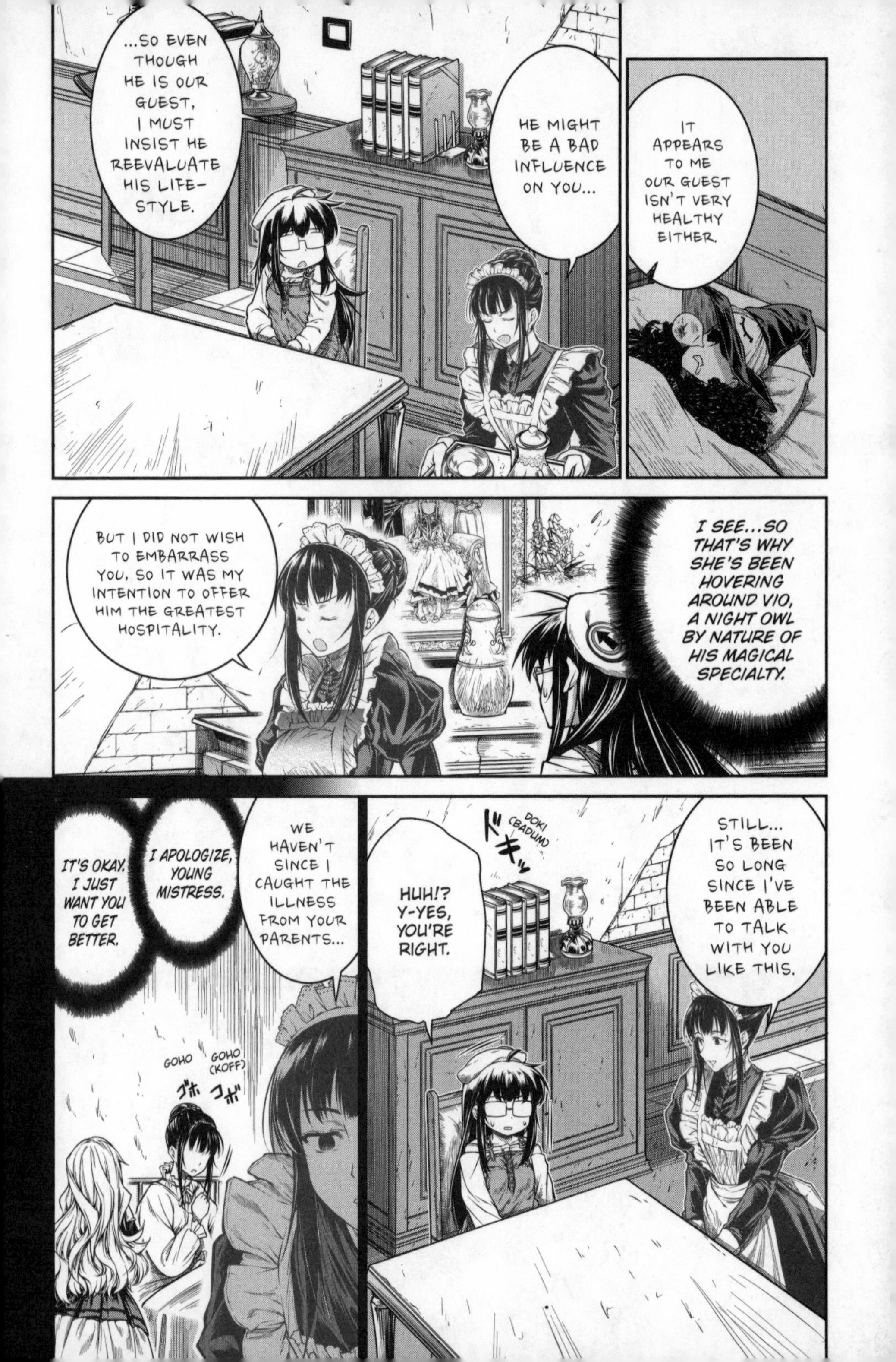
IT APPEARS TO ME OUR GUEST ISN'T VERY HEALTHY EITHER.
HE MIGHT BE A BAD INFLUENCE ON YOU...
...SO EVEN THOUGH HE IS OUR GUEST, I MUST INSIST HE REEVALUATE HIS LIFE-STYLE.
I SEE...SO THAT'S WHY SHE'S BEEN HOVERING AROUND VIO, A NIGHT OWL BY NATURE OF HIS MAGICAL SPECIALTY.
BUT I DID NOT WISH TO EMBARRASS YOU, SO IT WAS MY INTENTION TO OFFER HIM THE GREATEST HOSPITALITY.
STILL... IT'S BEEN SO LONG SINCE I'VE BEEN ABLE TO TALK WITH YOU LIKE THIS.
DOKI (BADUM)
HUH!? Y-YES, YOU'RE RIGHT.
WE HAVEN'T SINCE I CAUGHT THE ILLNESS FROM YOUR PARENTS...
GOHO GOHO (KOFF)
I APOLOGIZE, YOUNG MISTRESS.
IT'S OKAY. I JUST WANT YOU TO GET BETTER.

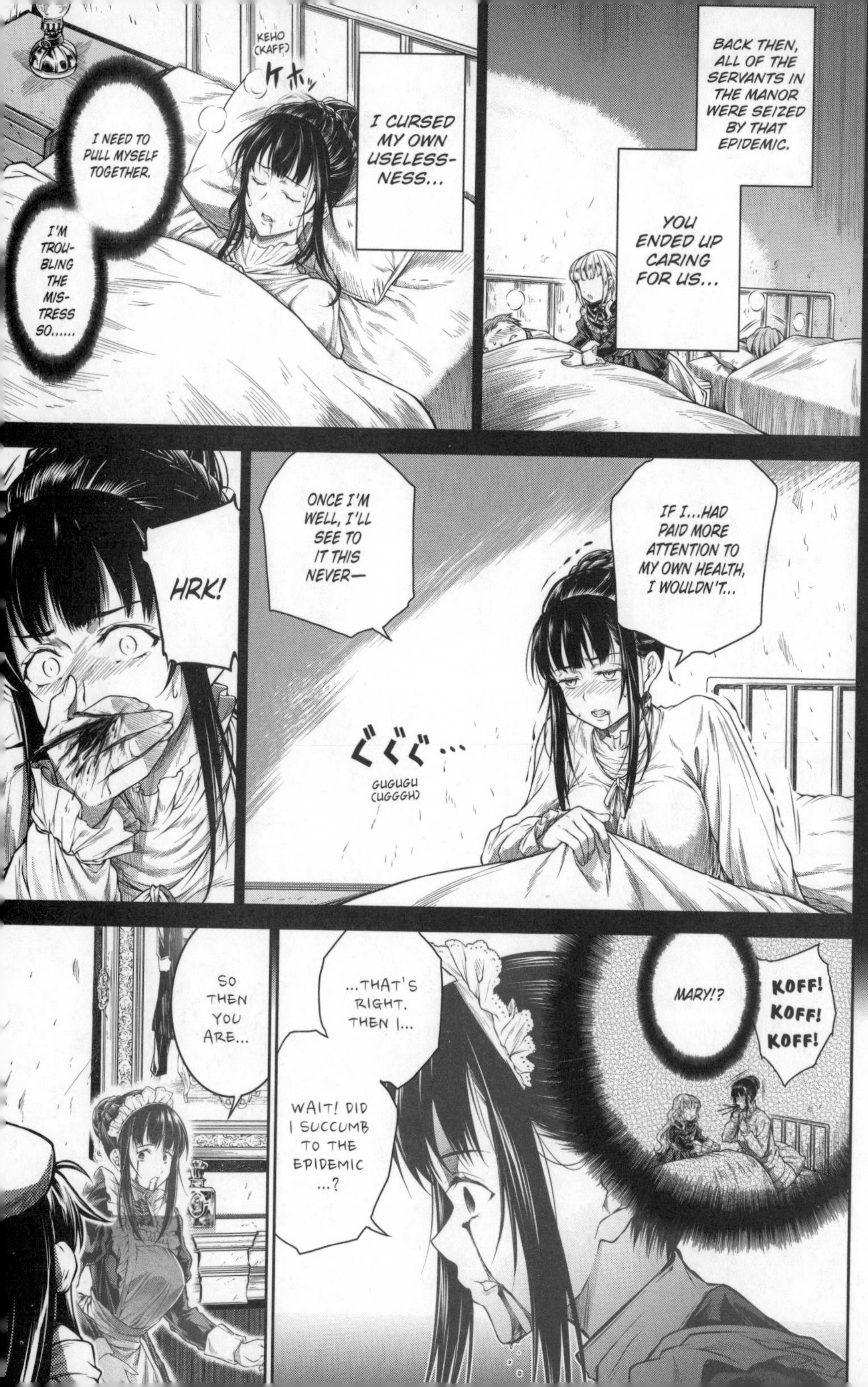
BACK THEN, ALL OF THE SERVANTS IN THE MANOR WERE SEIZED BY THAT EPIDEMIC.
YOU ENDED UP CARING FOR US...
I CURSED MY OWN USELESSNESS...
ケホッ
KEHO (KAFF)
I NEED TO PULL MYSELF TOGETHER.
I'M TROUBLING THE MISTRESS SO......
IF I...HAD PAID MORE ATTENTION TO MY OWN HEALTH, I WOULDN'T...
ONCE I'M WELL, I'LL SEE TO IT THIS NEVER—
ぐぐぐ…
GUGUGU (UGGGH)
HRK!
KOFF! KOFF! KOFF!
MARY!?
...THAT'S RIGHT. THEN I...
WAIT! DID I SUCCUMB TO THE EPIDEMIC...?
SO THEN YOU ARE...

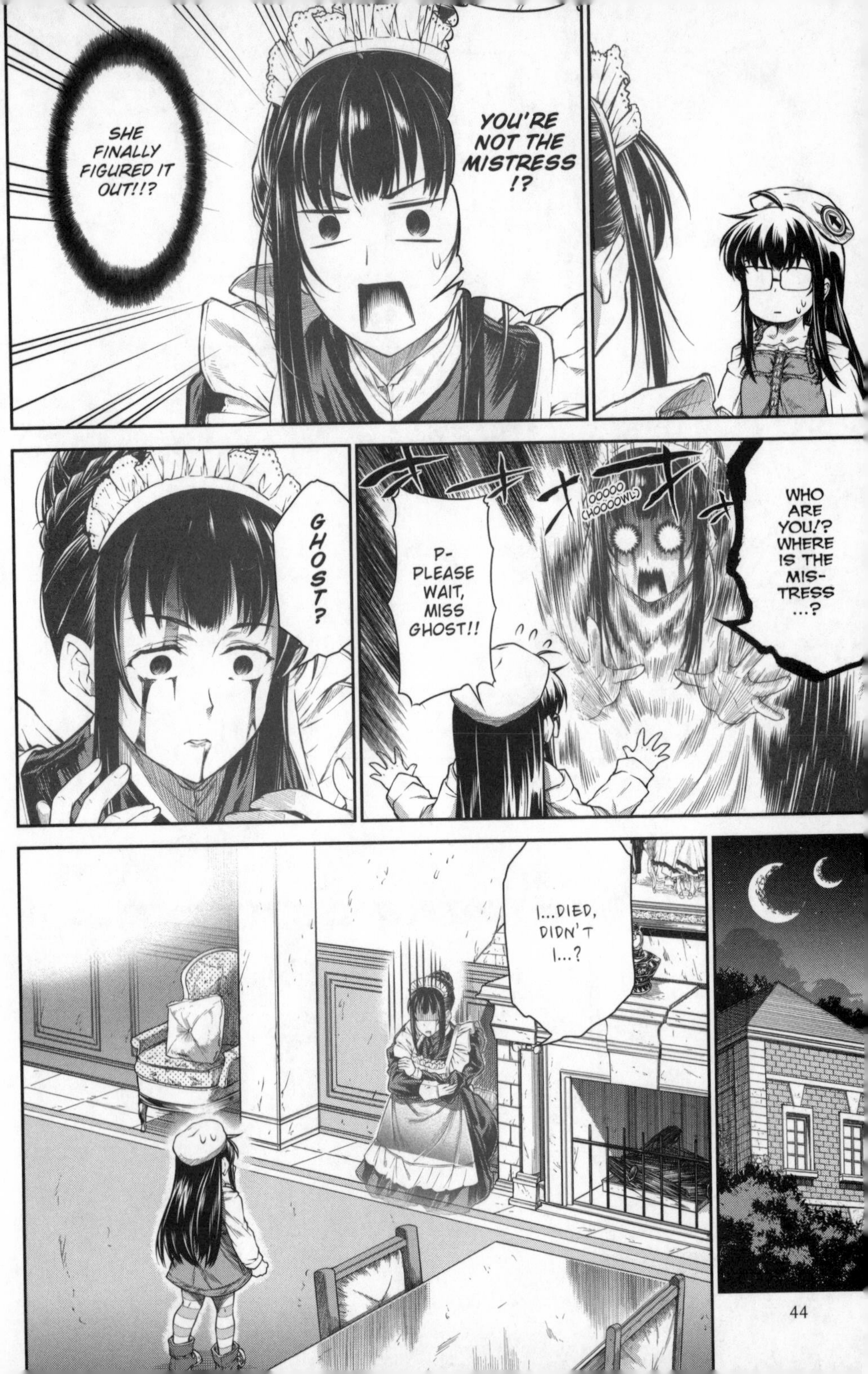
YOU'RE NOT THE MISTRESS!?
SHE FINALLY FIGURED IT OUT!!?
WHO ARE YOU!? WHERE IS THE MIS-TRESS...?
!OOOOO (HOOOOWL!)
P-PLEASE WAIT, MISS GHOST!!
GHOST?
I...DIED, DIDN'T I...?

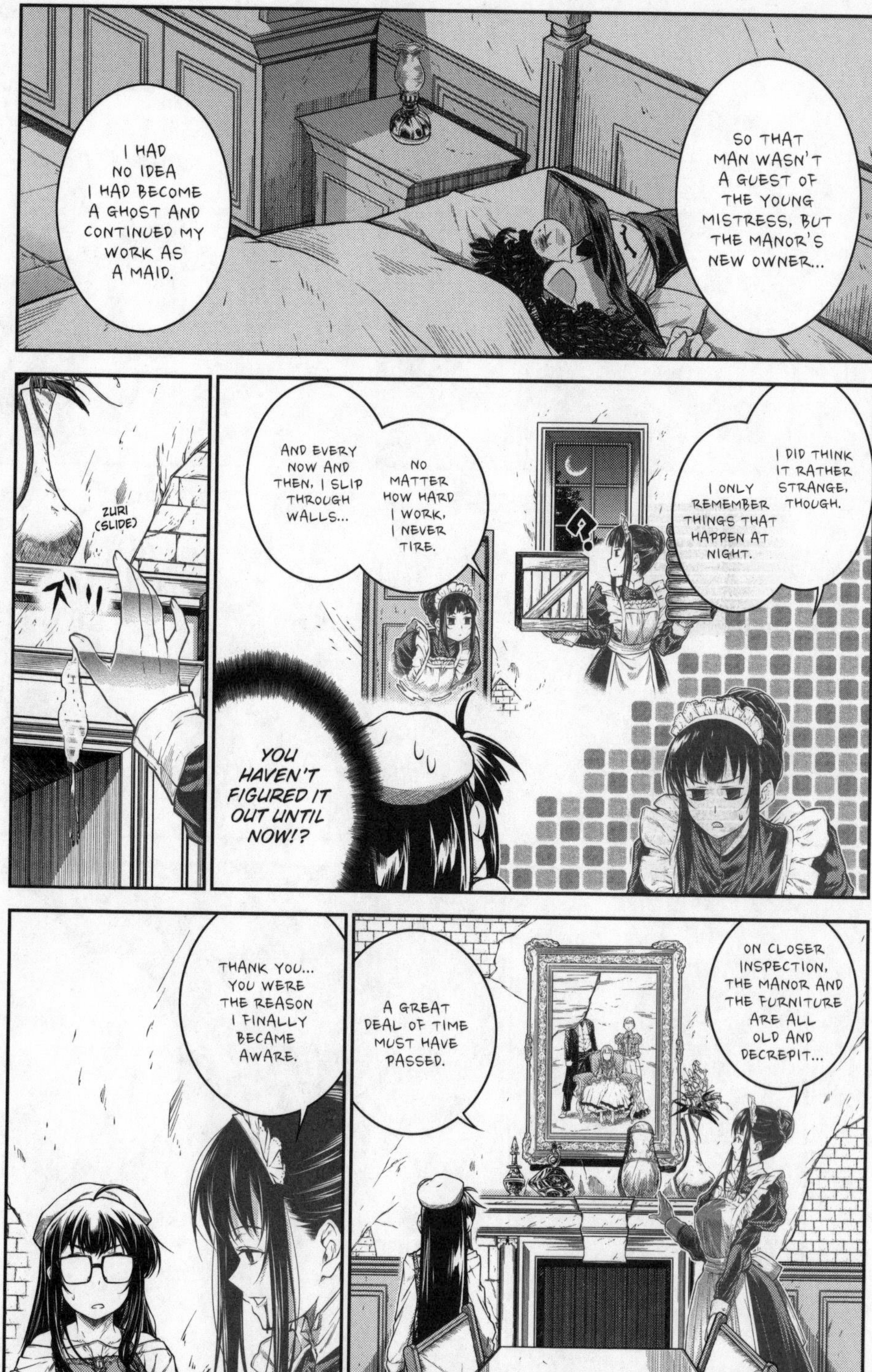
SO THAT MAN WASN'T A GUEST OF THE YOUNG MISTRESS, BUT THE MANOR'S NEW OWNER...
I HAD NO IDEA I HAD BECOME A GHOST AND CONTINUED MY WORK AS A MAID.
I DID THINK IT RATHER STRANGE, THOUGH.
I ONLY REMEMBER THINGS THAT HAPPEN AT NIGHT.
NO MATTER HOW HARD I WORK, I NEVER TIRE.
AND EVERY NOW AND THEN, I SLIP THROUGH WALLS...
YOU HAVEN'T FIGURED IT OUT UNTIL NOW!?
ZURI (SLIDE)
ズリ
ON CLOSER INSPECTION, THE MANOR AND THE FURNITURE ARE ALL OLD AND DECREPIT...
A GREAT DEAL OF TIME MUST HAVE PASSED.
THANK YOU... YOU WERE THE REASON I FINALLY BECAME AWARE.

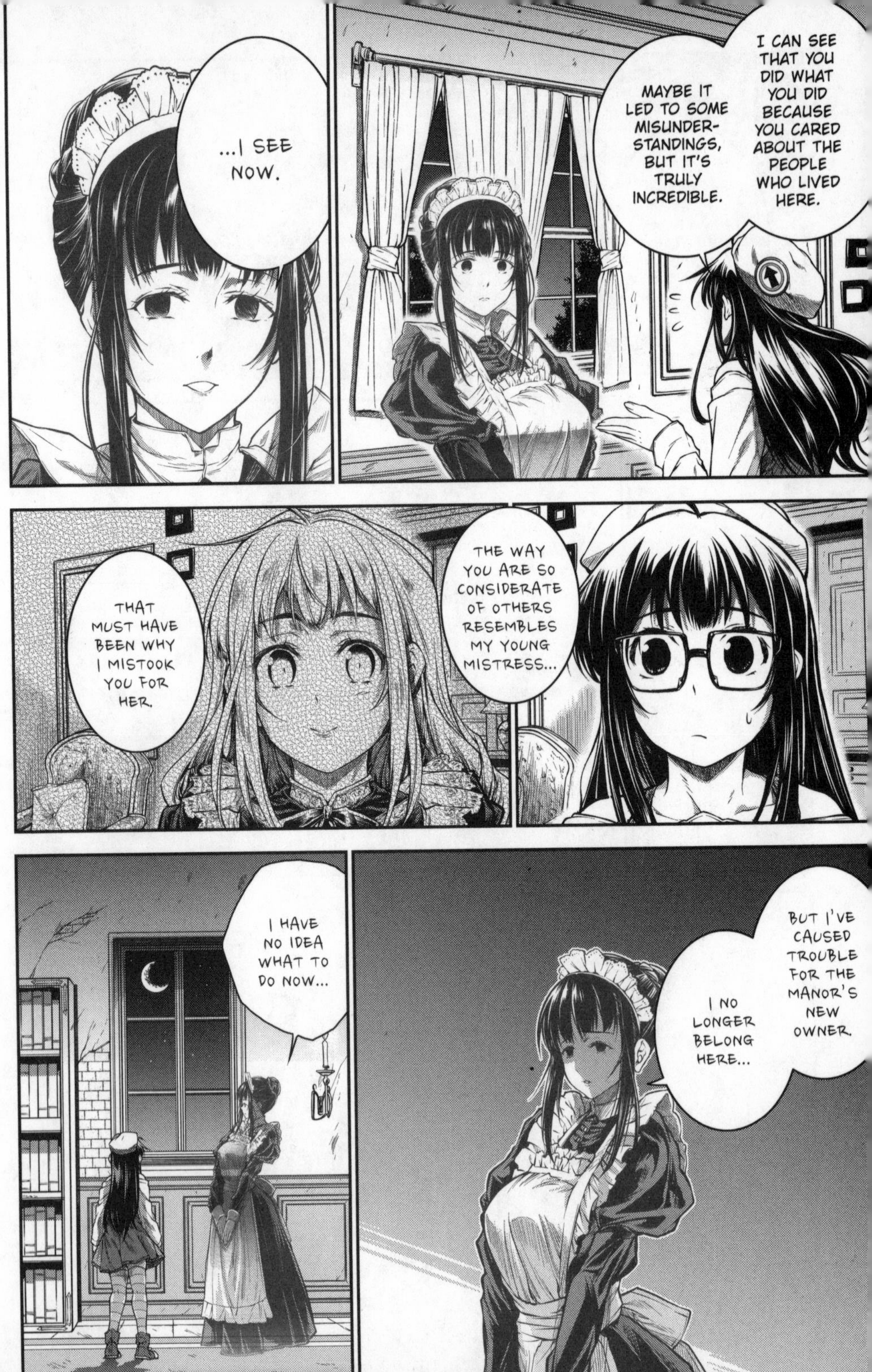
I CAN SEE THAT YOU DID WHAT YOU DID BECAUSE YOU CARED ABOUT THE PEOPLE WHO LIVED HERE.
MAYBE IT LED TO SOME MISUNDER-STANDINGS, BUT IT'S TRULY INCREDIBLE.
...I SEE NOW.
THE WAY YOU ARE SO CONSIDERATE OF OTHERS RESEMBLES MY YOUNG MISTRESS...
THAT MUST HAVE BEEN WHY I MISTOOK YOU FOR HER.
BUT I'VE CAUSED TROUBLE FOR THE MANOR'S NEW OWNER.
I NO LONGER BELONG HERE...
I HAVE NO IDEA WHAT TO DO NOW...

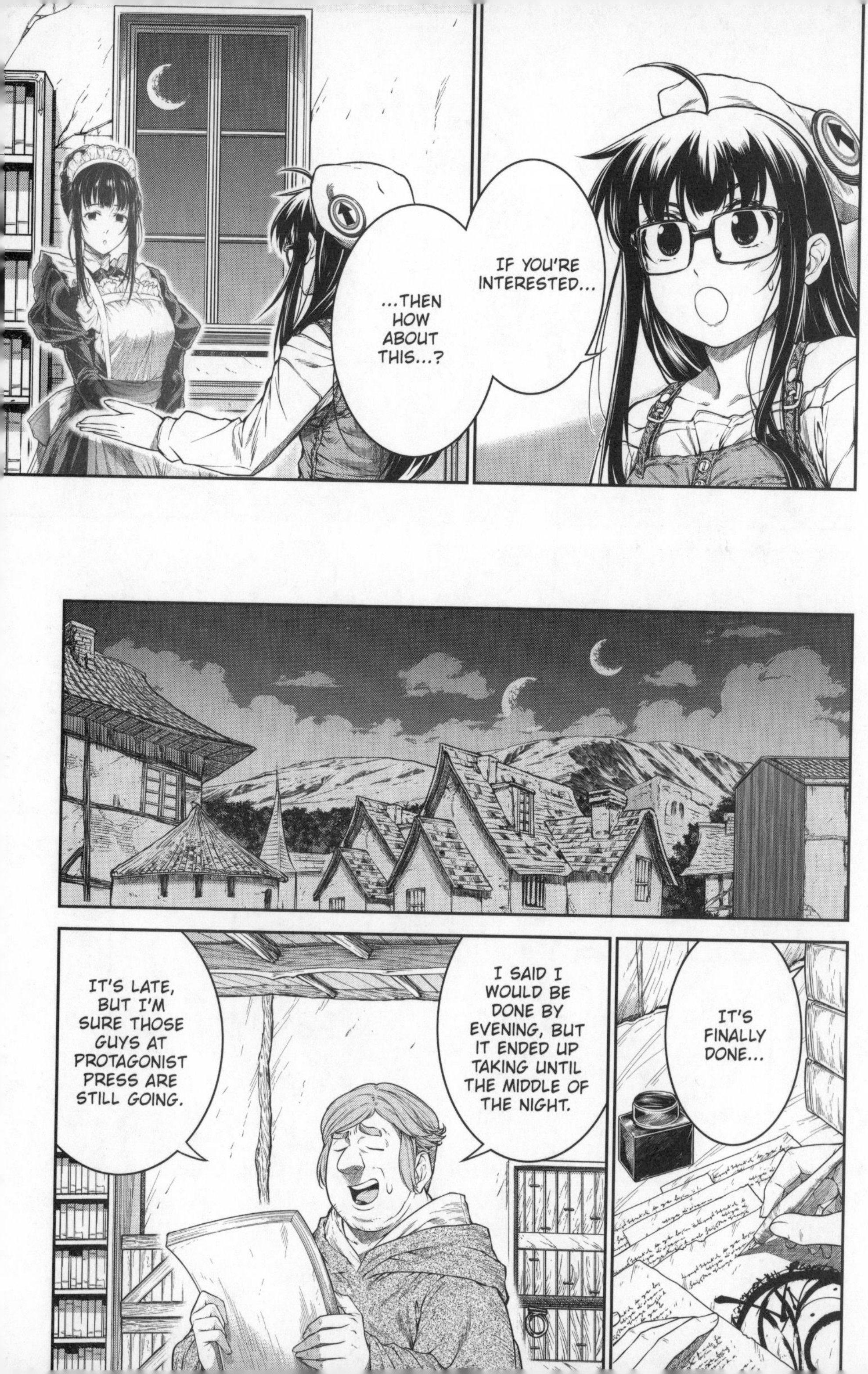
IF YOU'RE INTERESTED...
...THEN HOW ABOUT THIS...?
IT'S FINALLY DONE...
I SAID I WOULD BE DONE BY EVENING, BUT IT ENDED UP TAKING UNTIL THE MIDDLE OF THE NIGHT.
IT'S LATE, BUT I'M SURE THOSE GUYS AT PROTAGONIST PRESS ARE STILL GOING.

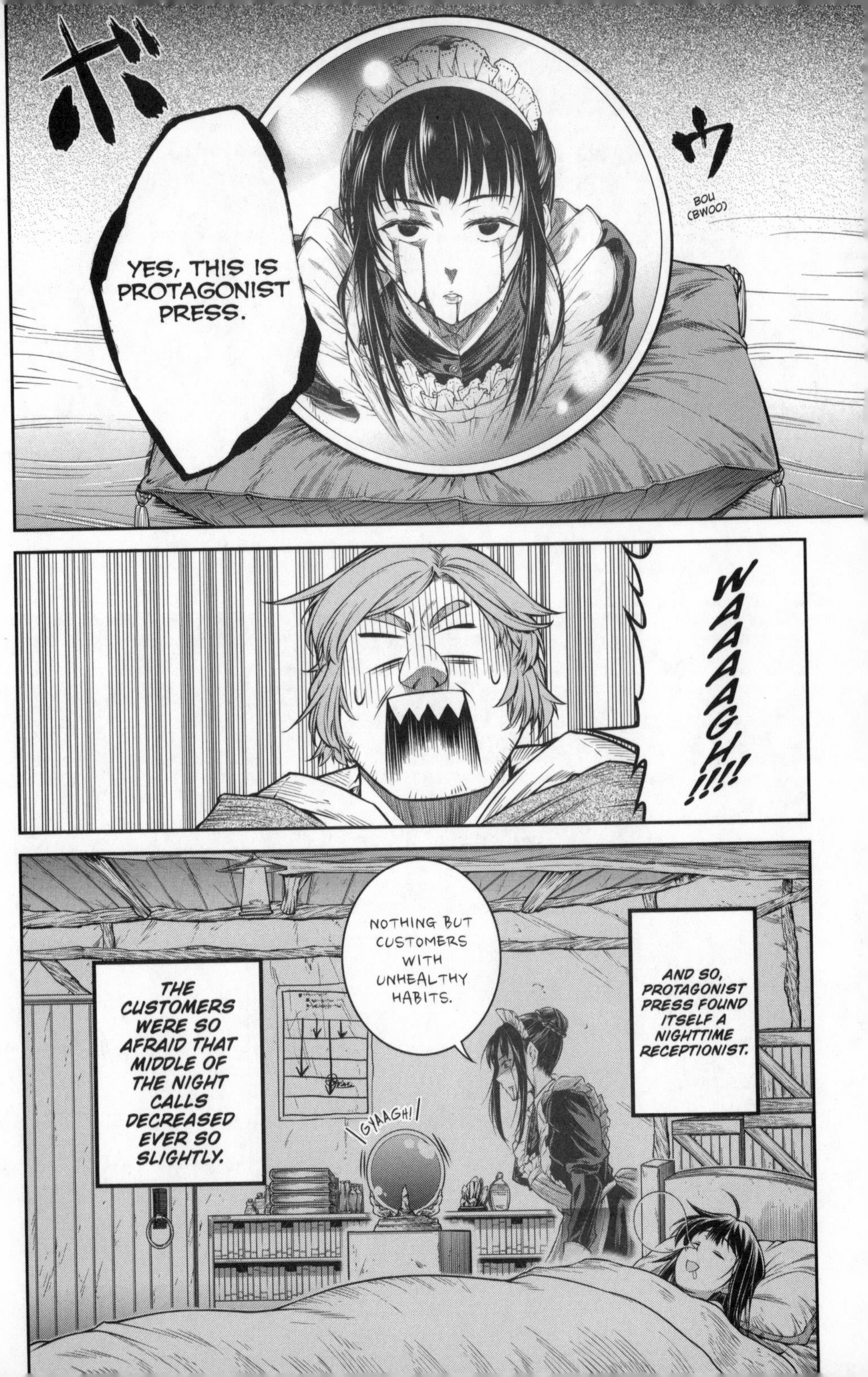
ボウ
BOU (BWOO)
YES, THIS IS PROTAGONIST PRESS.
WAAAAAGH!!!!
AND SO, PROTAGONIST PRESS FOUND ITSELF A NIGHTTIME RECEPTIONIST.
NOTHING BUT CUSTOMERS WITH UNHEALTHY HABITS.
GYAAGH!
THE CUSTOMERS WERE SO AFRAID THAT MIDDLE OF THE NIGHT CALLS DECREASED EVER SO SLIGHTLY.

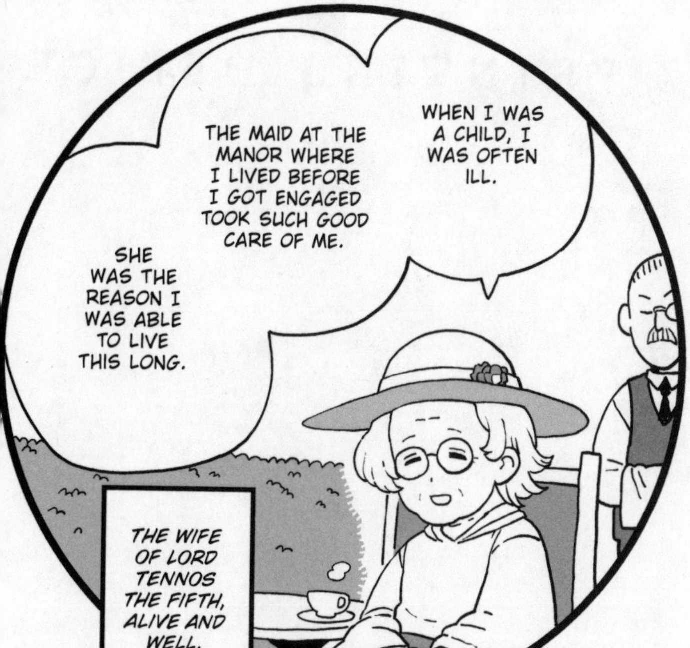
WHEN I WAS A CHILD, I WAS OFTEN ILL.
THE MAID AT THE MANOR WHERE I LIVED BEFORE I GOT ENGAGED TOOK SUCH GOOD CARE OF ME.
SHE WAS THE REASON I WAS ABLE TO LIVE THIS LONG.
THE WIFE OF LORD TENNOS THE FIFTH, ALIVE AND WELL.

A WITCH'S PRINTING OFFICE

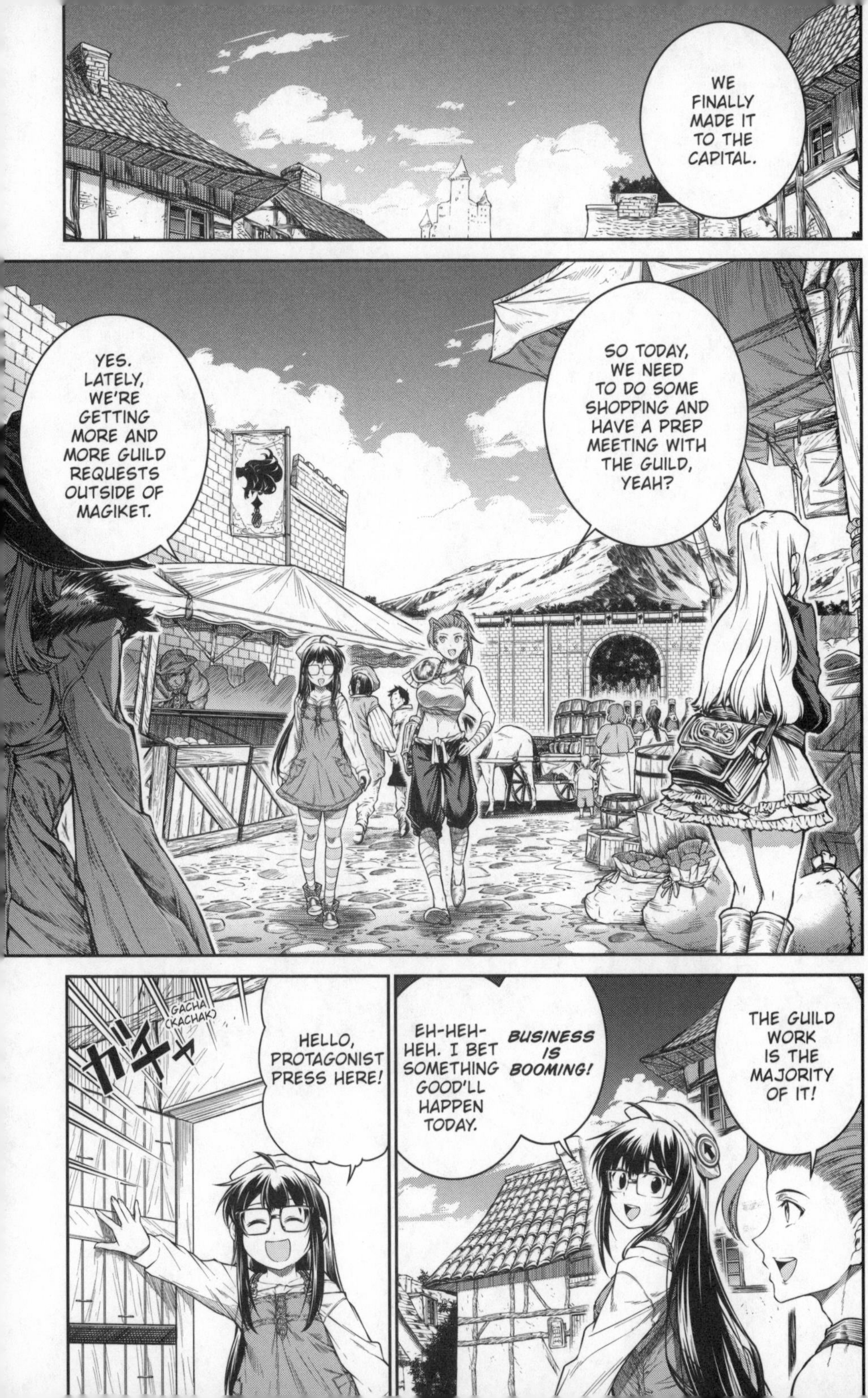
WE FINALLY MADE IT TO THE CAPITAL.
SO TODAY, WE NEED TO DO SOME SHOPPING AND HAVE A PREP MEETING WITH THE GUILD, YEAH?
YES. LATELY, WE'RE GETTING MORE AND MORE GUILD REQUESTS OUTSIDE OF MAGIKET.
THE GUILD WORK IS THE MAJORITY OF IT!
BUSINESS IS BOOMING!
EH-HEH-HEH. I BET SOMETHING GOOD'LL HAPPEN TODAY.
ガチャ
GACHA (KACHAK)
HELLO, PROTAGONIST PRESS HERE!

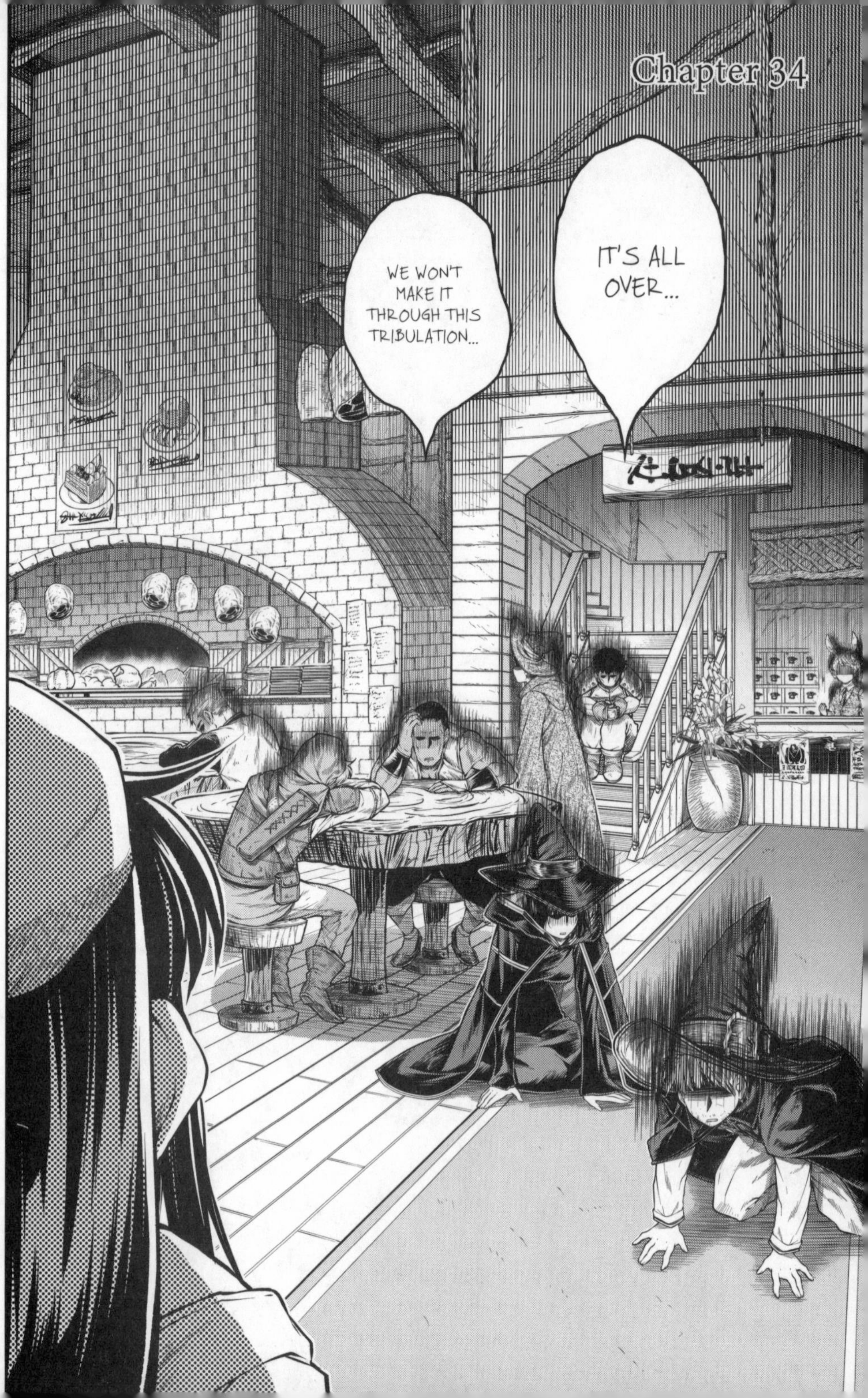
Chapter 34
IT'S ALL OVER...
WE WON'T MAKE IT THROUGH THIS TRIBULATION...

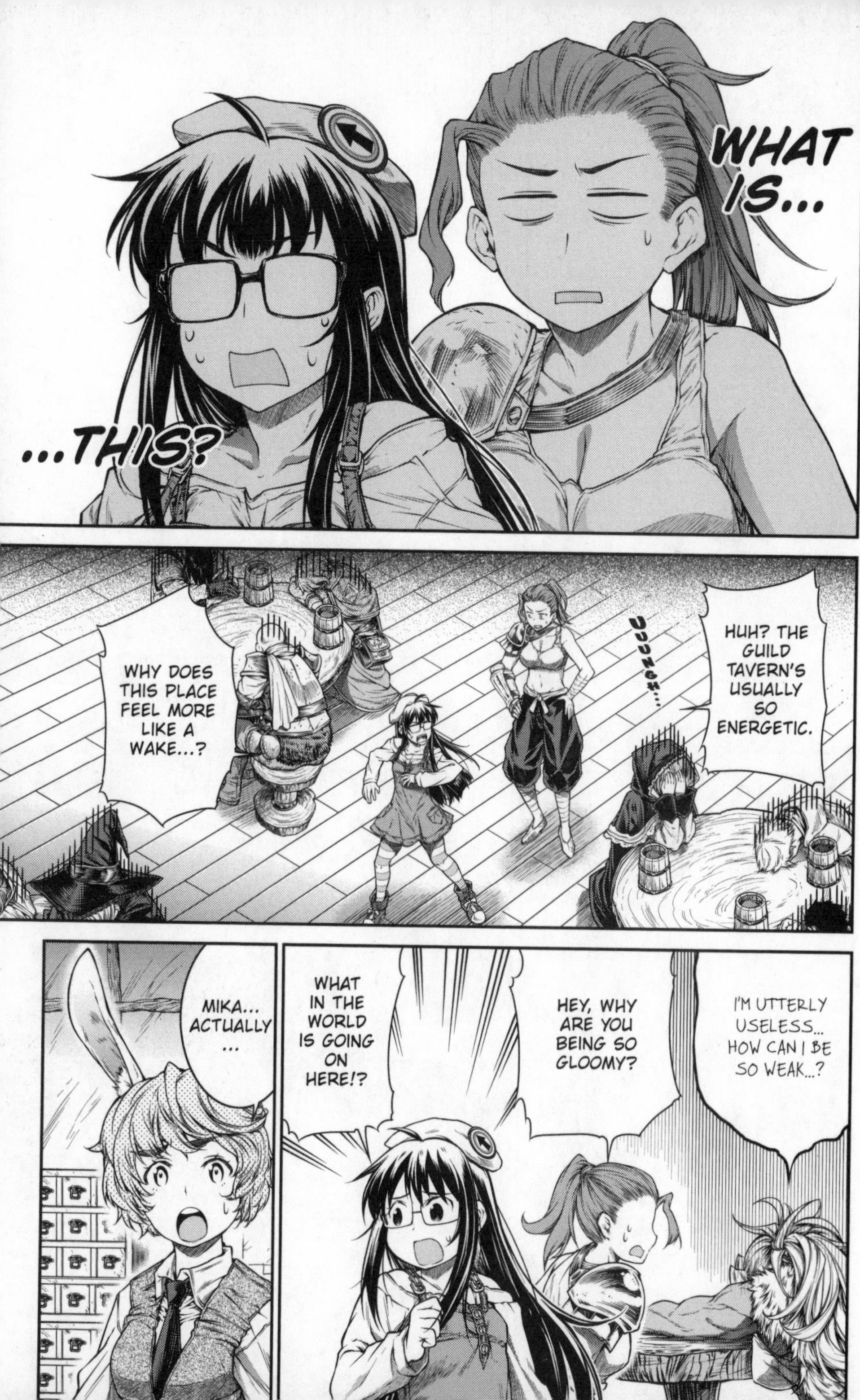
WHAT IS...
...THIS?
HUH? THE GUILD TAVERN'S USUALLY SO ENERGETIC.
UUUNGH...
WHY DOES THIS PLACE FEEL MORE LIKE A WAKE...?
I'M UTTERLY USELESS... HOW CAN I BE SO WEAK...?
HEY, WHY ARE YOU BEING SO GLOOMY?
WHAT IN THE WORLD IS GOING ON HERE!?
MIKA... ACTUALLY ...

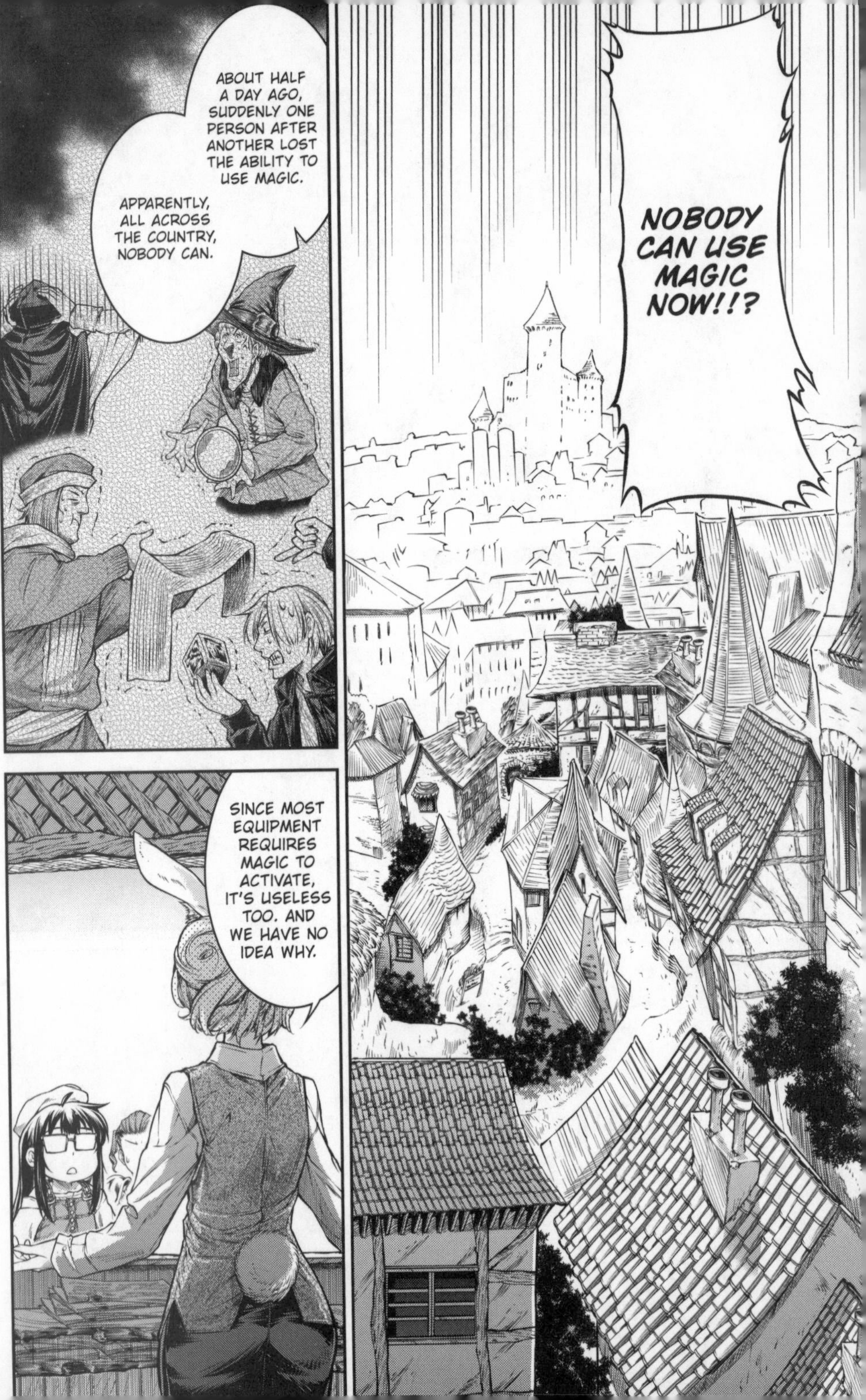
NOBODY CAN USE MAGIC NOW!!?
ABOUT HALF A DAY AGO, SUDDENLY ONE PERSON AFTER ANOTHER LOST THE ABILITY TO USE MAGIC.
APPARENTLY, ALL ACROSS THE COUNTRY, NOBODY CAN.
SINCE MOST EQUIPMENT REQUIRES MAGIC TO ACTIVATE, IT'S USELESS TOO. AND WE HAVE NO IDEA WHY.

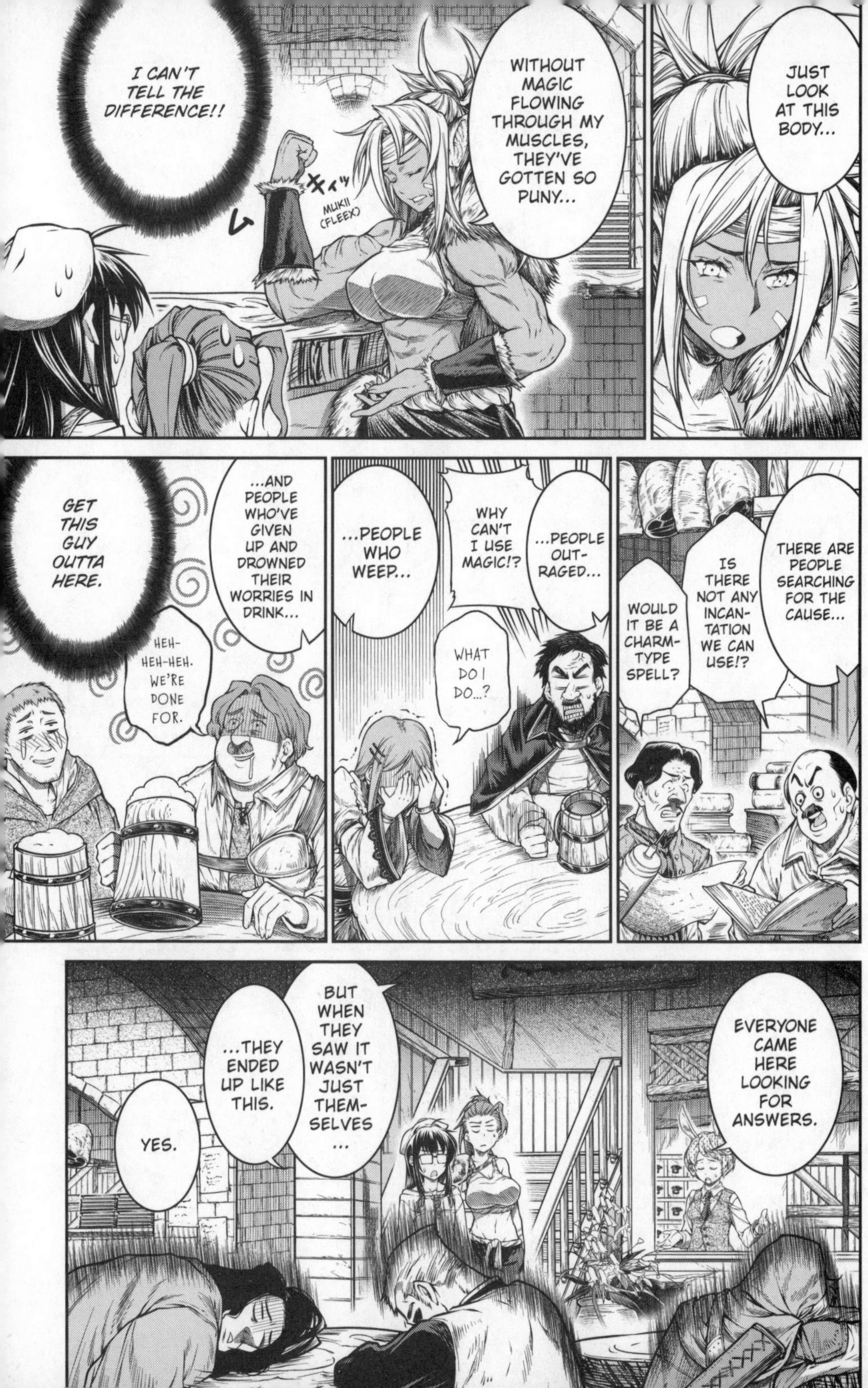
JUST LOOK AT THIS BODY...
WITHOUT MAGIC FLOWING THROUGH MY MUSCLES, THEY'VE GOTTEN SO PUNY...
キィッ
MUKII (FLEEX)
ム
I CAN'T TELL THE DIFFERENCE!!
THERE ARE PEOPLE SEARCHING FOR THE CAUSE...
IS THERE NOT ANY INCAN-TATION WE CAN USE!?
WOULD IT BE A CHARM-TYPE SPELL?
...PEOPLE OUT-RAGED...
WHY CAN'T I USE MAGIC!?
...PEOPLE WHO WEEP...
WHAT DO I DO...?
...AND PEOPLE WHO'VE GIVEN UP AND DROWNED THEIR WORRIES IN DRINK...
GET THIS GUY OUTTA HERE.
HEH-HEH-HEH. WE'RE DONE FOR.
EVERYONE CAME HERE LOOKING FOR ANSWERS.
BUT WHEN THEY SAW IT WASN'T JUST THEM-SELVES ...
...THEY ENDED UP LIKE THIS.
YES.

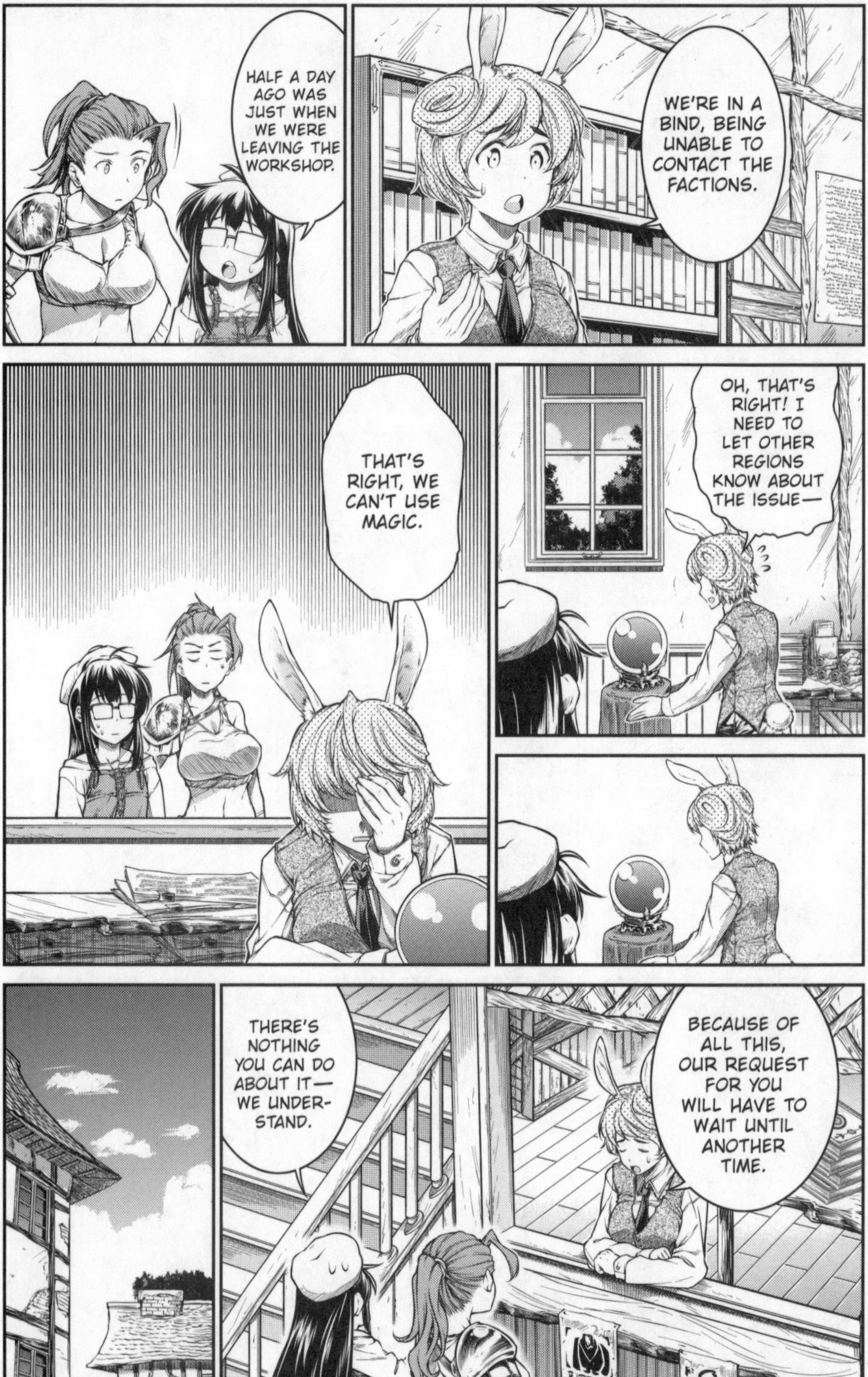
WE'RE IN A BIND, BEING UNABLE TO CONTACT THE FACTIONS.
HALF A DAY AGO WAS JUST WHEN WE WERE LEAVING THE WORKSHOP.
OH, THAT'S RIGHT! I NEED TO LET OTHER REGIONS KNOW ABOUT THE ISSUE—
THAT'S RIGHT, WE CAN'T USE MAGIC.
BECAUSE OF ALL THIS, OUR REQUEST FOR YOU WILL HAVE TO WAIT UNTIL ANOTHER TIME.
THERE'S NOTHING YOU CAN DO ABOUT IT— WE UNDER-STAND.

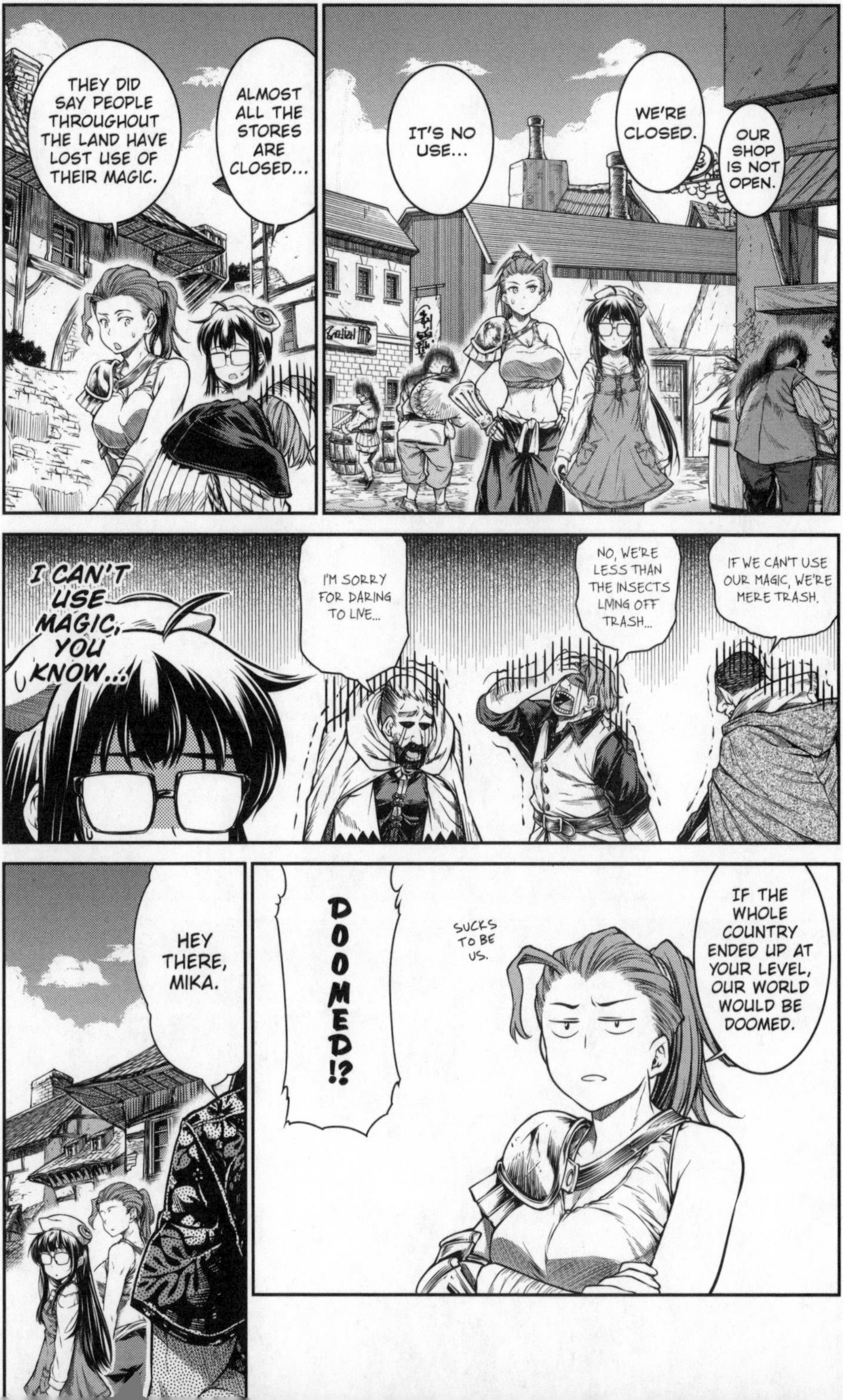
OUR SHOP IS NOT OPEN.
WE'RE CLOSED.
IT'S NO USE...
ALMOST ALL THE STORES ARE CLOSED...
THEY DID SAY PEOPLE THROUGHOUT THE LAND HAVE LOST USE OF THEIR MAGIC.
IF WE CAN'T USE OUR MAGIC, WE'RE MERE TRASH.
NO, WE'RE LESS THAN THE INSECTS LIVING OFF TRASH...
I'M SORRY FOR DARING TO LIVE...
I CAN'T USE MAGIC, YOU KNOW...
IF THE WHOLE COUNTRY ENDED UP AT YOUR LEVEL, OUR WORLD WOULD BE DOOMED.
SUCKS TO BE US.
DOOMED!?
HEY THERE, MIKA.

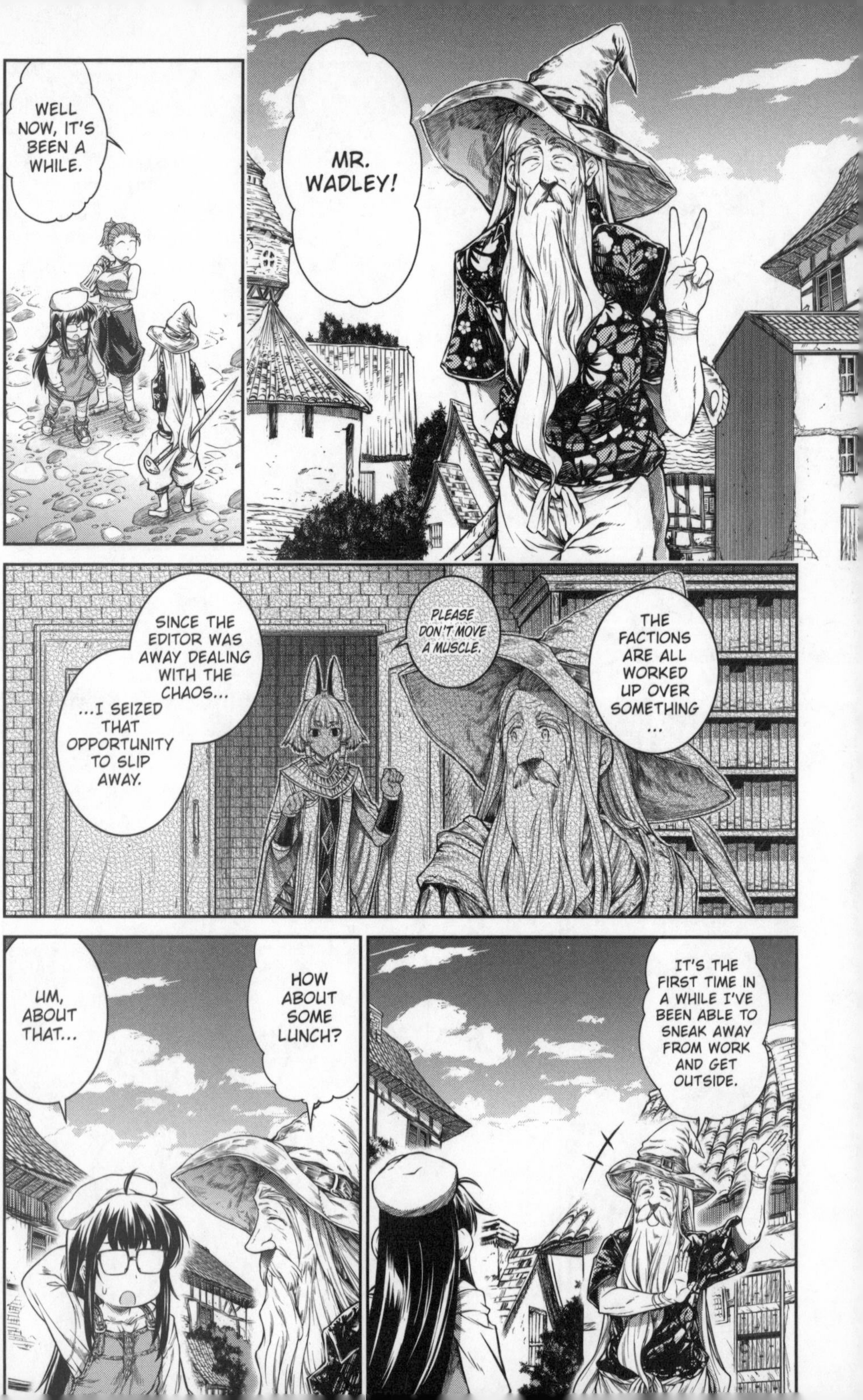
MR. WADLEY!
WELL NOW, IT'S BEEN A WHILE.
THE FACTIONS ARE ALL WORKED UP OVER SOMETHING...
PLEASE DON'T MOVE A MUSCLE.
SINCE THE EDITOR WAS AWAY DEALING WITH THE CHAOS...
...I SEIZED THAT OPPORTUNITY TO SLIP AWAY.
IT'S THE FIRST TIME IN A WHILE I'VE BEEN ABLE TO SNEAK AWAY FROM WORK AND GET OUTSIDE.
HOW ABOUT SOME LUNCH?
UM, ABOUT THAT...

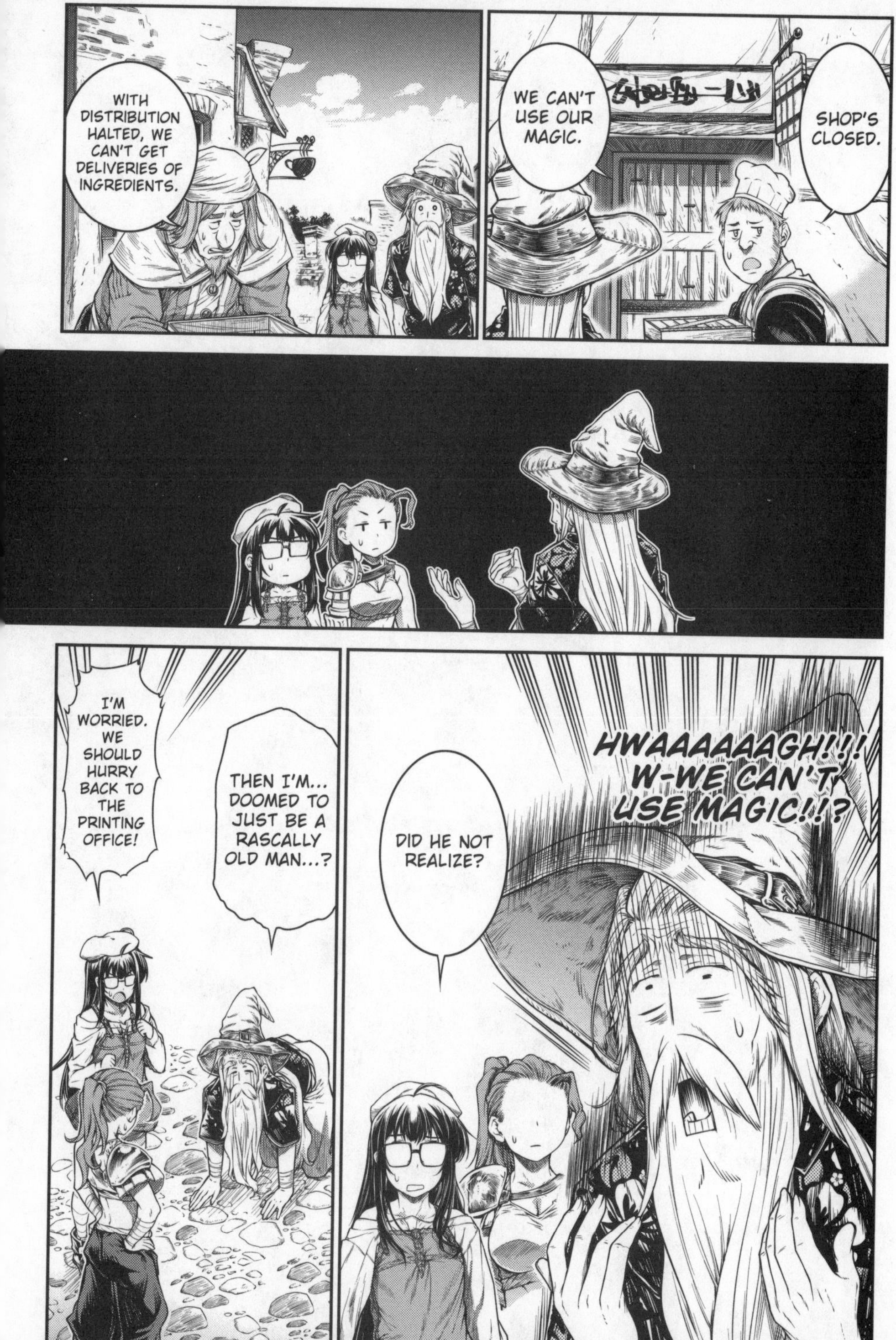
SHOP'S CLOSED.
WE CAN'T USE OUR MAGIC.
WITH DISTRIBUTION HALTED, WE CAN'T GET DELIVERIES OF INGREDIENTS.
HWAAAAAAGH!!! W-WE CAN'T USE MAGIC!!?
DID HE NOT REALIZE?
THEN I'M... DOOMED TO JUST BE A RASCALLY OLD MAN...?
I'M WORRIED. WE SHOULD HURRY BACK TO THE PRINTING OFFICE!

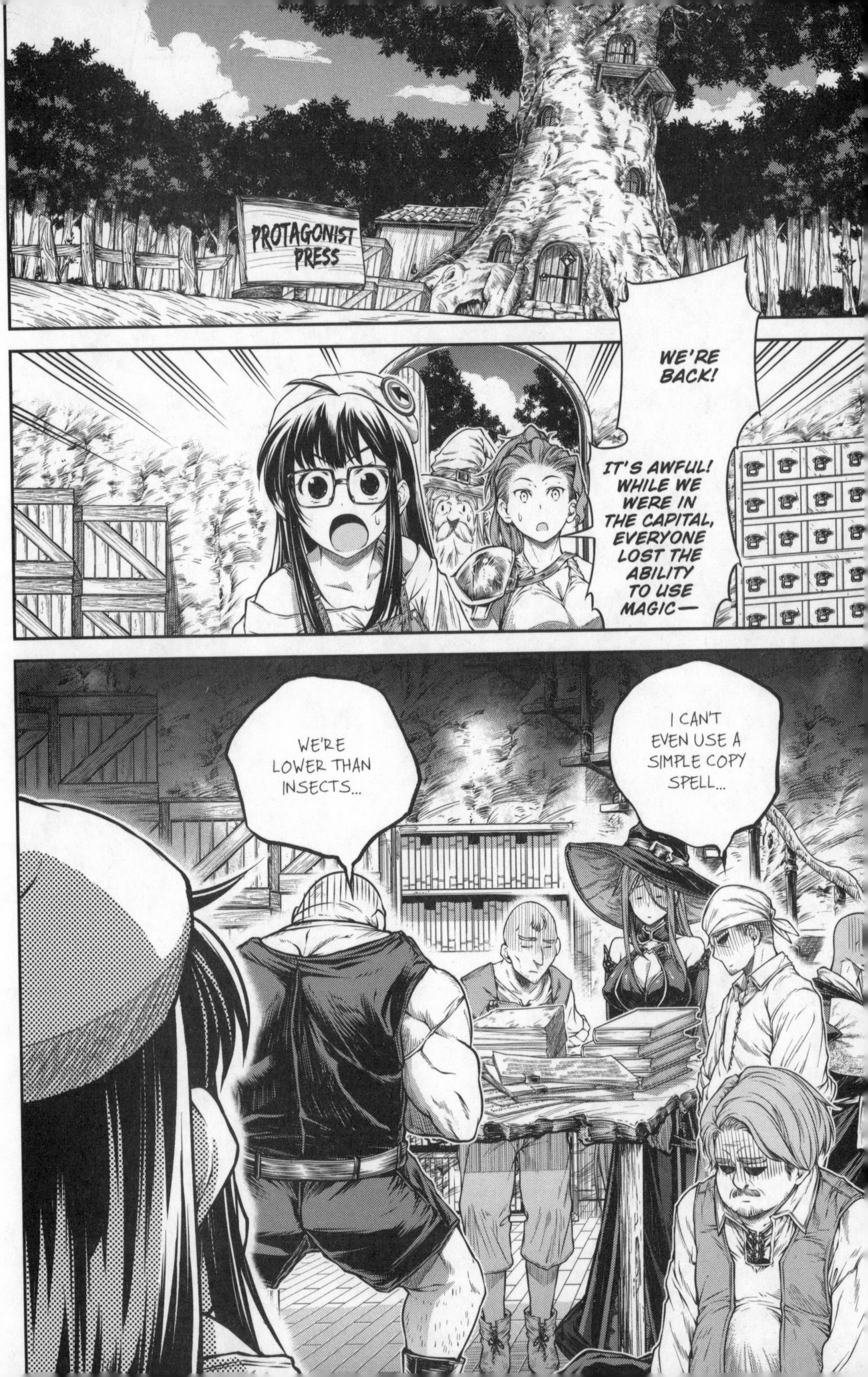
PROTAGONIST PRESS
WE'RE BACK!
IT'S AWFUL! WHILE WE WERE IN THE CAPITAL, EVERYONE LOST THE ABILITY TO USE MAGIC—
I CAN'T EVEN USE A SIMPLE COPY SPELL...
WE'RE LOWER THAN INSECTS...

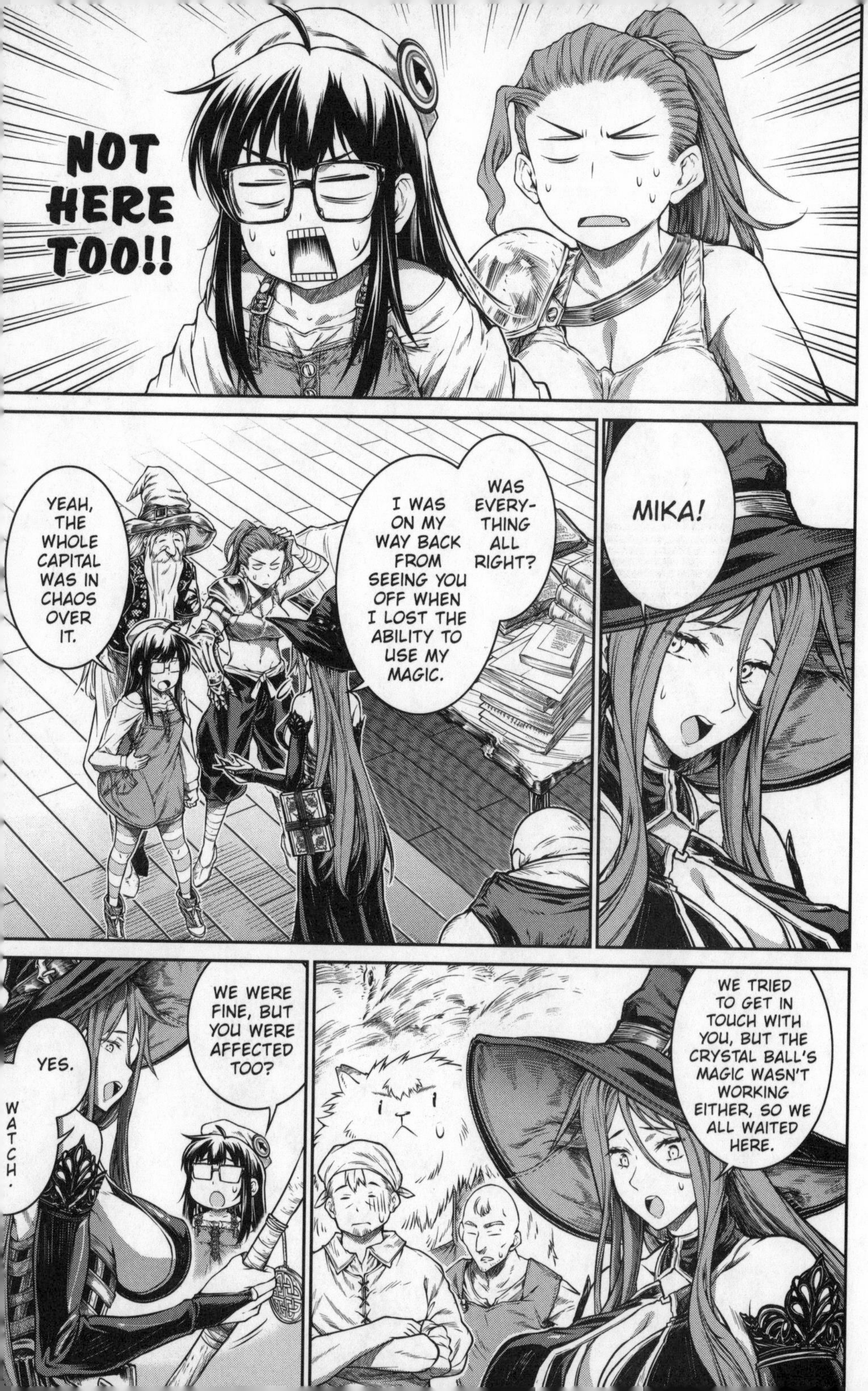
NOT HERE TOO!!
MIKA!
WAS EVERYTHING ALL RIGHT?
I WAS ON MY WAY BACK FROM SEEING YOU OFF WHEN I LOST THE ABILITY TO USE MY MAGIC.
YEAH, THE WHOLE CAPITAL WAS IN CHAOS OVER IT.
WE TRIED TO GET IN TOUCH WITH YOU, BUT THE CRYSTAL BALL'S MAGIC WASN'T WORKING EITHER, SO WE ALL WAITED HERE.
WE WERE FINE, BUT YOU WERE AFFECTED TOO?
YES.
WATCH.

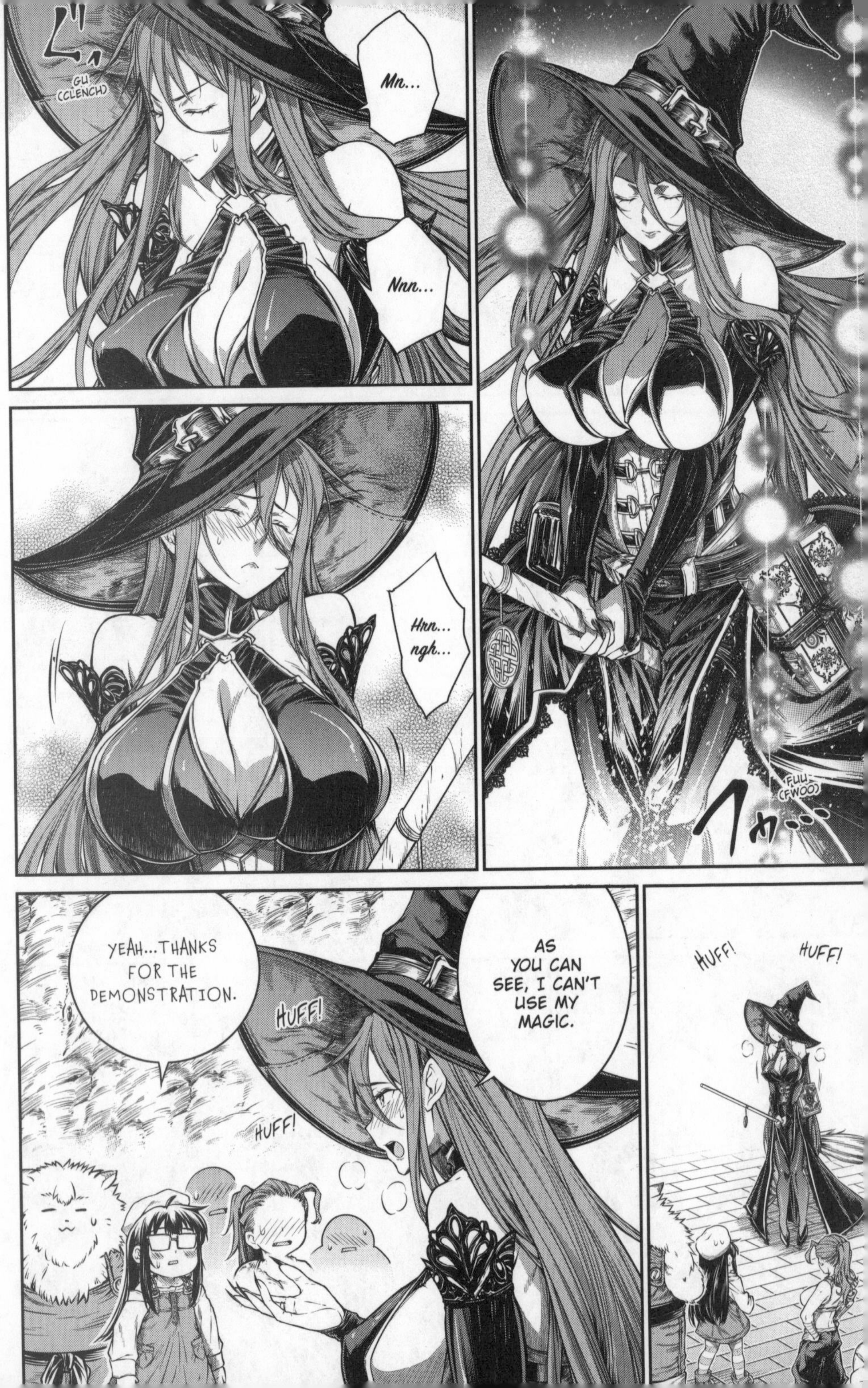
FUU (FWOO)
GU (CLENCH)
Mn...
Nnn...
Hrn... ngh...
HUFF!
HUFF!
AS YOU CAN SEE, I CAN'T USE MY MAGIC.
HUFF!
YEAH...THANKS FOR THE DEMONSTRATION.
HUFF!

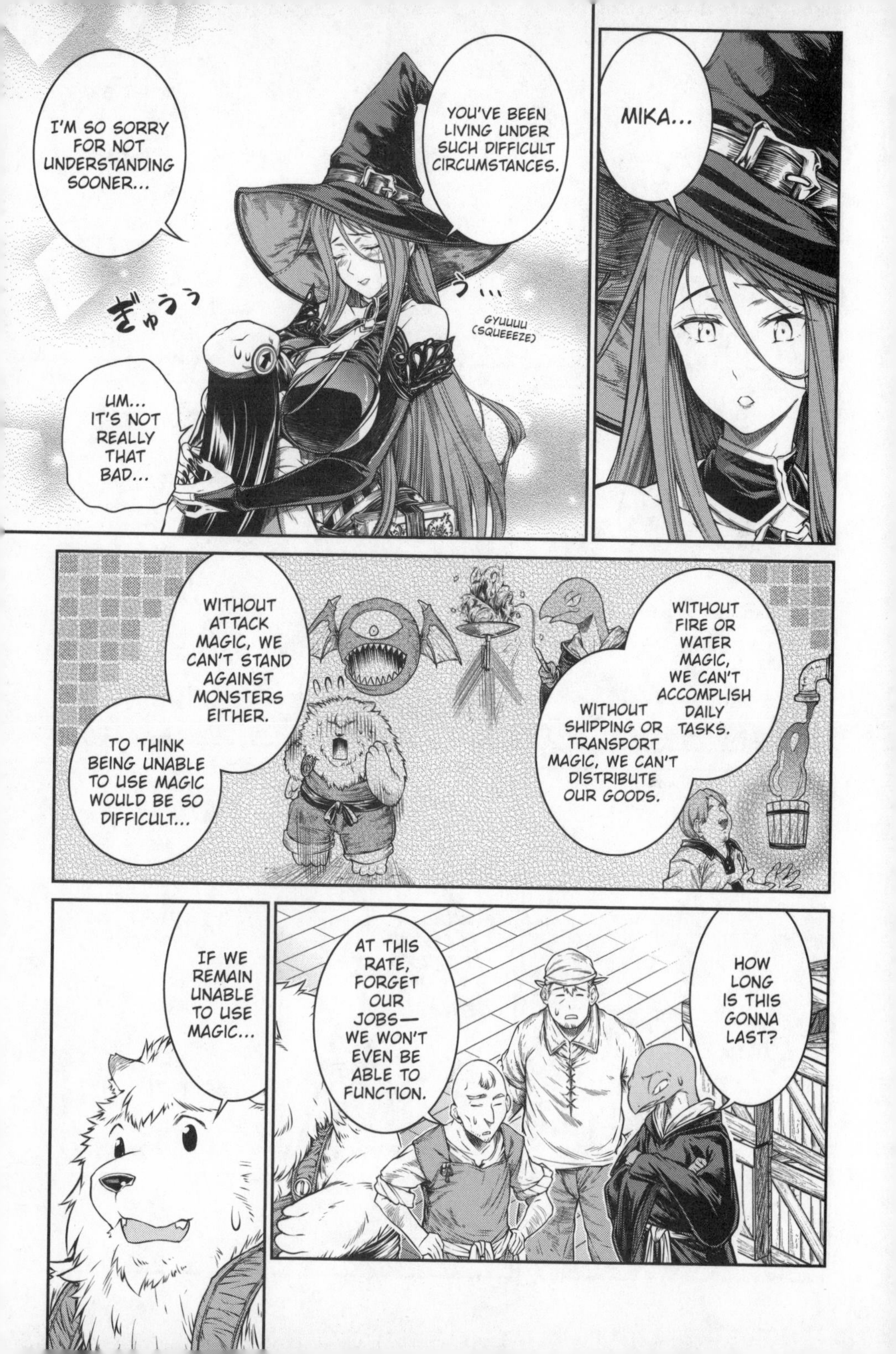
MIKA...
YOU'VE BEEN LIVING UNDER SUCH DIFFICULT CIRCUMSTANCES.
I'M SO SORRY FOR NOT UNDERSTANDING SOONER...
う...
ぎゅううう
GYUUUU (SQUEEEZE)
UM... IT'S NOT REALLY THAT BAD...
WITHOUT FIRE OR WATER MAGIC, WE CAN'T ACCOMPLISH DAILY TASKS.
WITHOUT SHIPPING OR TRANSPORT MAGIC, WE CAN'T DISTRIBUTE OUR GOODS.
WITHOUT ATTACK MAGIC, WE CAN'T STAND AGAINST MONSTERS EITHER.
TO THINK BEING UNABLE TO USE MAGIC WOULD BE SO DIFFICULT...
HOW LONG IS THIS GONNA LAST?
AT THIS RATE, FORGET OUR JOBS— WE WON'T EVEN BE ABLE TO FUNCTION.
IF WE REMAIN UNABLE TO USE MAGIC...

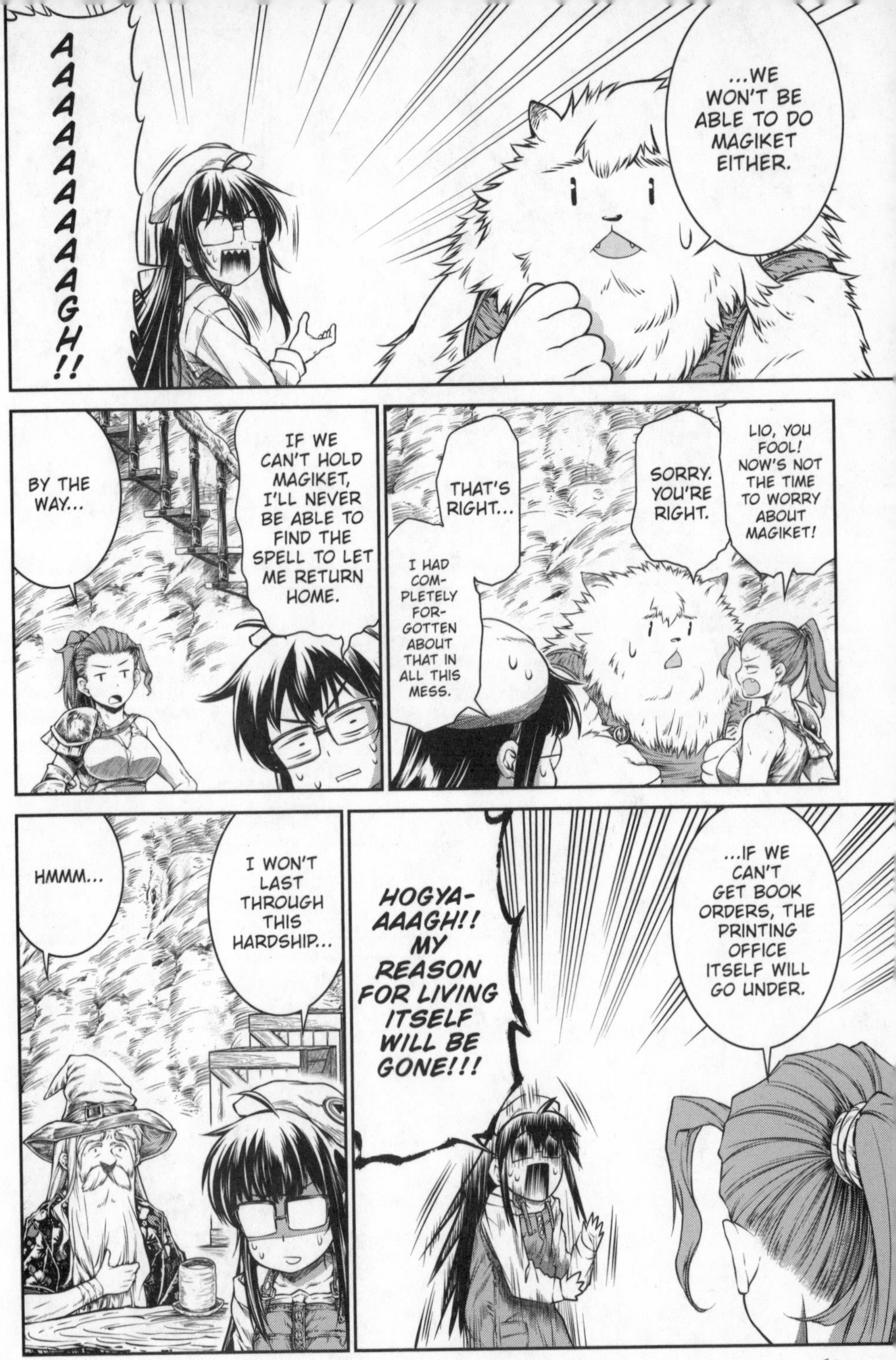
...WE WON'T BE ABLE TO DO MAGIKET EITHER.
AAAAAAAAAGH!!
LIO, YOU FOOL! NOW'S NOT THE TIME TO WORRY ABOUT MAGIKET!
SORRY. YOU'RE RIGHT.
THAT'S RIGHT...
I HAD COMPLETELY FORGOTTEN ABOUT THAT IN ALL THIS MESS.
IF WE CAN'T HOLD MAGIKET, I'LL NEVER BE ABLE TO FIND THE SPELL TO LET ME RETURN HOME.
BY THE WAY...
...IF WE CAN'T GET BOOK ORDERS, THE PRINTING OFFICE ITSELF WILL GO UNDER.
HOGYA-AAAGH!! MY REASON FOR LIVING ITSELF WILL BE GONE!!!
I WON'T LAST THROUGH THIS HARDSHIP...
HMMM...

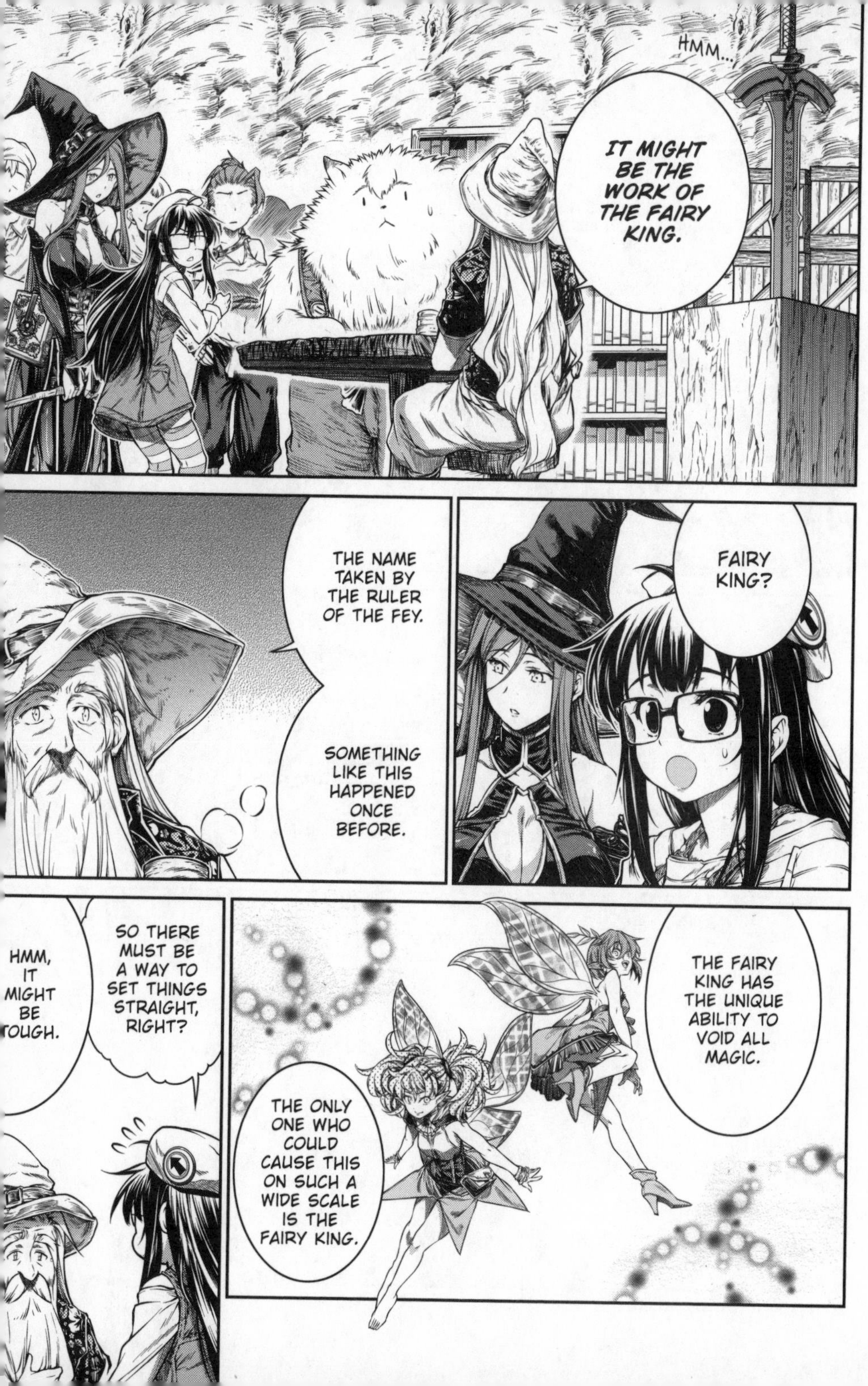
HMM...
IT MIGHT BE THE WORK OF THE FAIRY KING.
FAIRY KING?
THE NAME TAKEN BY THE RULER OF THE FEY.
SOMETHING LIKE THIS HAPPENED ONCE BEFORE.
THE FAIRY KING HAS THE UNIQUE ABILITY TO VOID ALL MAGIC.
THE ONLY ONE WHO COULD CAUSE THIS ON SUCH A WIDE SCALE IS THE FAIRY KING.
SO THERE MUST BE A WAY TO SET THINGS STRAIGHT, RIGHT?
HMM, IT MIGHT BE TOUGH.

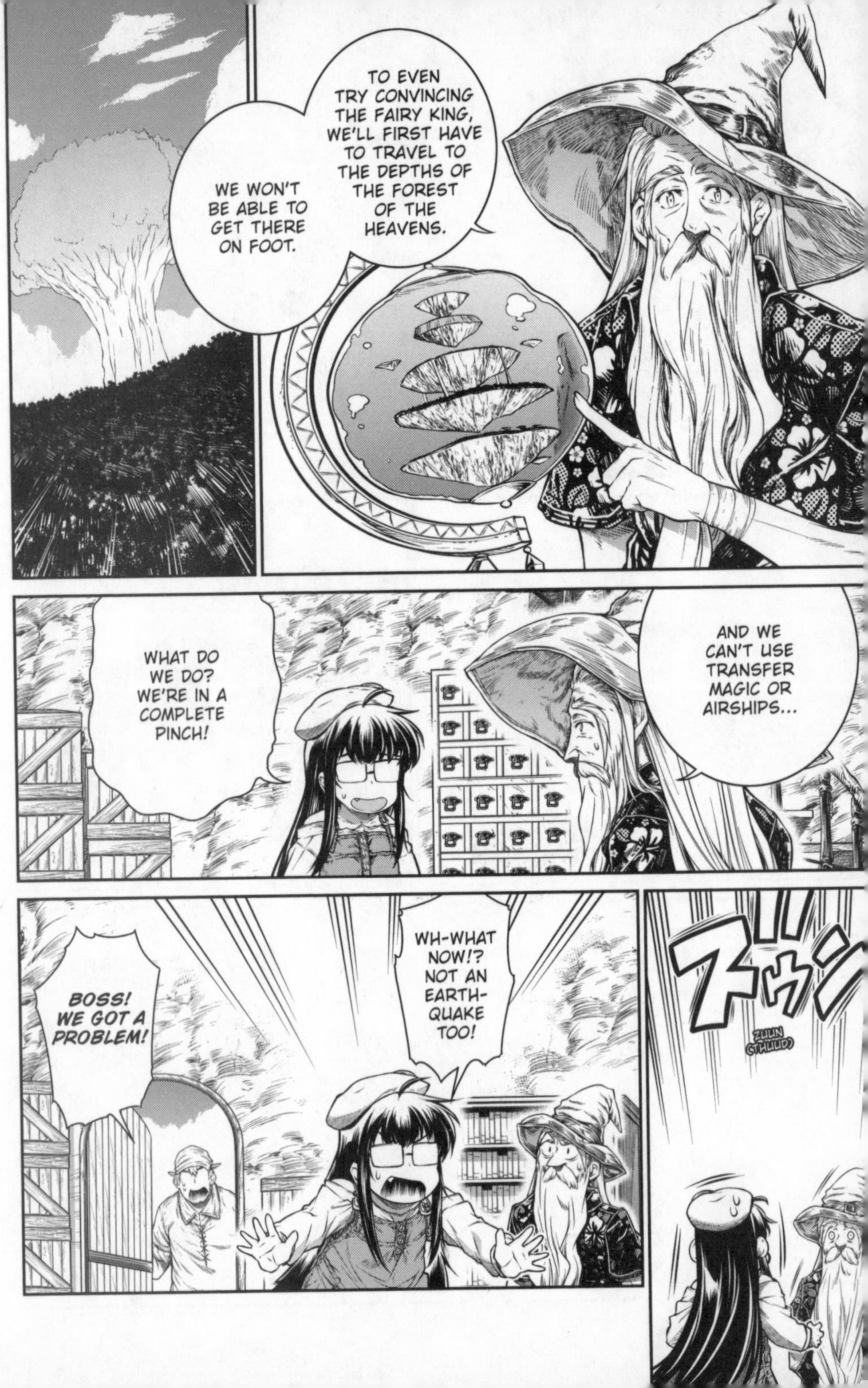
TO EVEN TRY CONVINCING THE FAIRY KING, WE'LL FIRST HAVE TO TRAVEL TO THE DEPTHS OF THE FOREST OF THE HEAVENS.
WE WON'T BE ABLE TO GET THERE ON FOOT.
AND WE CAN'T USE TRANSFER MAGIC OR AIRSHIPS...
WHAT DO WE DO? WE'RE IN A COMPLETE PINCH!
ZUUN (THUUD)
WH-WHAT NOW!? NOT AN EARTH-QUAKE TOO!
BOSS! WE GOT A PROBLEM!

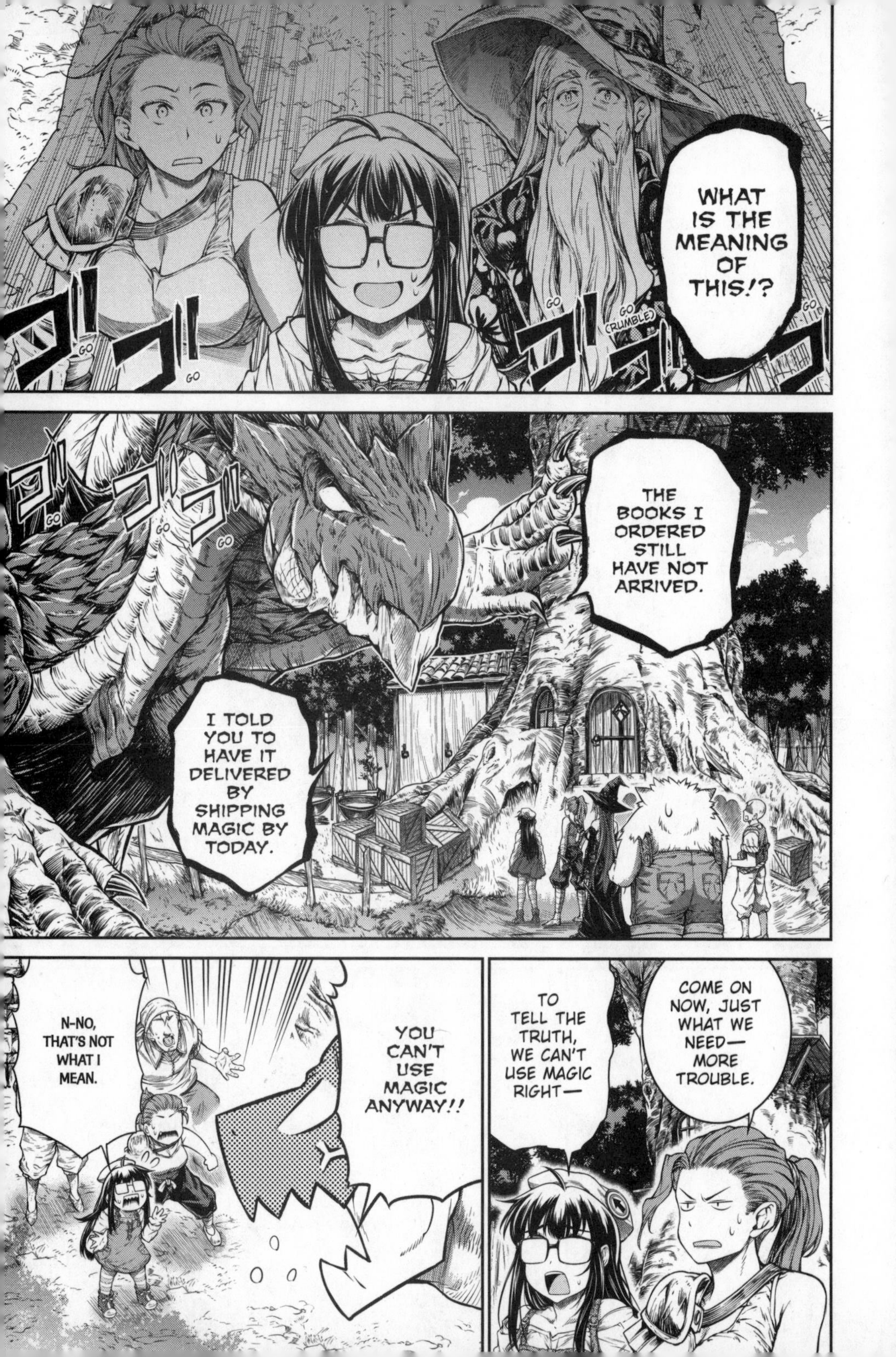
WHAT IS THE MEANING OF THIS!?
GO
GO (RUMBLE)
GO
GO
GO
THE BOOKS I ORDERED STILL HAVE NOT ARRIVED.
GO
GO
GO
I TOLD YOU TO HAVE IT DELIVERED BY SHIPPING MAGIC BY TODAY.
COME ON NOW, JUST WHAT WE NEED—MORE TROUBLE.
TO TELL THE TRUTH, WE CAN'T USE MAGIC RIGHT—
YOU CAN'T USE MAGIC ANYWAY!!
N-NO, THAT'S NOT WHAT I MEAN.

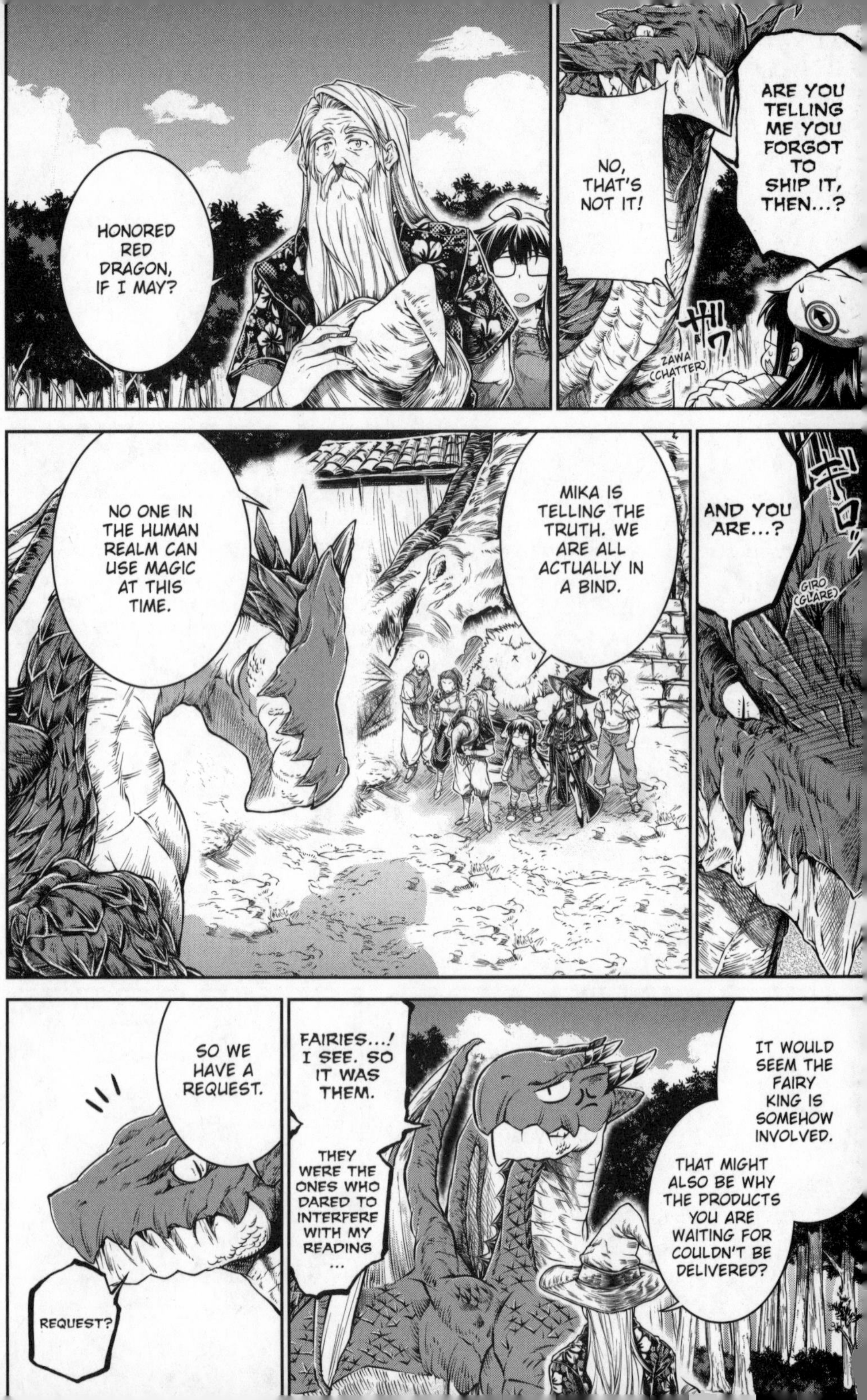
ARE YOU TELLING ME YOU FORGOT TO SHIP IT, THEN...?
NO, THAT'S NOT IT!
ザワ
ZAWA (CHATTER)
HONORED RED DRAGON, IF I MAY?
ギロッ
AND YOU ARE...?
GIRO (GLARE)
MIKA IS TELLING THE TRUTH. WE ARE ALL ACTUALLY IN A BIND.
NO ONE IN THE HUMAN REALM CAN USE MAGIC AT THIS TIME.
IT WOULD SEEM THE FAIRY KING IS SOMEHOW INVOLVED.
THAT MIGHT ALSO BE WHY THE PRODUCTS YOU ARE WAITING FOR COULDN'T BE DELIVERED?
FAIRIES...! I SEE. SO IT WAS THEM.
THEY WERE THE ONES WHO DARED TO INTERFERE WITH MY READING...
SO WE HAVE A REQUEST.
REQUEST?

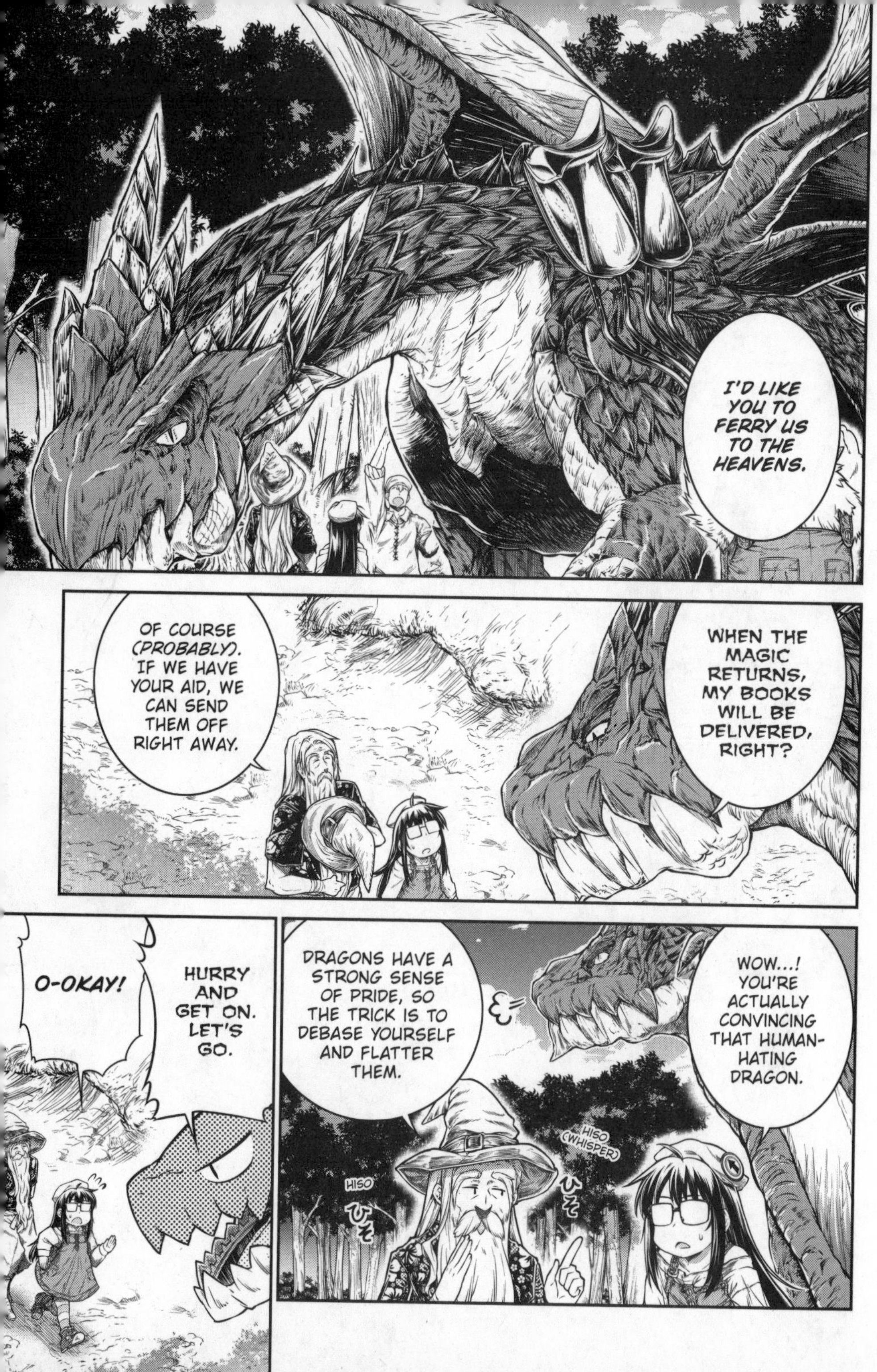
I'D LIKE YOU TO FERRY US TO THE HEAVENS.
WHEN THE MAGIC RETURNS, MY BOOKS WILL BE DELIVERED, RIGHT?
OF COURSE (PROBABLY). IF WE HAVE YOUR AID, WE CAN SEND THEM OFF RIGHT AWAY.
WOW...! YOU'RE ACTUALLY CONVINCING THAT HUMAN-HATING DRAGON.
HISO (WHISPER)
DRAGONS HAVE A STRONG SENSE OF PRIDE, SO THE TRICK IS TO DEBASE YOURSELF AND FLATTER THEM.
HISO
HURRY AND GET ON. LET'S GO.
O-OKAY!

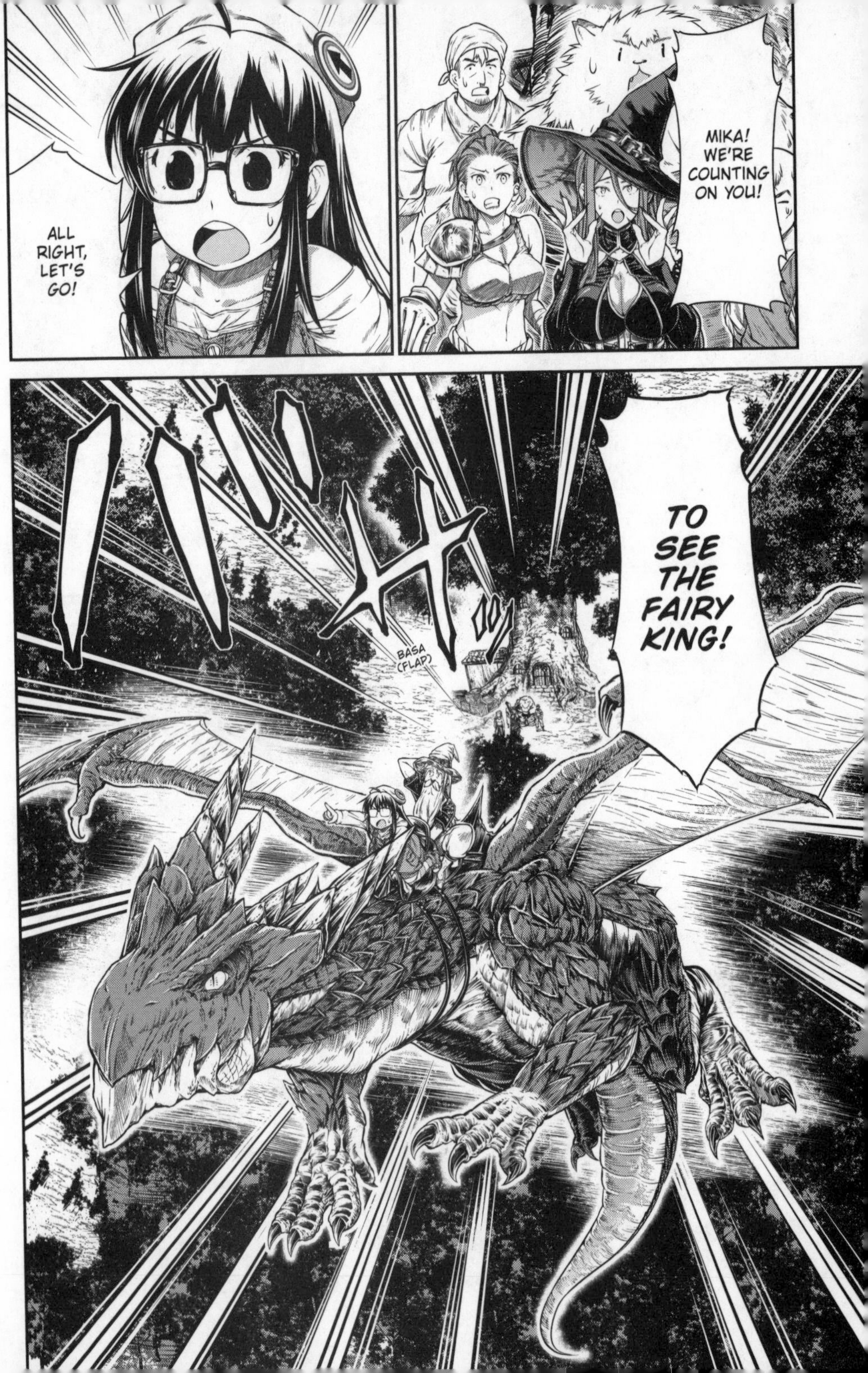
MIKA! WE'RE COUNTING ON YOU!
ALL RIGHT, LET'S GO!
TO SEE THE FAIRY KING!
BASA (FLAP)

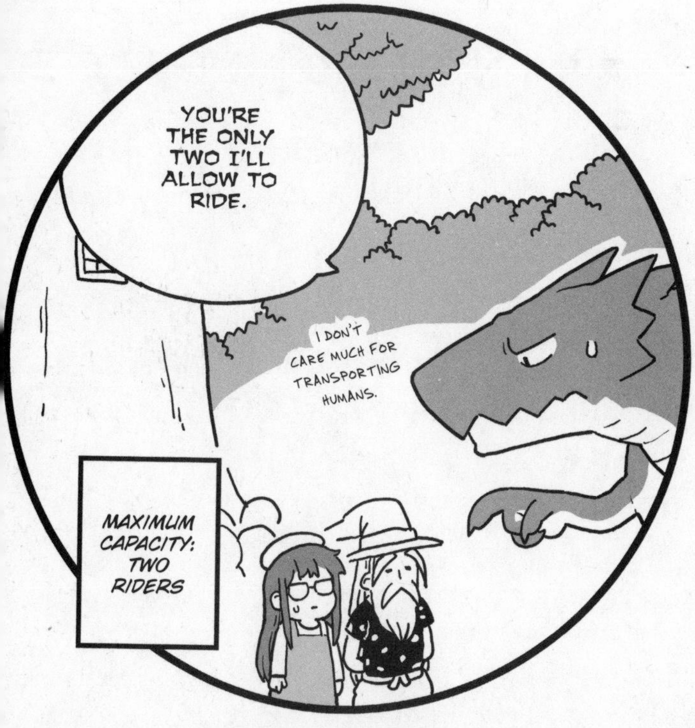
YOU'RE THE ONLY TWO I'LL ALLOW TO RIDE.
I DON'T CARE MUCH FOR TRANSPORTING HUMANS.
MAXIMUM CAPACITY: TWO RIDERS

A WITCH'S PRINTING OFFICE

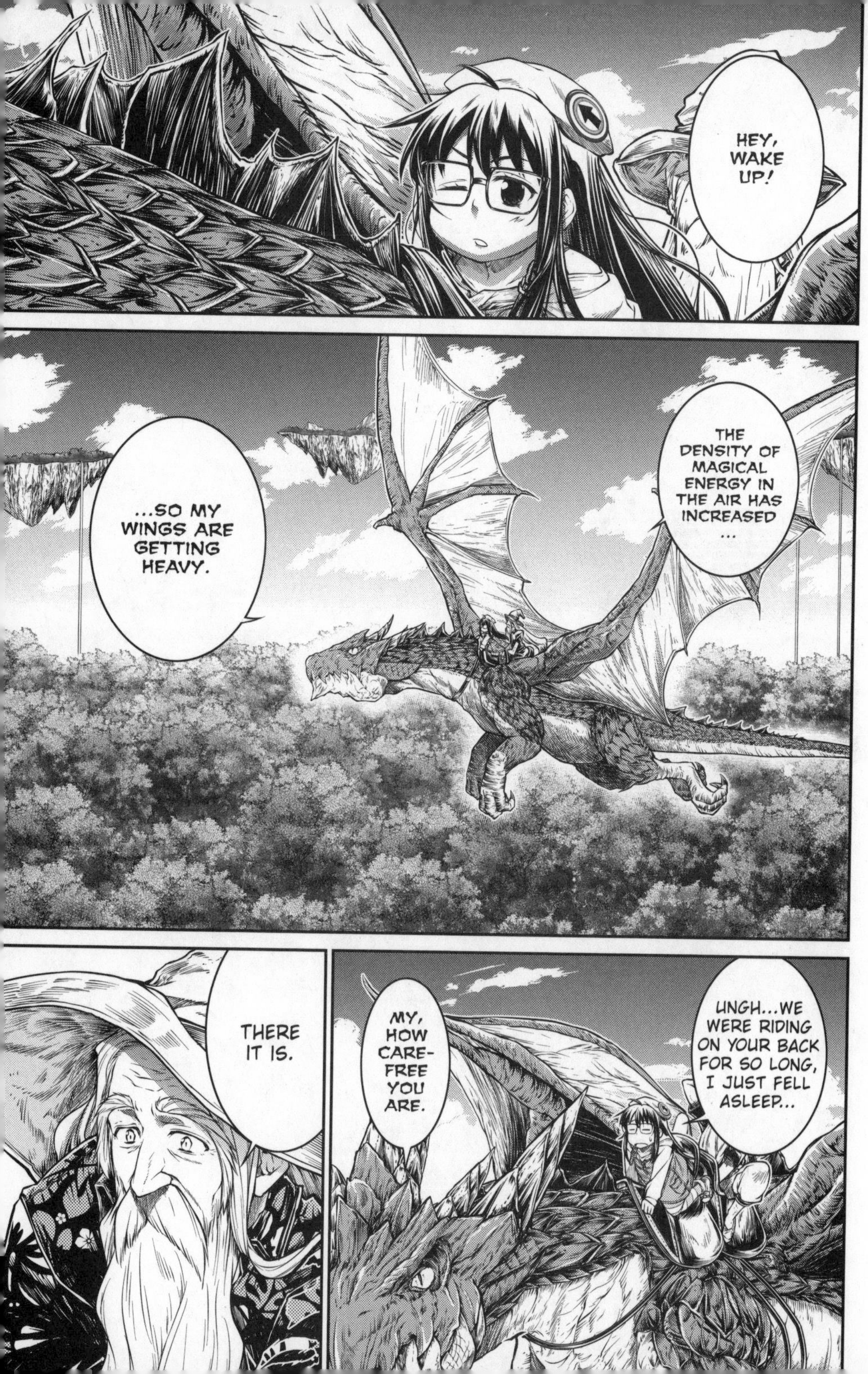
HEY, WAKE UP!
THE DENSITY OF MAGICAL ENERGY IN THE AIR HAS INCREASED...
...SO MY WINGS ARE GETTING HEAVY.
UNGH...WE WERE RIDING ON YOUR BACK FOR SO LONG, I JUST FELL ASLEEP...
MY, HOW CARE-FREE YOU ARE.
THERE IT IS.

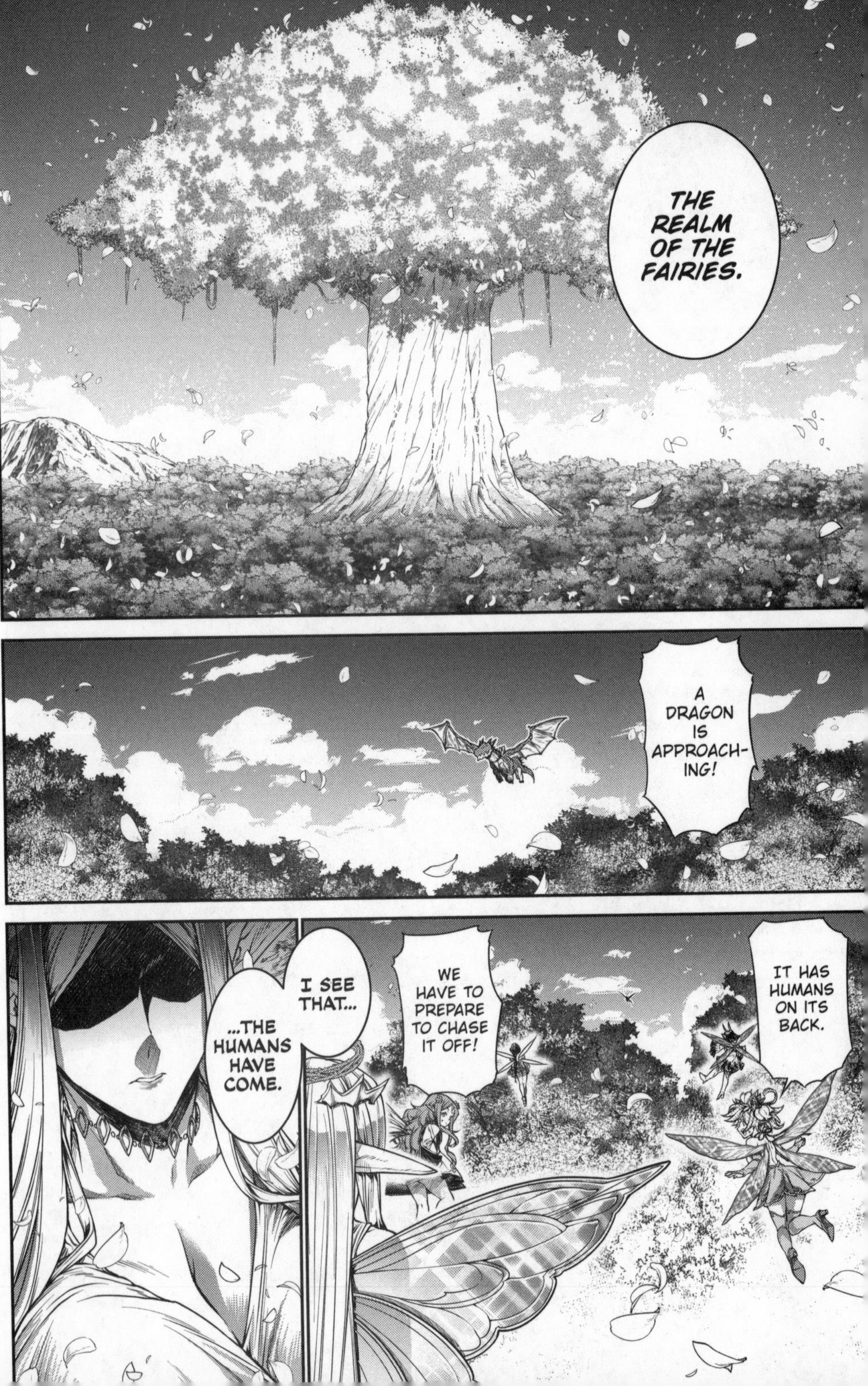
THE REALM OF THE FAIRIES.
A DRAGON IS APPROACH-ING!
IT HAS HUMANS ON ITS BACK.
WE HAVE TO PREPARE TO CHASE IT OFF!
I SEE THAT...
...THE HUMANS HAVE COME.

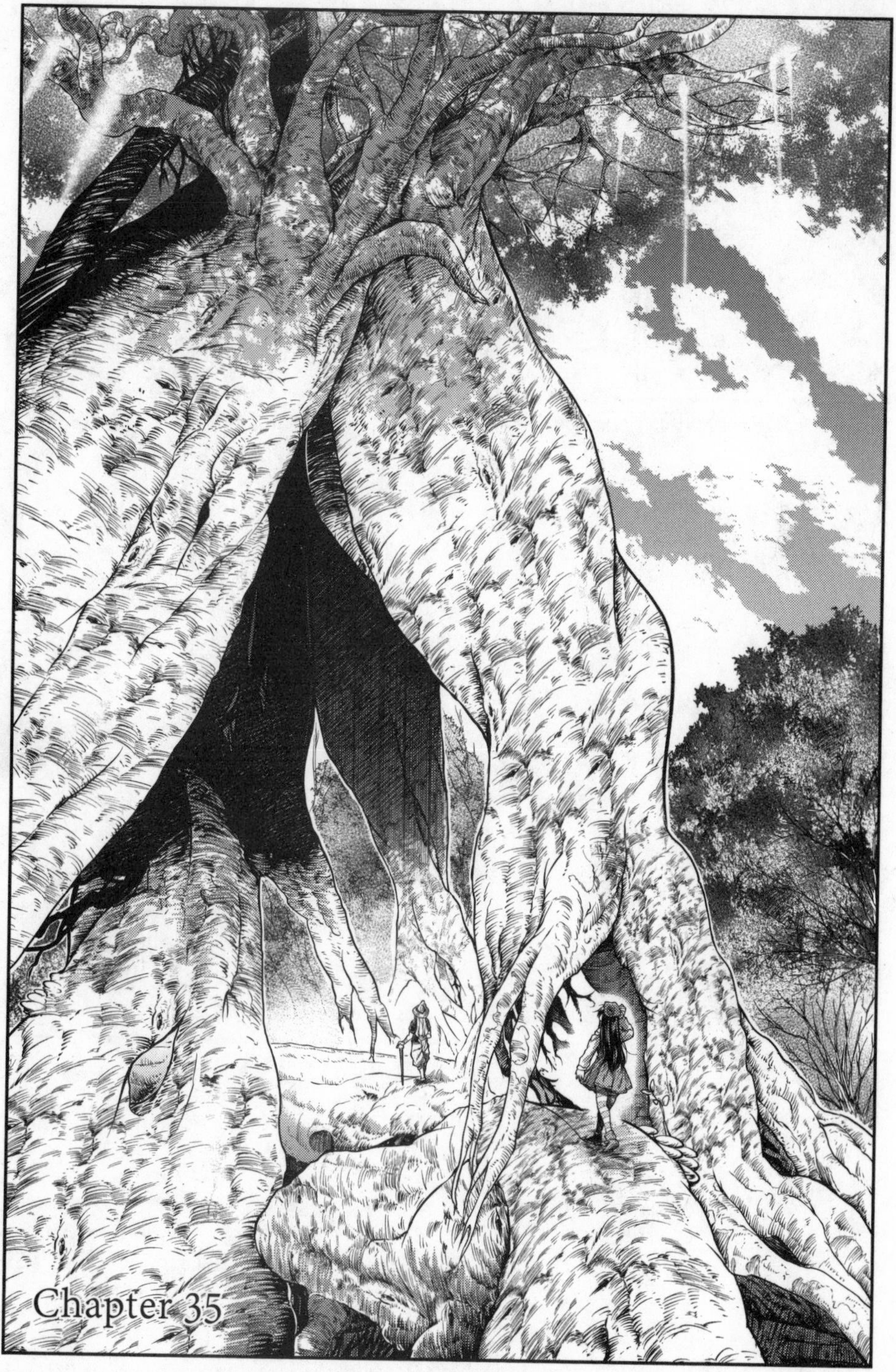
Chapter 35

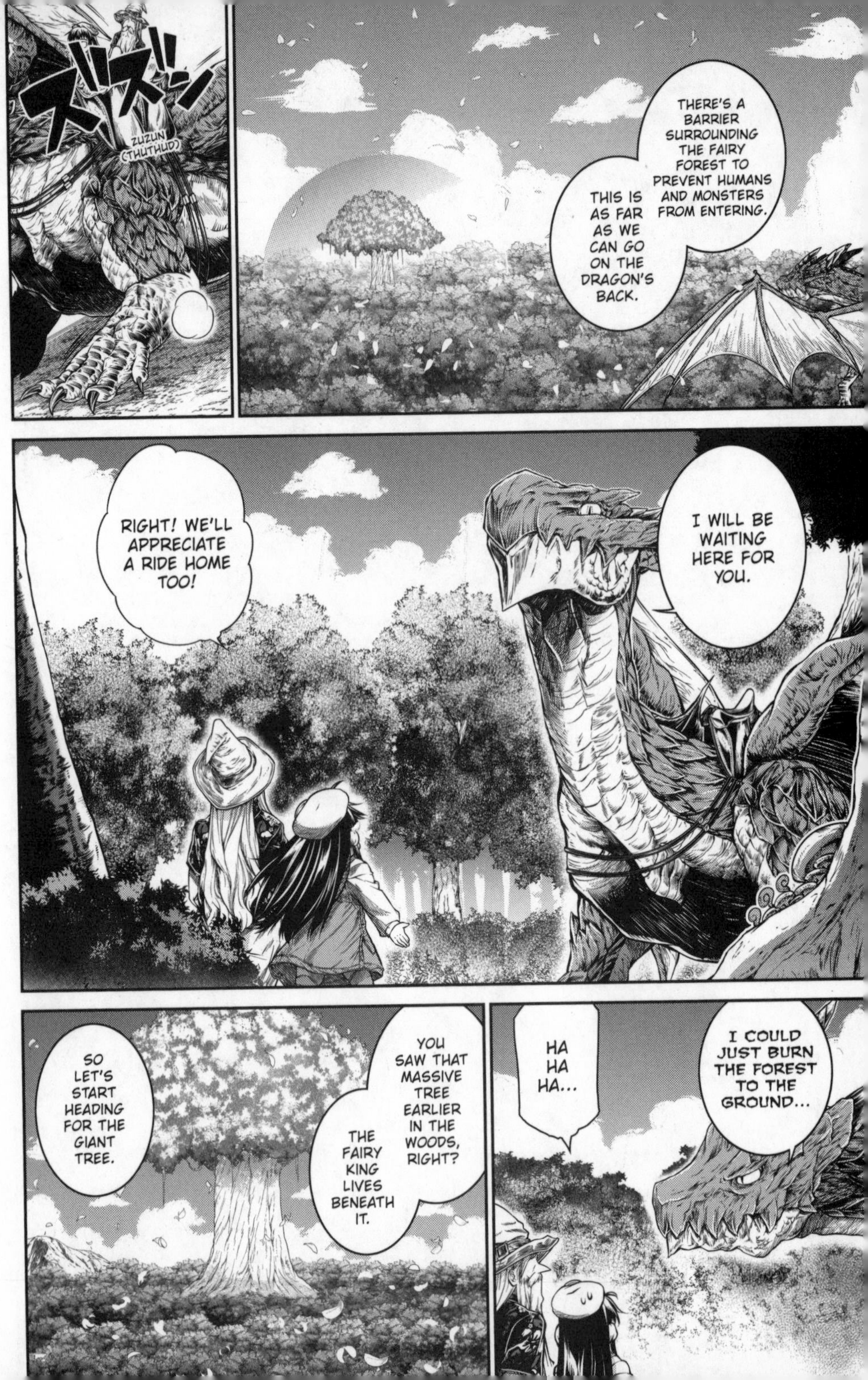
THERE'S A BARRIER SURROUNDING THE FAIRY FOREST TO PREVENT HUMANS AND MONSTERS FROM ENTERING.
THIS IS AS FAR AS WE CAN GO ON THE DRAGON'S BACK.
ズズン
ZUZUN (THUTHUD)
I WILL BE WAITING HERE FOR YOU.
RIGHT! WE'LL APPRECIATE A RIDE HOME TOO!
I COULD JUST BURN THE FOREST TO THE GROUND...
HA HA HA...
YOU SAW THAT MASSIVE TREE EARLIER IN THE WOODS, RIGHT?
THE FAIRY KING LIVES BENEATH IT.
SO LET'S START HEADING FOR THE GIANT TREE.

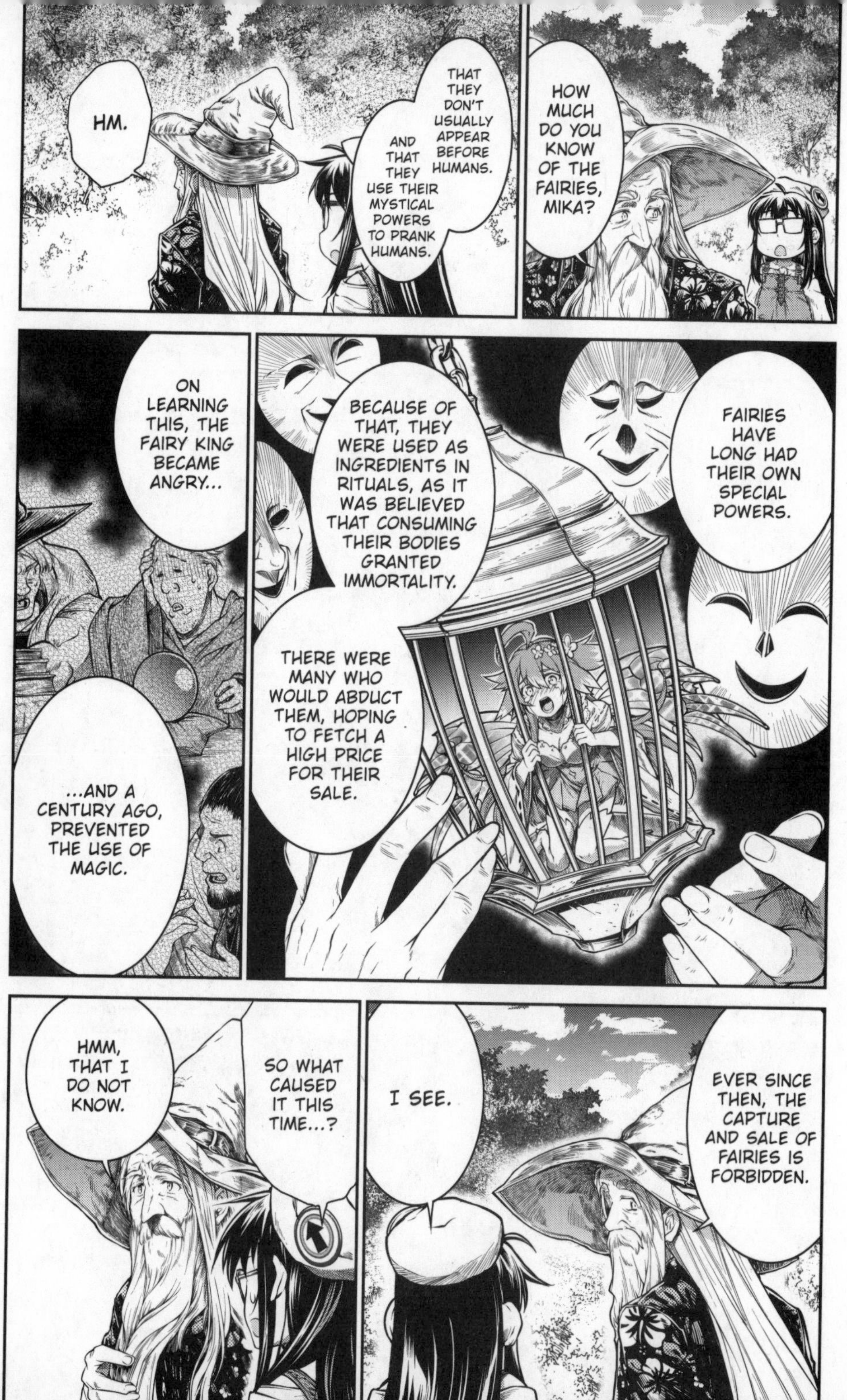
HOW MUCH DO YOU KNOW OF THE FAIRIES, MIKA?
THAT THEY DON'T USUALLY APPEAR BEFORE HUMANS.
AND THAT THEY USE THEIR MYSTICAL POWERS TO PRANK HUMANS.
HM.
FAIRIES HAVE LONG HAD THEIR OWN SPECIAL POWERS.
BECAUSE OF THAT, THEY WERE USED AS INGREDIENTS IN RITUALS, AS IT WAS BELIEVED THAT CONSUMING THEIR BODIES GRANTED IMMORTALITY.
THERE WERE MANY WHO WOULD ABDUCT THEM, HOPING TO FETCH A HIGH PRICE FOR THEIR SALE.
ON LEARNING THIS, THE FAIRY KING BECAME ANGRY...
...AND A CENTURY AGO, PREVENTED THE USE OF MAGIC.
EVER SINCE THEN, THE CAPTURE AND SALE OF FAIRIES IS FORBIDDEN.
I SEE.
SO WHAT CAUSED IT THIS TIME...?
HMM, THAT I DO NOT KNOW.

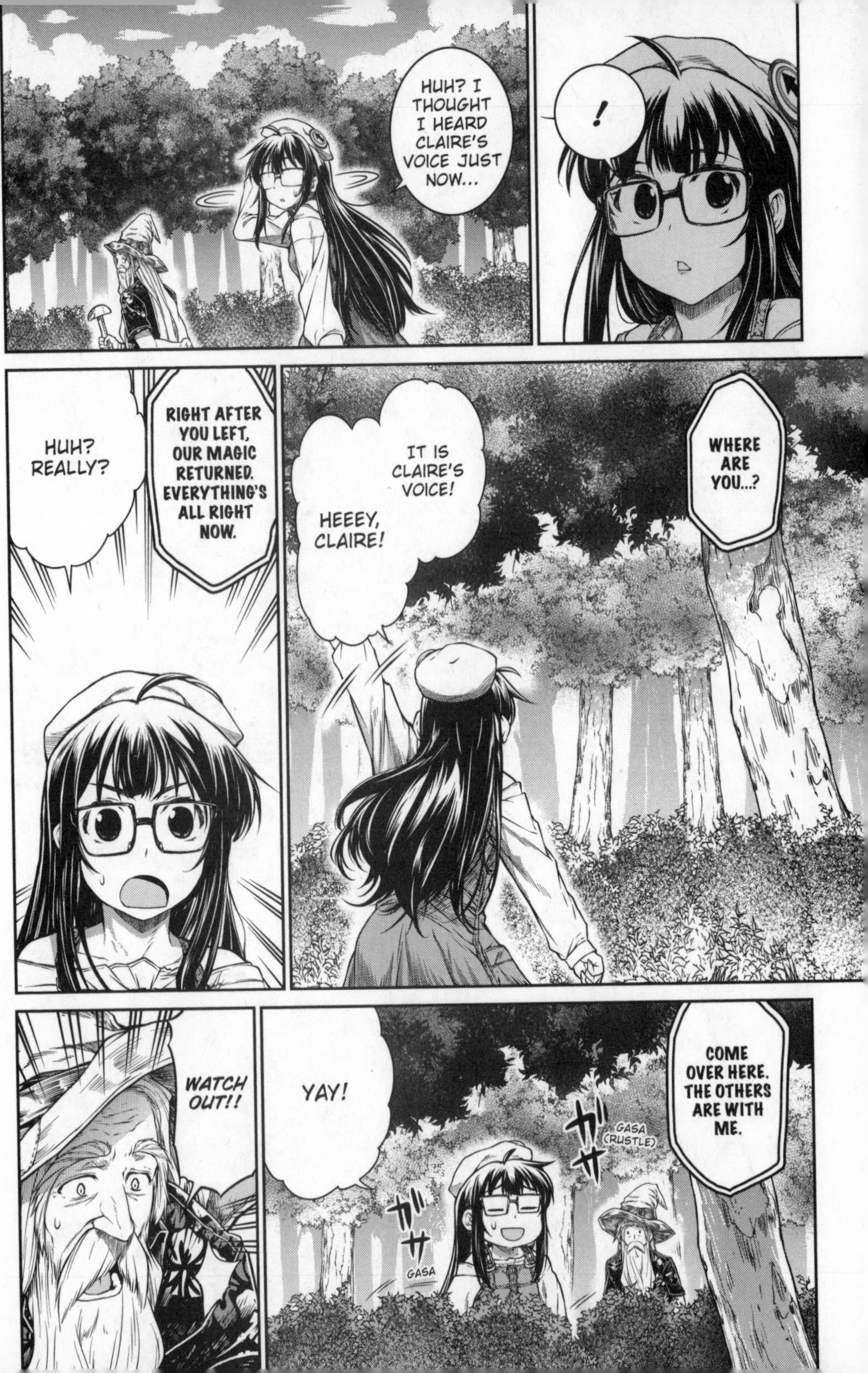
!
HUH? I THOUGHT I HEARD CLAIRE'S VOICE JUST NOW...
WHERE ARE YOU...?
IT IS CLAIRE'S VOICE!
HEEEY, CLAIRE!
RIGHT AFTER YOU LEFT, OUR MAGIC RETURNED. EVERYTHING'S ALL RIGHT NOW.
HUH? REALLY?
COME OVER HERE. THE OTHERS ARE WITH ME.
GASA (RUSTLE)
GASA
YAY!
WATCH OUT!!

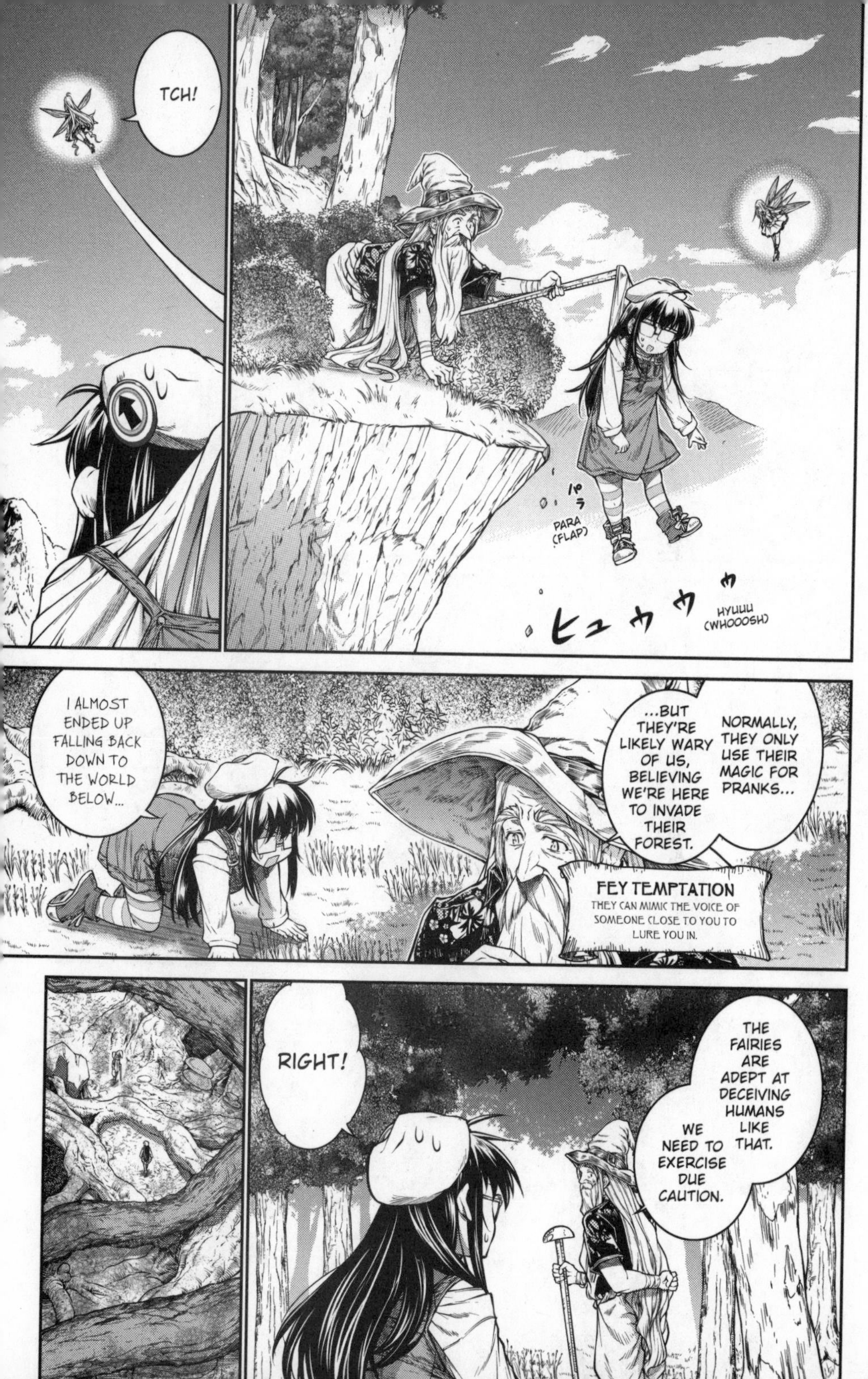
パラ
PARA (FLAP)
ヒュウウゥ
HYUUU (WHOOOSH)
TCH!
NORMALLY, THEY ONLY USE THEIR MAGIC FOR PRANKS...
...BUT THEY'RE LIKELY WARY OF US, BELIEVING WE'RE HERE TO INVADE THEIR FOREST.
FEY TEMPTATION
THEY CAN MIMIC THE VOICE OF SOMEONE CLOSE TO YOU TO LURE YOU IN.
I ALMOST ENDED UP FALLING BACK DOWN TO THE WORLD BELOW...
THE FAIRIES ARE ADEPT AT DECEIVING HUMANS LIKE THAT.
WE NEED TO EXERCISE DUE CAUTION.
RIGHT!

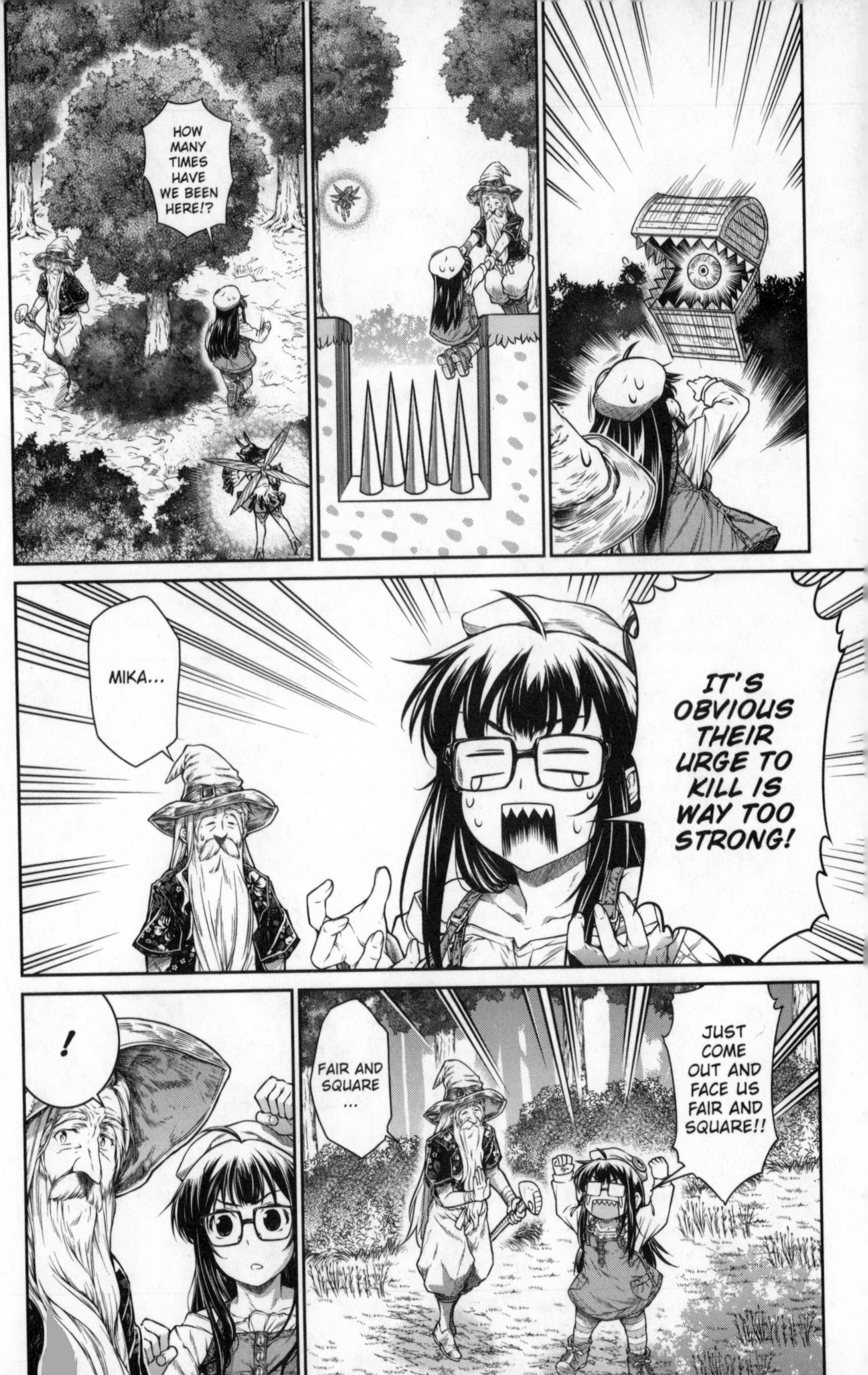
HOW MANY TIMES HAVE WE BEEN HERE!?
IT'S OBVIOUS THEIR URGE TO KILL IS WAY TOO STRONG!
MIKA...
JUST COME OUT AND FACE US FAIR AND SQUARE!!
FAIR AND SQUARE ...
!

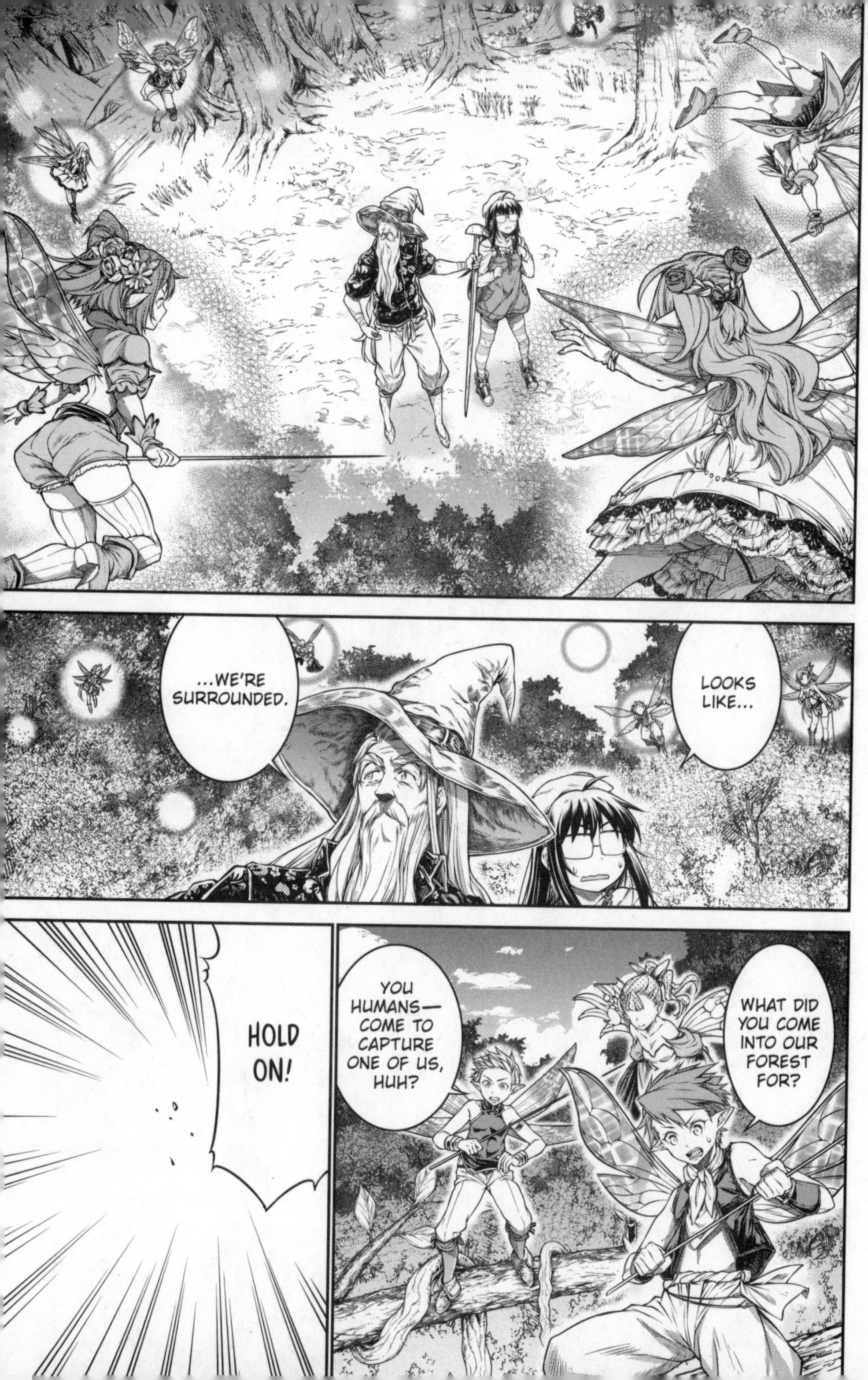
LOOKS LIKE...
...WE'RE SURROUNDED.
WHAT DID YOU COME INTO OUR FOREST FOR?
YOU HUMANS—COME TO CAPTURE ONE OF US, HUH?
HOLD ON!

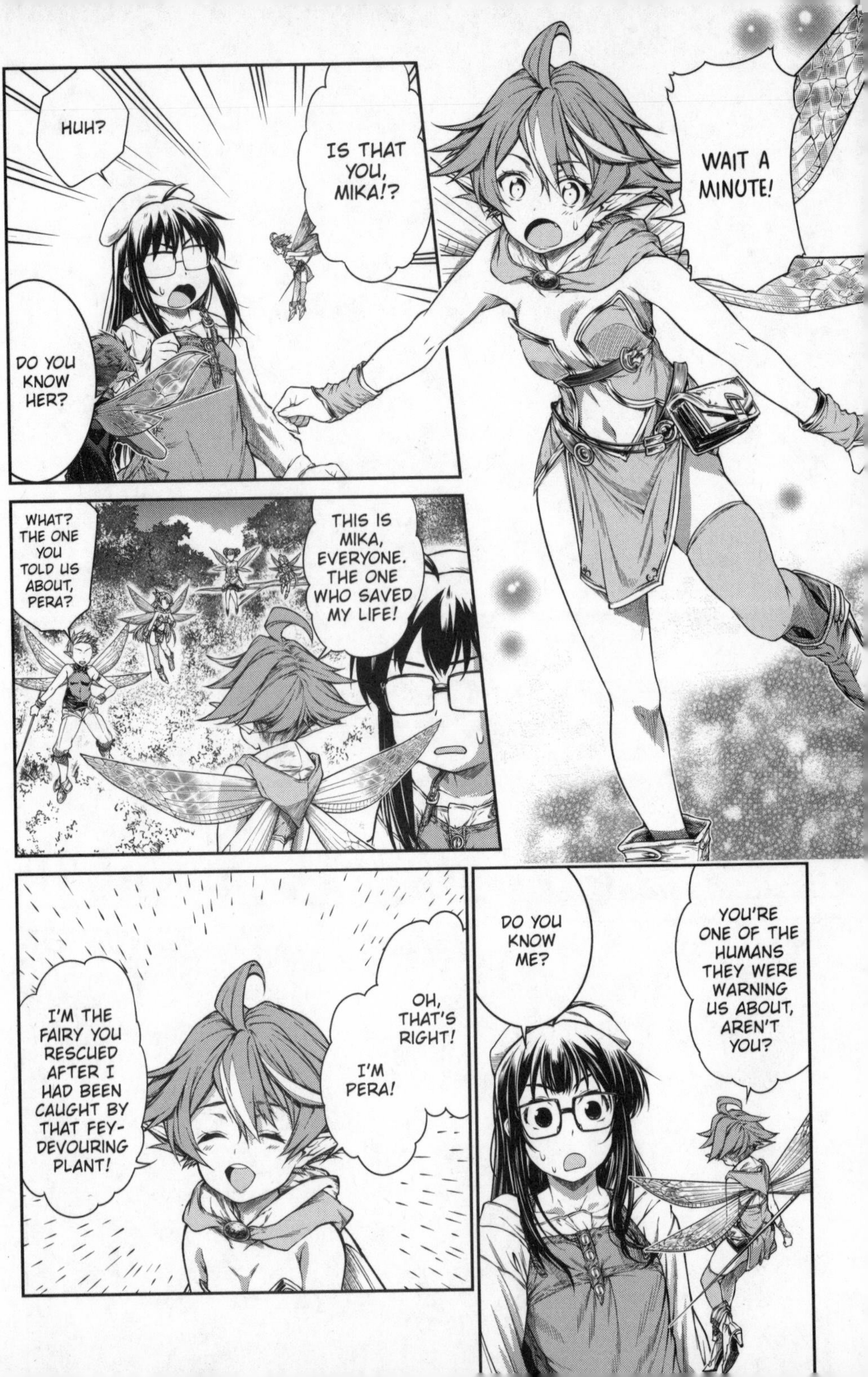
WAIT A MINUTE!
IS THAT YOU, MIKA!?
HUH?
DO YOU KNOW HER?
THIS IS MIKA, EVERYONE. THE ONE WHO SAVED MY LIFE!
WHAT? THE ONE YOU TOLD US ABOUT, PERA?
YOU'RE ONE OF THE HUMANS THEY WERE WARNING US ABOUT, AREN'T YOU?
DO YOU KNOW ME?
OH, THAT'S RIGHT!
I'M PERA!
I'M THE FAIRY YOU RESCUED AFTER I HAD BEEN CAUGHT BY THAT FEY-DEVOURING PLANT!

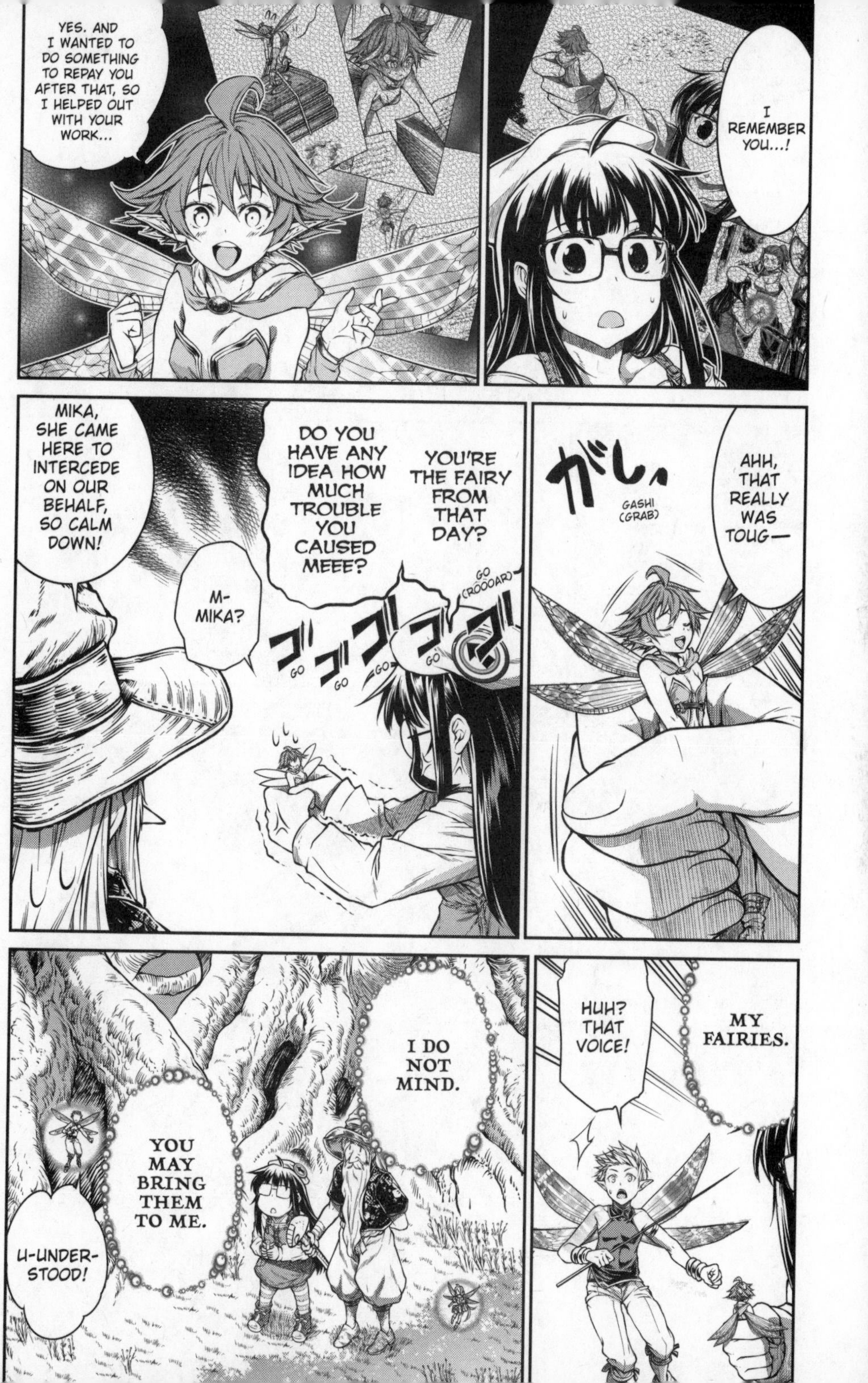
I REMEMBER YOU...!
YES. AND I WANTED TO DO SOMETHING TO REPAY YOU AFTER THAT, SO I HELPED OUT WITH YOUR WORK...
AHH, THAT REALLY WAS TOUG—
がし
GASHI (GRAB)
YOU'RE THE FAIRY FROM THAT DAY?
DO YOU HAVE ANY IDEA HOW MUCH TROUBLE YOU CAUSED MEEE?
GO (ROOOAR)
ゴゴゴゴ
GO GO GO GO
M-MIKA?
MIKA, SHE CAME HERE TO INTERCEDE ON OUR BEHALF, SO CALM DOWN!
MY FAIRIES.
HUH? THAT VOICE!
I DO NOT MIND.
YOU MAY BRING THEM TO ME.
U-UNDERSTOOD!

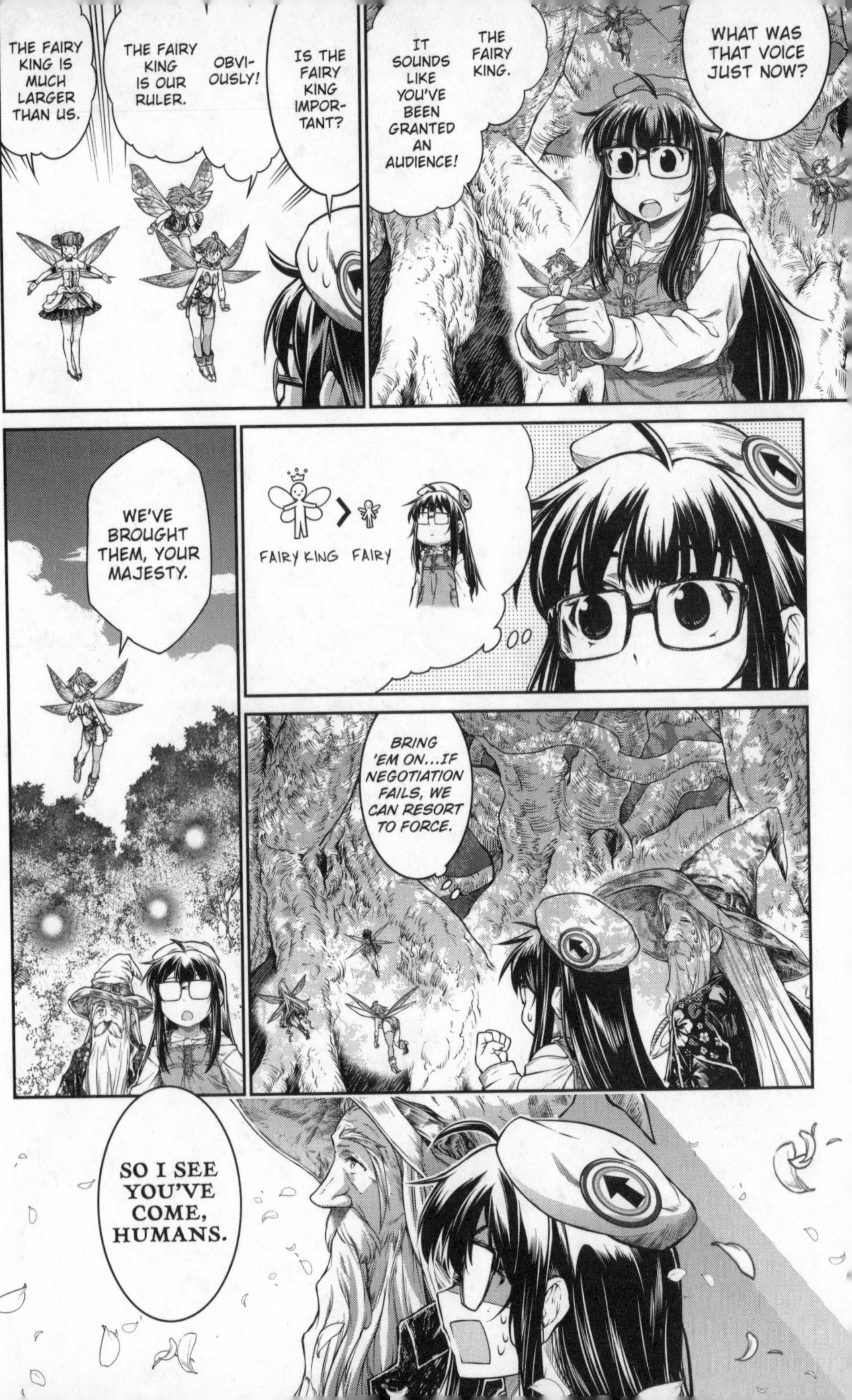
WHAT WAS THAT VOICE JUST NOW?
THE FAIRY KING.
IT SOUNDS LIKE YOU'VE BEEN GRANTED AN AUDIENCE!
IS THE FAIRY KING IMPORTANT?
OBVIOUSLY!
THE FAIRY KING IS OUR RULER.
THE FAIRY KING IS MUCH LARGER THAN US.
FAIRY KING
FAIRY
BRING 'EM ON...IF NEGOTIATION FAILS, WE CAN RESORT TO FORCE.
WE'VE BROUGHT THEM, YOUR MAJESTY.
SO I SEE YOU'VE COME, HUMANS.

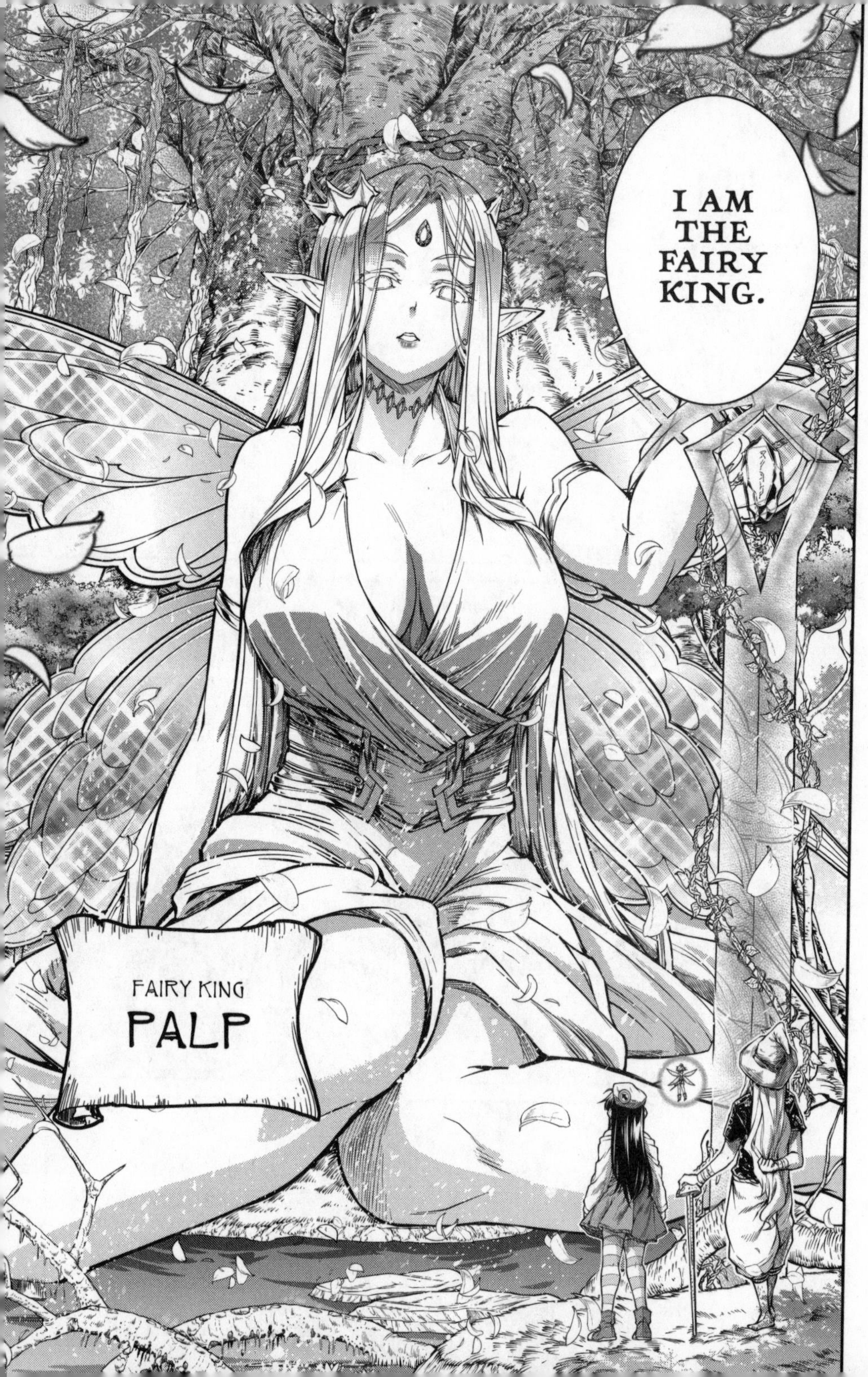
I AM THE FAIRY KING.
FAIRY KING PALP

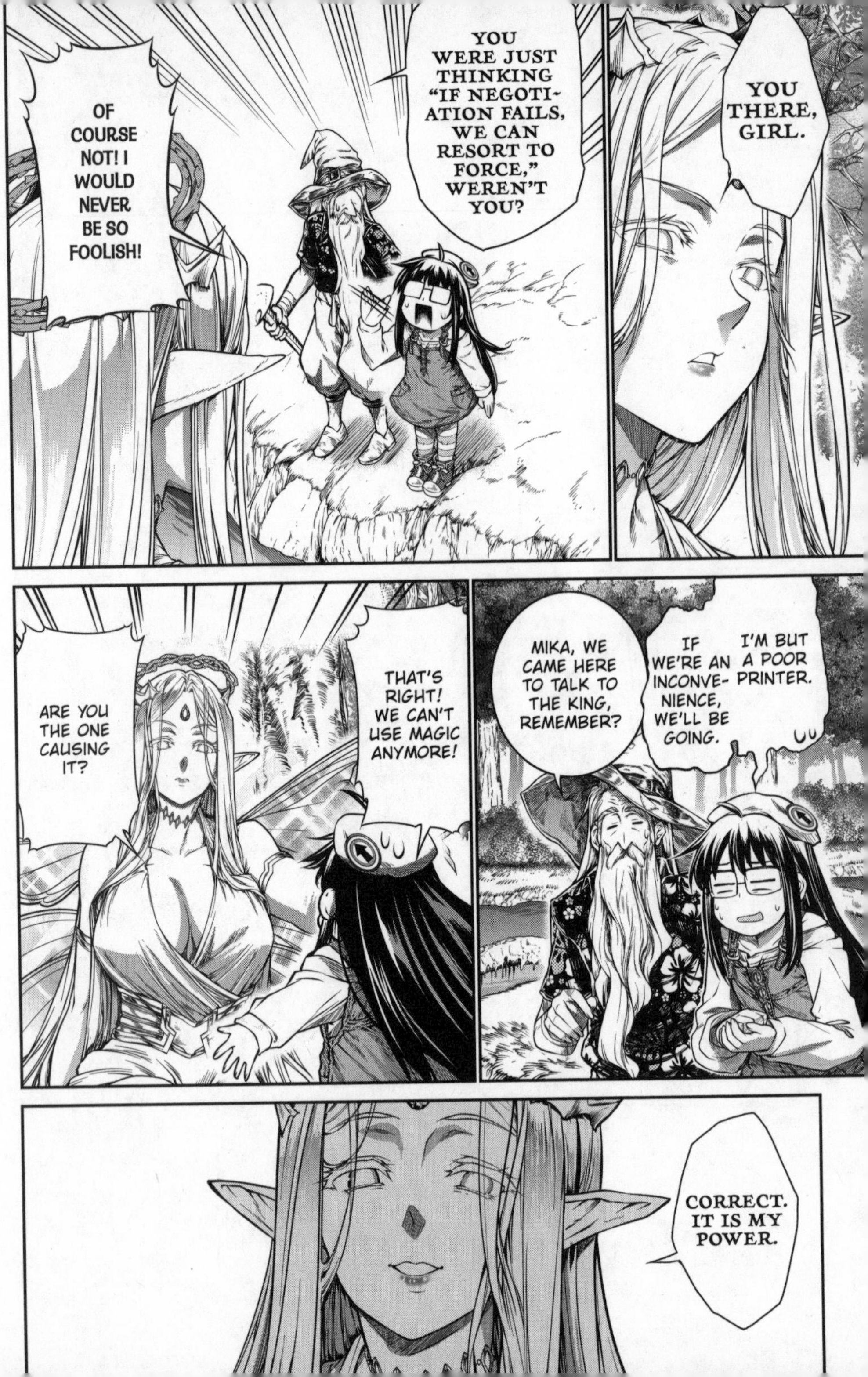
YOU THERE, GIRL.
YOU WERE JUST THINKING "IF NEGOTIATION FAILS, WE CAN RESORT TO FORCE," WEREN'T YOU?
OF COURSE NOT! I WOULD NEVER BE SO FOOLISH!
I'M BUT A POOR PRINTER.
IF WE'RE AN INCONVENIENCE, WE'LL BE GOING.
MIKA, WE CAME HERE TO TALK TO THE KING, REMEMBER?
THAT'S RIGHT! WE CAN'T USE MAGIC ANYMORE!
ARE YOU THE ONE CAUSING IT?
CORRECT. IT IS MY POWER.

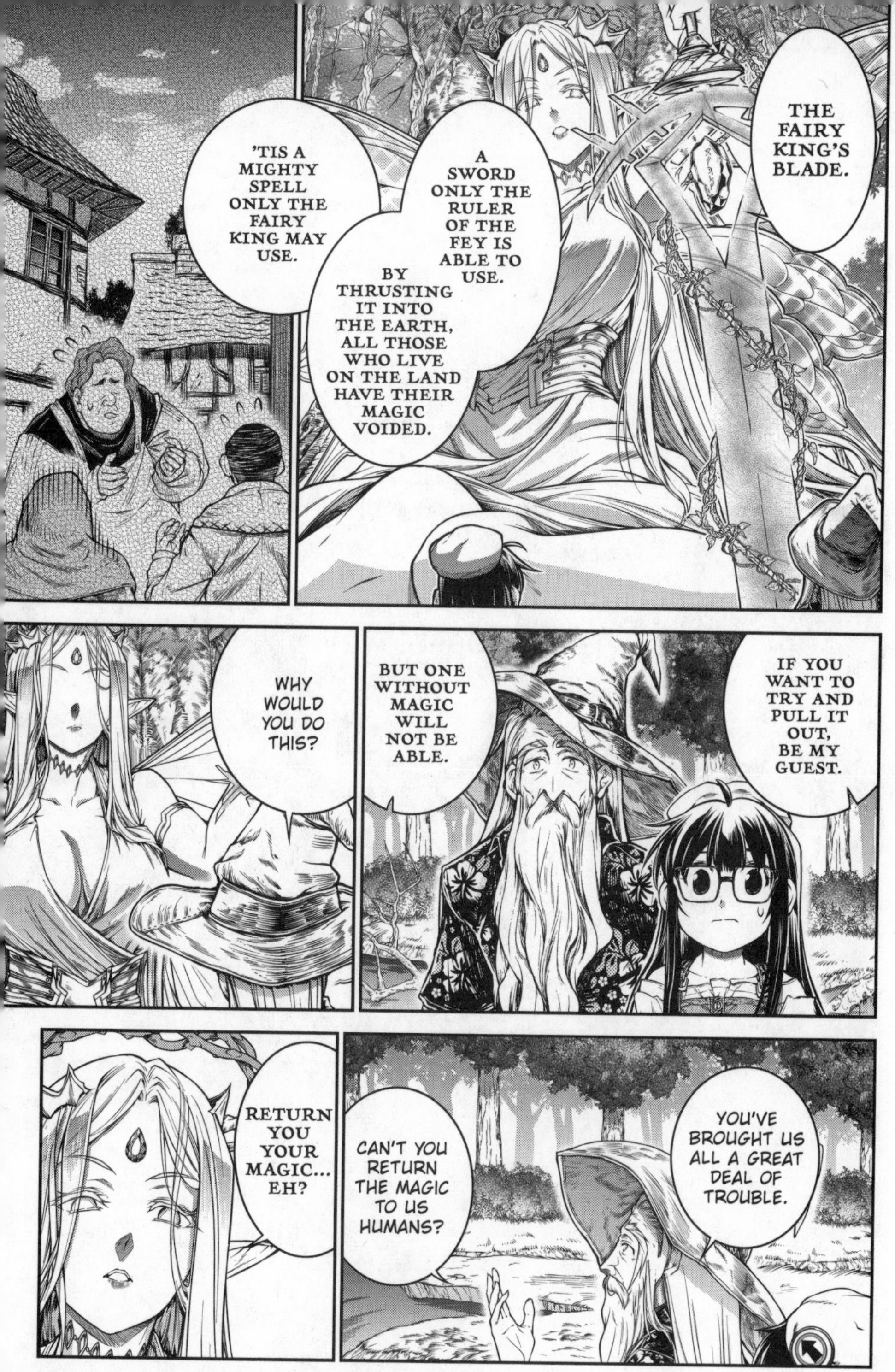
THE FAIRY KING'S BLADE.
A SWORD ONLY THE RULER OF THE FEY IS ABLE TO USE.
BY THRUSTING IT INTO THE EARTH, ALL THOSE WHO LIVE ON THE LAND HAVE THEIR MAGIC VOIDED.
'TIS A MIGHTY SPELL ONLY THE FAIRY KING MAY USE.
IF YOU WANT TO TRY AND PULL IT OUT, BE MY GUEST.
BUT ONE WITHOUT MAGIC WILL NOT BE ABLE.
WHY WOULD YOU DO THIS?
YOU'VE BROUGHT US ALL A GREAT DEAL OF TROUBLE.
CAN'T YOU RETURN THE MAGIC TO US HUMANS?
RETURN YOU YOUR MAGIC... EH?

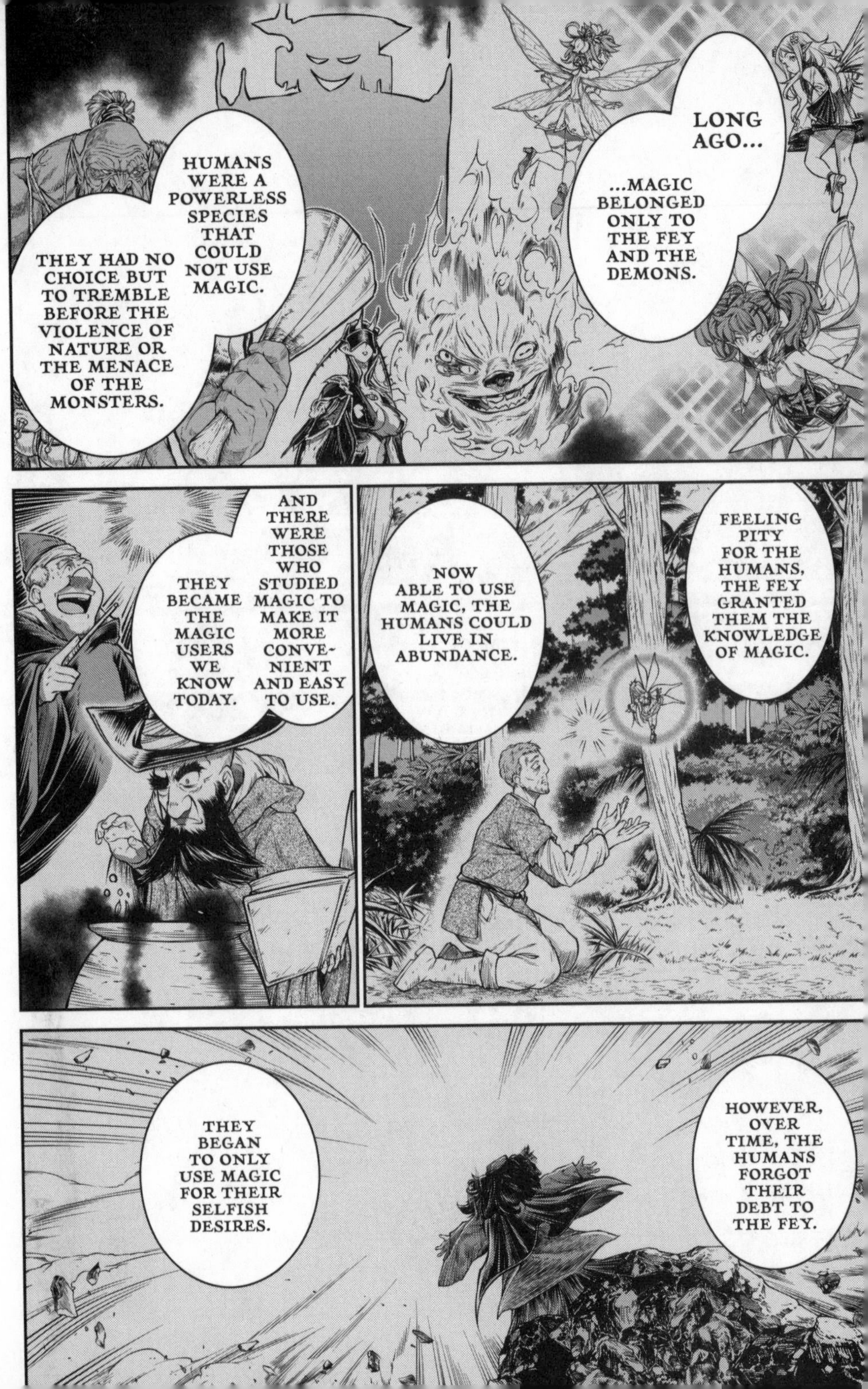
LONG AGO...
...MAGIC BELONGED ONLY TO THE FEY AND THE DEMONS.
HUMANS WERE A POWERLESS SPECIES THAT COULD NOT USE MAGIC.
THEY HAD NO CHOICE BUT TO TREMBLE BEFORE THE VIOLENCE OF NATURE OR THE MENACE OF THE MONSTERS.
FEELING PITY FOR THE HUMANS, THE FEY GRANTED THEM THE KNOWLEDGE OF MAGIC.
NOW ABLE TO USE MAGIC, THE HUMANS COULD LIVE IN ABUNDANCE.
AND THERE WERE THOSE WHO STUDIED MAGIC TO MAKE IT MORE CONVE-NIENT AND EASY TO USE.
THEY BECAME THE MAGIC USERS WE KNOW TODAY.
HOWEVER, OVER TIME, THE HUMANS FORGOT THEIR DEBT TO THE FEY.
THEY BEGAN TO ONLY USE MAGIC FOR THEIR SELFISH DESIRES.

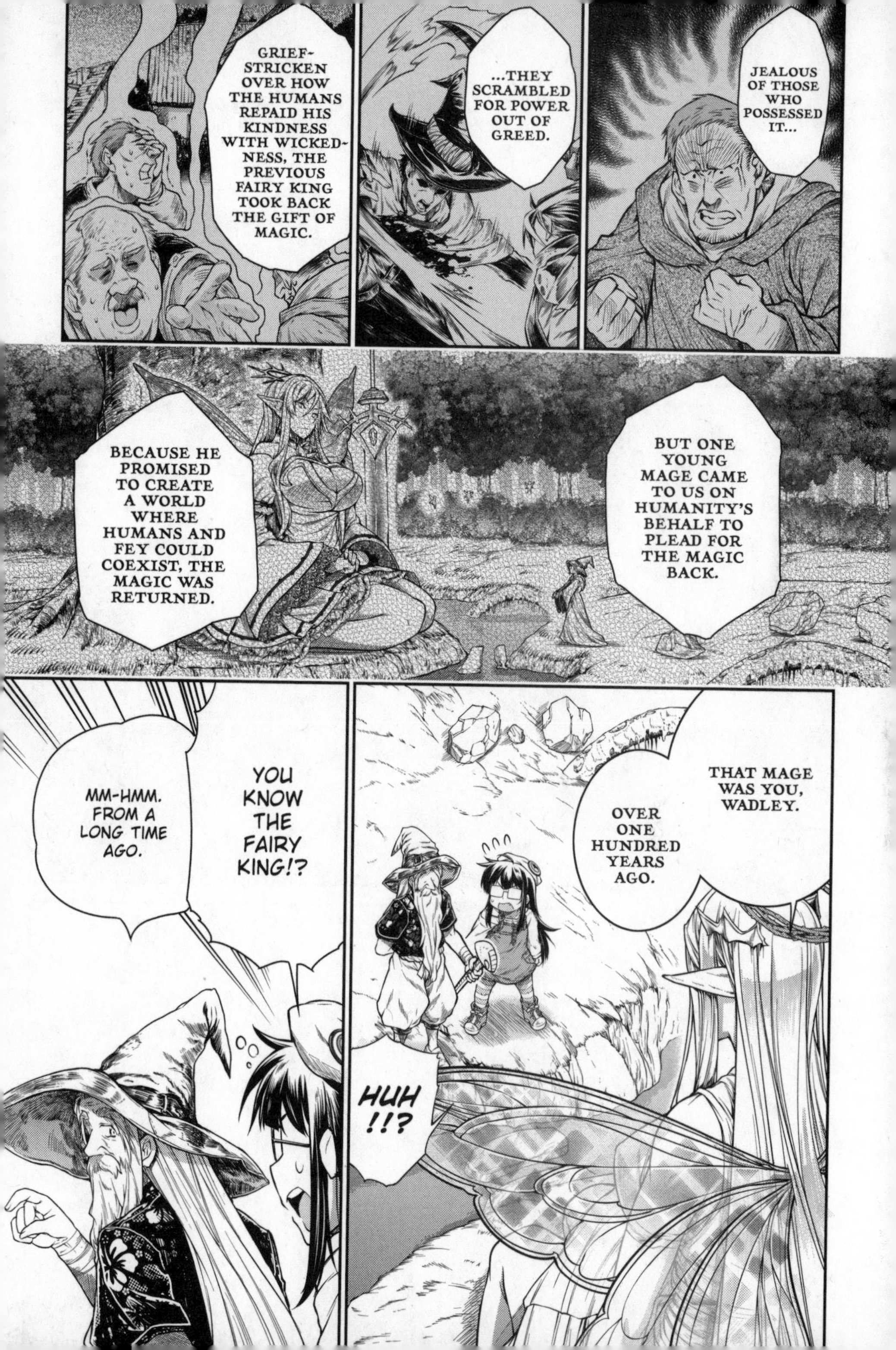
JEALOUS OF THOSE WHO POSSESSED IT...
...THEY SCRAMBLED FOR POWER OUT OF GREED.
GRIEF-STRICKEN OVER HOW THE HUMANS REPAID HIS KINDNESS WITH WICKEDNESS, THE PREVIOUS FAIRY KING TOOK BACK THE GIFT OF MAGIC.
BUT ONE YOUNG MAGE CAME TO US ON HUMANITY'S BEHALF TO PLEAD FOR THE MAGIC BACK.
BECAUSE HE PROMISED TO CREATE A WORLD WHERE HUMANS AND FEY COULD COEXIST, THE MAGIC WAS RETURNED.
THAT MAGE WAS YOU, WADLEY.
OVER ONE HUNDRED YEARS AGO.
HUH!!?
YOU KNOW THE FAIRY KING!?
MM-HMM. FROM A LONG TIME AGO.

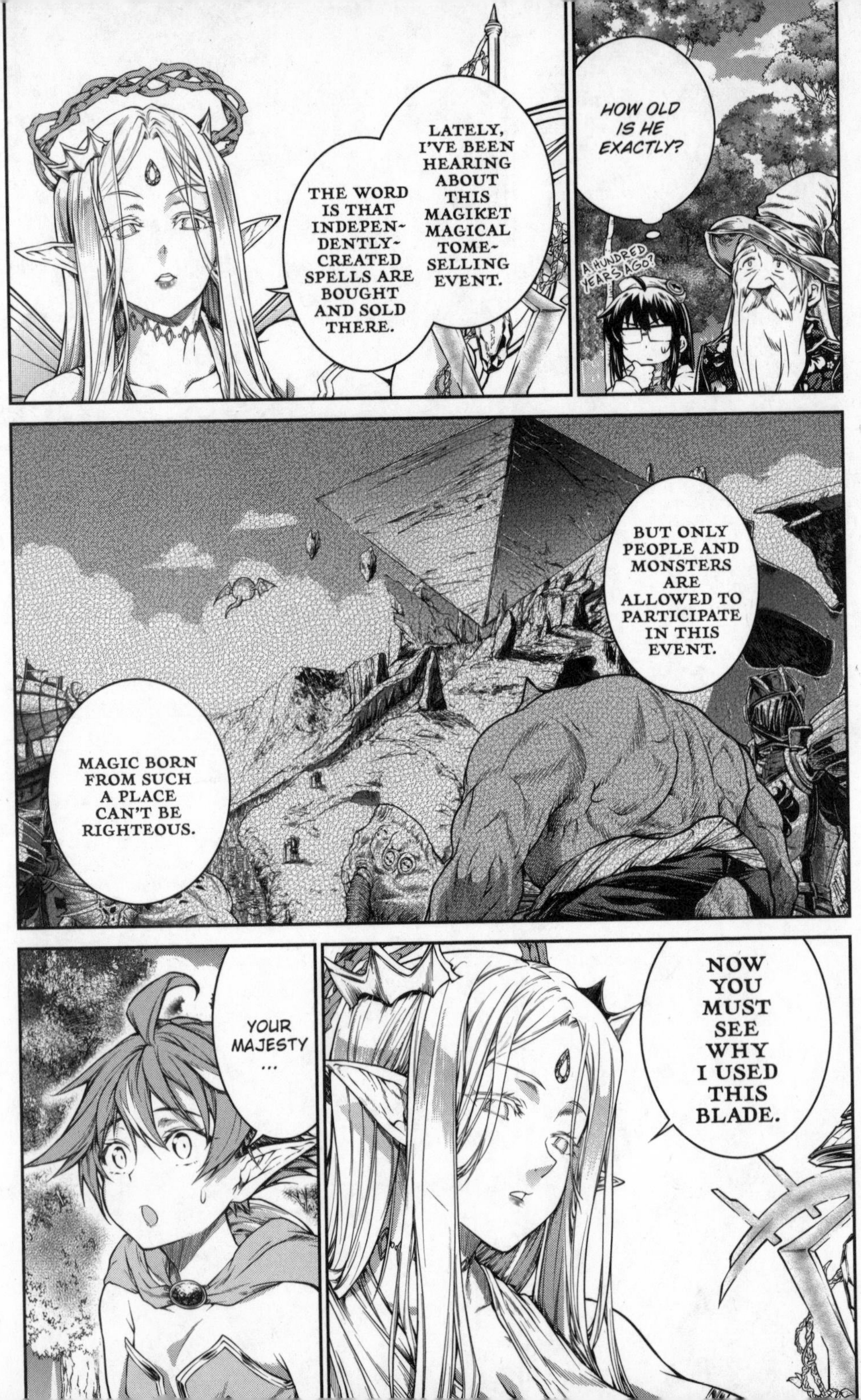
HOW OLD IS HE EXACTLY?
A HUNDRED YEARS AGO?
LATELY, I'VE BEEN HEARING ABOUT THIS MAGIKET MAGICAL TOME-SELLING EVENT.
THE WORD IS THAT INDEPEN-DENTLY-CREATED SPELLS ARE BOUGHT AND SOLD THERE.
BUT ONLY PEOPLE AND MONSTERS ARE ALLOWED TO PARTICIPATE IN THIS EVENT.
MAGIC BORN FROM SUCH A PLACE CAN'T BE RIGHTEOUS.
NOW YOU MUST SEE WHY I USED THIS BLADE.
YOUR MAJESTY ...

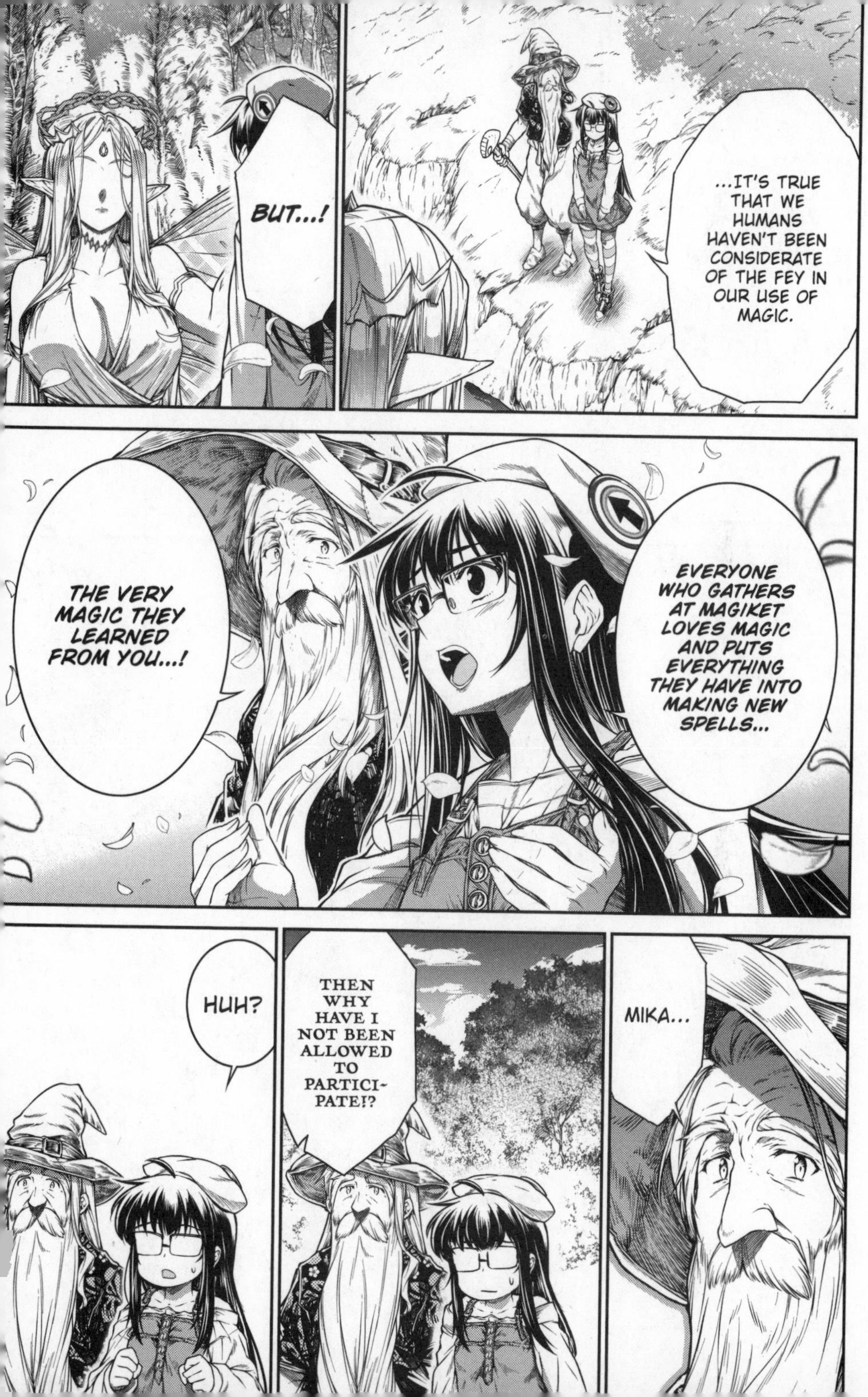
...IT'S TRUE THAT WE HUMANS HAVEN'T BEEN CONSIDERATE OF THE FEY IN OUR USE OF MAGIC.
BUT...!
EVERYONE WHO GATHERS AT MAGIKET LOVES MAGIC AND PUTS EVERYTHING THEY HAVE INTO MAKING NEW SPELLS...
THE VERY MAGIC THEY LEARNED FROM YOU...!
MIKA...
THEN WHY HAVE I NOT BEEN ALLOWED TO PARTICI-PATE!?
HUH?

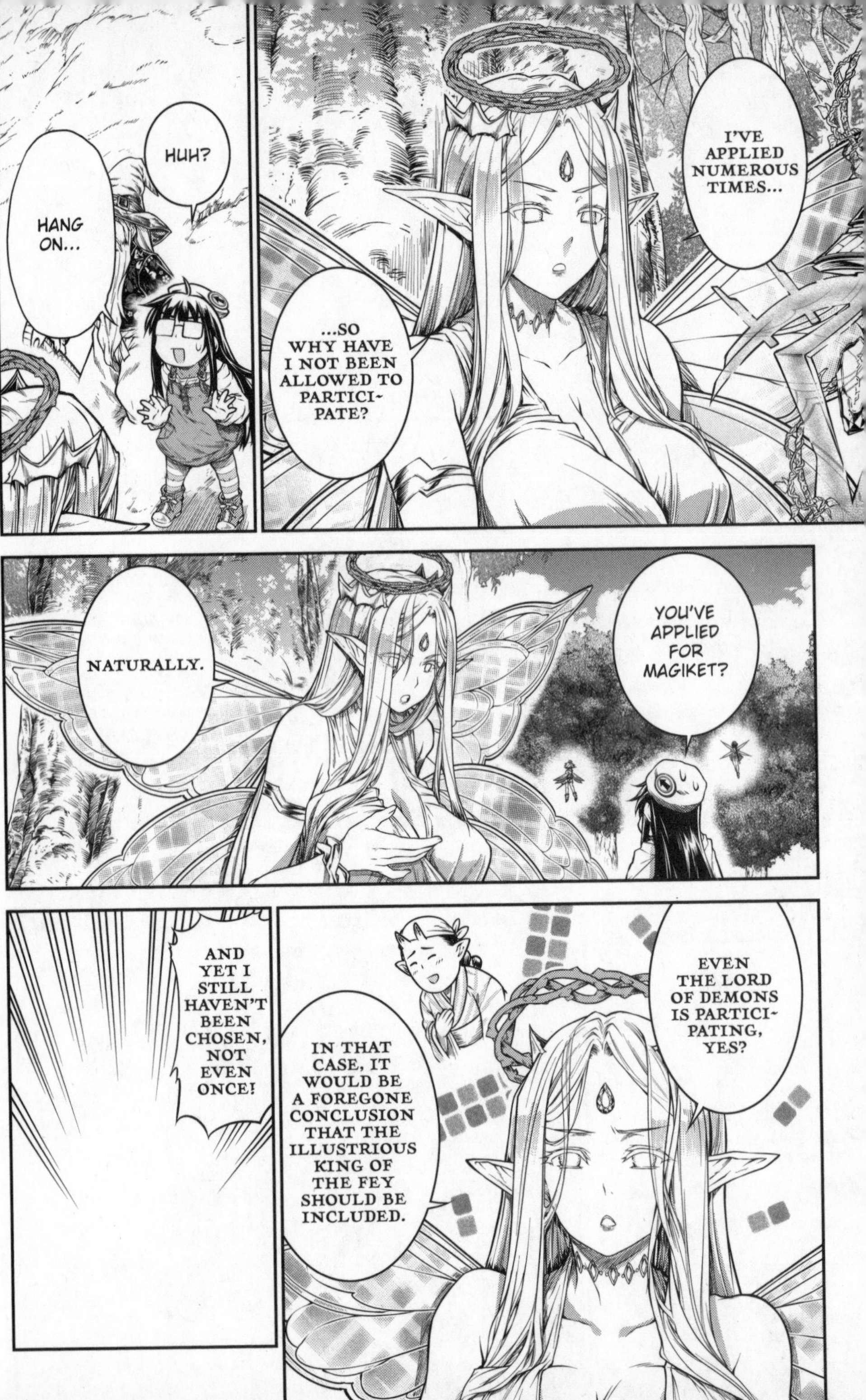
I'VE APPLIED NUMEROUS TIMES...
...SO WHY HAVE I NOT BEEN ALLOWED TO PARTICI-PATE?
HUH?
HANG ON...
YOU'VE APPLIED FOR MAGIKET?
NATURALLY.
EVEN THE LORD OF DEMONS IS PARTICI-PATING, YES?
IN THAT CASE, IT WOULD BE A FOREGONE CONCLUSION THAT THE ILLUSTRIOUS KING OF THE FEY SHOULD BE INCLUDED.
AND YET I STILL HAVEN'T BEEN CHOSEN, NOT EVEN ONCE!

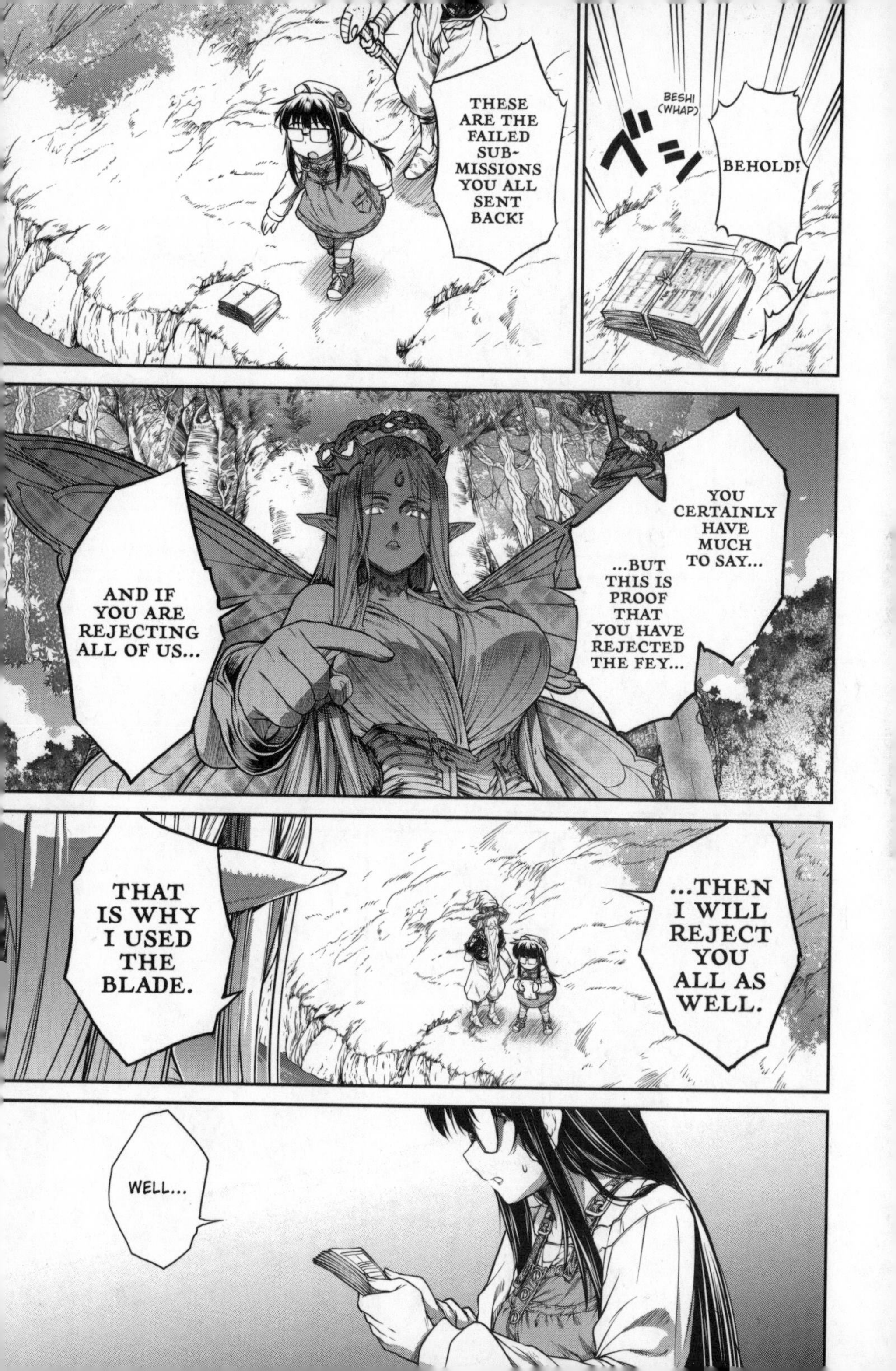
BESHI (WHAP)
ベシ
BEHOLD!
THESE ARE THE FAILED SUB-MISSIONS YOU ALL SENT BACK!
YOU CERTAINLY HAVE MUCH TO SAY...
...BUT THIS IS PROOF THAT YOU HAVE REJECTED THE FEY...
AND IF YOU ARE REJECTING ALL OF US...
...THEN I WILL REJECT YOU ALL AS WELL.
THAT IS WHY I USED THE BLADE.
WELL...

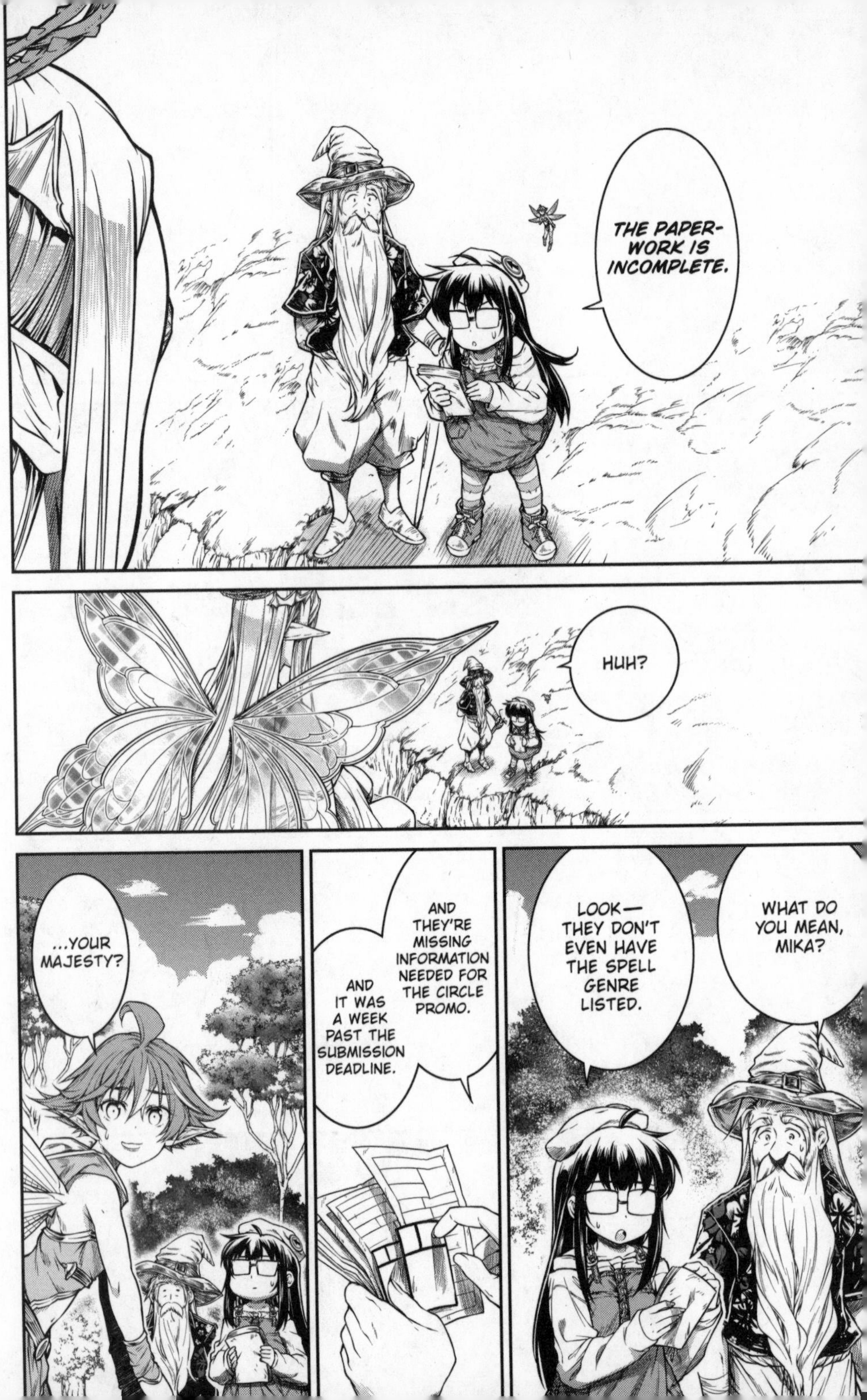
THE PAPER-WORK IS INCOMPLETE.
HUH?
WHAT DO YOU MEAN, MIKA?
LOOK—THEY DON'T EVEN HAVE THE SPELL GENRE LISTED.
AND THEY'RE MISSING INFORMATION NEEDED FOR THE CIRCLE PROMO.
AND IT WAS A WEEK PAST THE SUBMISSION DEADLINE.
...YOUR MAJESTY?

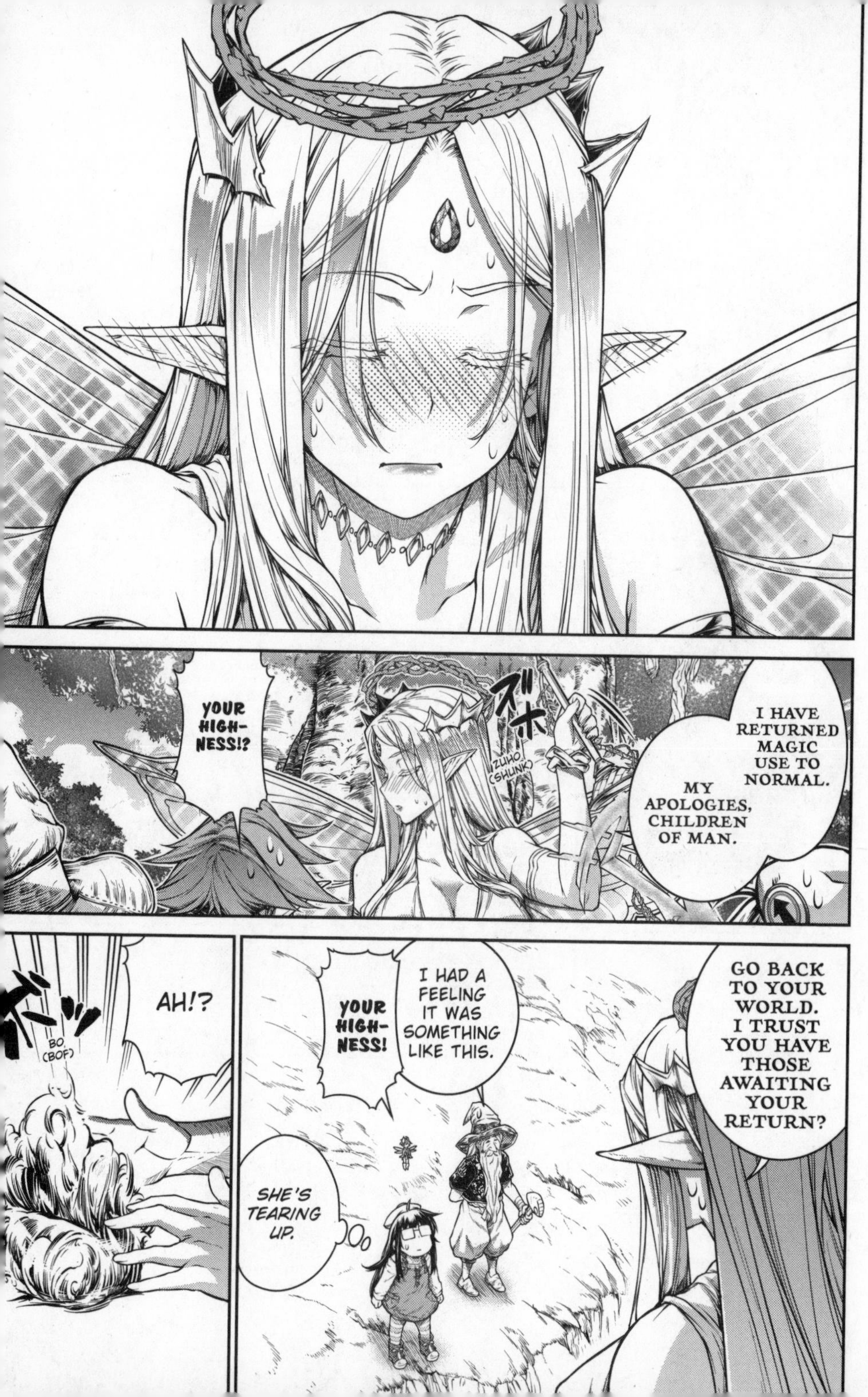
I HAVE RETURNED MAGIC USE TO NORMAL.
MY APOLOGIES, CHILDREN OF MAN.
ズホ
ZUHO (SHUNK)
YOUR HIGHNESS!?
GO BACK TO YOUR WORLD. I TRUST YOU HAVE THOSE AWAITING YOUR RETURN?
I HAD A FEELING IT WAS SOMETHING LIKE THIS.
YOUR HIGHNESS!
SHE'S TEARING UP.
AH!?
BO (BOF)

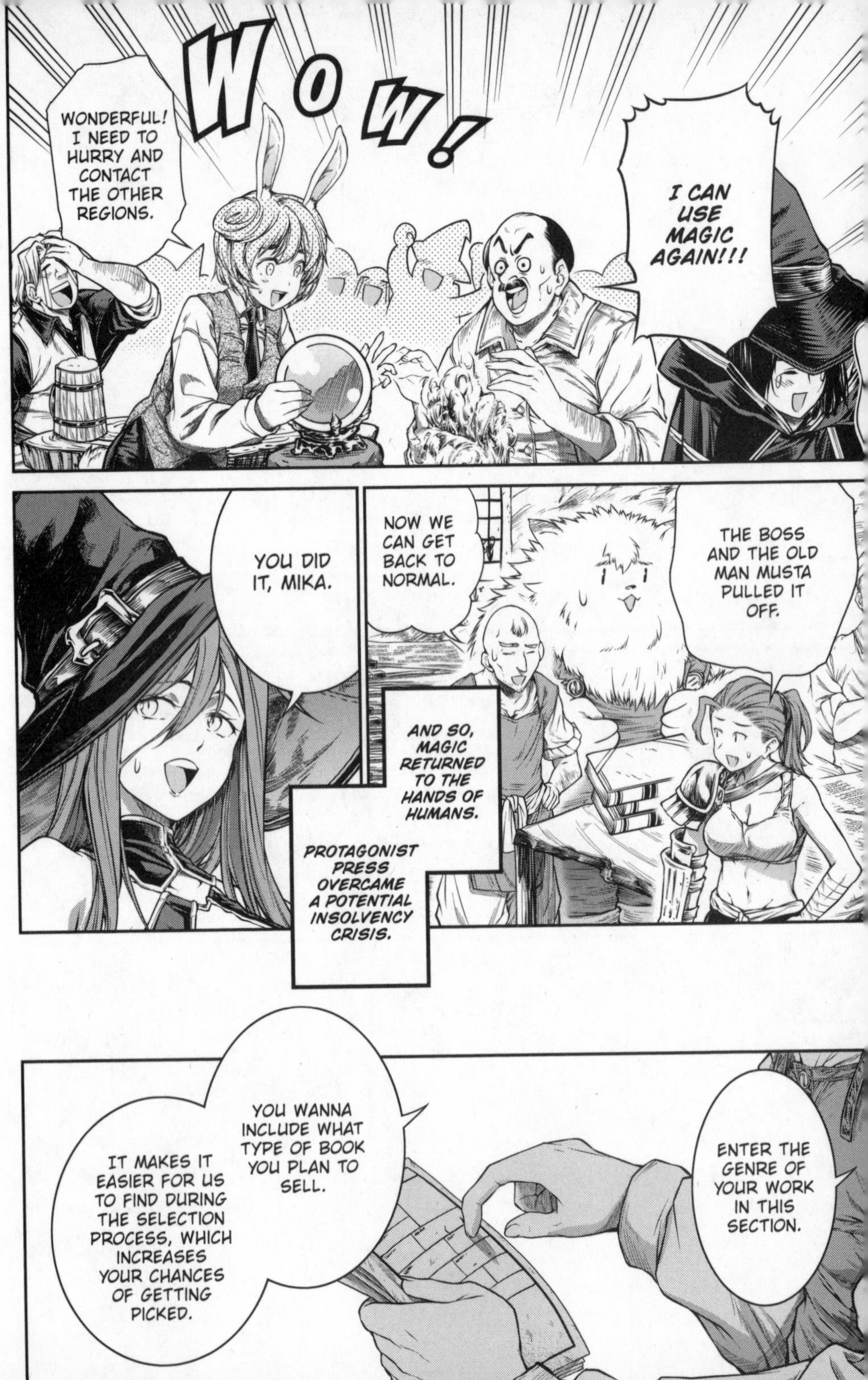
I CAN USE MAGIC AGAIN!!!
WOW!
WONDERFUL! I NEED TO HURRY AND CONTACT THE OTHER REGIONS.
THE BOSS AND THE OLD MAN MUSTA PULLED IT OFF.
NOW WE CAN GET BACK TO NORMAL.
YOU DID IT, MIKA.
AND SO, MAGIC RETURNED TO THE HANDS OF HUMANS.
PROTAGONIST PRESS OVERCAME A POTENTIAL INSOLVENCY CRISIS.
ENTER THE GENRE OF YOUR WORK IN THIS SECTION.
YOU WANNA INCLUDE WHAT TYPE OF BOOK YOU PLAN TO SELL.
IT MAKES IT EASIER FOR US TO FIND DURING THE SELECTION PROCESS, WHICH INCREASES YOUR CHANCES OF GETTING PICKED.

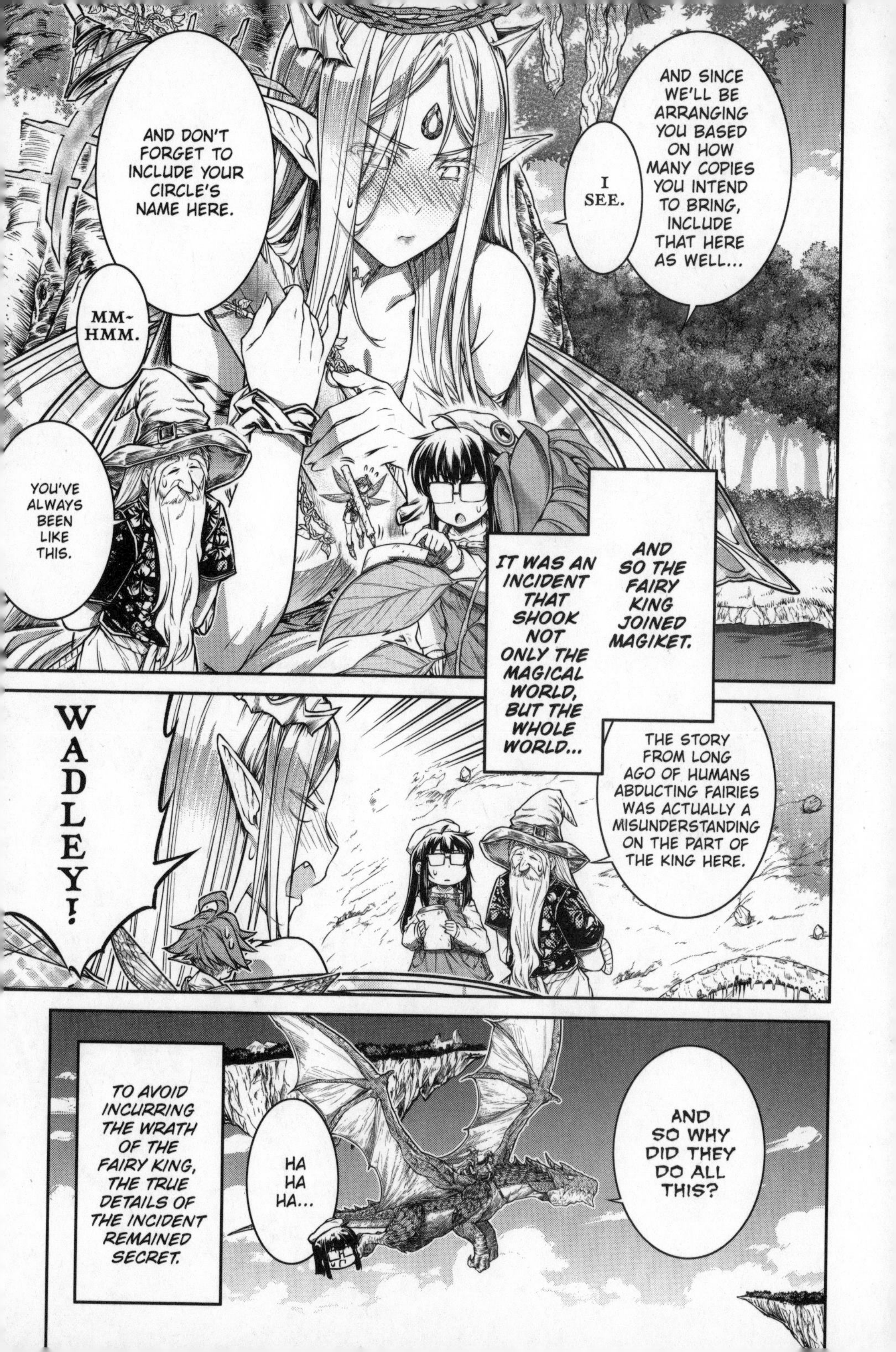
AND SINCE WE'LL BE ARRANGING YOU BASED ON HOW MANY COPIES YOU INTEND TO BRING, INCLUDE THAT HERE AS WELL...
I SEE.
AND DON'T FORGET TO INCLUDE YOUR CIRCLE'S NAME HERE.
MM-HMM.
YOU'VE ALWAYS BEEN LIKE THIS.
AND SO THE FAIRY KING JOINED MAGIKET.
IT WAS AN INCIDENT THAT SHOOK NOT ONLY THE MAGICAL WORLD, BUT THE WHOLE WORLD...
THE STORY FROM LONG AGO OF HUMANS ABDUCTING FAIRIES WAS ACTUALLY A MISUNDERSTANDING ON THE PART OF THE KING HERE.
WADLEY!
AND SO WHY DID THEY DO ALL THIS?
HA HA HA...
TO AVOID INCURRING THE WRATH OF THE FAIRY KING, THE TRUE DETAILS OF THE INCIDENT REMAINED SECRET.

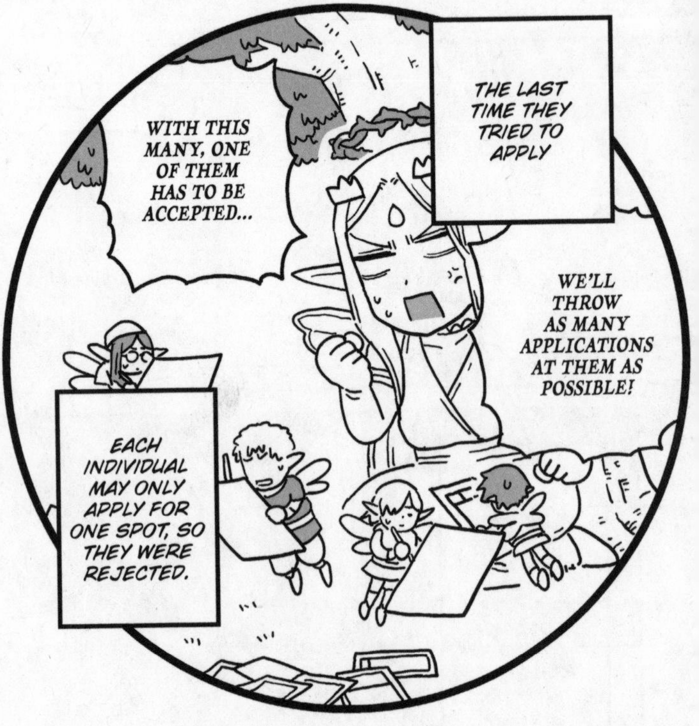
THE LAST TIME THEY TRIED TO APPLY
WITH THIS MANY, ONE OF THEM HAS TO BE ACCEPTED...
WE'LL THROW AS MANY APPLICATIONS AT THEM AS POSSIBLE!
EACH INDIVIDUAL MAY ONLY APPLY FOR ONE SPOT, SO THEY WERE REJECTED.

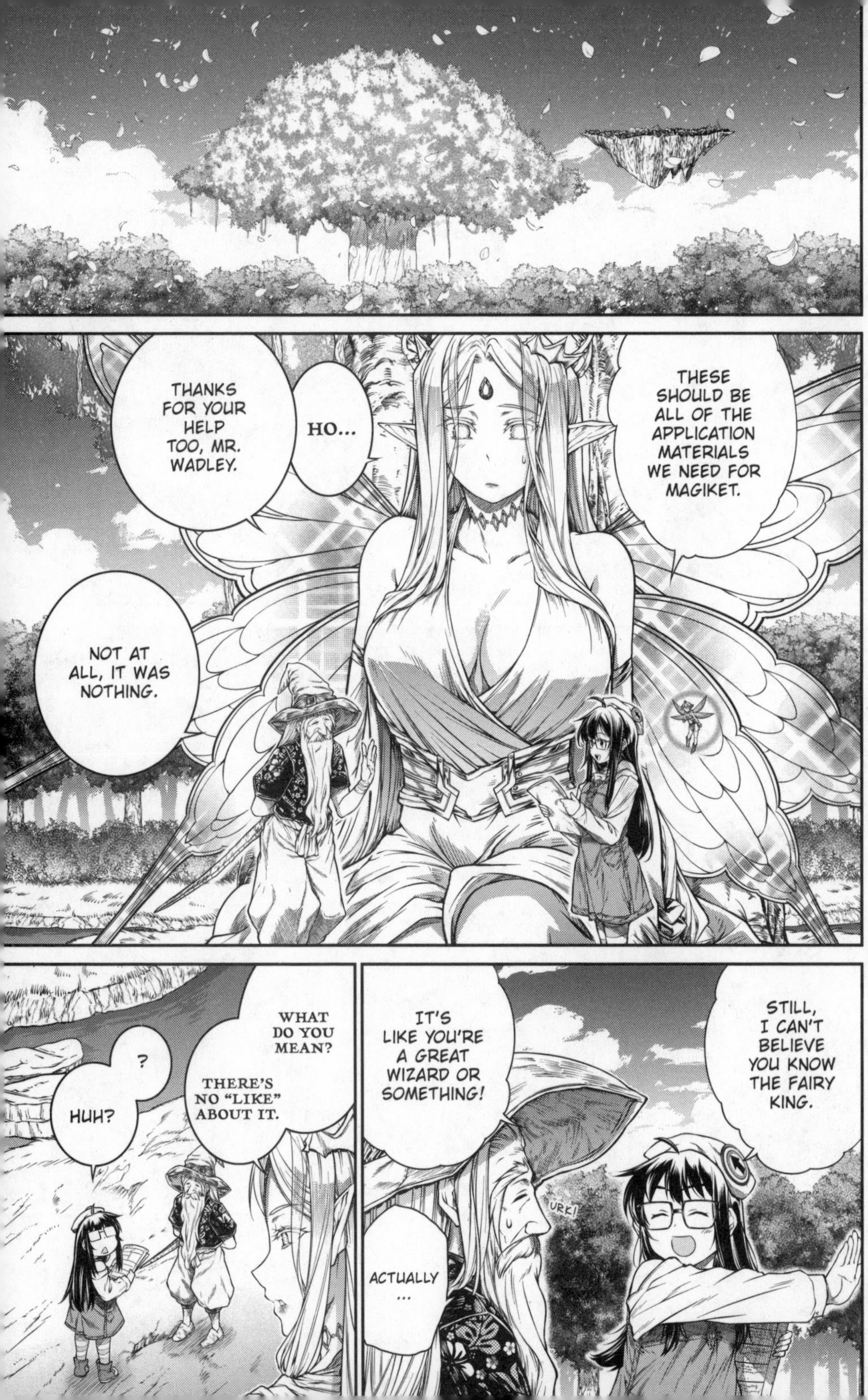
THESE SHOULD BE ALL OF THE APPLICATION MATERIALS WE NEED FOR MAGIKET.
HO...
THANKS FOR YOUR HELP TOO, MR. WADLEY.
NOT AT ALL, IT WAS NOTHING.
STILL, I CAN'T BELIEVE YOU KNOW THE FAIRY KING.
URK!
IT'S LIKE YOU'RE A GREAT WIZARD OR SOMETHING!
ACTUALLY ...
WHAT DO YOU MEAN?
THERE'S NO "LIKE" ABOUT IT.
?
HUH?

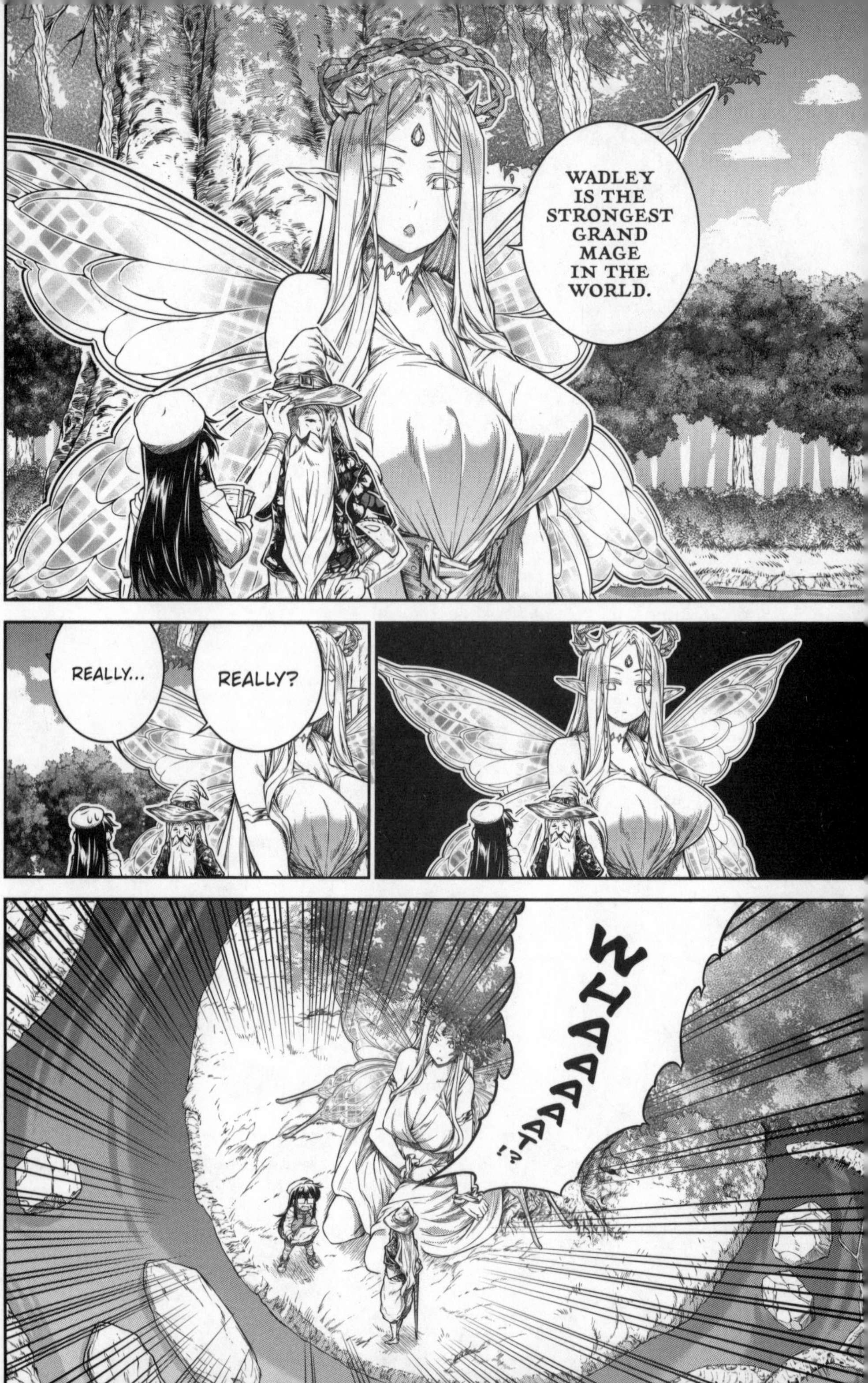
WADLEY IS THE STRONGEST GRAND MAGE IN THE WORLD.
REALLY?
REALLY...
WHAAAAAAT!?

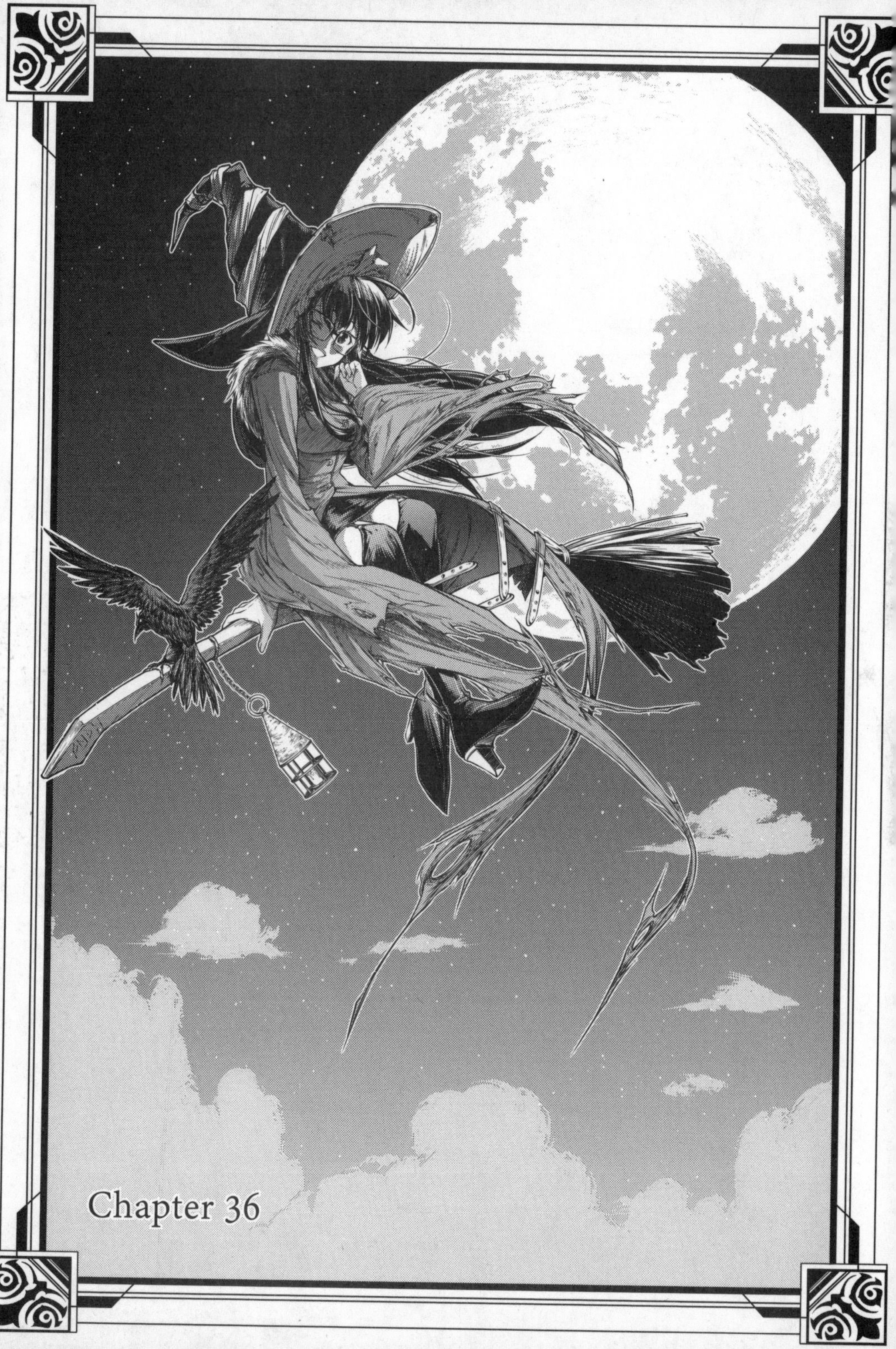Chapter 36

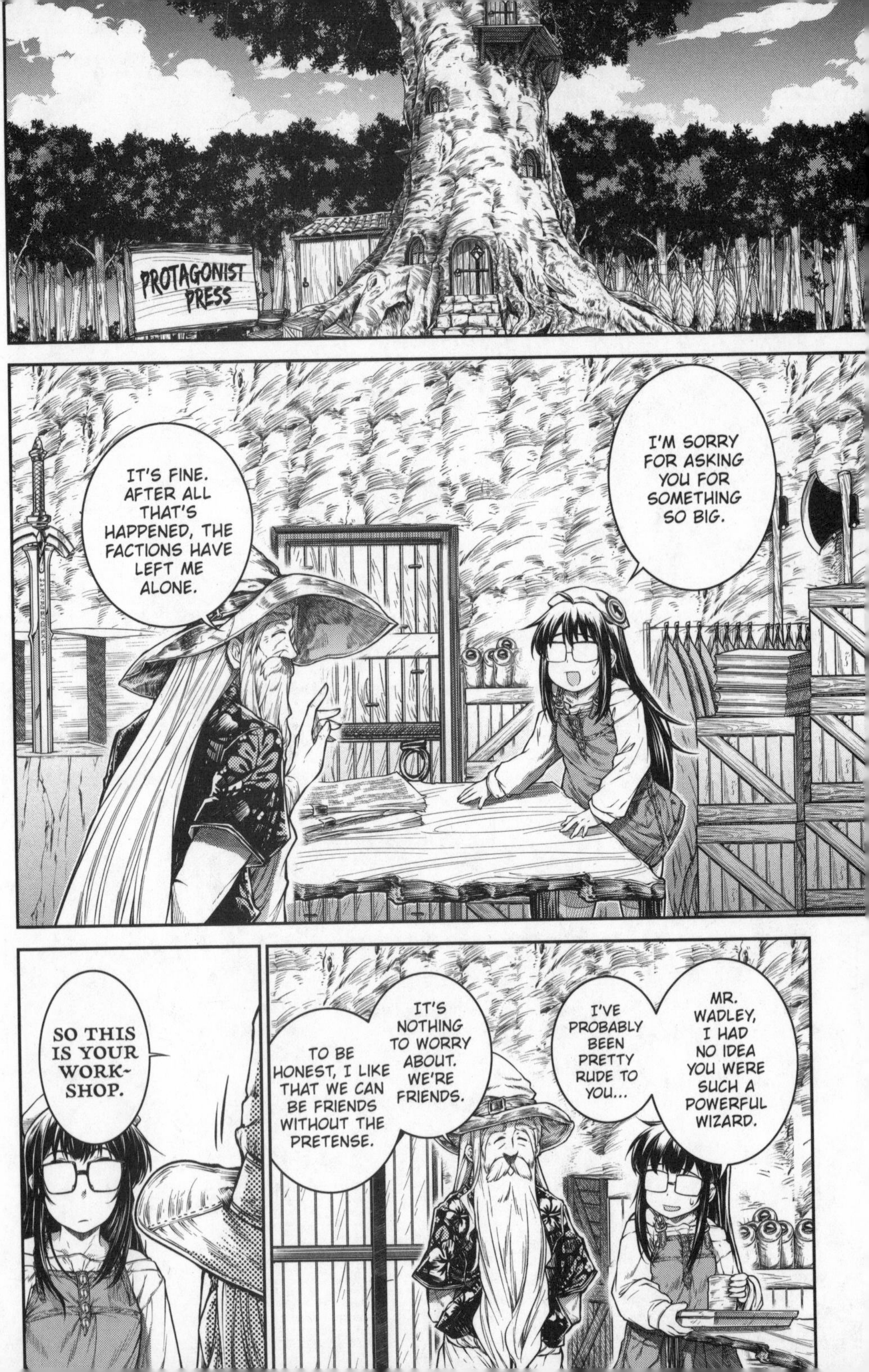
PROTAGONIST PRESS
I'M SORRY FOR ASKING YOU FOR SOMETHING SO BIG.
IT'S FINE. AFTER ALL THAT'S HAPPENED, THE FACTIONS HAVE LEFT ME ALONE.
MR. WADLEY, I HAD NO IDEA YOU WERE SUCH A POWERFUL WIZARD.
I'VE PROBABLY BEEN PRETTY RUDE TO YOU...
IT'S NOTHING TO WORRY ABOUT. WE'RE FRIENDS.
TO BE HONEST, I LIKE THAT WE CAN BE FRIENDS WITHOUT THE PRETENSE.
SO THIS IS YOUR WORK-SHOP.

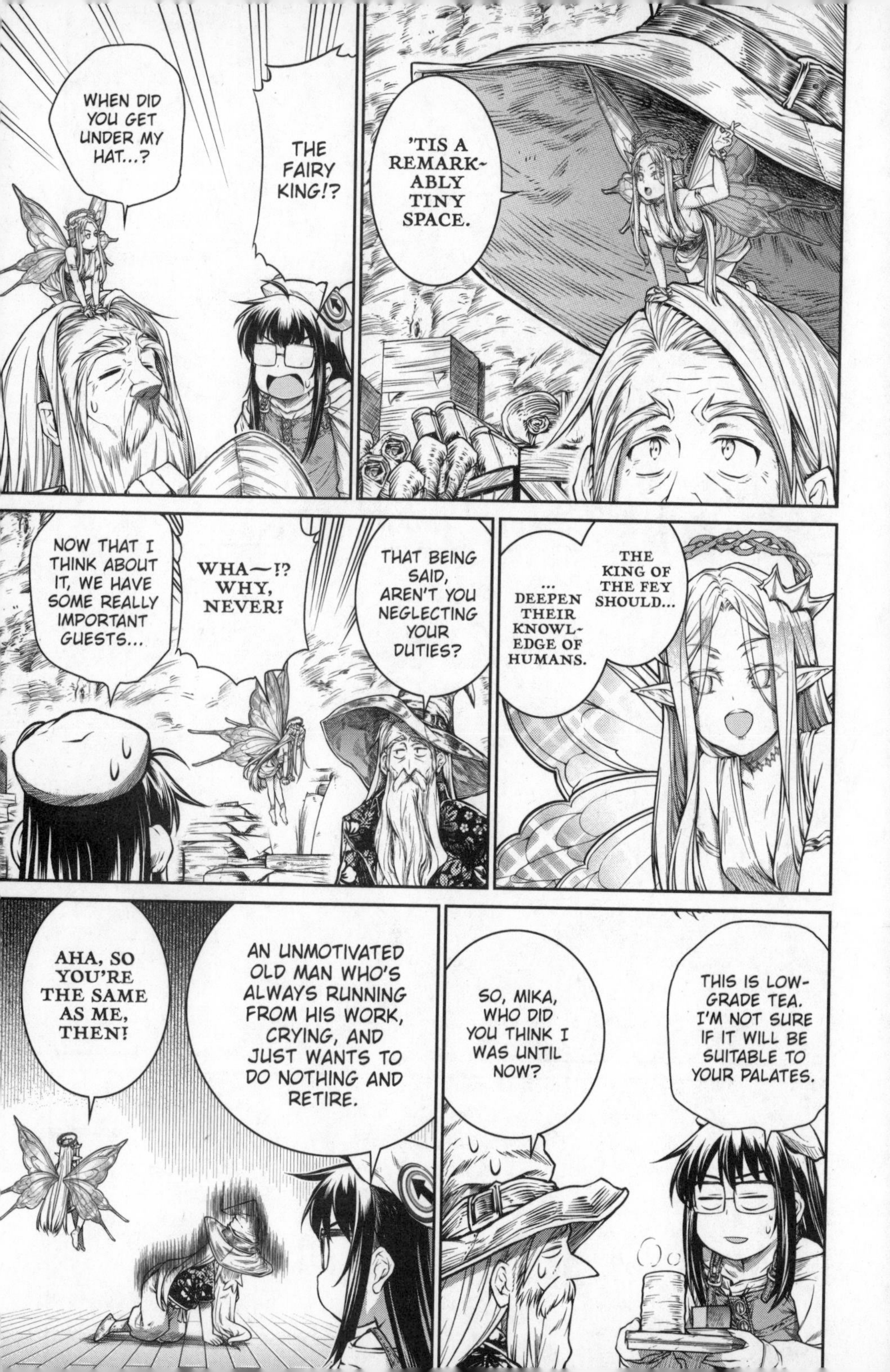
'TIS A REMARKABLY TINY SPACE.
THE FAIRY KING!?
WHEN DID YOU GET UNDER MY HAT...?
THE KING OF THE FEY SHOULD...
... DEEPEN THEIR KNOWLEDGE OF HUMANS.
THAT BEING SAID, AREN'T YOU NEGLECTING YOUR DUTIES?
WHA—!? WHY, NEVER!
NOW THAT I THINK ABOUT IT, WE HAVE SOME REALLY IMPORTANT GUESTS...
THIS IS LOW-GRADE TEA. I'M NOT SURE IF IT WILL BE SUITABLE TO YOUR PALATES.
SO, MIKA, WHO DID YOU THINK I WAS UNTIL NOW?
AN UNMOTIVATED OLD MAN WHO'S ALWAYS RUNNING FROM HIS WORK, CRYING, AND JUST WANTS TO DO NOTHING AND RETIRE.
AHA, SO YOU'RE THE SAME AS ME, THEN!

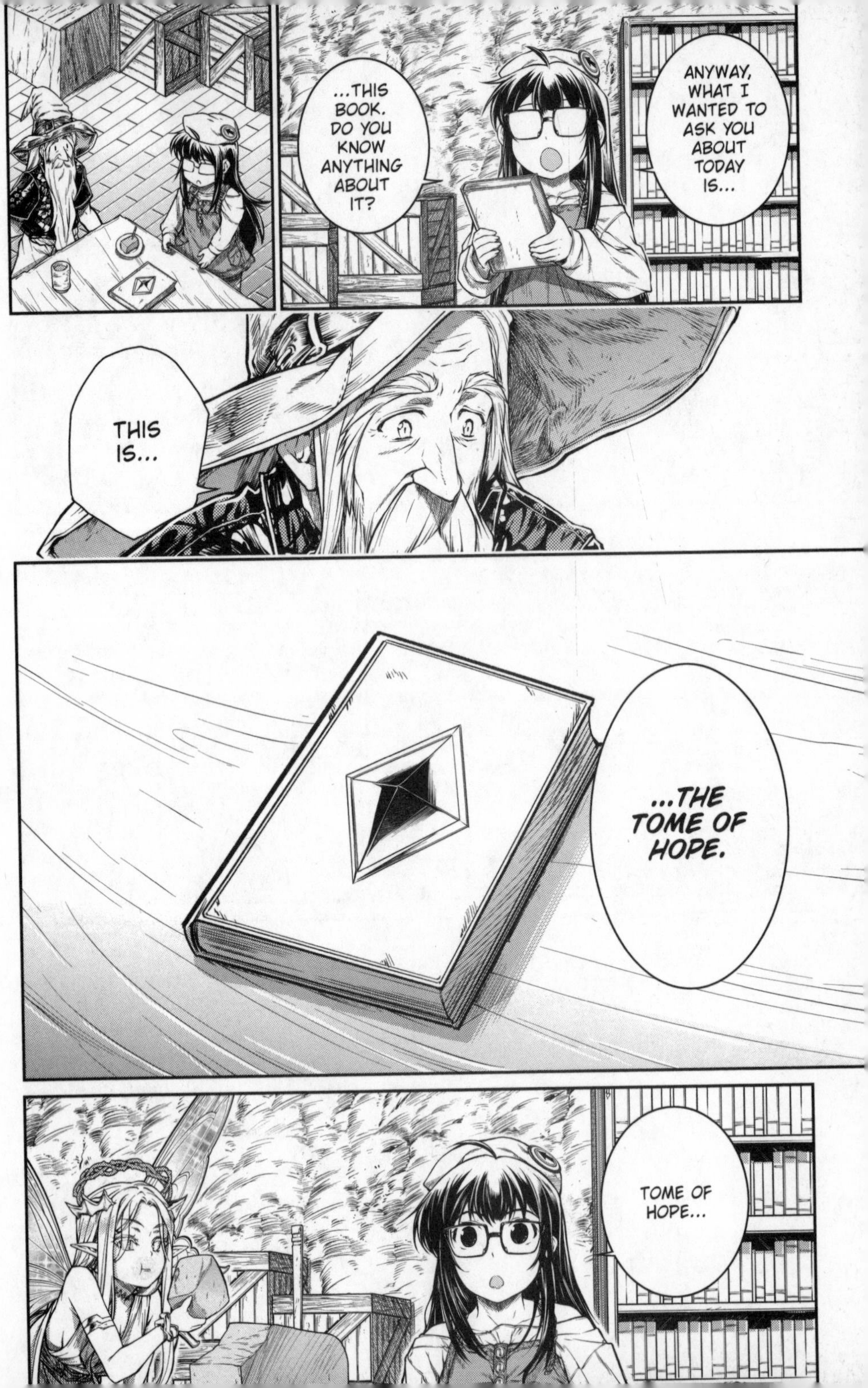
ANYWAY, WHAT I WANTED TO ASK YOU ABOUT TODAY IS...
...THIS BOOK. DO YOU KNOW ANYTHING ABOUT IT?
THIS IS...
...THE TOME OF HOPE.
TOME OF HOPE...

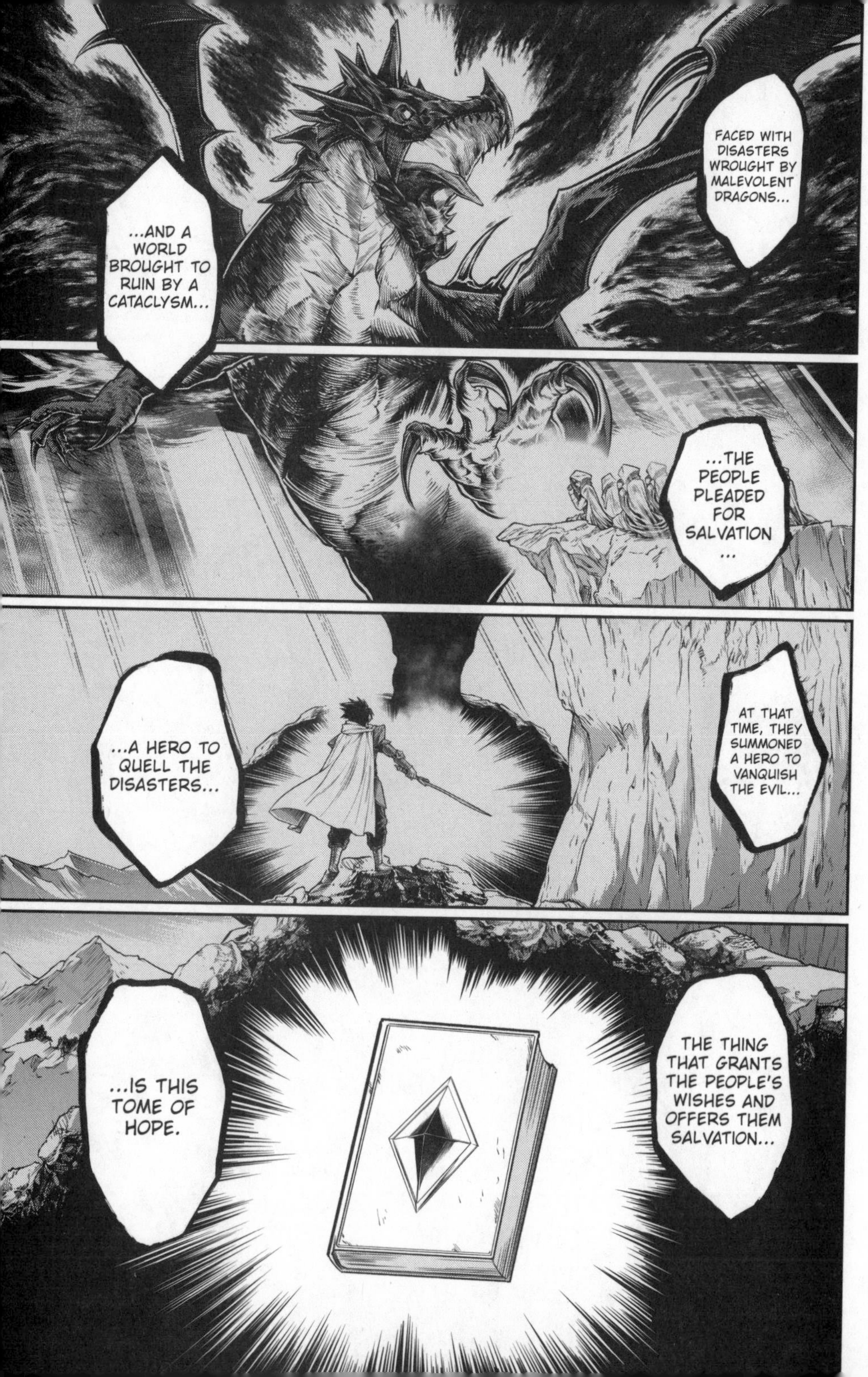
FACED WITH DISASTERS WROUGHT BY MALEVOLENT DRAGONS...
...AND A WORLD BROUGHT TO RUIN BY A CATACLYSM...
...THE PEOPLE PLEADED FOR SALVATION...
AT THAT TIME, THEY SUMMONED A HERO TO VANQUISH THE EVIL...
...A HERO TO QUELL THE DISASTERS...
THE THING THAT GRANTS THE PEOPLE'S WISHES AND OFFERS THEM SALVATION...
...IS THIS TOME OF HOPE.

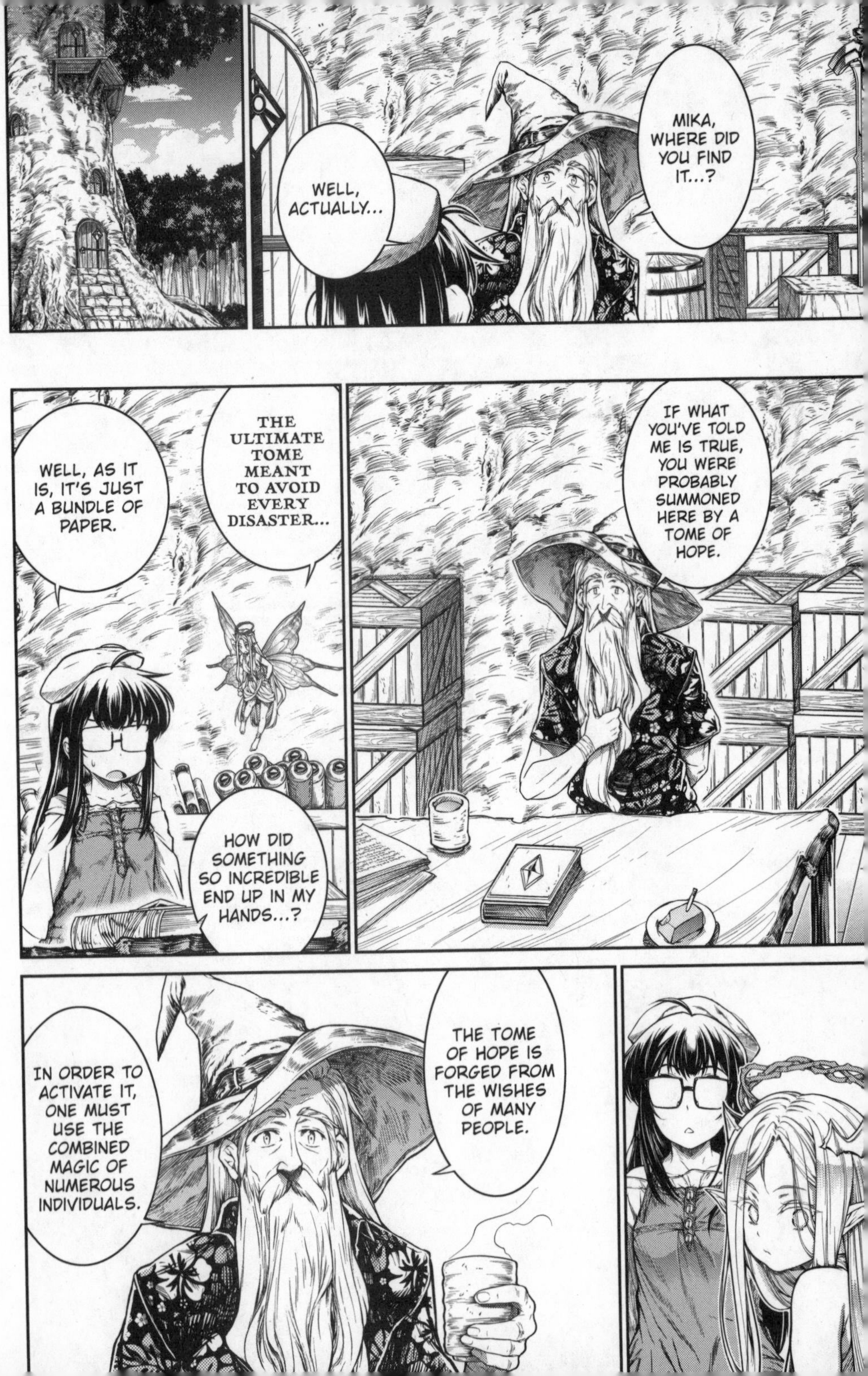
MIKA, WHERE DID YOU FIND IT...?
WELL, ACTUALLY...
IF WHAT YOU'VE TOLD ME IS TRUE, YOU WERE PROBABLY SUMMONED HERE BY A TOME OF HOPE.
THE ULTIMATE TOME MEANT TO AVOID EVERY DISASTER...
WELL, AS IT IS, IT'S JUST A BUNDLE OF PAPER.
HOW DID SOMETHING SO INCREDIBLE END UP IN MY HANDS...?
THE TOME OF HOPE IS FORGED FROM THE WISHES OF MANY PEOPLE.
IN ORDER TO ACTIVATE IT, ONE MUST USE THE COMBINED MAGIC OF NUMEROUS INDIVIDUALS.

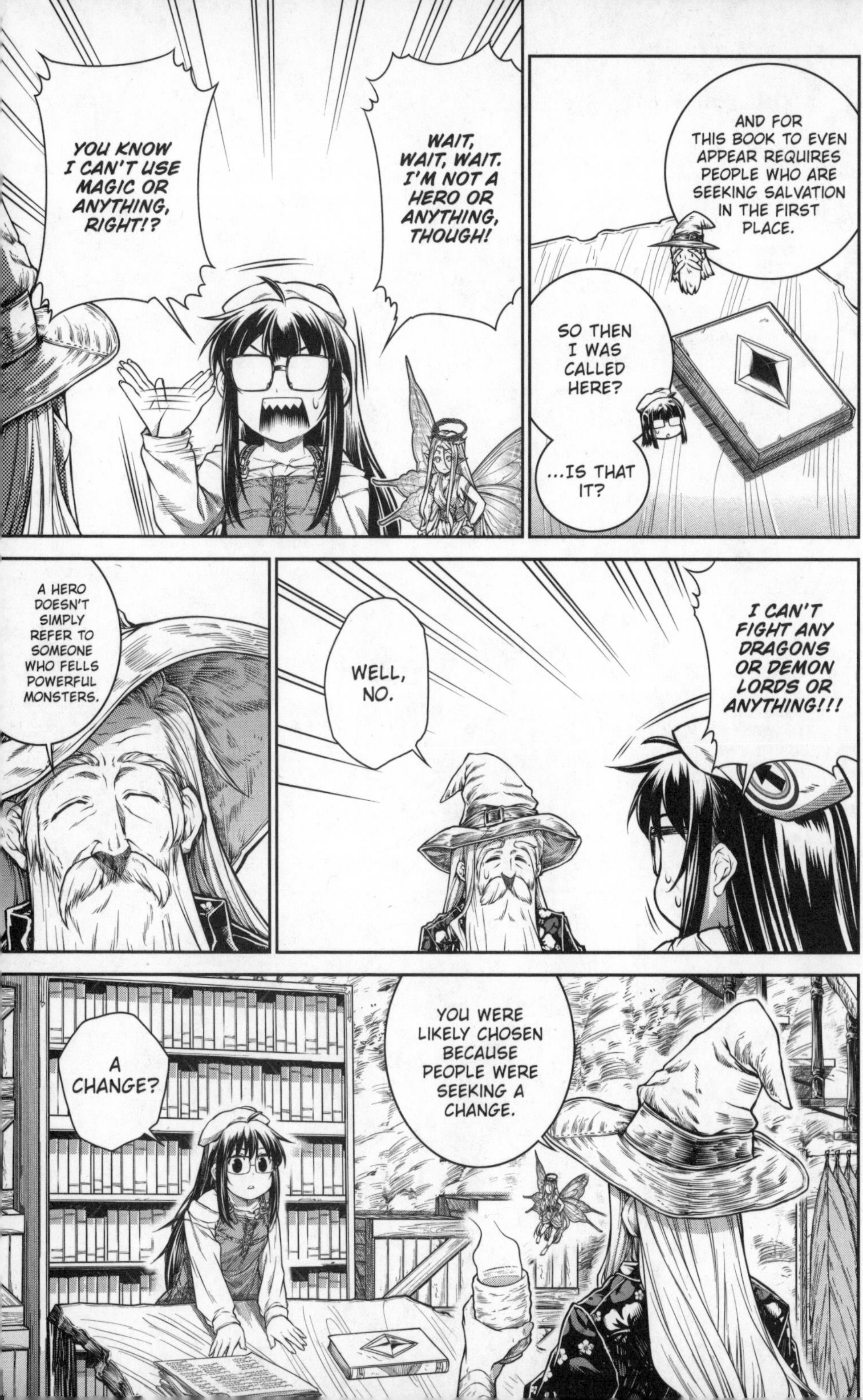
AND FOR THIS BOOK TO EVEN APPEAR REQUIRES PEOPLE WHO ARE SEEKING SALVATION IN THE FIRST PLACE.
SO THEN I WAS CALLED HERE?
...IS THAT IT?
WAIT, WAIT, WAIT. I'M NOT A HERO OR ANYTHING, THOUGH!
YOU KNOW I CAN'T USE MAGIC OR ANYTHING, RIGHT!?
I CAN'T FIGHT ANY DRAGONS OR DEMON LORDS OR ANYTHING!!!
WELL, NO.
A HERO DOESN'T SIMPLY REFER TO SOMEONE WHO FELLS POWERFUL MONSTERS.
YOU WERE LIKELY CHOSEN BECAUSE PEOPLE WERE SEEKING A CHANGE.
A CHANGE?

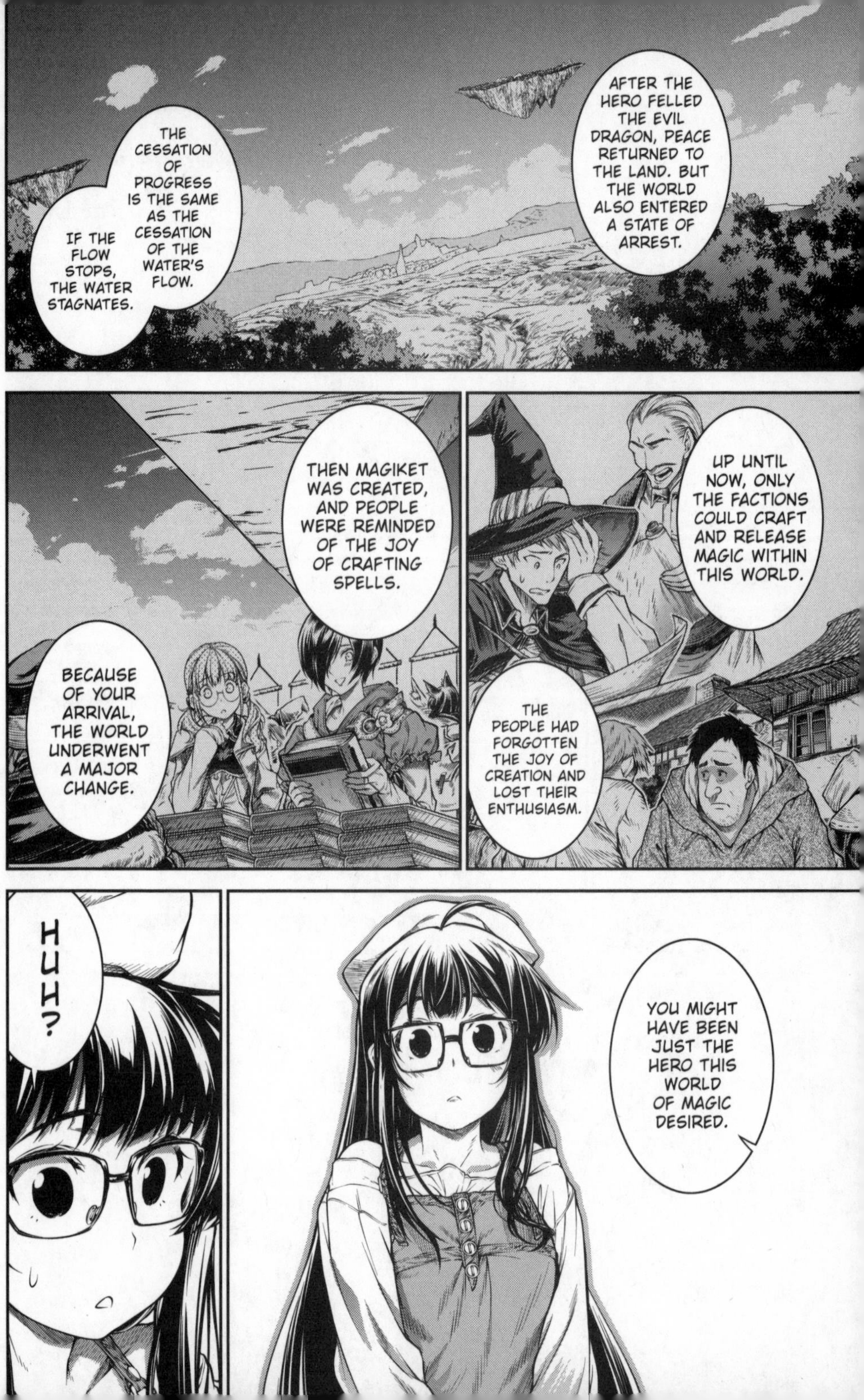
AFTER THE HERO FELLED THE EVIL DRAGON, PEACE RETURNED TO THE LAND. BUT THE WORLD ALSO ENTERED A STATE OF ARREST.
THE CESSATION OF PROGRESS IS THE SAME AS THE CESSATION OF THE WATER'S FLOW.
IF THE FLOW STOPS, THE WATER STAGNATES.
UP UNTIL NOW, ONLY THE FACTIONS COULD CRAFT AND RELEASE MAGIC WITHIN THIS WORLD.
THE PEOPLE HAD FORGOTTEN THE JOY OF CREATION AND LOST THEIR ENTHUSIASM.
THEN MAGIKET WAS CREATED, AND PEOPLE WERE REMINDED OF THE JOY OF CRAFTING SPELLS.
BECAUSE OF YOUR ARRIVAL, THE WORLD UNDERWENT A MAJOR CHANGE.
YOU MIGHT HAVE BEEN JUST THE HERO THIS WORLD OF MAGIC DESIRED.
HUH?

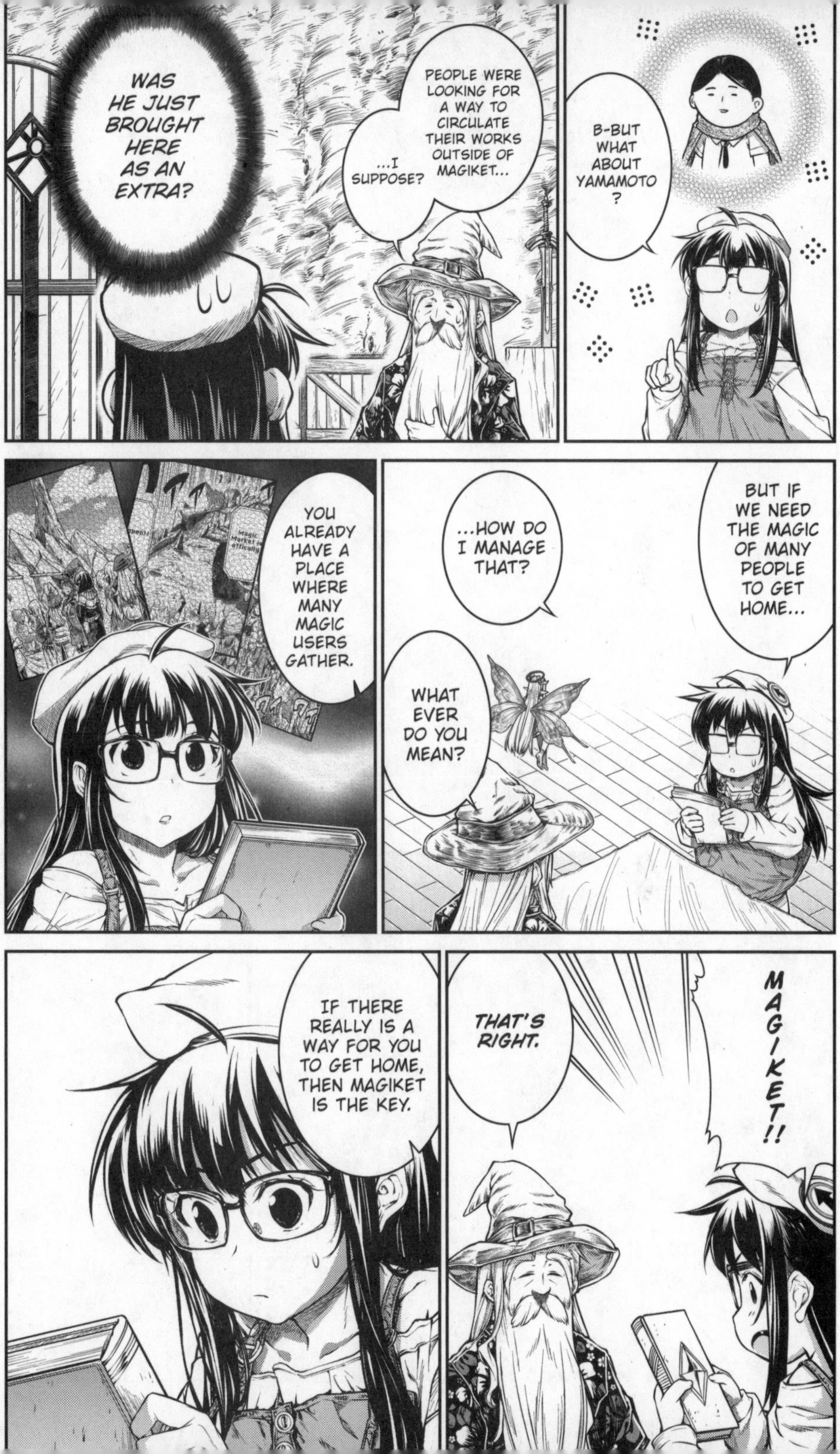
B-BUT WHAT ABOUT YAMAMOTO?
PEOPLE WERE LOOKING FOR A WAY TO CIRCULATE THEIR WORKS OUTSIDE OF MAGIKET...
...I SUPPOSE?
WAS HE JUST BROUGHT HERE AS AN EXTRA?
BUT IF WE NEED THE MAGIC OF MANY PEOPLE TO GET HOME...
...HOW DO I MANAGE THAT?
WHAT EVER DO YOU MEAN?
YOU ALREADY HAVE A PLACE WHERE MANY MAGIC USERS GATHER.
MAGIKET!!
THAT'S RIGHT.
IF THERE REALLY IS A WAY FOR YOU TO GET HOME, THEN MAGIKET IS THE KEY.

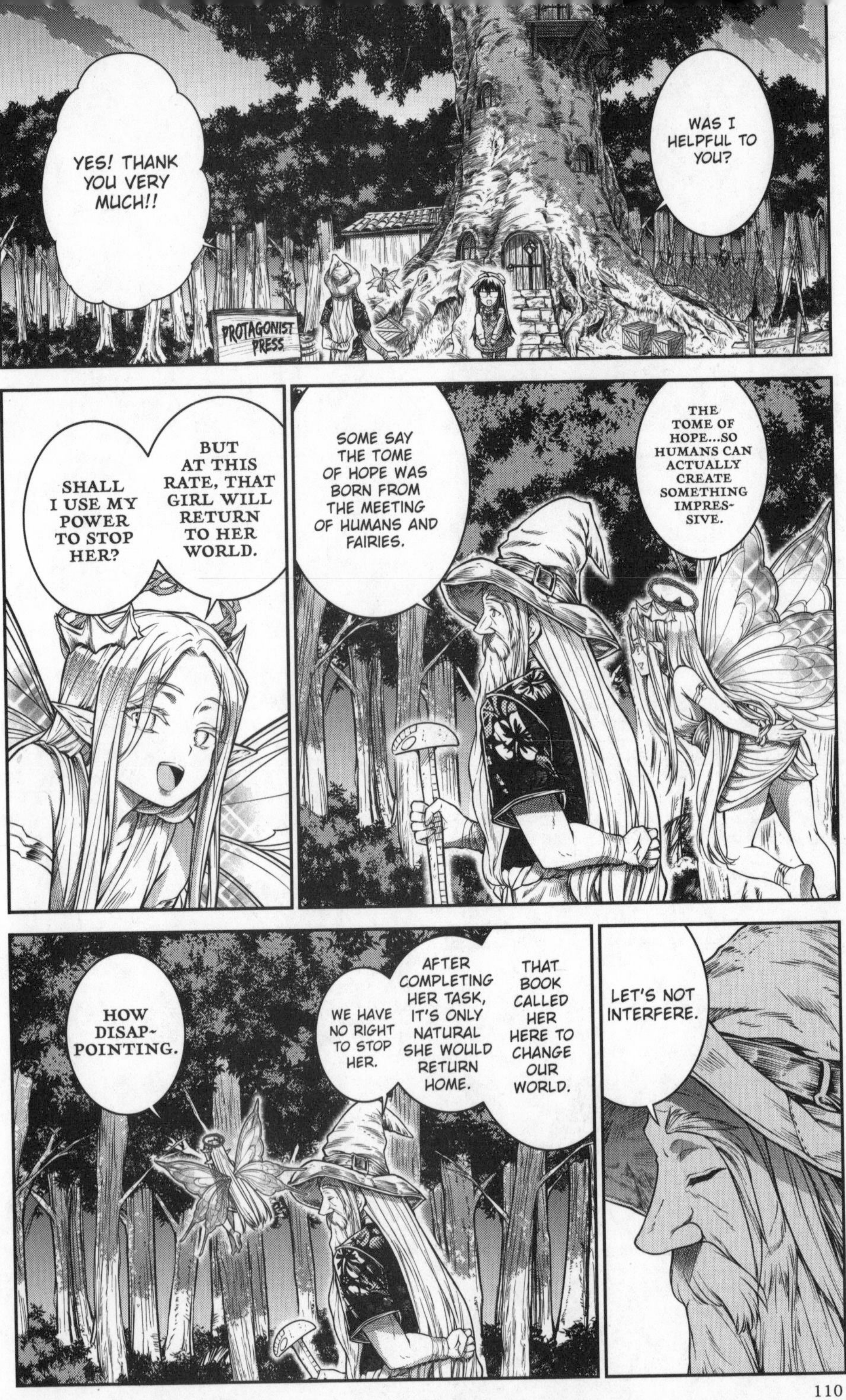

WAS I HELPFUL TO YOU?
YES! THANK YOU VERY MUCH!!
PROTAGONIST PRESS
THE TOME OF HOPE...SO HUMANS CAN ACTUALLY CREATE SOMETHING IMPRESSIVE.
SOME SAY THE TOME OF HOPE WAS BORN FROM THE MEETING OF HUMANS AND FAIRIES.
BUT AT THIS RATE, THAT GIRL WILL RETURN TO HER WORLD.
SHALL I USE MY POWER TO STOP HER?
LET'S NOT INTERFERE.
THAT BOOK CALLED HER HERE TO CHANGE OUR WORLD.
AFTER COMPLETING HER TASK, IT'S ONLY NATURAL SHE WOULD RETURN HOME.
WE HAVE NO RIGHT TO STOP HER.
HOW DISAPPOINTING.

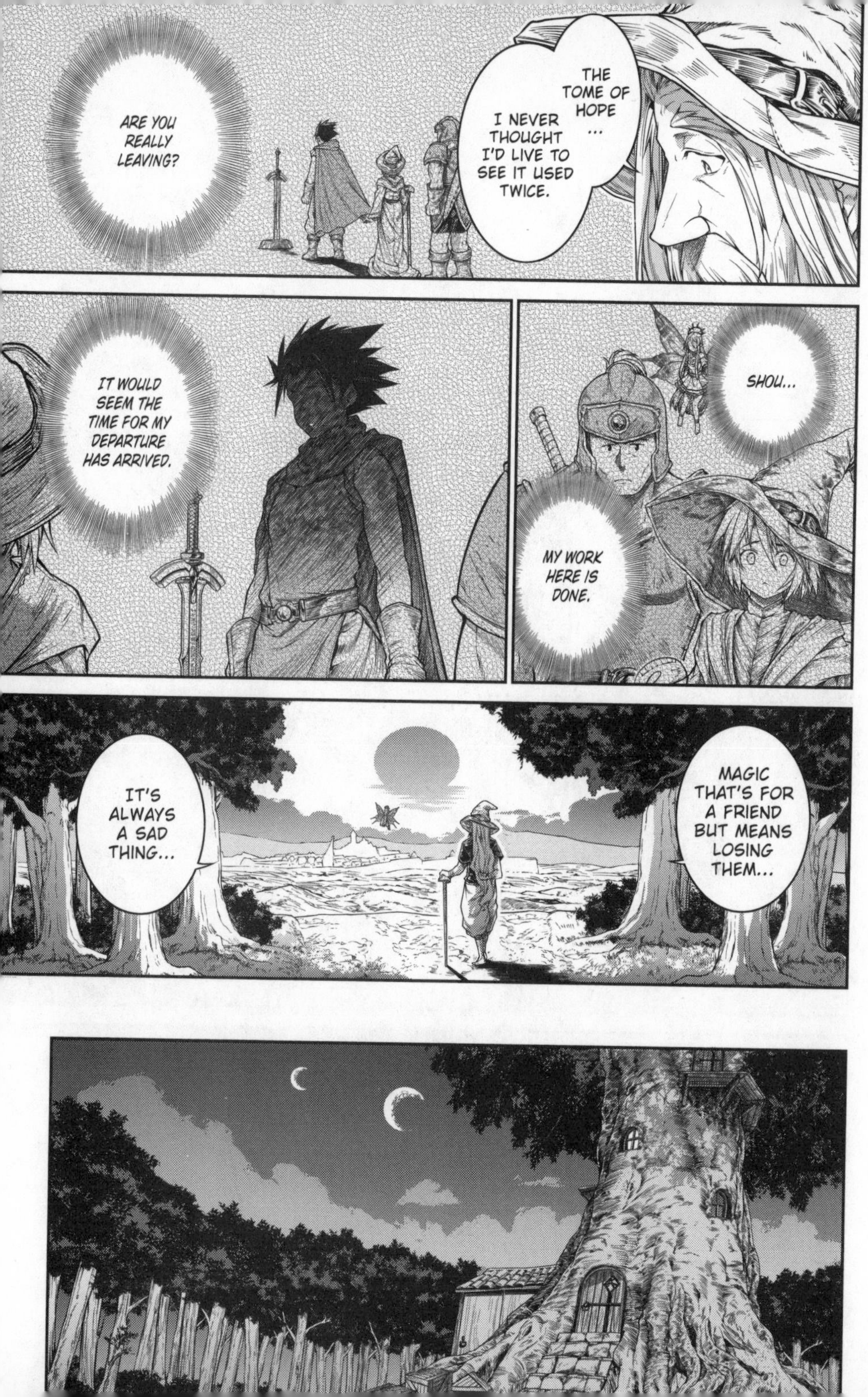
THE TOME OF HOPE...
I NEVER THOUGHT I'D LIVE TO SEE IT USED TWICE.
ARE YOU REALLY LEAVING?
SHOU...
MY WORK HERE IS DONE.
IT WOULD SEEM THE TIME FOR MY DEPARTURE HAS ARRIVED.
MAGIC THAT'S FOR A FRIEND BUT MEANS LOSING THEM...
IT'S ALWAYS A SAD THING...

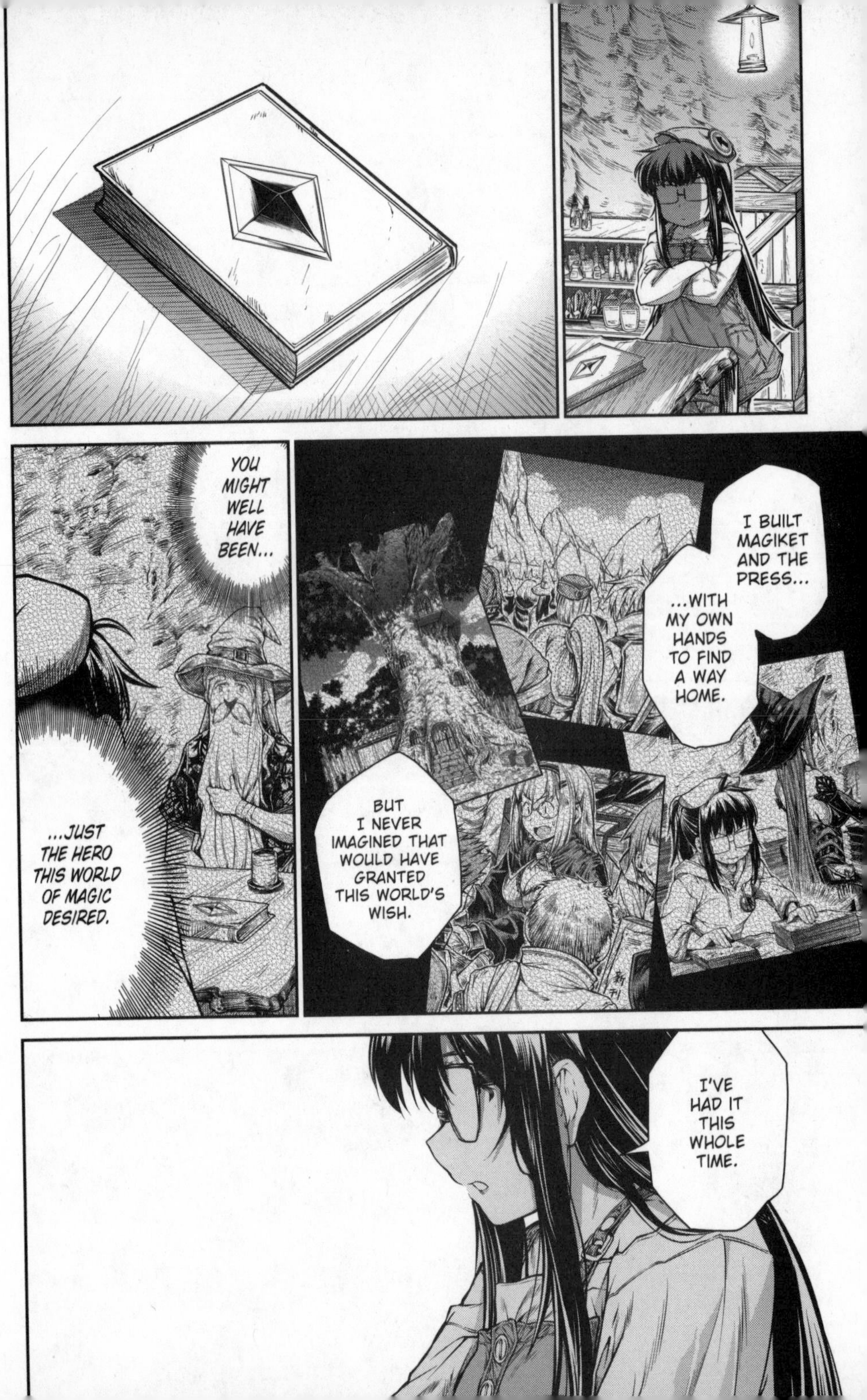
I BUILT MAGIKET AND THE PRESS...
...WITH MY OWN HANDS TO FIND A WAY HOME.
BUT I NEVER IMAGINED THAT WOULD HAVE GRANTED THIS WORLD'S WISH.
YOU MIGHT WELL HAVE BEEN...
...JUST THE HERO THIS WORLD OF MAGIC DESIRED.
I'VE HAD IT THIS WHOLE TIME.

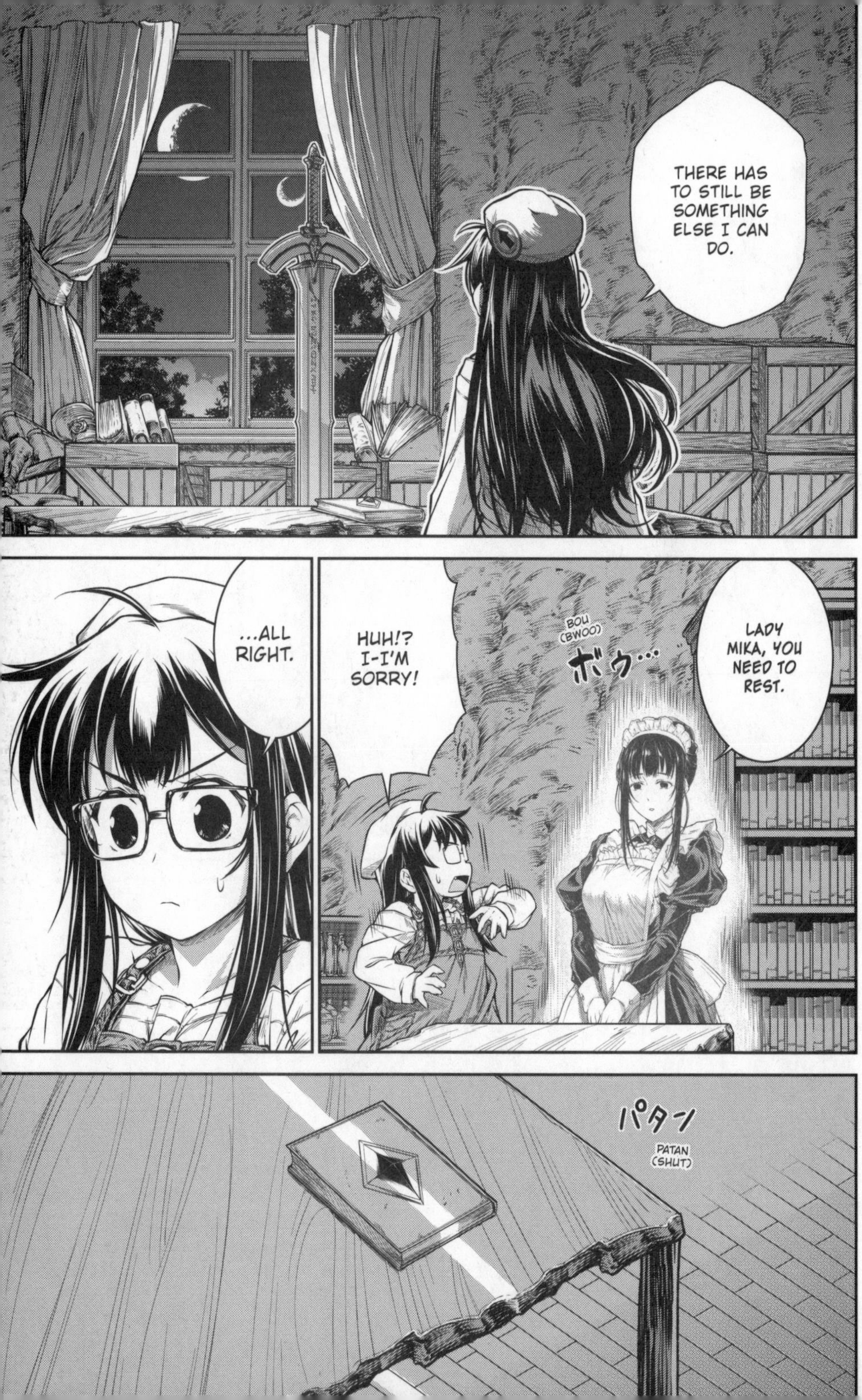
THERE HAS TO STILL BE SOMETHING ELSE I CAN DO.
LADY MIKA, YOU NEED TO REST.
ボゥ…
BOU (BWOO)
HUH!? I-I'M SORRY!
...ALL RIGHT.
パタン
PATAN (SHUT)

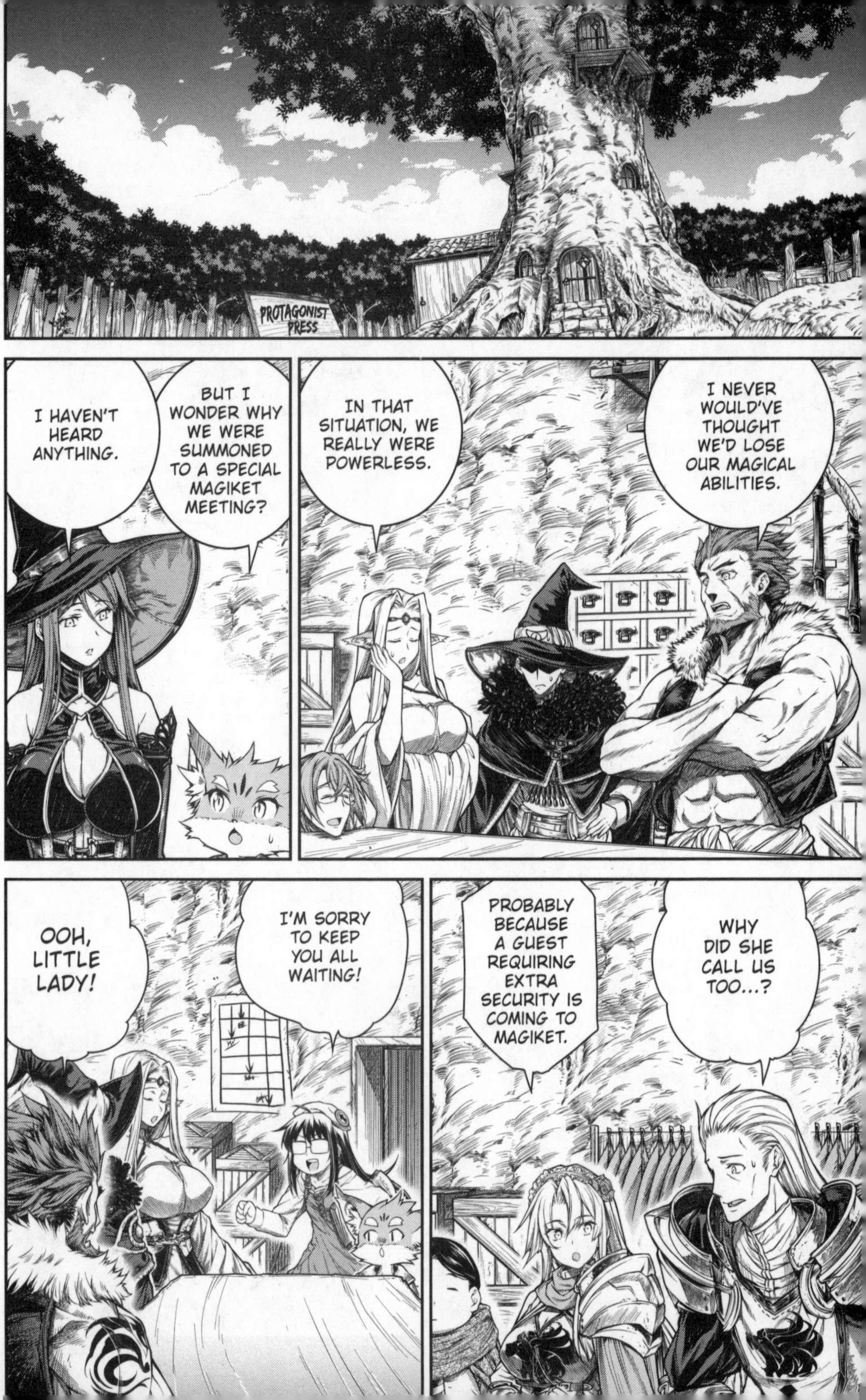
PROTAGONIST PRESS
I NEVER WOULD'VE THOUGHT WE'D LOSE OUR MAGICAL ABILITIES.
IN THAT SITUATION, WE REALLY WERE POWERLESS.
BUT I WONDER WHY WE WERE SUMMONED TO A SPECIAL MAGIKET MEETING?
I HAVEN'T HEARD ANYTHING.
WHY DID SHE CALL US TOO...?
PROBABLY BECAUSE A GUEST REQUIRING EXTRA SECURITY IS COMING TO MAGIKET.
I'M SORRY TO KEEP YOU ALL WAITING!
OOH, LITTLE LADY!

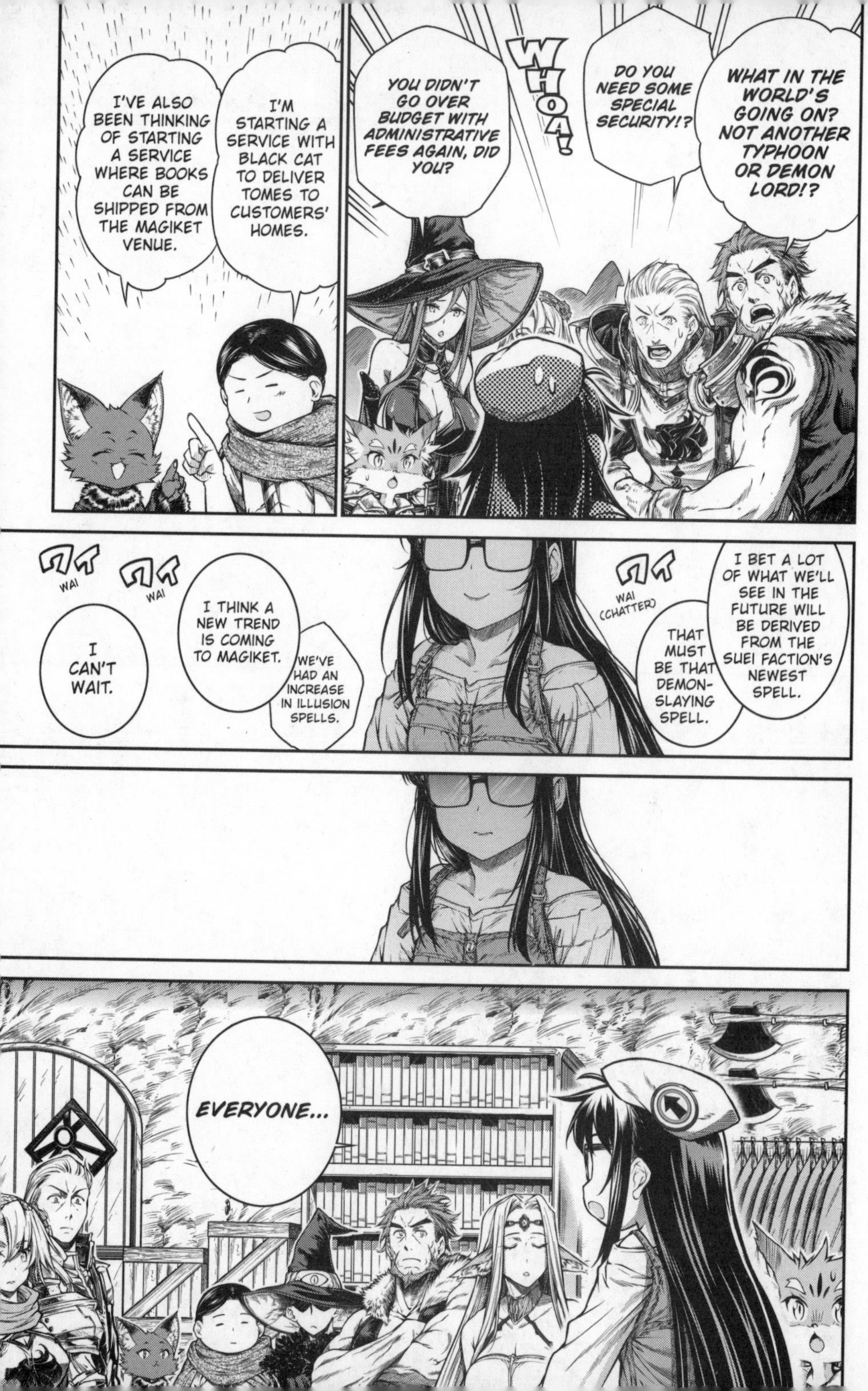
WHAT IN THE WORLD'S GOING ON? NOT ANOTHER TYPHOON OR DEMON LORD!?
DO YOU NEED SOME SPECIAL SECURITY!?
WHOA!
YOU DIDN'T GO OVER BUDGET WITH ADMINISTRATIVE FEES AGAIN, DID YOU?
I'M STARTING A SERVICE WITH BLACK CAT TO DELIVER TOMES TO CUSTOMERS' HOMES.
I'VE ALSO BEEN THINKING OF STARTING A SERVICE WHERE BOOKS CAN BE SHIPPED FROM THE MAGIKET VENUE.
I BET A LOT OF WHAT WE'LL SEE IN THE FUTURE WILL BE DERIVED FROM THE SUEI FACTION'S NEWEST SPELL.
ワイ
WAI (CHATTER)
THAT MUST BE THAT DEMON-SLAYING SPELL.
WE'VE HAD AN INCREASE IN ILLUSION SPELLS.
I THINK A NEW TREND IS COMING TO MAGIKET.
ワイ
WAI
ワイ
WAI
I CAN'T WAIT.
EVERYONE...

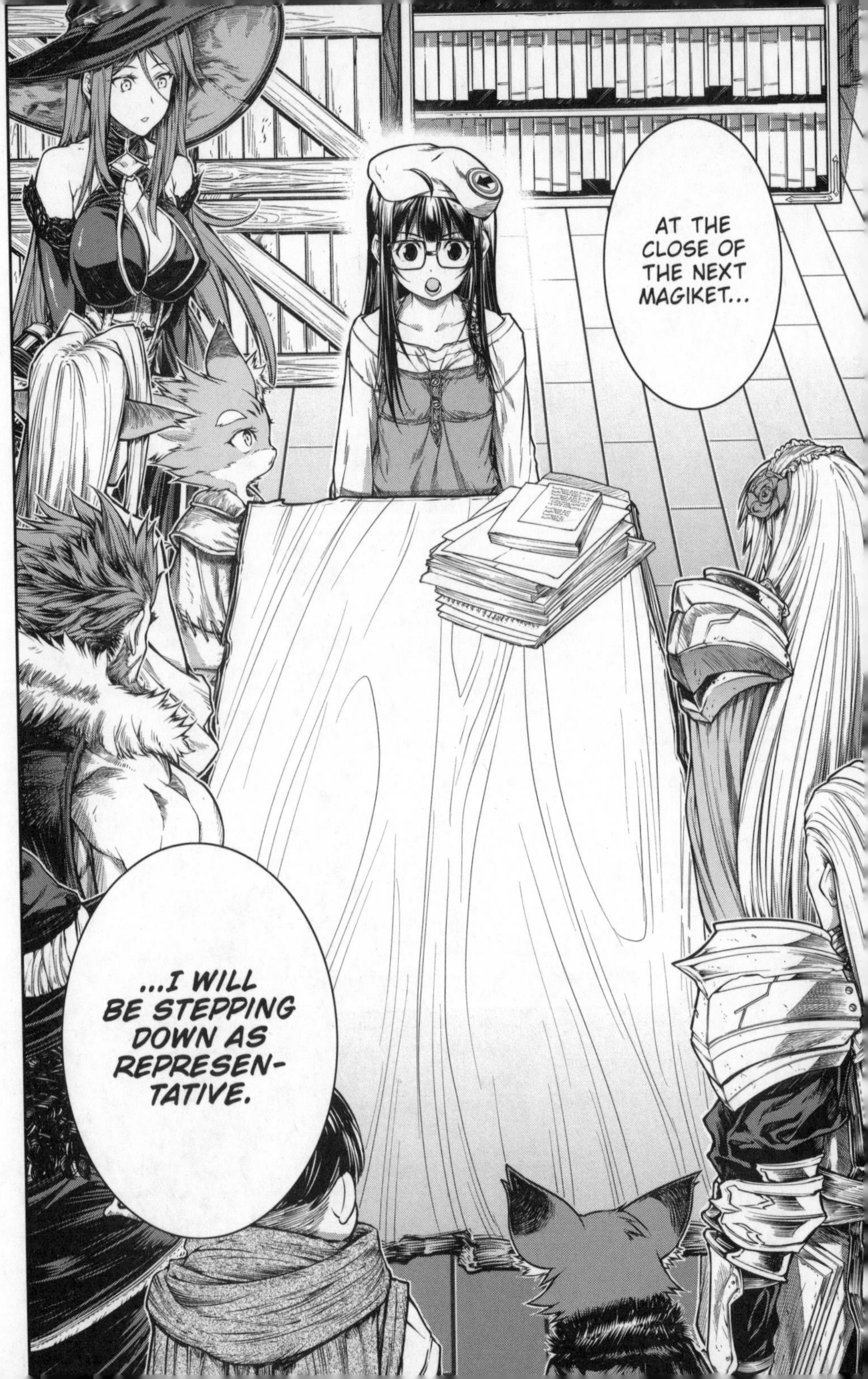
AT THE CLOSE OF THE NEXT MAGIKET...
...I WILL BE STEPPING DOWN AS REPRESEN-TATIVE.

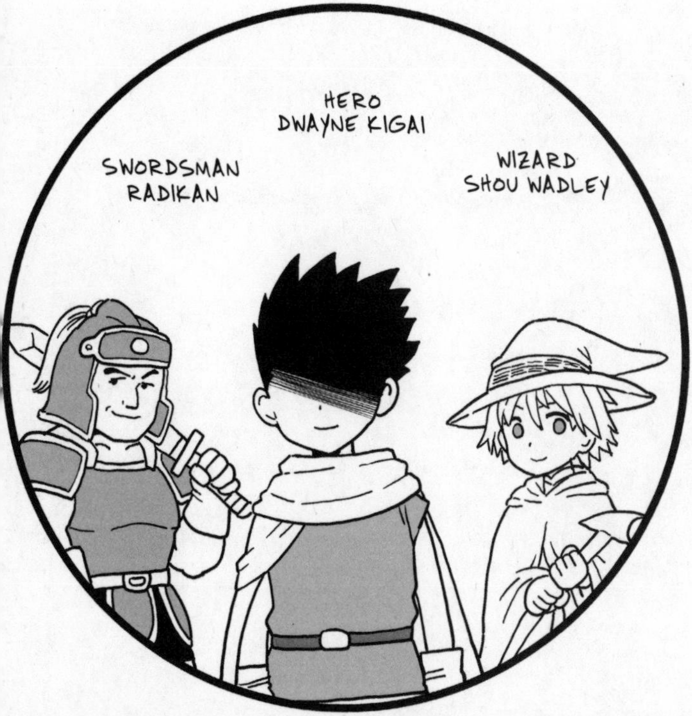
HERO
DWAYNE KIGAI
WIZARD
SHOU WADLEY
SWORDSMAN
RADIKAN

TRANSLATION NOTES

General
The faction names such as Suei, Kadoka, and Sugak are all references to actual Japanese publishers!

Page 20 – True Demon Lord
The idea of a final boss whose true self is disguised as one of two support units—with the "main body" being a decoy—is famously found in the role-playing game *Chrono Trigger*.

Page 85 – Palp
Based on the word "pulp," as in paper—the fundamental resource of manga.

Page 115 – Black Cat
Black Cat (or Black Cat Shipping) is based on the Japanese delivery service Yamato Transport, which features black cats in its logo.

Page 115 – Demon-Slaying Spell
This is a reference to the popular manga *Demon Slayer: Kimetsu no Yaiba*.

Page 117 – Shou Wadley, Dwayne Kigai, Radikan
All three of these names are references to Akihabara. As seen in earlier volumes, "Shou Wadley" is from *Showa-doori* (a major street in Akihabara). "Dwayne Kigai" is from *Denki Gai*, or "Electric Town" (a nickname for Akihabara originally from the post–World War II period, when the area first became known as a go-to place for electronics). "Radikan" is from Radio Kaikan (the first high-rise building in Akihabara and a well-known landmark).

In addition, all three of their outfits are derived from character classes in the role-playing game *Dragon Quest III*. Shou is a mage, Dwayne is a hero, and Radikan is a warrior.

Page 156 – Magazine hiatus
A Witch's Printing Office began serialization in *Dengeki G's Comic*, which became an online publication after 2019.

Page 158 – Orange Devil
This monster is based on a recurring boss in the *Mega Man* franchise, the Yellow Devil, which attacks by splitting itself into pieces and flying across the room.

Page 158 – Op Lily
This monster is a reference to an enemy from the *Phantasy Star* games that is known as a newbie killer due to its strong magic.

Final Chapter

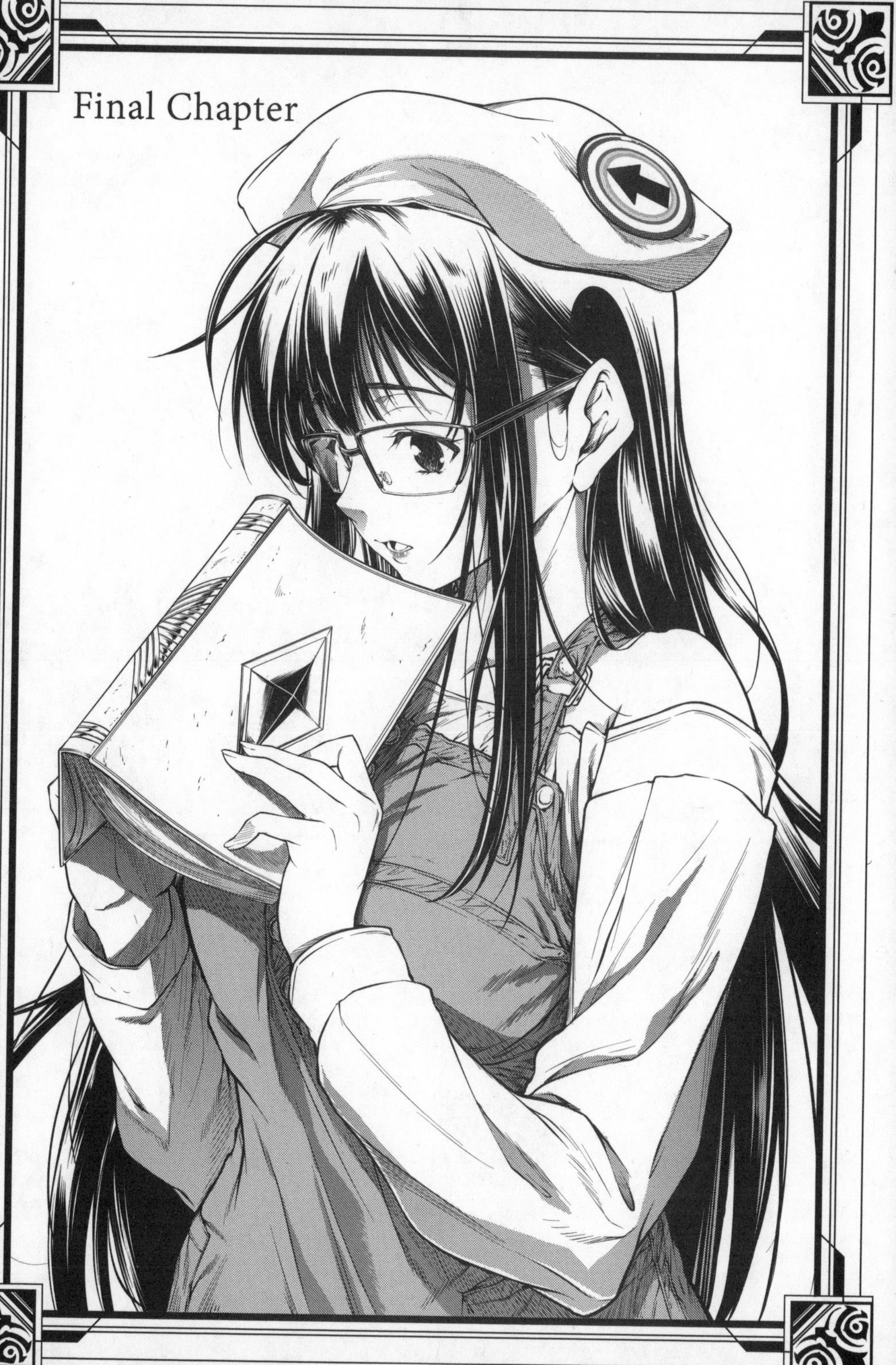

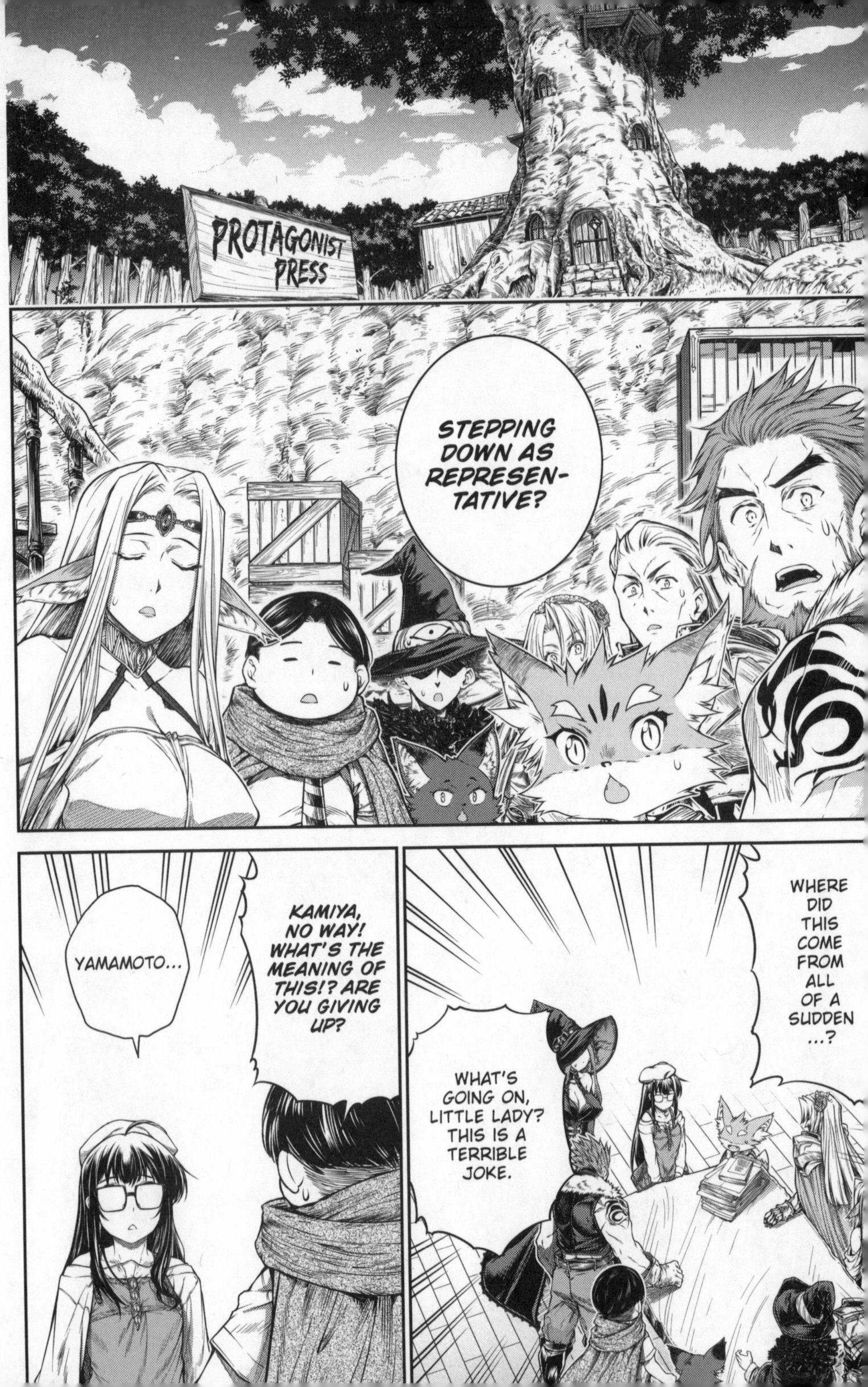
PROTAGONIST PRESS
STEPPING DOWN AS REPRESEN-TATIVE?
WHERE DID THIS COME FROM ALL OF A SUDDEN...?
WHAT'S GOING ON, LITTLE LADY? THIS IS A TERRIBLE JOKE.
KAMIYA, NO WAY! WHAT'S THE MEANING OF THIS!? ARE YOU GIVING UP?
YAMAMOTO...

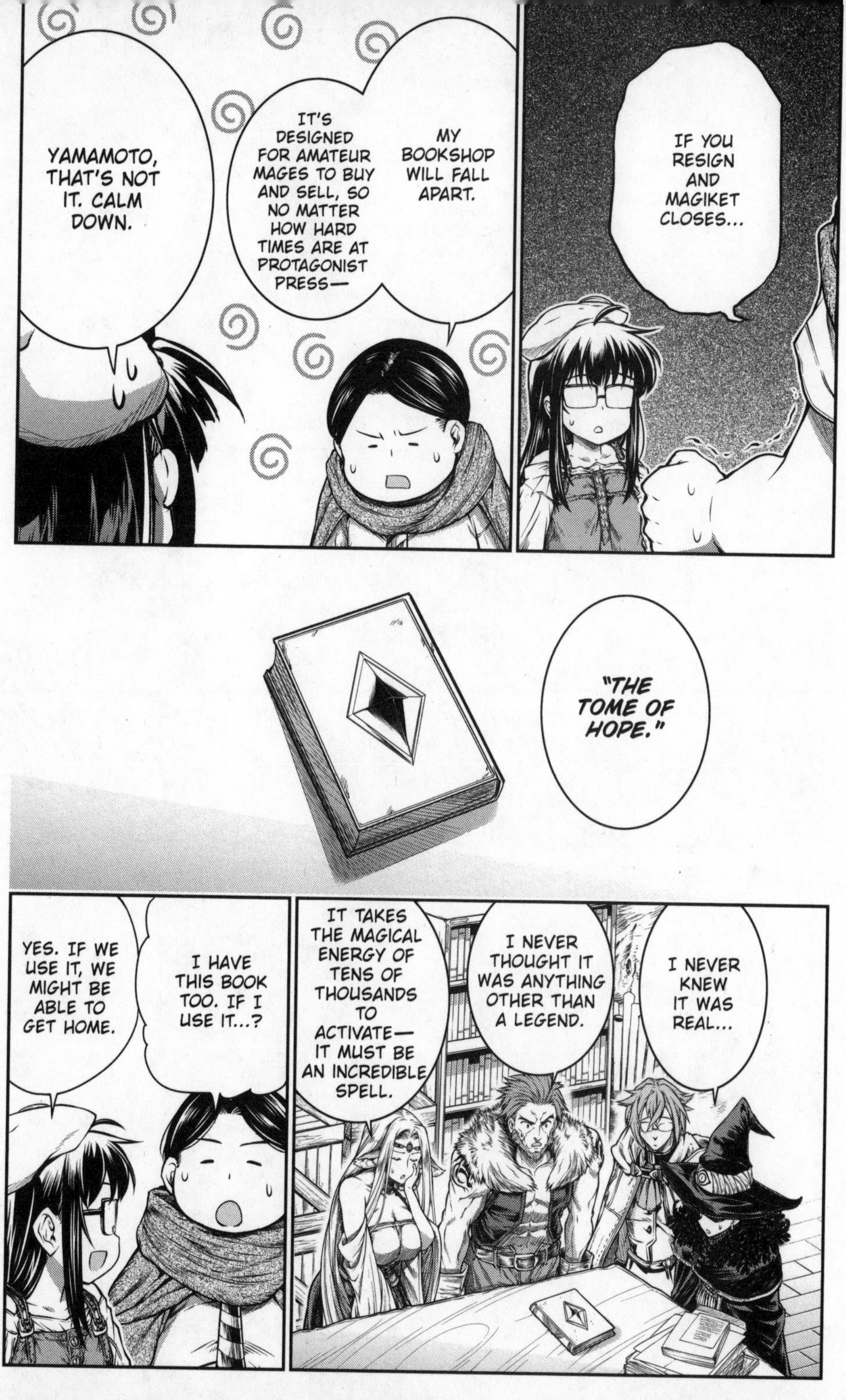
IF YOU RESIGN AND MAGIKET CLOSES...
MY BOOKSHOP WILL FALL APART.
IT'S DESIGNED FOR AMATEUR MAGES TO BUY AND SELL, SO NO MATTER HOW HARD TIMES ARE AT PROTAGONIST PRESS—
YAMAMOTO, THAT'S NOT IT. CALM DOWN.
"THE TOME OF HOPE."
I NEVER KNEW IT WAS REAL...
I NEVER THOUGHT IT WAS ANYTHING OTHER THAN A LEGEND.
IT TAKES THE MAGICAL ENERGY OF TENS OF THOUSANDS TO ACTIVATE— IT MUST BE AN INCREDIBLE SPELL.
I HAVE THIS BOOK TOO. IF I USE IT...?
YES. IF WE USE IT, WE MIGHT BE ABLE TO GET HOME.

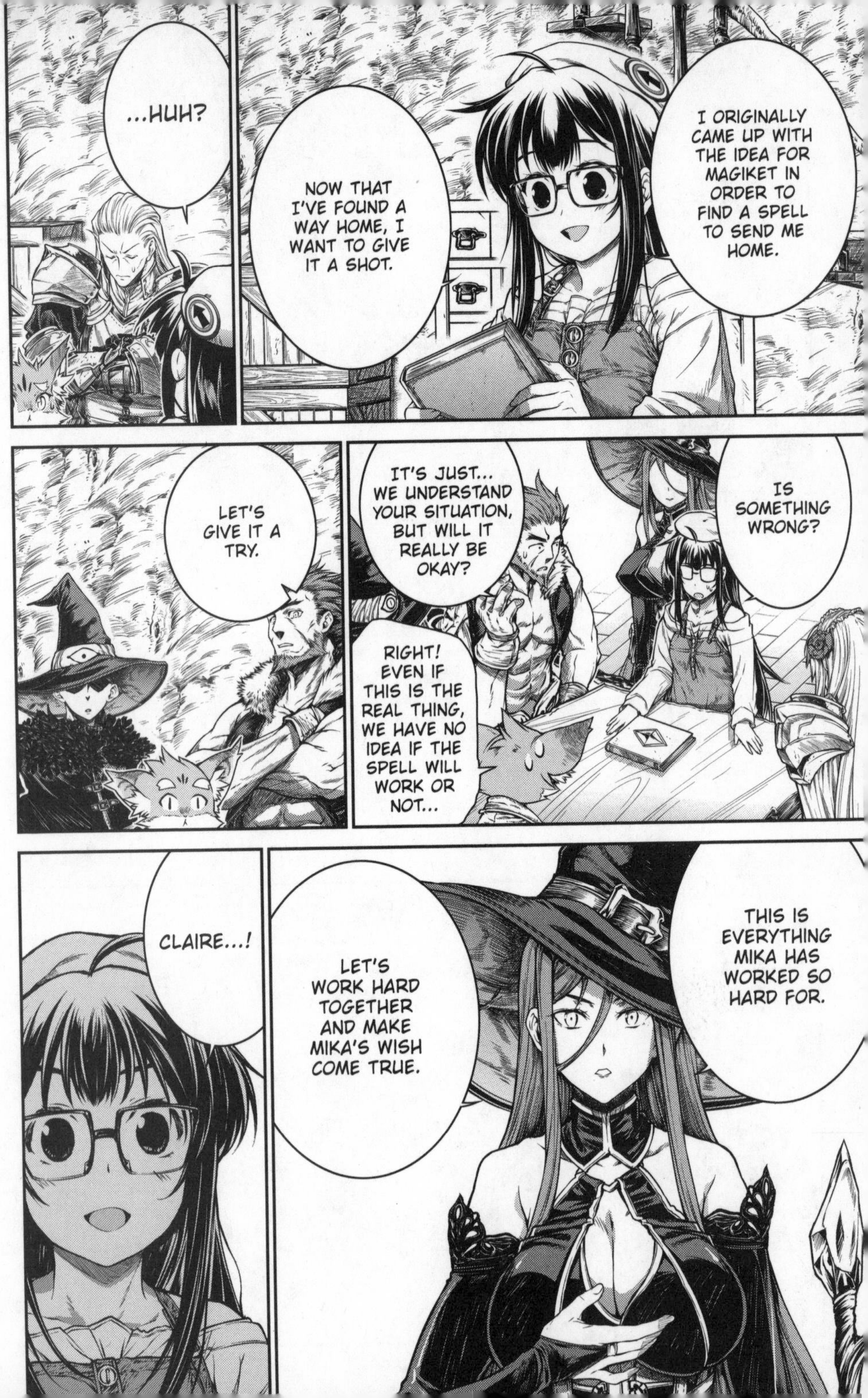
I ORIGINALLY CAME UP WITH THE IDEA FOR MAGIKET IN ORDER TO FIND A SPELL TO SEND ME HOME.
NOW THAT I'VE FOUND A WAY HOME, I WANT TO GIVE IT A SHOT.
...HUH?
IS SOMETHING WRONG?
IT'S JUST... WE UNDERSTAND YOUR SITUATION, BUT WILL IT REALLY BE OKAY?
RIGHT! EVEN IF THIS IS THE REAL THING, WE HAVE NO IDEA IF THE SPELL WILL WORK OR NOT...
LET'S GIVE IT A TRY.
THIS IS EVERYTHING MIKA HAS WORKED SO HARD FOR.
LET'S WORK HARD TOGETHER AND MAKE MIKA'S WISH COME TRUE.
CLAIRE...!

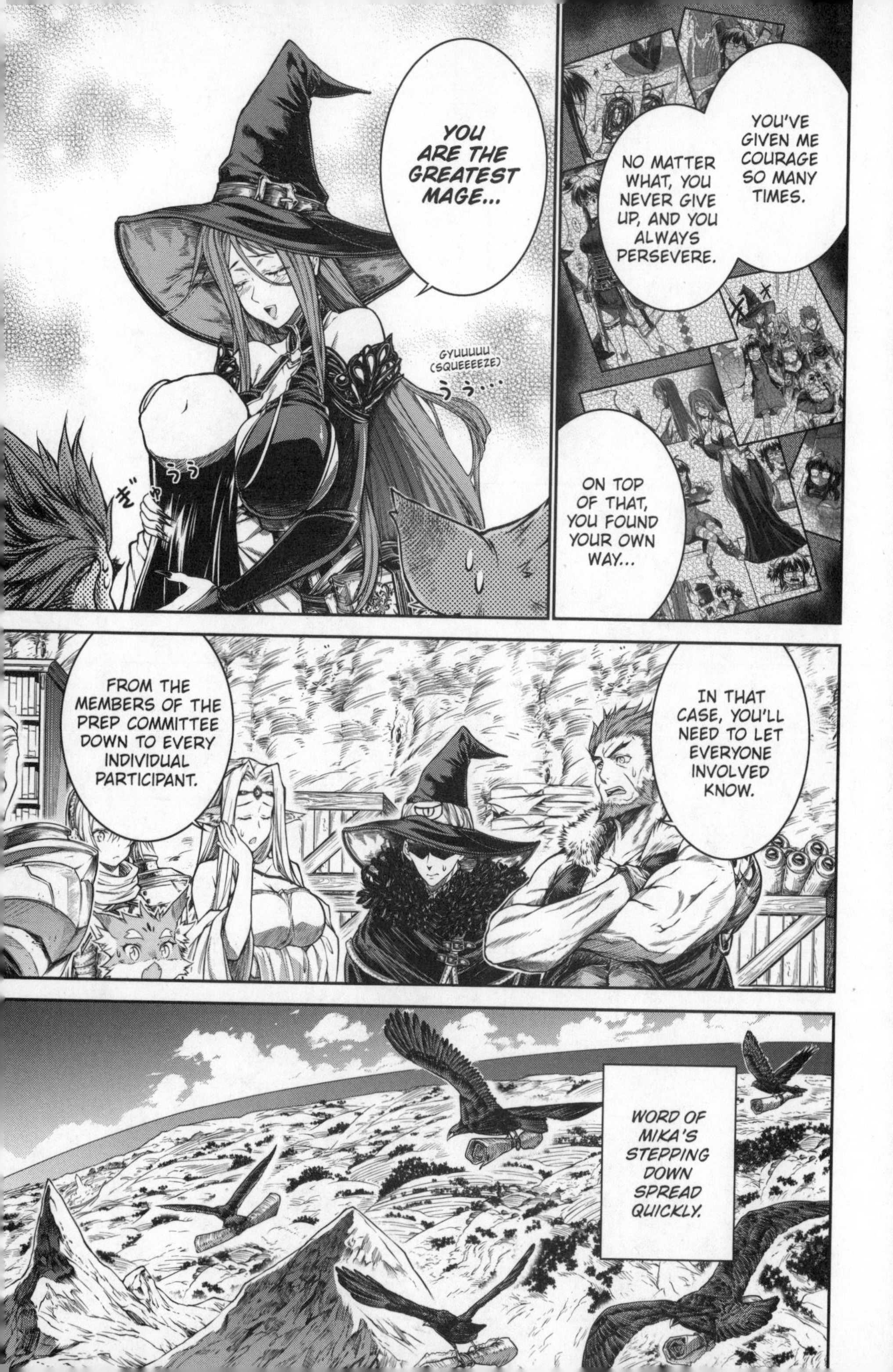
YOU'VE GIVEN ME COURAGE SO MANY TIMES.
NO MATTER WHAT, YOU NEVER GIVE UP, AND YOU ALWAYS PERSEVERE.
ON TOP OF THAT, YOU FOUND YOUR OWN WAY...
YOU ARE THE GREATEST MAGE...
GYUUUUU (SQUEEEEZE)
ぎゅううう
うぅ…
IN THAT CASE, YOU'LL NEED TO LET EVERYONE INVOLVED KNOW.
FROM THE MEMBERS OF THE PREP COMMITTEE DOWN TO EVERY INDIVIDUAL PARTICIPANT.
WORD OF MIKA'S STEPPING DOWN SPREAD QUICKLY.

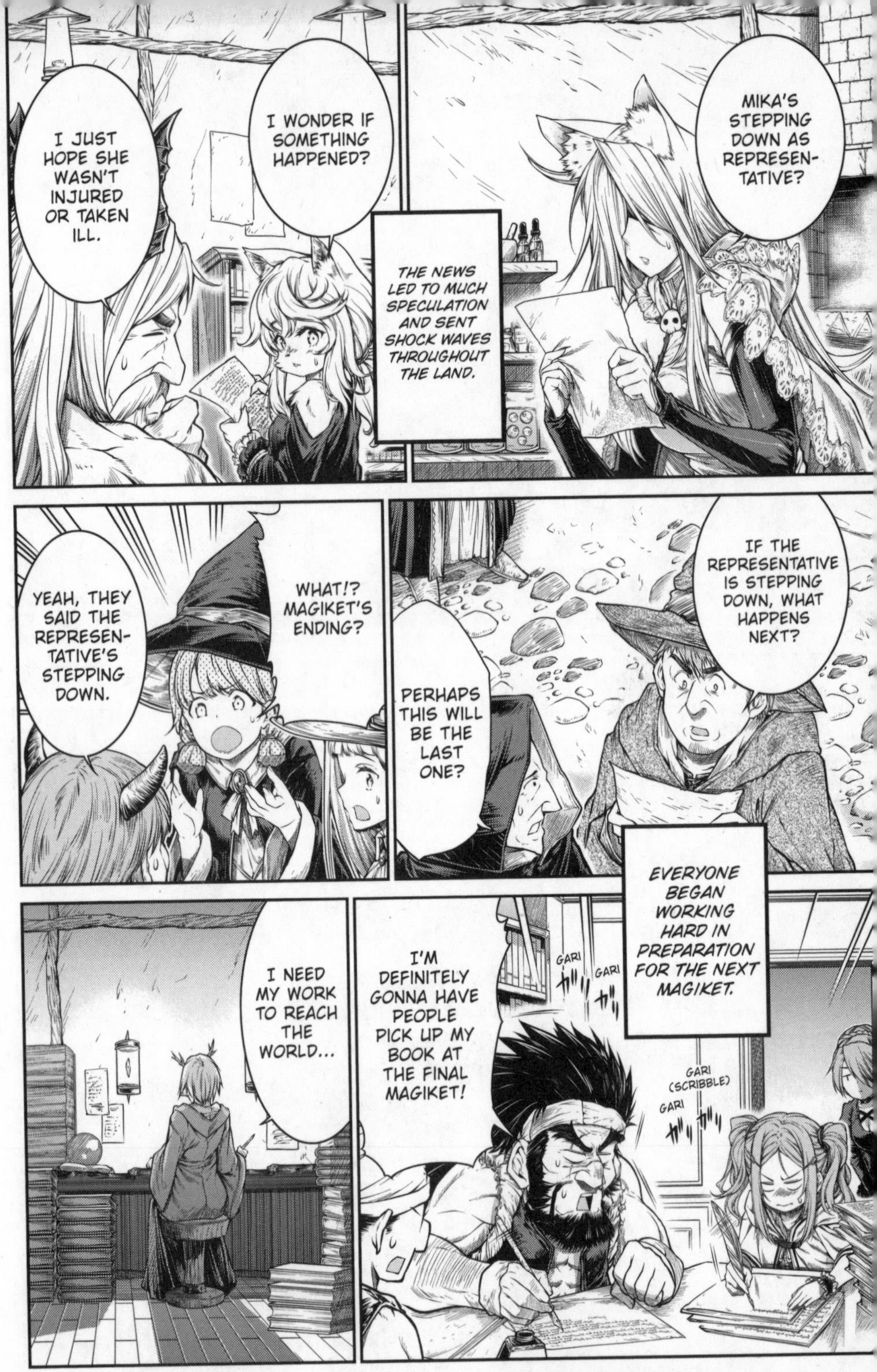

MIKA'S STEPPING DOWN AS REPRESEN-TATIVE?
THE NEWS LED TO MUCH SPECULATION AND SENT SHOCK WAVES THROUGHOUT THE LAND.
I WONDER IF SOMETHING HAPPENED?
I JUST HOPE SHE WASN'T INJURED OR TAKEN ILL.
IF THE REPRESENTATIVE IS STEPPING DOWN, WHAT HAPPENS NEXT?
PERHAPS THIS WILL BE THE LAST ONE?
WHAT!? MAGIKET'S ENDING?
YEAH, THEY SAID THE REPRESEN-TATIVE'S STEPPING DOWN.
EVERYONE BEGAN WORKING HARD IN PREPARATION FOR THE NEXT MAGIKET.
GARI (SCRIBBLE)
GARI
GARI
GARI
I'M DEFINITELY GONNA HAVE PEOPLE PICK UP MY BOOK AT THE FINAL MAGIKET!
I NEED MY WORK TO REACH THE WORLD...

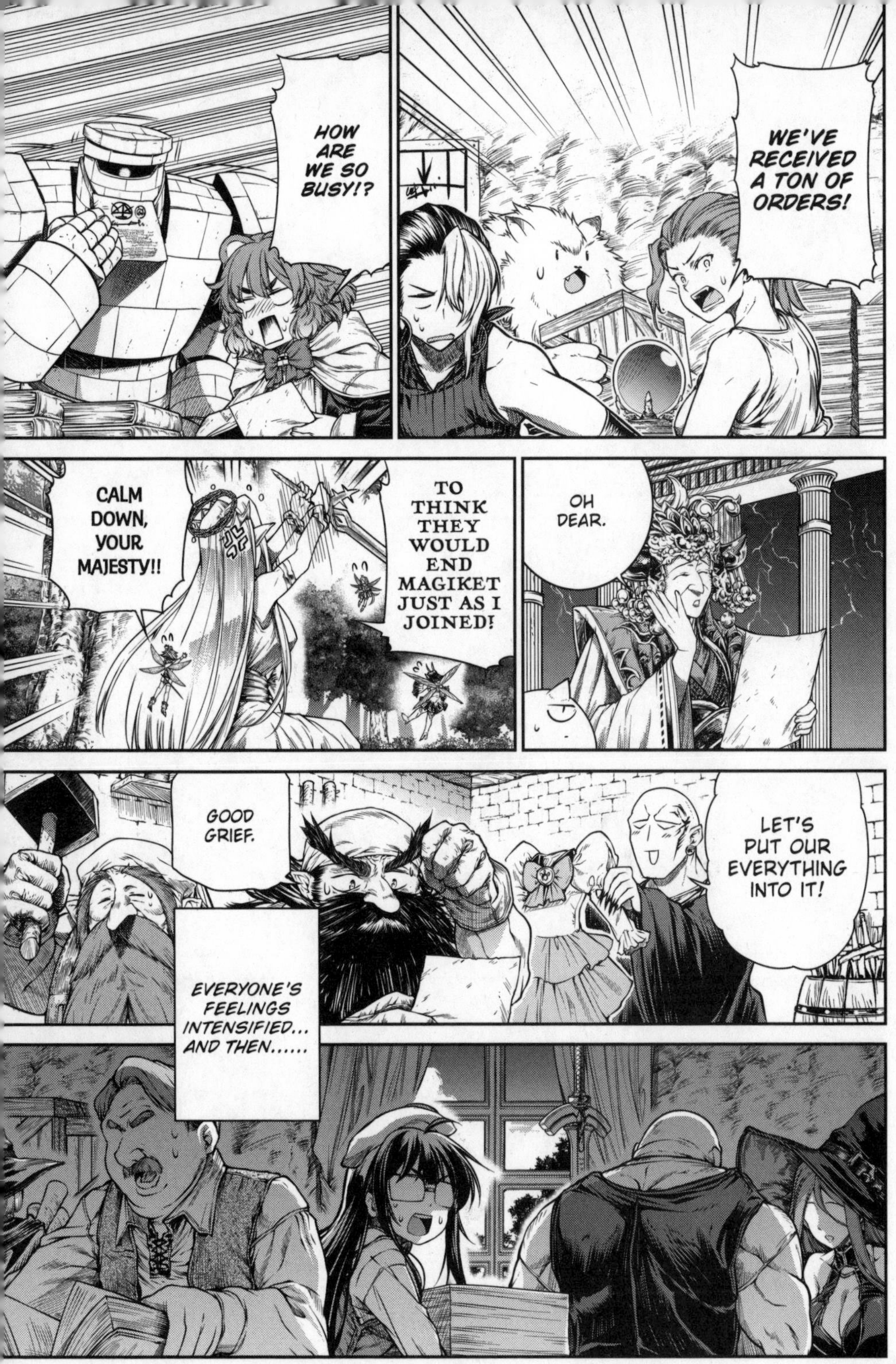
WE'VE RECEIVED A TON OF ORDERS!
HOW ARE WE SO BUSY!?
OH DEAR.
TO THINK THEY WOULD END MAGIKET JUST AS I JOINED!
CALM DOWN, YOUR MAJESTY!!
LET'S PUT OUR EVERYTHING INTO IT!
GOOD GRIEF.
EVERYONE'S FEELINGS INTENSIFIED... AND THEN......

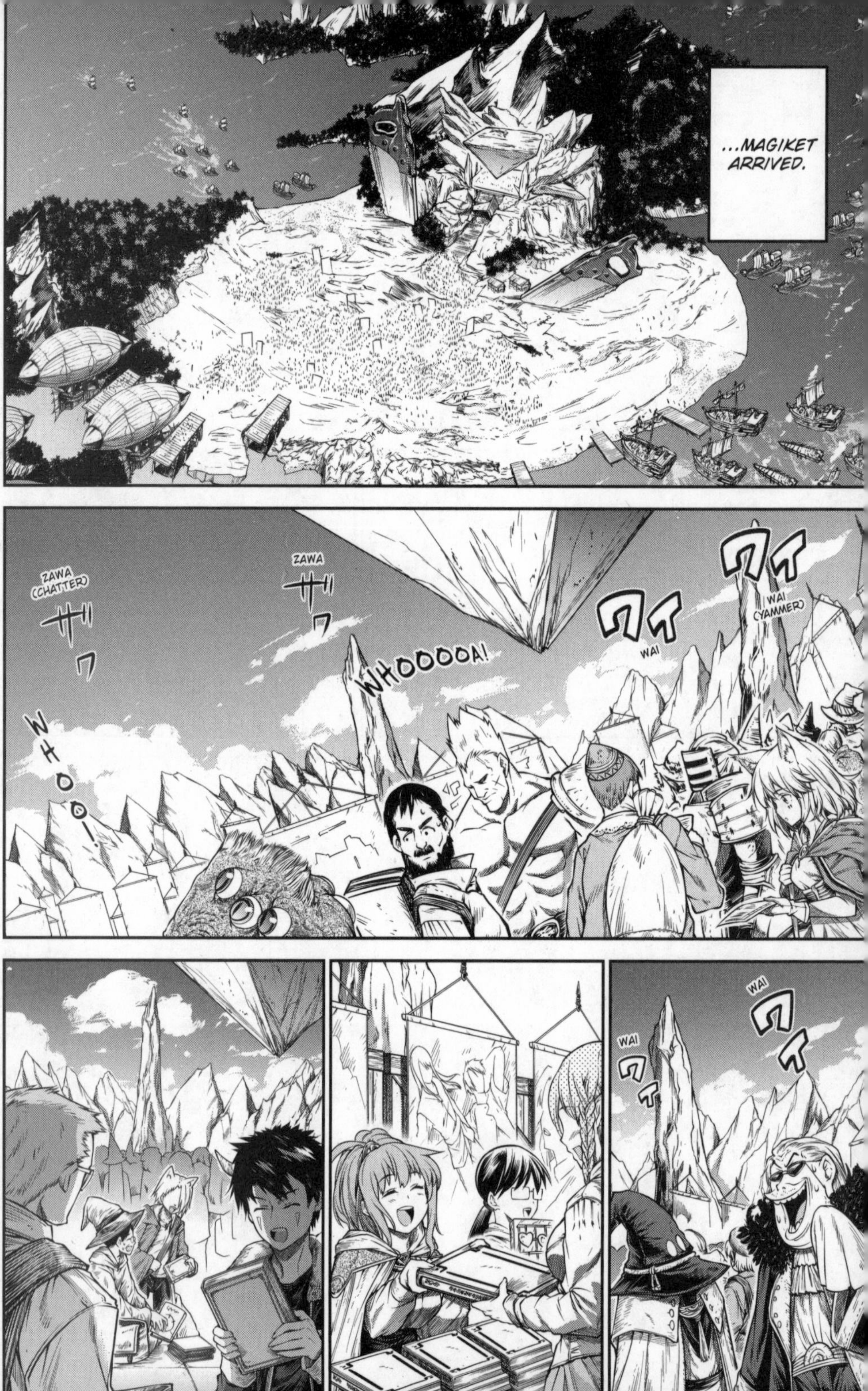
...MAGIKET ARRIVED.
ワイ
WAI (YAMMER)
ワイ
WAI
WHOOOOA!
ZAWA
ザワ
ZAWA (CHATTER)
ザワ
WHOO!
WAI
ワイ
WAI
ワイ

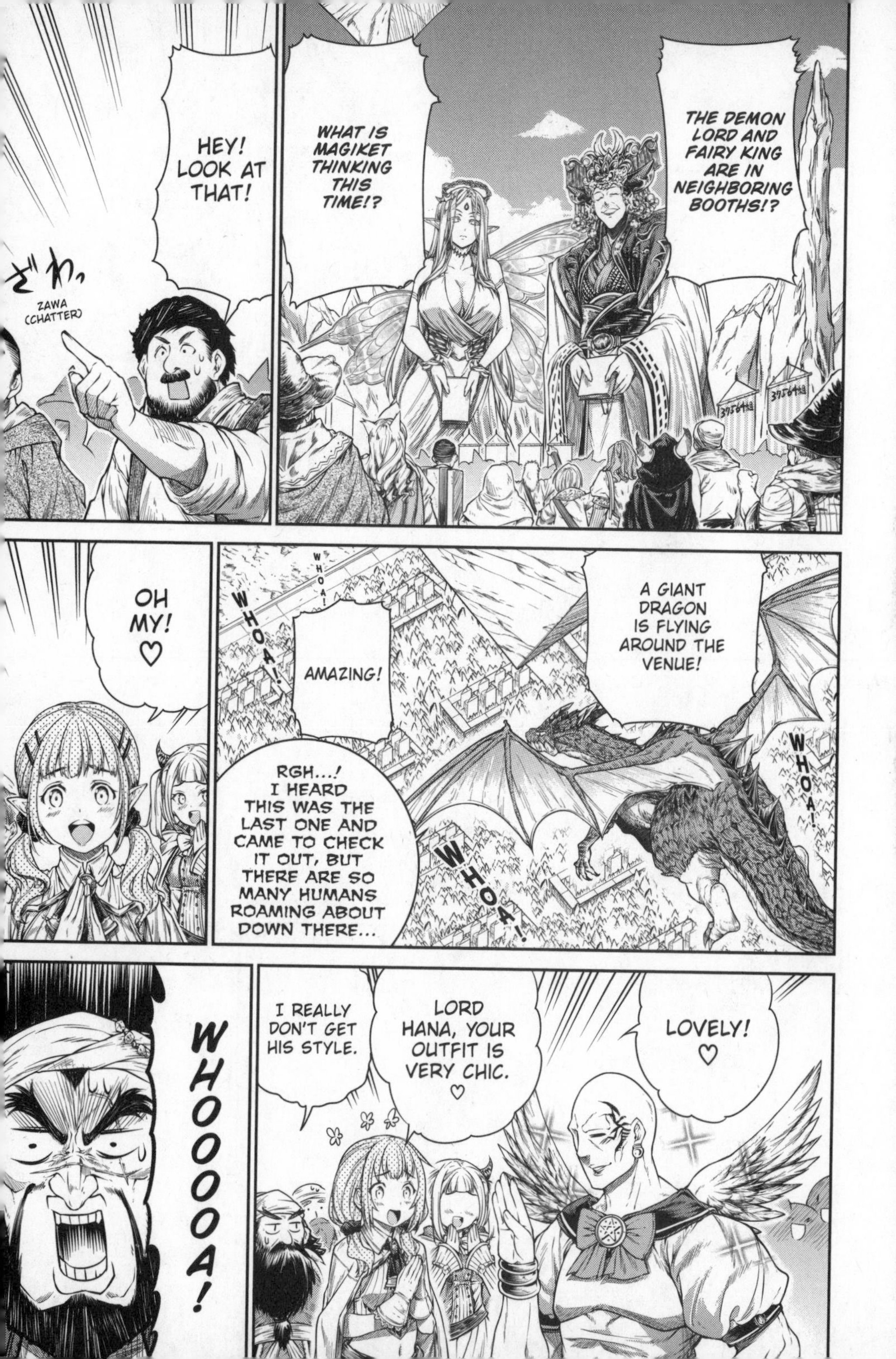
THE DEMON LORD AND FAIRY KING ARE IN NEIGHBORING BOOTHS!?
WHAT IS MAGIKET THINKING THIS TIME!?
HEY! LOOK AT THAT!
ざわっ
ZAWA (CHATTER)
A GIANT DRAGON IS FLYING AROUND THE VENUE!
WHOA!
WHOA!
AMAZING!
WHOA!
RGH...! I HEARD THIS WAS THE LAST ONE AND CAME TO CHECK IT OUT, BUT THERE ARE SO MANY HUMANS ROAMING ABOUT DOWN THERE...
WHOA!
OH MY! ♡
LOVELY! ♡
LORD HANA, YOUR OUTFIT IS VERY CHIC. ♡
I REALLY DON'T GET HIS STYLE.
WHOOOOOA!

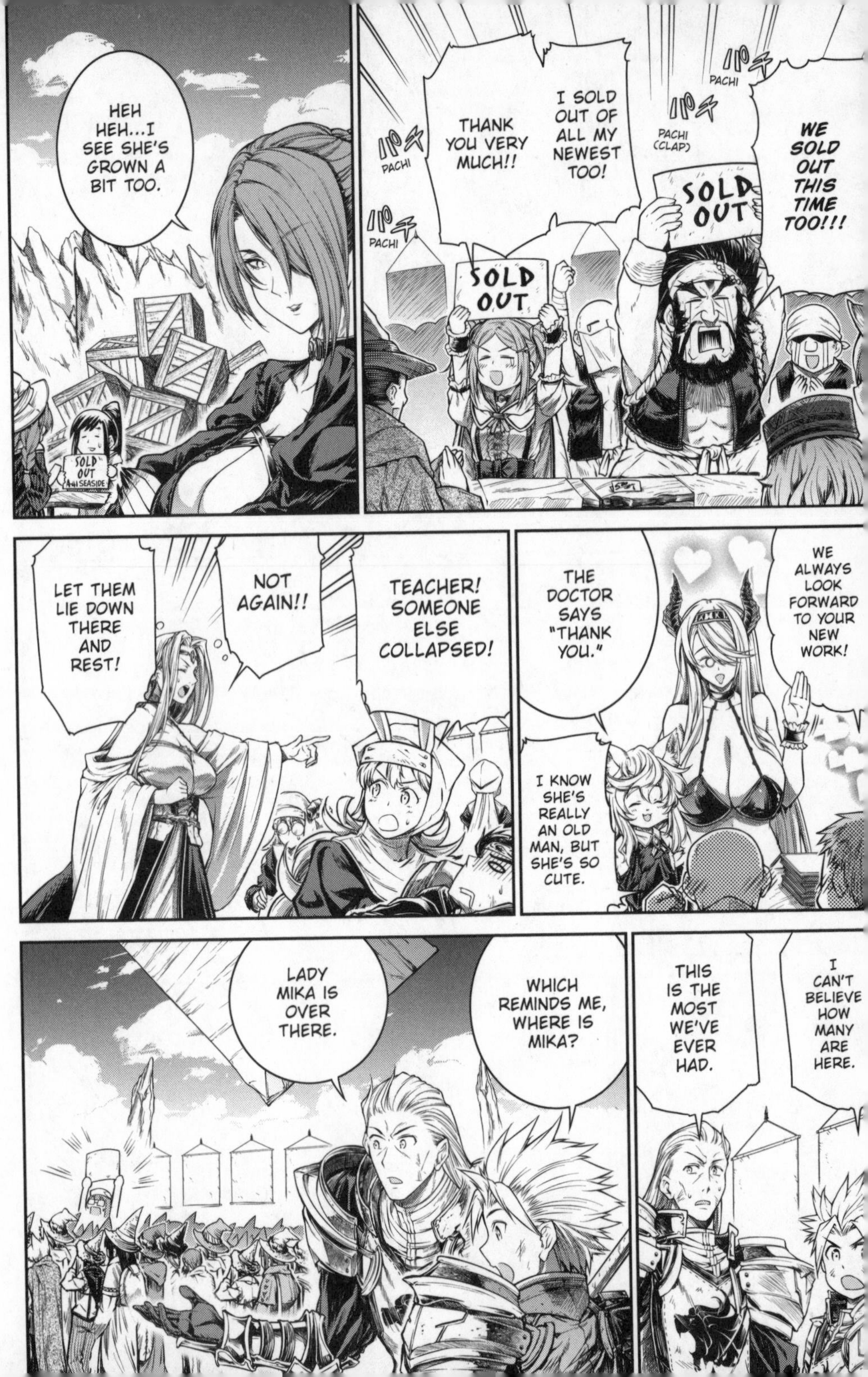
WE SOLD OUT THIS TIME TOO!!!
PACHI
PACHI (CLAP)
SOLD OUT
I SOLD OUT OF ALL MY NEWEST TOO!
THANK YOU VERY MUCH!!
PACHI
PACHI
SOLD OUT
HEH HEH...I SEE SHE'S GROWN A BIT TOO.
SOLD OUT A-41 SEASIDE
WE ALWAYS LOOK FORWARD TO YOUR NEW WORK!
THE DOCTOR SAYS "THANK YOU."
I KNOW SHE'S REALLY AN OLD MAN, BUT SHE'S SO CUTE.
TEACHER! SOMEONE ELSE COLLAPSED!
NOT AGAIN!!
LET THEM LIE DOWN THERE AND REST!
I CAN'T BELIEVE HOW MANY ARE HERE.
THIS IS THE MOST WE'VE EVER HAD.
WHICH REMINDS ME, WHERE IS MIKA?
LADY MIKA IS OVER THERE.

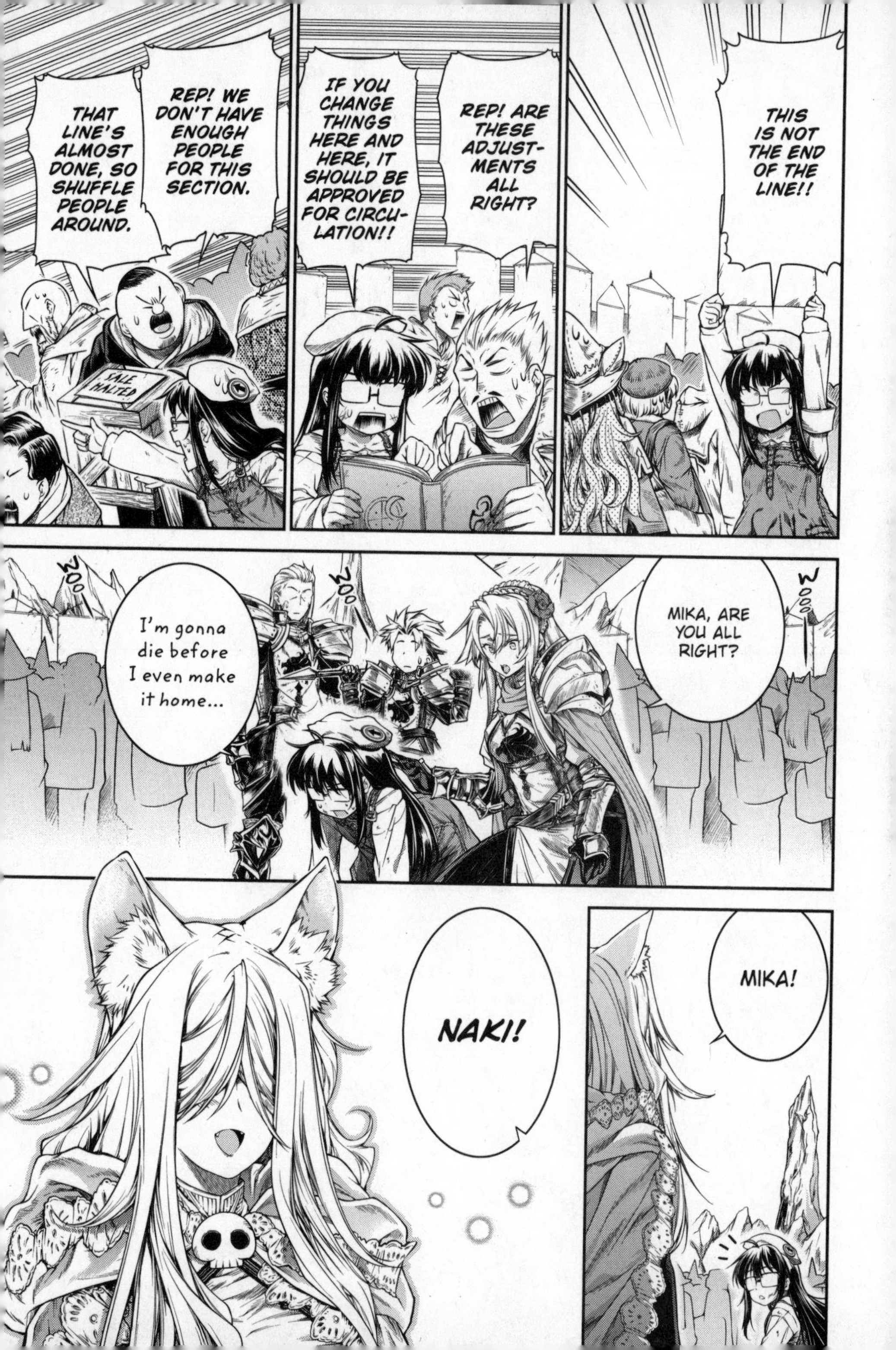
THIS IS NOT THE END OF THE LINE!!
REP! ARE THESE ADJUSTMENTS ALL RIGHT?
IF YOU CHANGE THINGS HERE AND HERE, IT SHOULD BE APPROVED FOR CIRCULATION!!
REP! WE DON'T HAVE ENOUGH PEOPLE FOR THIS SECTION.
THAT LINE'S ALMOST DONE, SO SHUFFLE PEOPLE AROUND.
SALE HALTED
WOOO
MIKA, ARE YOU ALL RIGHT?
WOOO
I'm gonna die before I even make it home...
WOOO
MIKA!
NAKI!

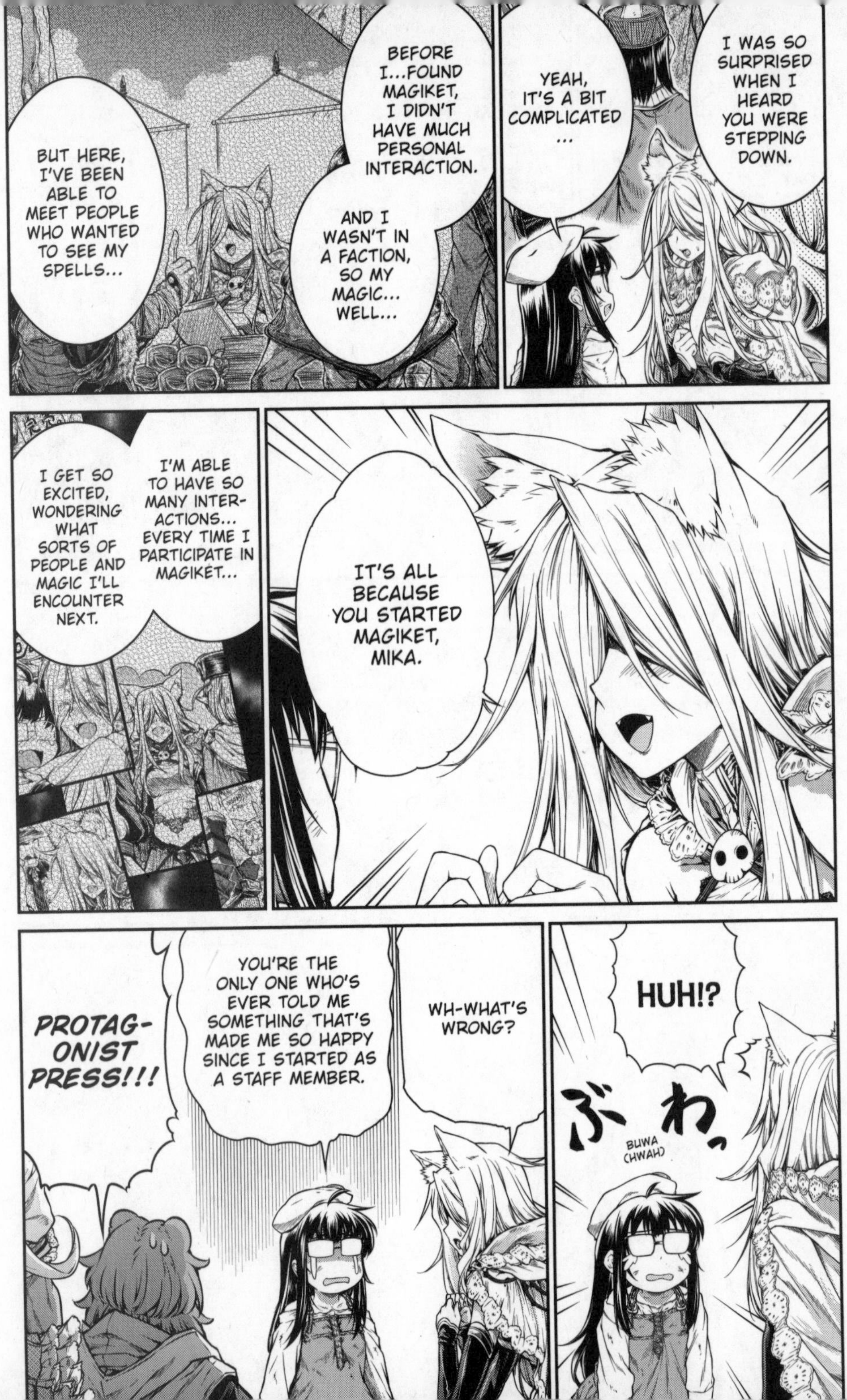
I WAS SO SURPRISED WHEN I HEARD YOU WERE STEPPING DOWN.
YEAH, IT'S A BIT COMPLICATED ...
BEFORE I...FOUND MAGIKET, I DIDN'T HAVE MUCH PERSONAL INTERACTION.
AND I WASN'T IN A FACTION, SO MY MAGIC... WELL...
BUT HERE, I'VE BEEN ABLE TO MEET PEOPLE WHO WANTED TO SEE MY SPELLS...
IT'S ALL BECAUSE YOU STARTED MAGIKET, MIKA.
I'M ABLE TO HAVE SO MANY INTER-ACTIONS... EVERY TIME I PARTICIPATE IN MAGIKET...
I GET SO EXCITED, WONDERING WHAT SORTS OF PEOPLE AND MAGIC I'LL ENCOUNTER NEXT.
HUH!?
ぶわっ
BUWA (HWAH)
WH-WHAT'S WRONG?
YOU'RE THE ONLY ONE WHO'S EVER TOLD ME SOMETHING THAT'S MADE ME SO HAPPY SINCE I STARTED AS A STAFF MEMBER.
PROTAG-ONIST PRESS!!!

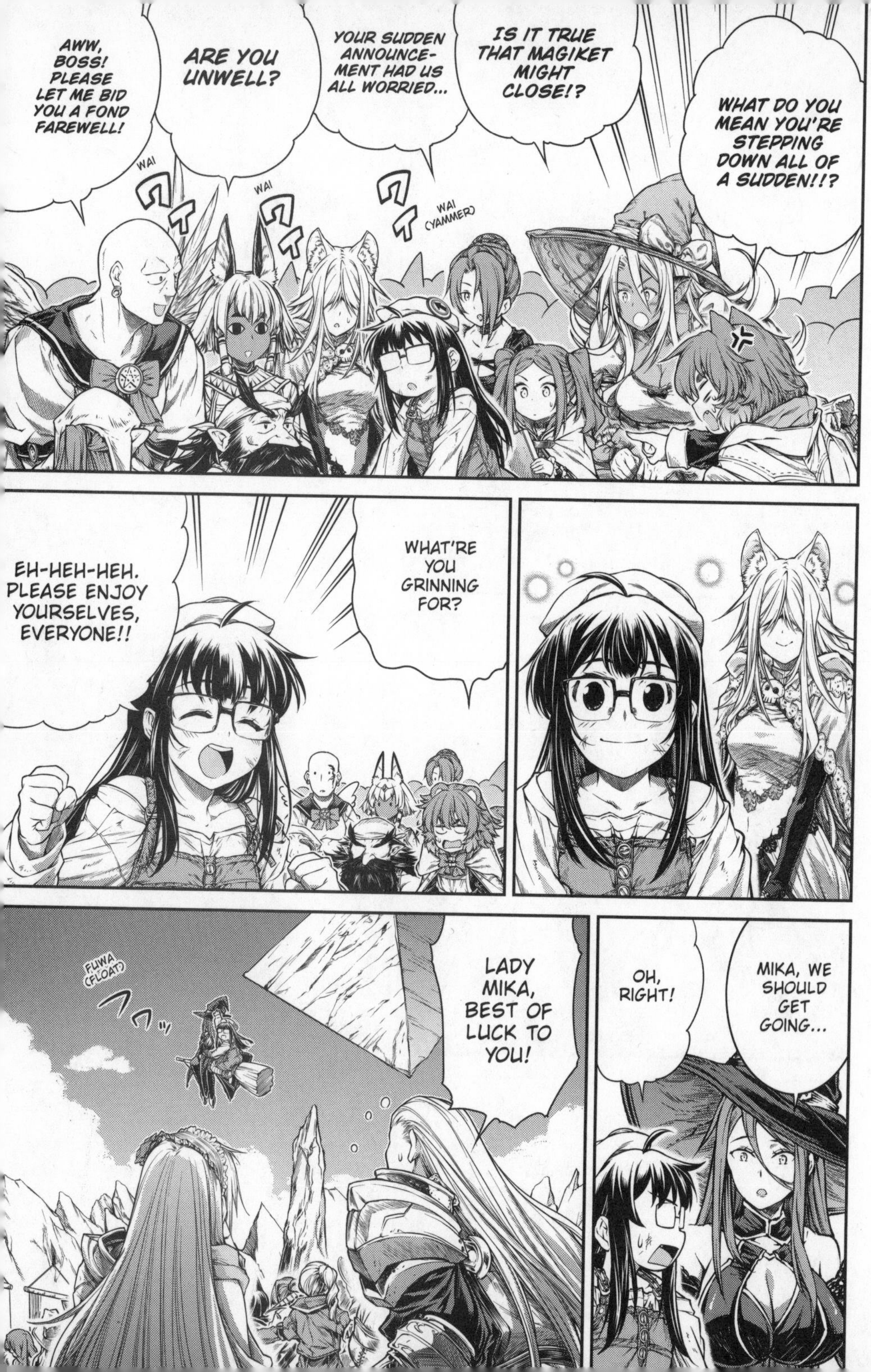
WHAT DO YOU MEAN YOU'RE STEPPING DOWN ALL OF A SUDDEN!!?
IS IT TRUE THAT MAGIKET MIGHT CLOSE!?
YOUR SUDDEN ANNOUNCEMENT HAD US ALL WORRIED...
ARE YOU UNWELL?
AWW, BOSS! PLEASE LET ME BID YOU A FOND FAREWELL!
WAI (YAMMER)
WAI
WAI
WHAT'RE YOU GRINNING FOR?
EH-HEH-HEH. PLEASE ENJOY YOURSELVES, EVERYONE!!
MIKA, WE SHOULD GET GOING...
OH, RIGHT!
LADY MIKA, BEST OF LUCK TO YOU!
FUWA (FLOAT)

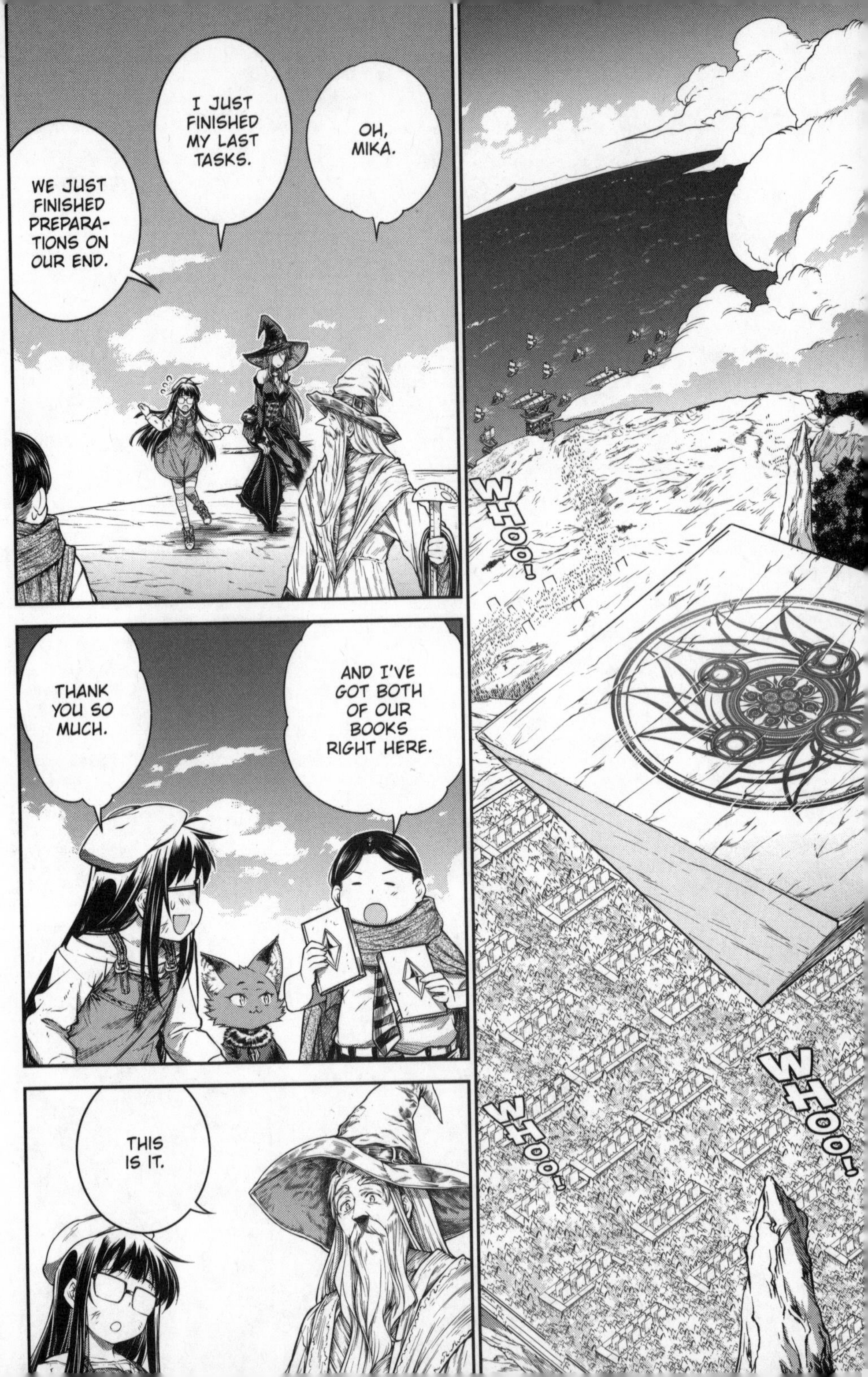
WHOOO!
WHOOO!
WHOO!
OH, MIKA.
I JUST FINISHED MY LAST TASKS.
WE JUST FINISHED PREPARA-TIONS ON OUR END.
AND I'VE GOT BOTH OF OUR BOOKS RIGHT HERE.
THANK YOU SO MUCH.
THIS IS IT.

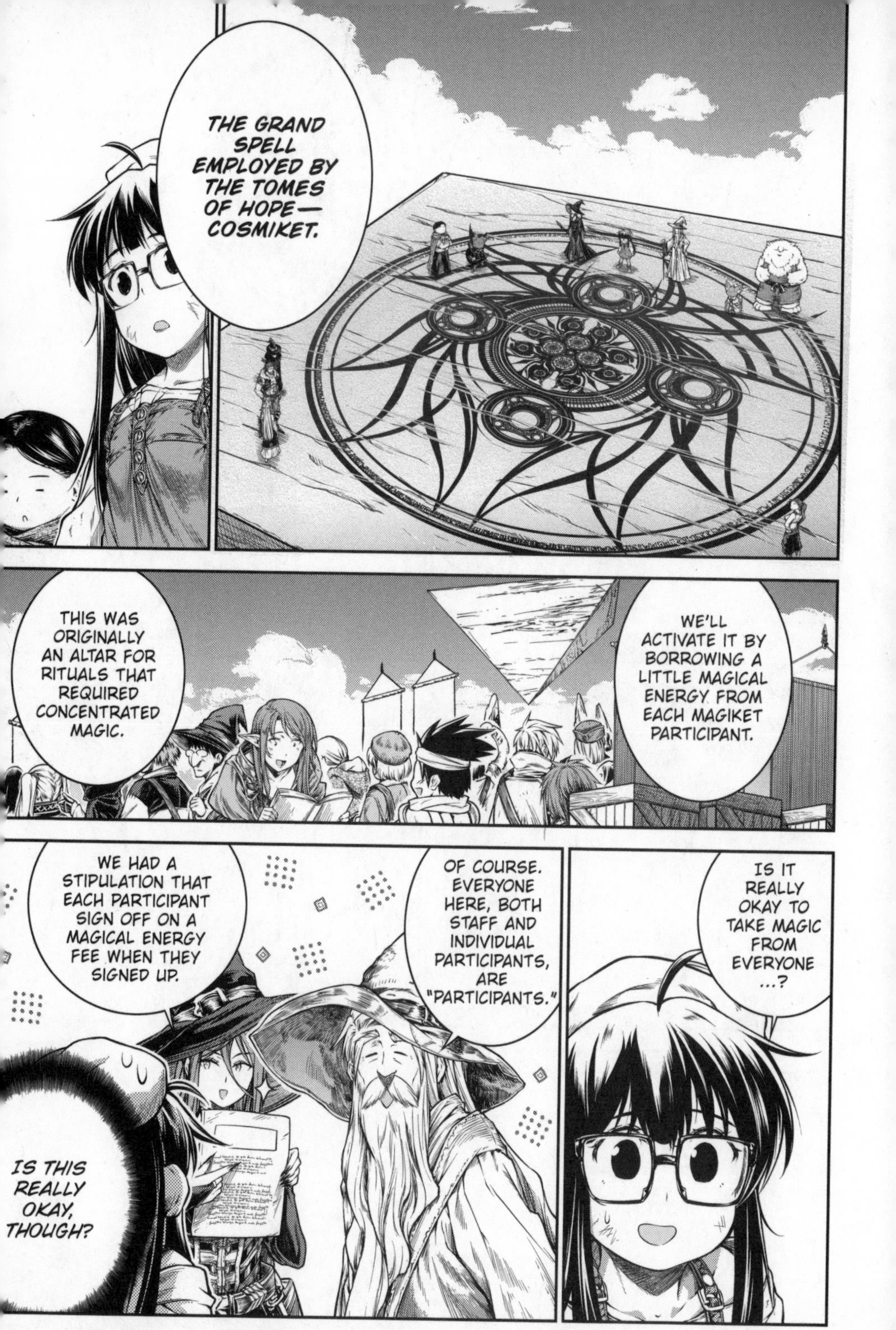
THE GRAND SPELL EMPLOYED BY THE TOMES OF HOPE—COSMIKET.
WE'LL ACTIVATE IT BY BORROWING A LITTLE MAGICAL ENERGY FROM EACH MAGIKET PARTICIPANT.
THIS WAS ORIGINALLY AN ALTAR FOR RITUALS THAT REQUIRED CONCENTRATED MAGIC.
IS IT REALLY OKAY TO TAKE MAGIC FROM EVERYONE ...?
OF COURSE. EVERYONE HERE, BOTH STAFF AND INDIVIDUAL PARTICIPANTS, ARE "PARTICIPANTS."
WE HAD A STIPULATION THAT EACH PARTICIPANT SIGN OFF ON A MAGICAL ENERGY FEE WHEN THEY SIGNED UP.
IS THIS REALLY OKAY, THOUGH?

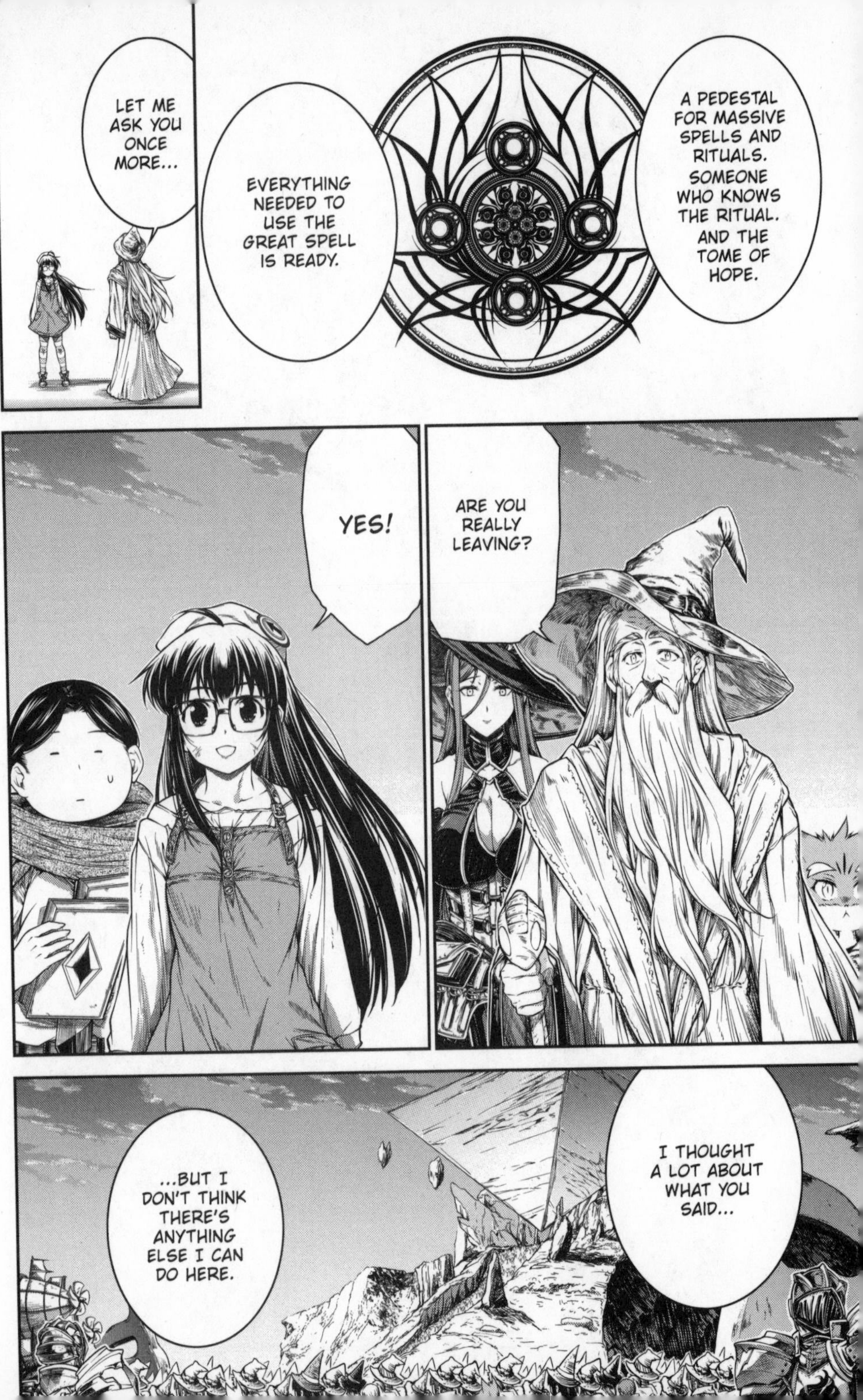
A PEDESTAL FOR MASSIVE SPELLS AND RITUALS. SOMEONE WHO KNOWS THE RITUAL. AND THE TOME OF HOPE.
EVERYTHING NEEDED TO USE THE GREAT SPELL IS READY.
LET ME ASK YOU ONCE MORE...
ARE YOU REALLY LEAVING?
YES!
I THOUGHT A LOT ABOUT WHAT YOU SAID...
...BUT I DON'T THINK THERE'S ANYTHING ELSE I CAN DO HERE.

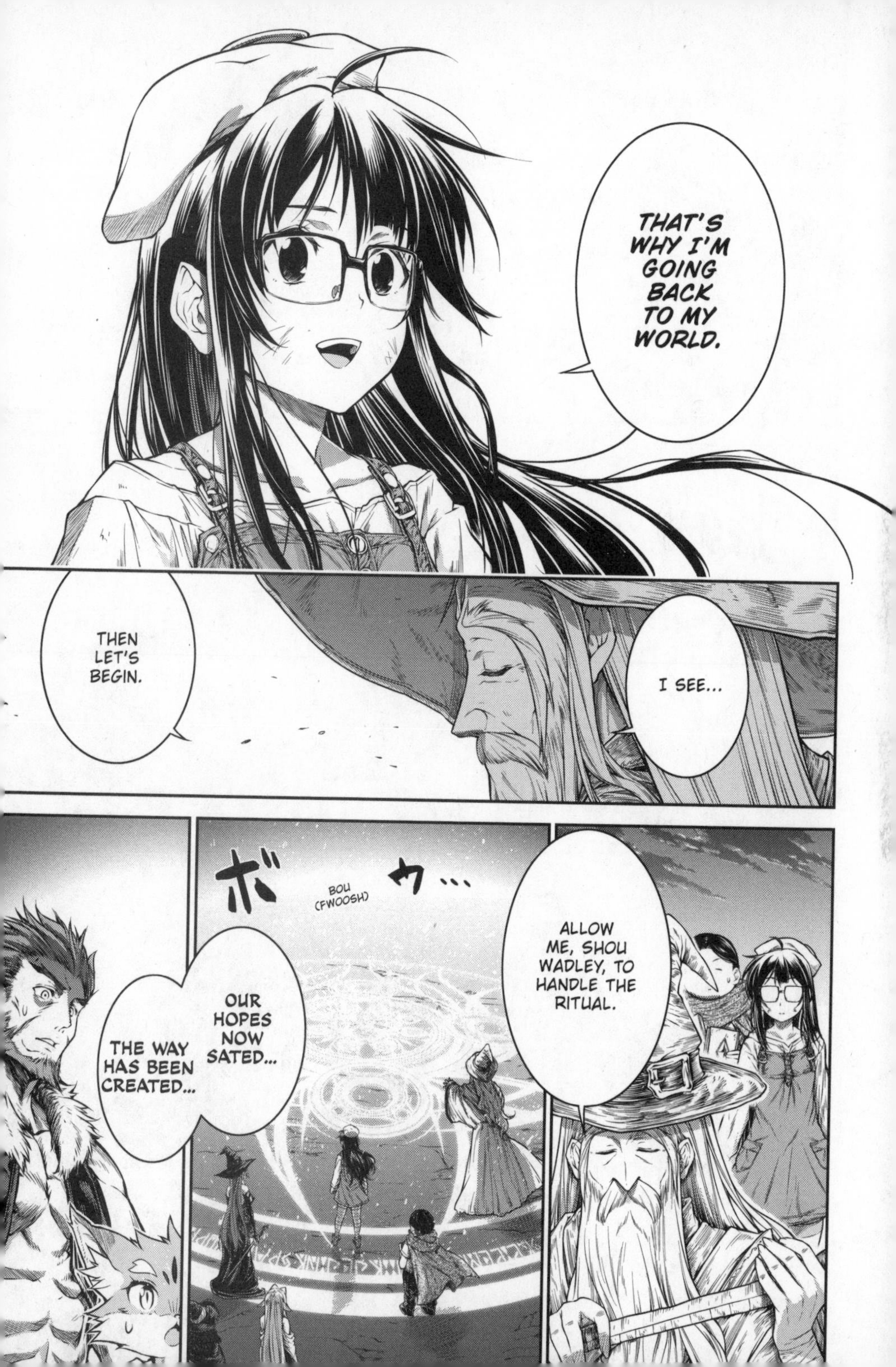
THAT'S WHY I'M GOING BACK TO MY WORLD.
I SEE...
THEN LET'S BEGIN.
ALLOW ME, SHOU WADLEY, TO HANDLE THE RITUAL.
ボウ…
BOU (FWOOSH)
OUR HOPES NOW SATED...
THE WAY HAS BEEN CREATED...

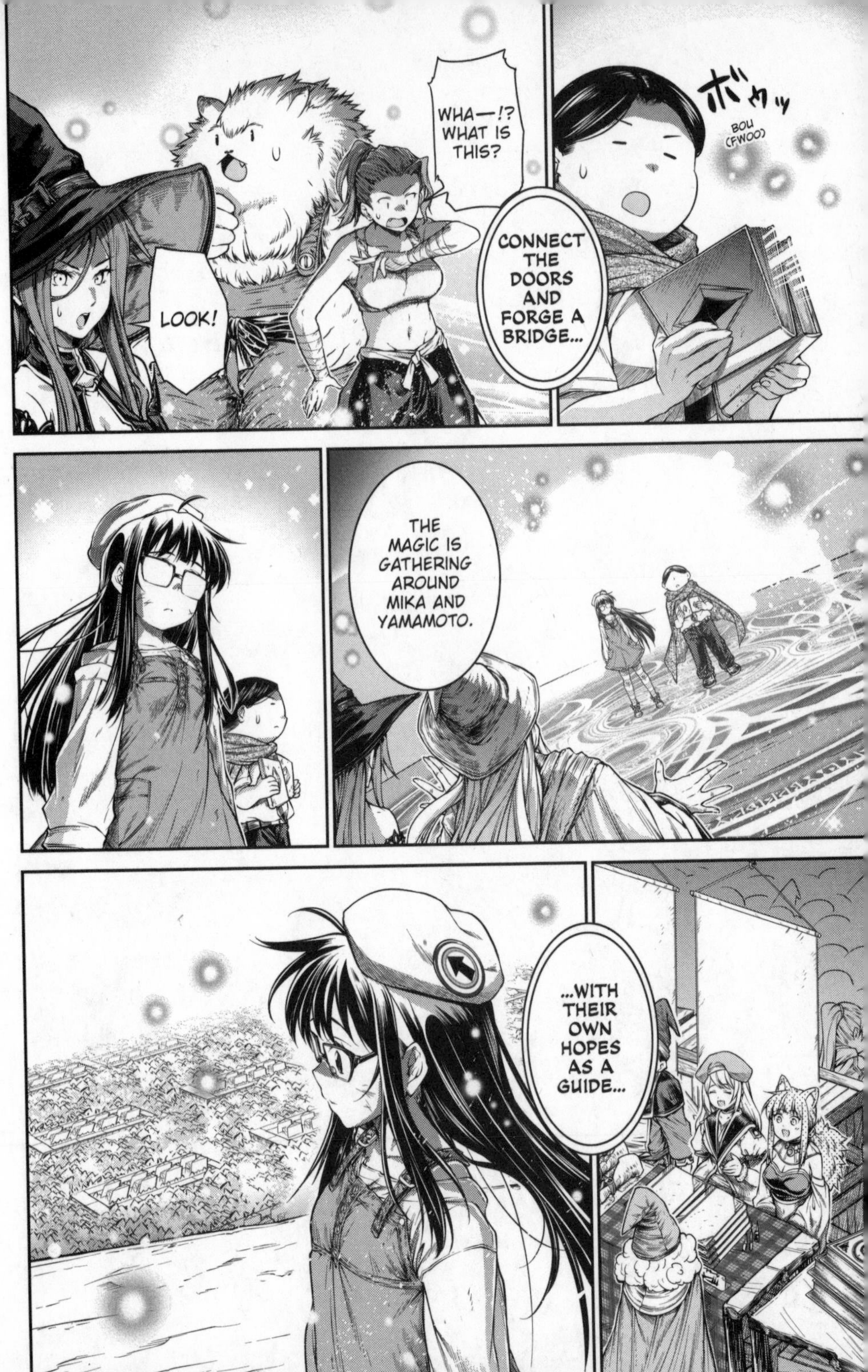
ボゥッ
BOU (FWOO)
CONNECT THE DOORS AND FORGE A BRIDGE...
WHA—!? WHAT IS THIS?
LOOK!
THE MAGIC IS GATHERING AROUND MIKA AND YAMAMOTO.
...WITH THEIR OWN HOPES AS A GUIDE...

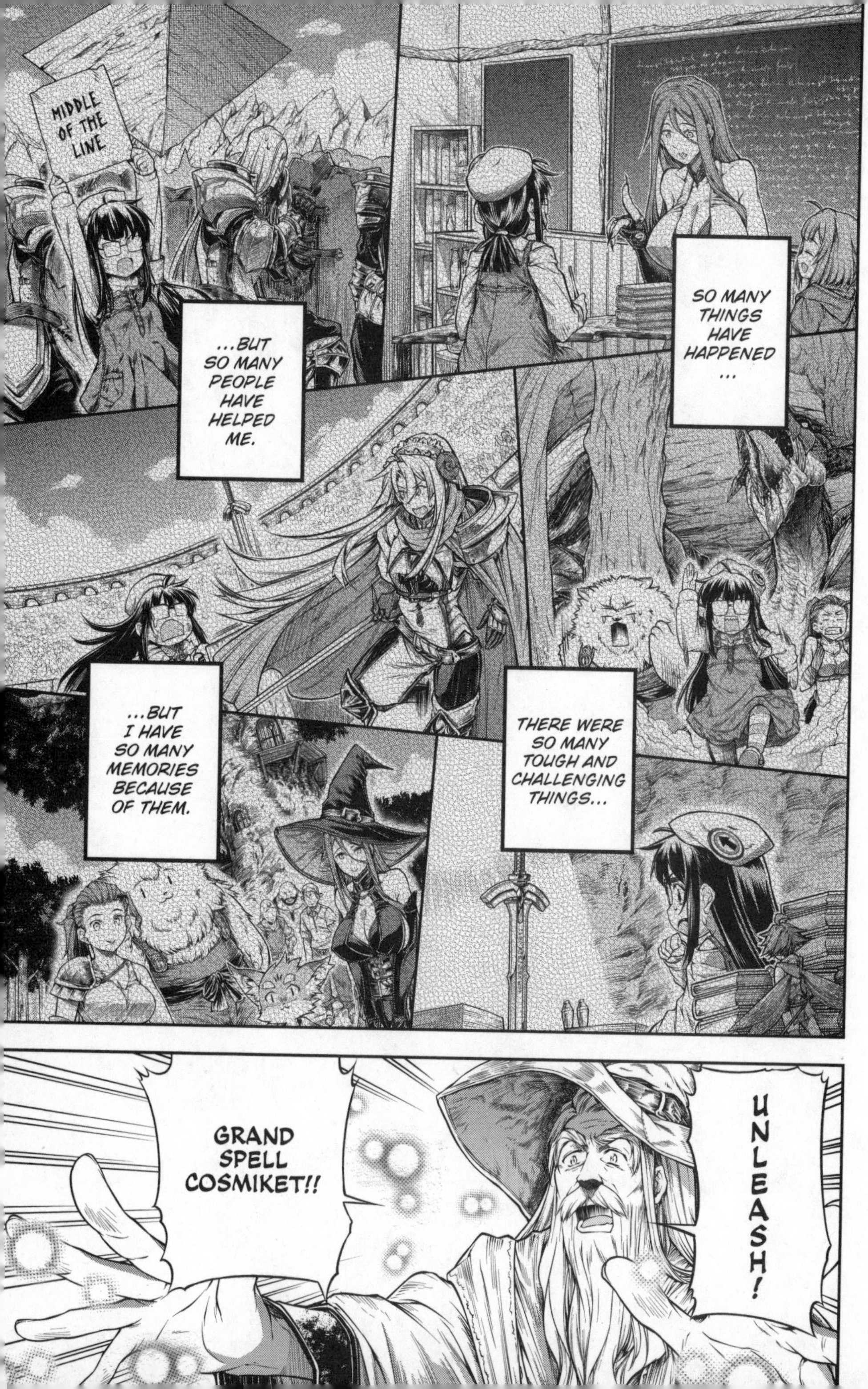
SO MANY THINGS HAVE HAPPENED...
MIDDLE OF THE LINE
...BUT SO MANY PEOPLE HAVE HELPED ME.
THERE WERE SO MANY TOUGH AND CHALLENGING THINGS...
...BUT I HAVE SO MANY MEMORIES BECAUSE OF THEM.
UNLEASH!
GRAND SPELL COSMIKET!!

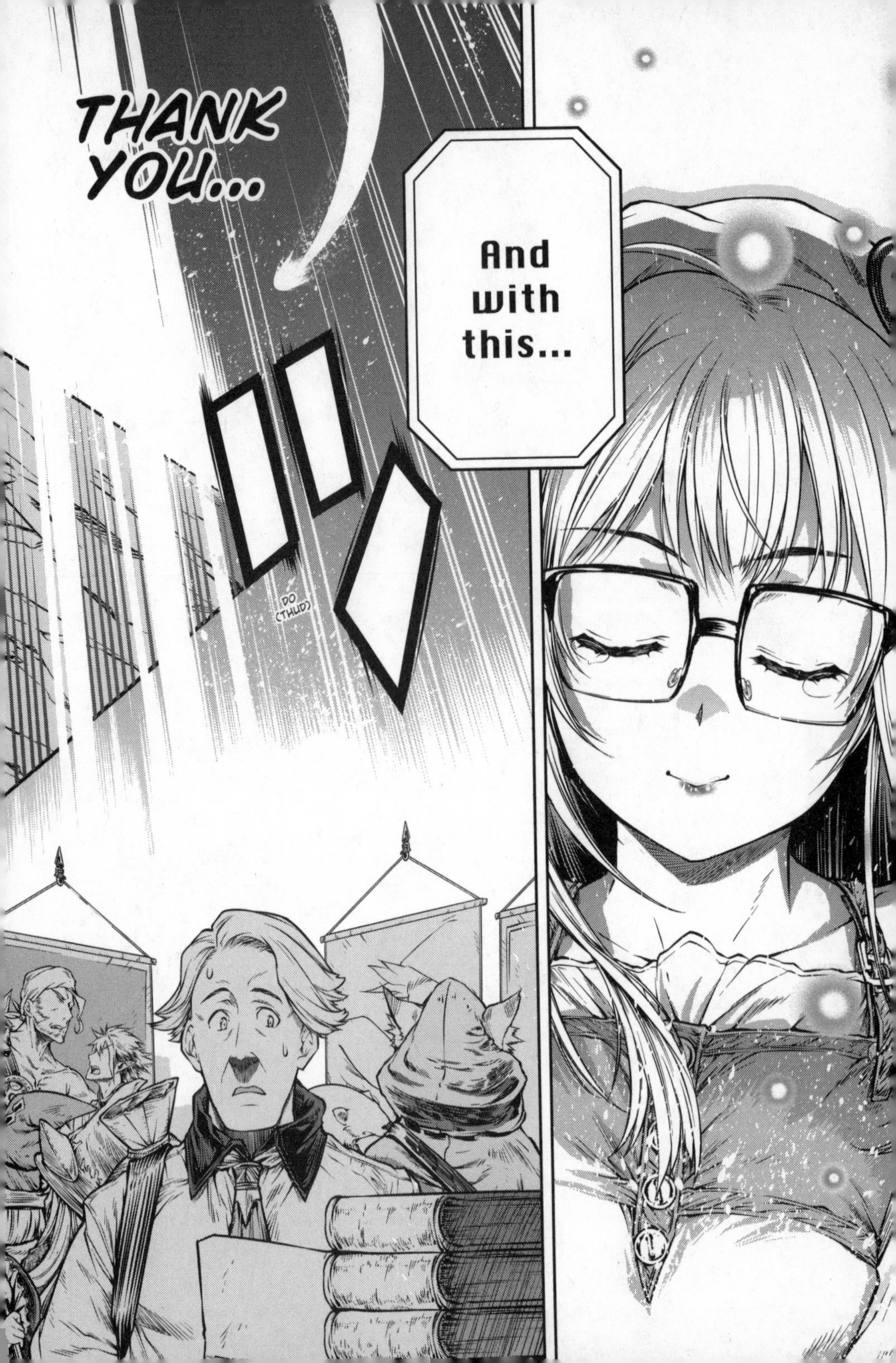
And with this...
THANK YOU...
DO
(THUD)

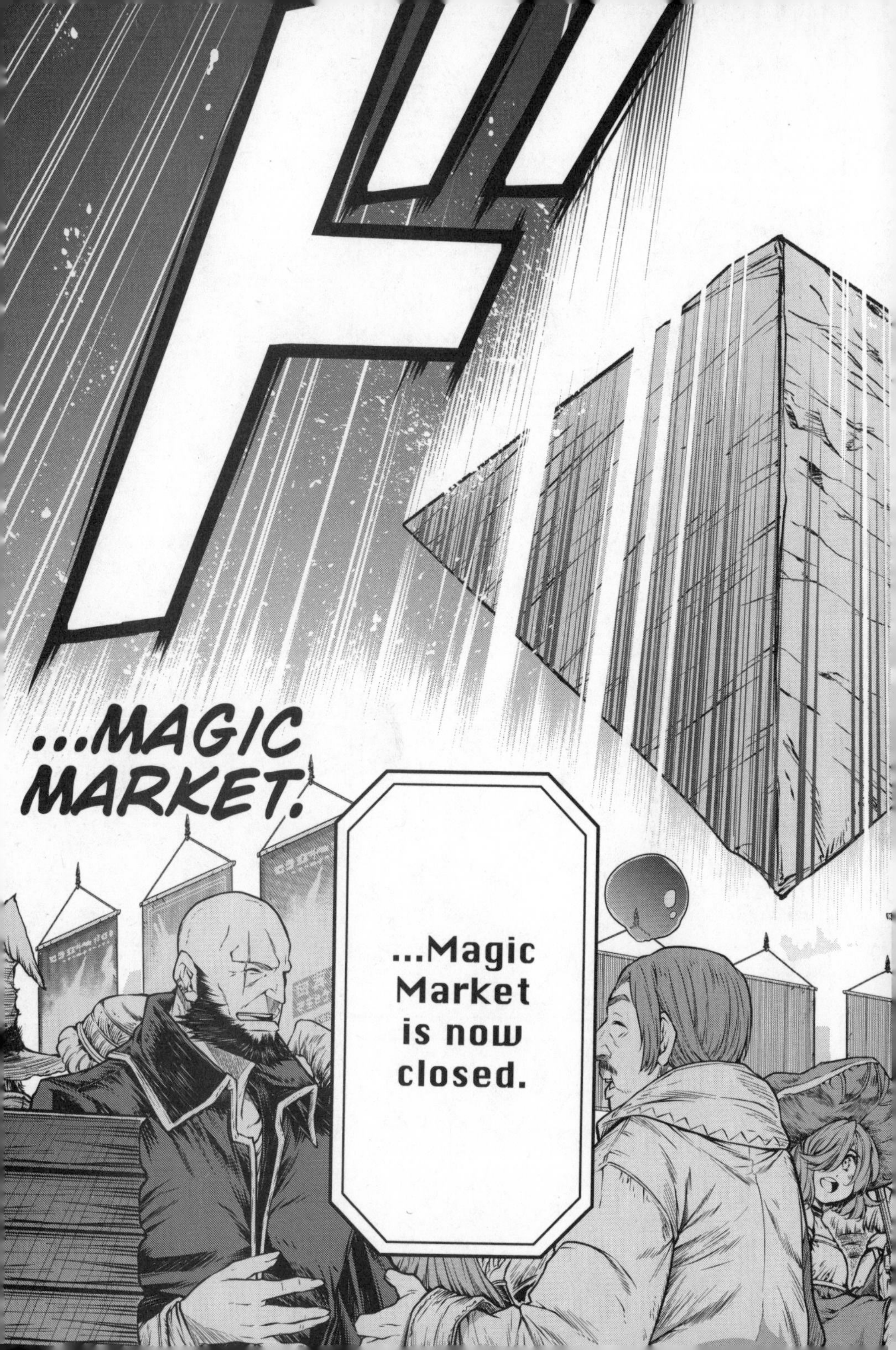
...MAGIC MARKET.
...Magic Market is now closed.

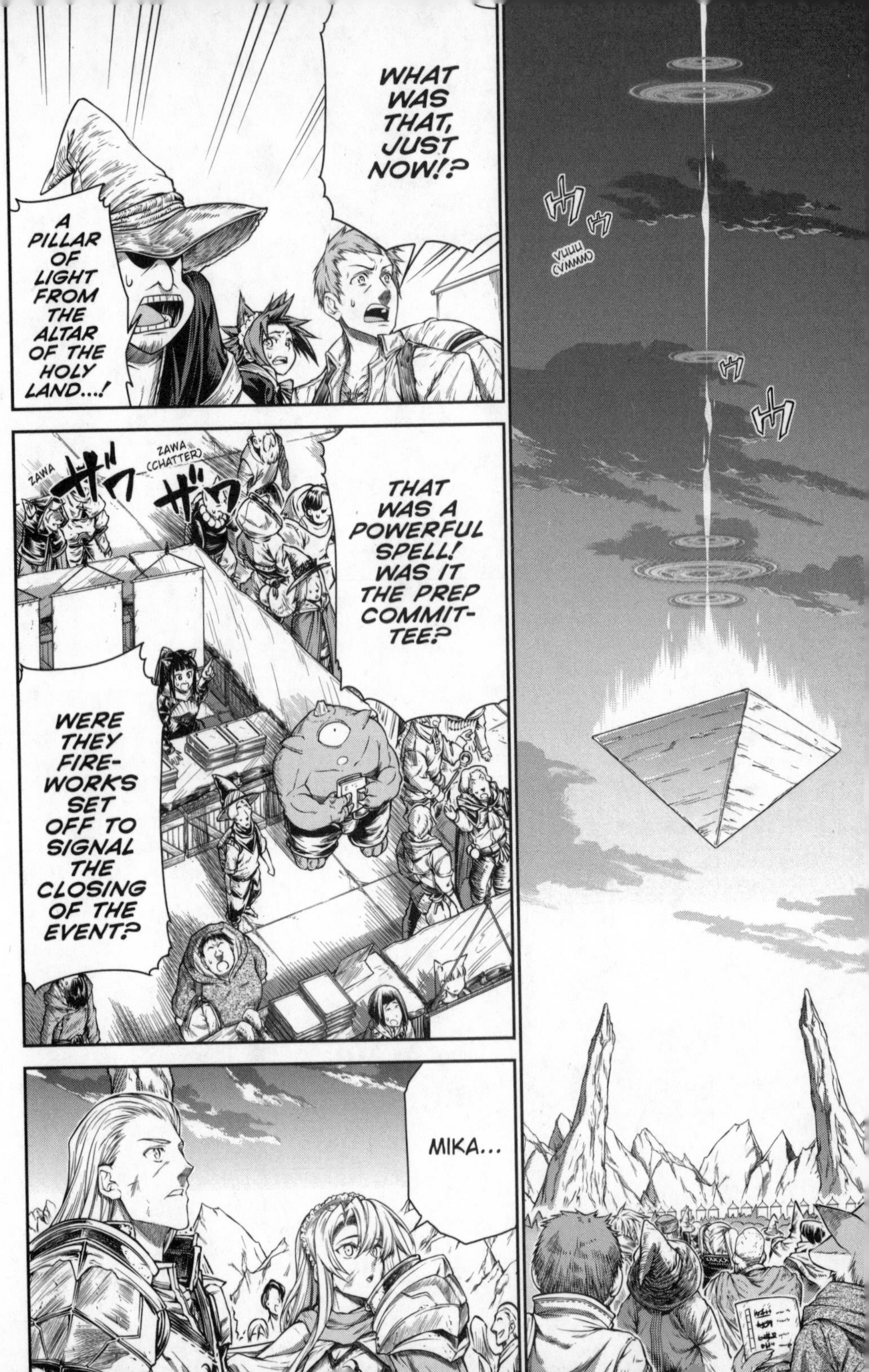
VUUU (VMMMM)
WHAT WAS THAT, JUST NOW!?
A PILLAR OF LIGHT FROM THE ALTAR OF THE HOLY LAND...!
ザワ
ZAWA
ザワ
ZAWA (CHATTER)
THAT WAS A POWERFUL SPELL! WAS IT THE PREP COMMITTEE?
WERE THEY FIREWORKS SET OFF TO SIGNAL THE CLOSING OF THE EVENT?
MIKA...

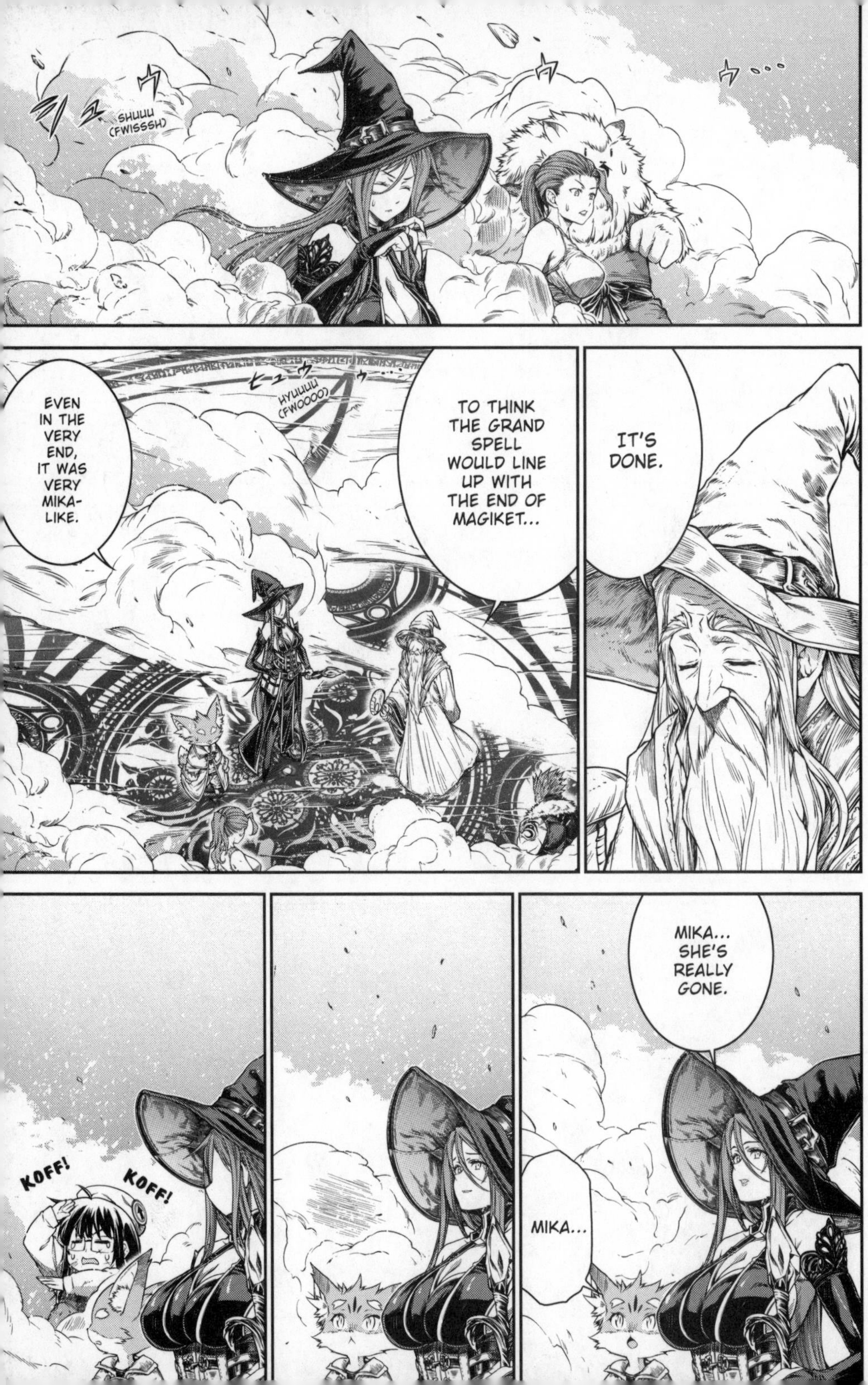
SHUUU (FWISSSH)
IT'S DONE.
TO THINK THE GRAND SPELL WOULD LINE UP WITH THE END OF MAGIKET...
HYUUUU (FWOOOO)
EVEN IN THE VERY END, IT WAS VERY MIKA-LIKE.
MIKA... SHE'S REALLY GONE.
MIKA...
KOFF! KOFF!

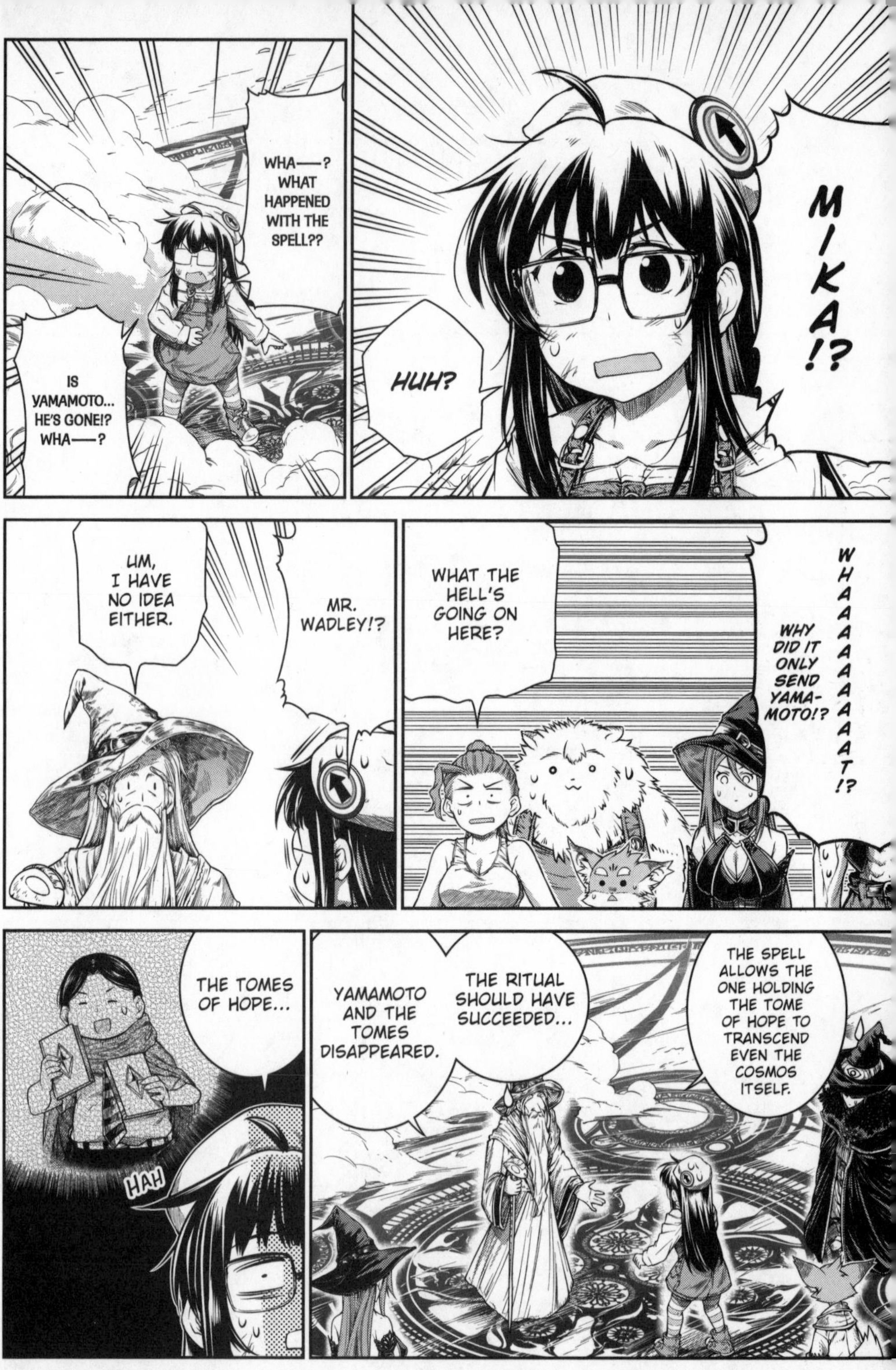
MIKA!?
HUH?
WHA—? WHAT HAPPENED WITH THE SPELL??
IS YAMAMOTO... HE'S GONE!? WHA—?
WHAAAAAAAAAAT!?
WHY DID IT ONLY SEND YAMA-MOTO!?
WHAT THE HELL'S GOING ON HERE?
MR. WADLEY!?
UM, I HAVE NO IDEA EITHER.
THE SPELL ALLOWS THE ONE HOLDING THE TOME OF HOPE TO TRANSCEND EVEN THE COSMOS ITSELF.
THE RITUAL SHOULD HAVE SUCCEEDED...
YAMAMOTO AND THE TOMES DISAPPEARED.
THE TOMES OF HOPE...
HAH

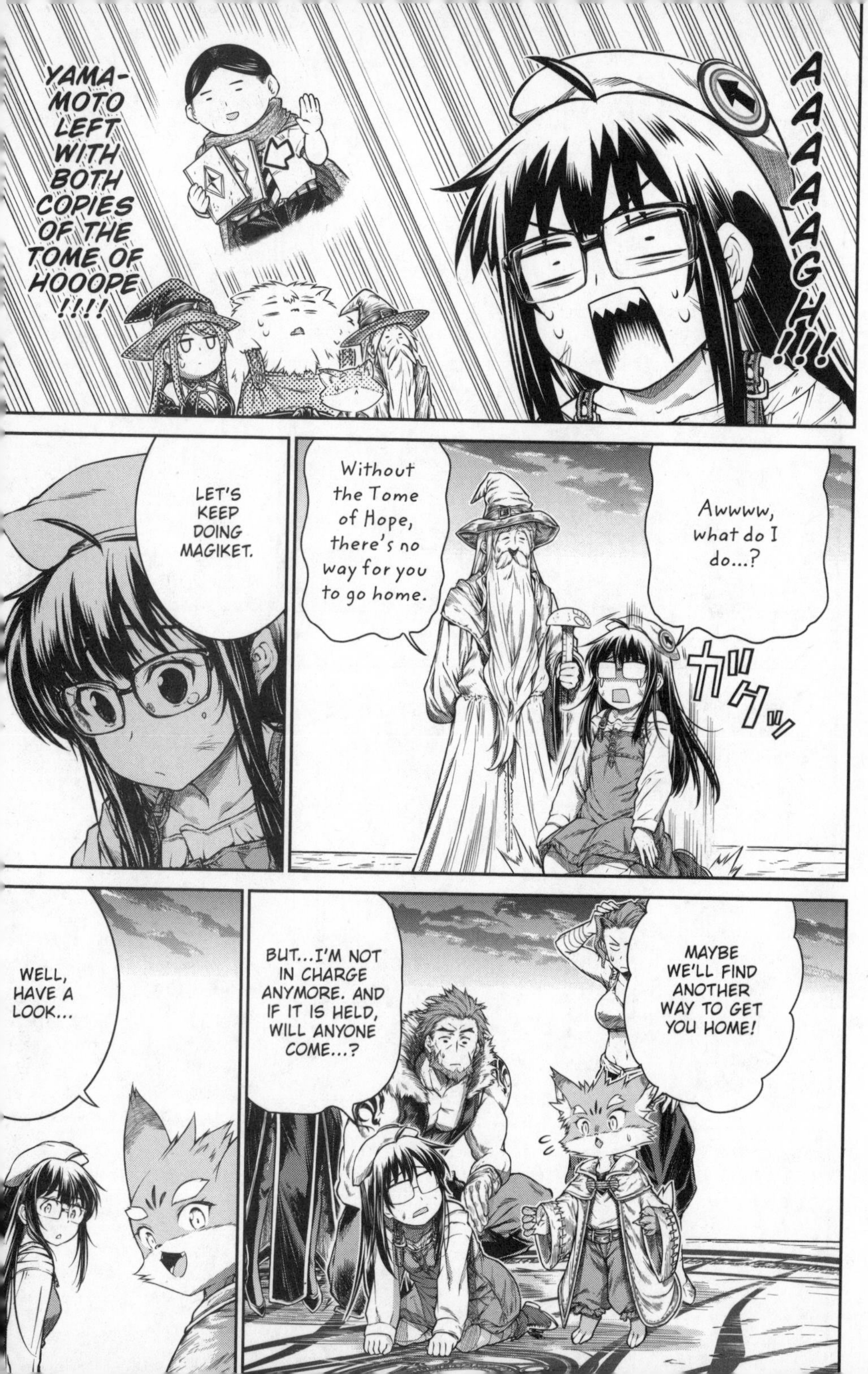
AAAAAGH!!!
YAMAMOTO LEFT WITH BOTH COPIES OF THE TOME OF HOOOPE!!!!
Awwww, what do I do...?
Without the Tome of Hope, there's no way for you to go home.
ガクッ
LET'S KEEP DOING MAGIKET.
MAYBE WE'LL FIND ANOTHER WAY TO GET YOU HOME!
BUT...I'M NOT IN CHARGE ANYMORE. AND IF IT IS HELD, WILL ANYONE COME...?
WELL, HAVE A LOOK...

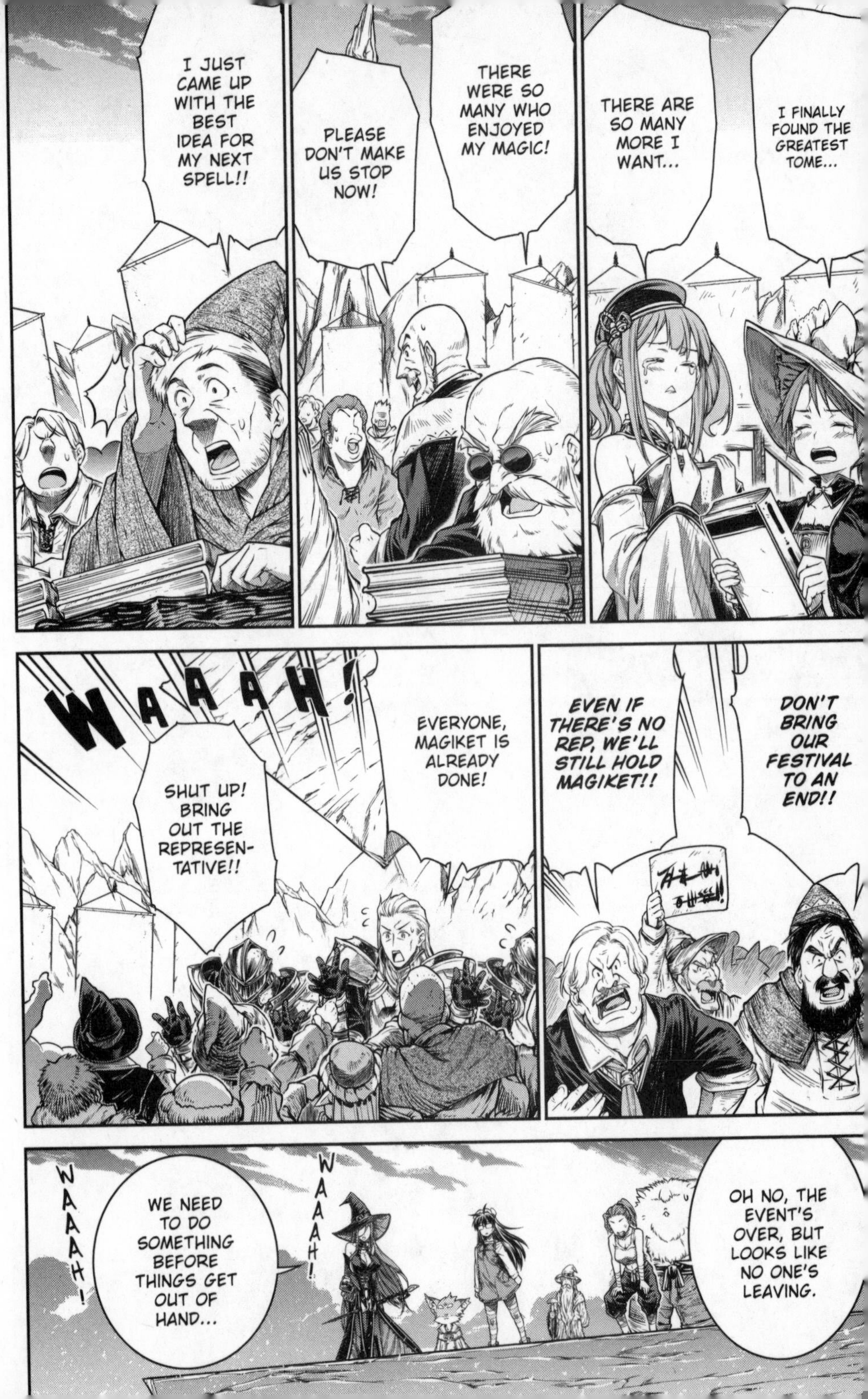
I FINALLY FOUND THE GREATEST TOME...
THERE ARE SO MANY MORE I WANT...
THERE WERE SO MANY WHO ENJOYED MY MAGIC!
PLEASE DON'T MAKE US STOP NOW!
I JUST CAME UP WITH THE BEST IDEA FOR MY NEXT SPELL!!
DON'T BRING OUR FESTIVAL TO AN END!!
EVEN IF THERE'S NO REP, WE'LL STILL HOLD MAGIKET!!
EVERYONE, MAGIKET IS ALREADY DONE!
WAAAAH!
SHUT UP! BRING OUT THE REPRESENTATIVE!!
OH NO, THE EVENT'S OVER, BUT LOOKS LIKE NO ONE'S LEAVING.
WAAAH!
WE NEED TO DO SOMETHING BEFORE THINGS GET OUT OF HAND...
WAAAAH!

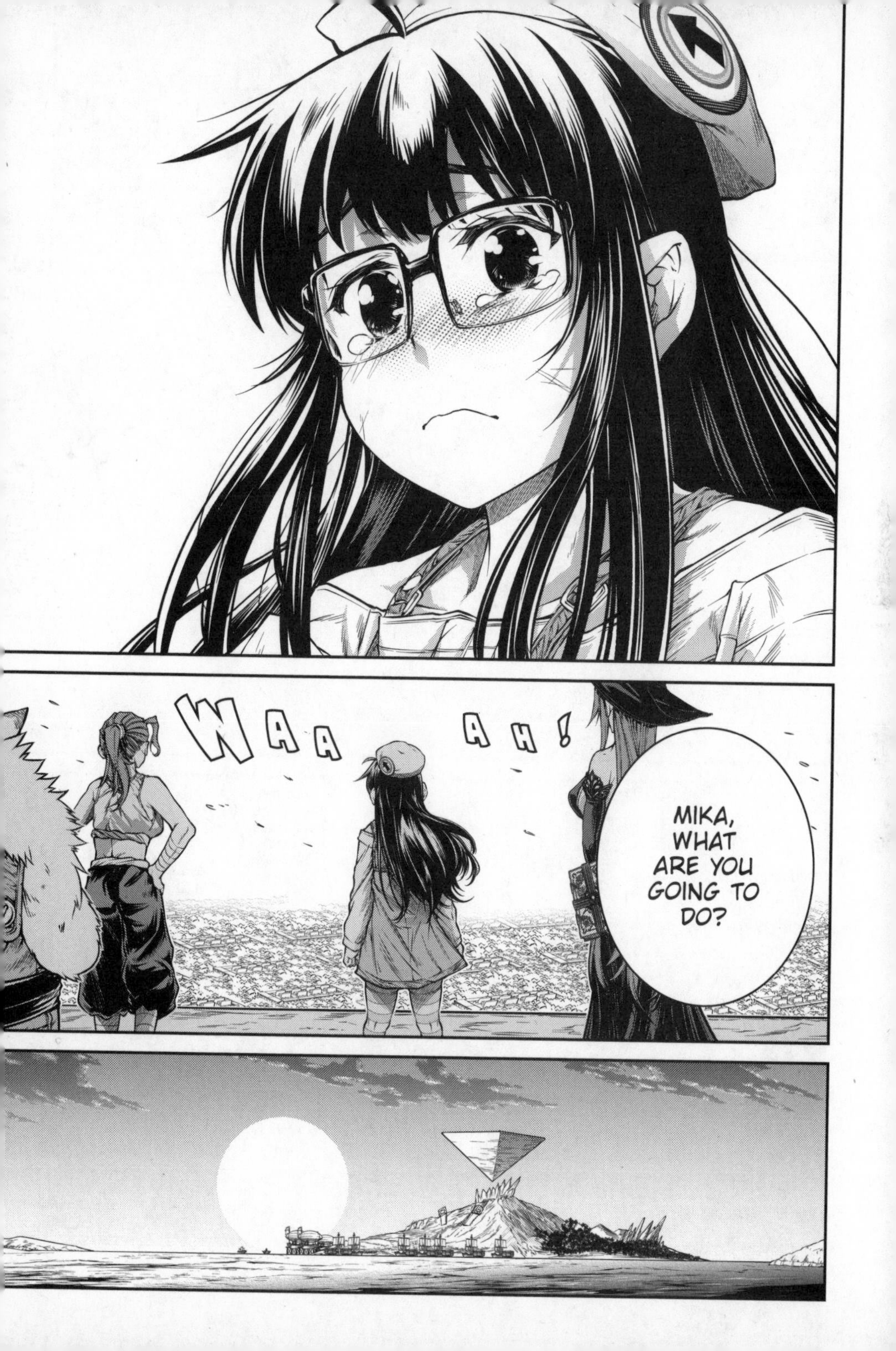
MIKA, WHAT ARE YOU GOING TO DO?
WAAAH!

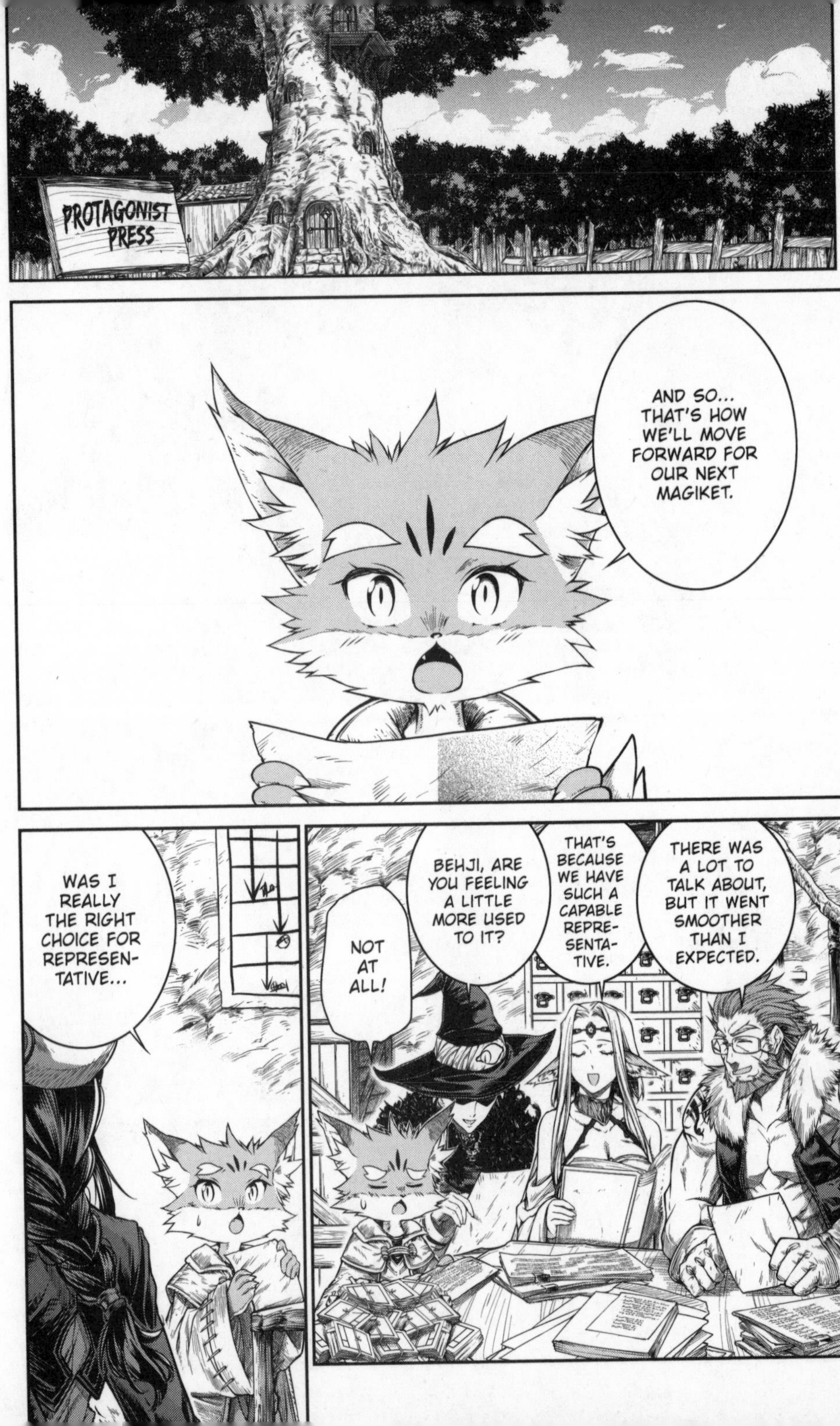
PROTAGONIST PRESS
AND SO... THAT'S HOW WE'LL MOVE FORWARD FOR OUR NEXT MAGIKET.
THERE WAS A LOT TO TALK ABOUT, BUT IT WENT SMOOTHER THAN I EXPECTED.
THAT'S BECAUSE WE HAVE SUCH A CAPABLE REPRESENTATIVE.
BEHJI, ARE YOU FEELING A LITTLE MORE USED TO IT?
NOT AT ALL!
WAS I REALLY THE RIGHT CHOICE FOR REPRESENTATIVE...

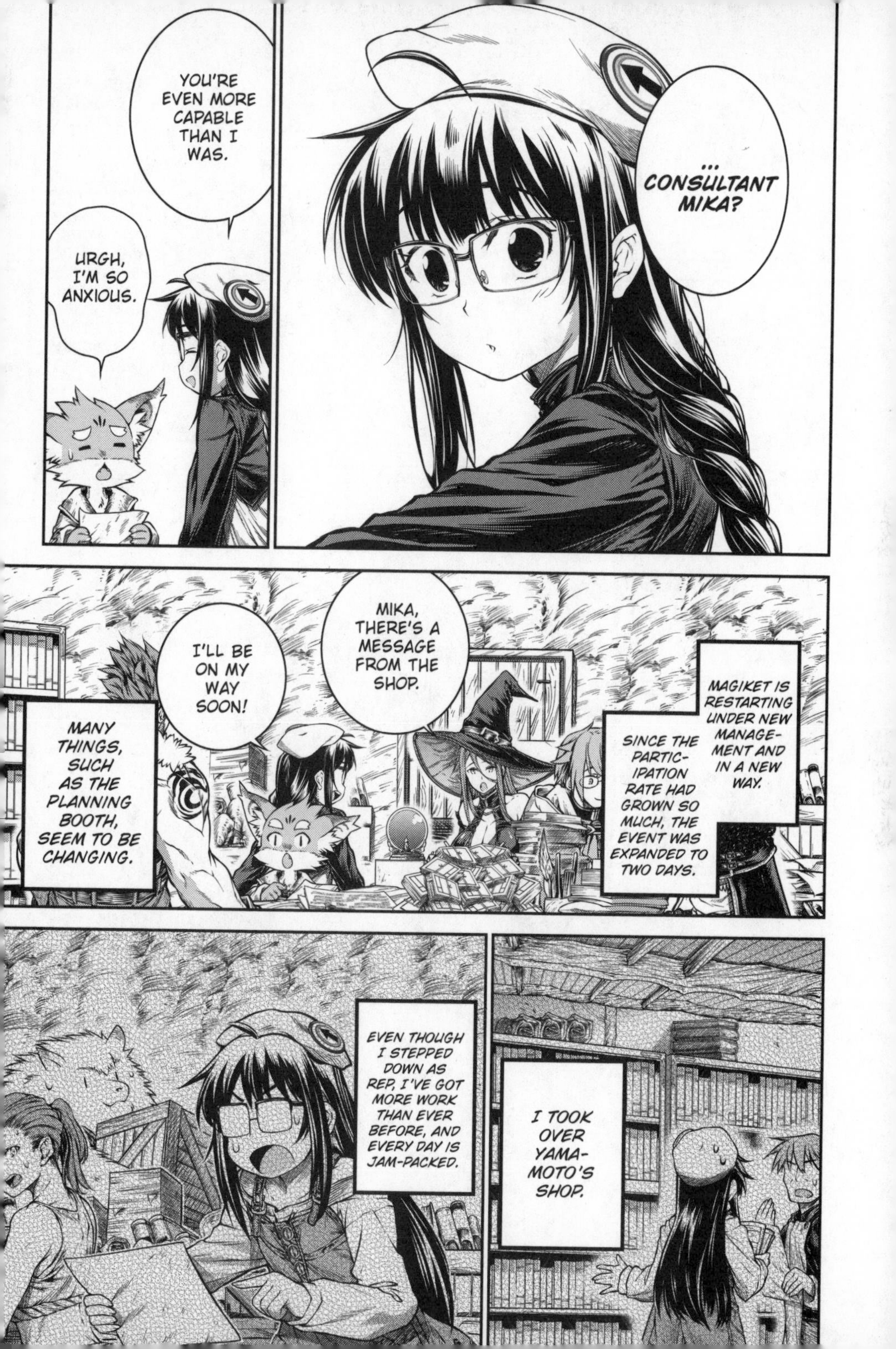
... CONSULTANT MIKA?
YOU'RE EVEN MORE CAPABLE THAN I WAS.
URGH, I'M SO ANXIOUS.
MAGIKET IS RESTARTING UNDER NEW MANAGE-MENT AND IN A NEW WAY.
SINCE THE PARTIC-IPATION RATE HAD GROWN SO MUCH, THE EVENT WAS EXPANDED TO TWO DAYS.
MIKA, THERE'S A MESSAGE FROM THE SHOP.
I'LL BE ON MY WAY SOON!
MANY THINGS, SUCH AS THE PLANNING BOOTH, SEEM TO BE CHANGING.
I TOOK OVER YAMA-MOTO'S SHOP.
EVEN THOUGH I STEPPED DOWN AS REP, I'VE GOT MORE WORK THAN EVER BEFORE, AND EVERY DAY IS JAM-PACKED.

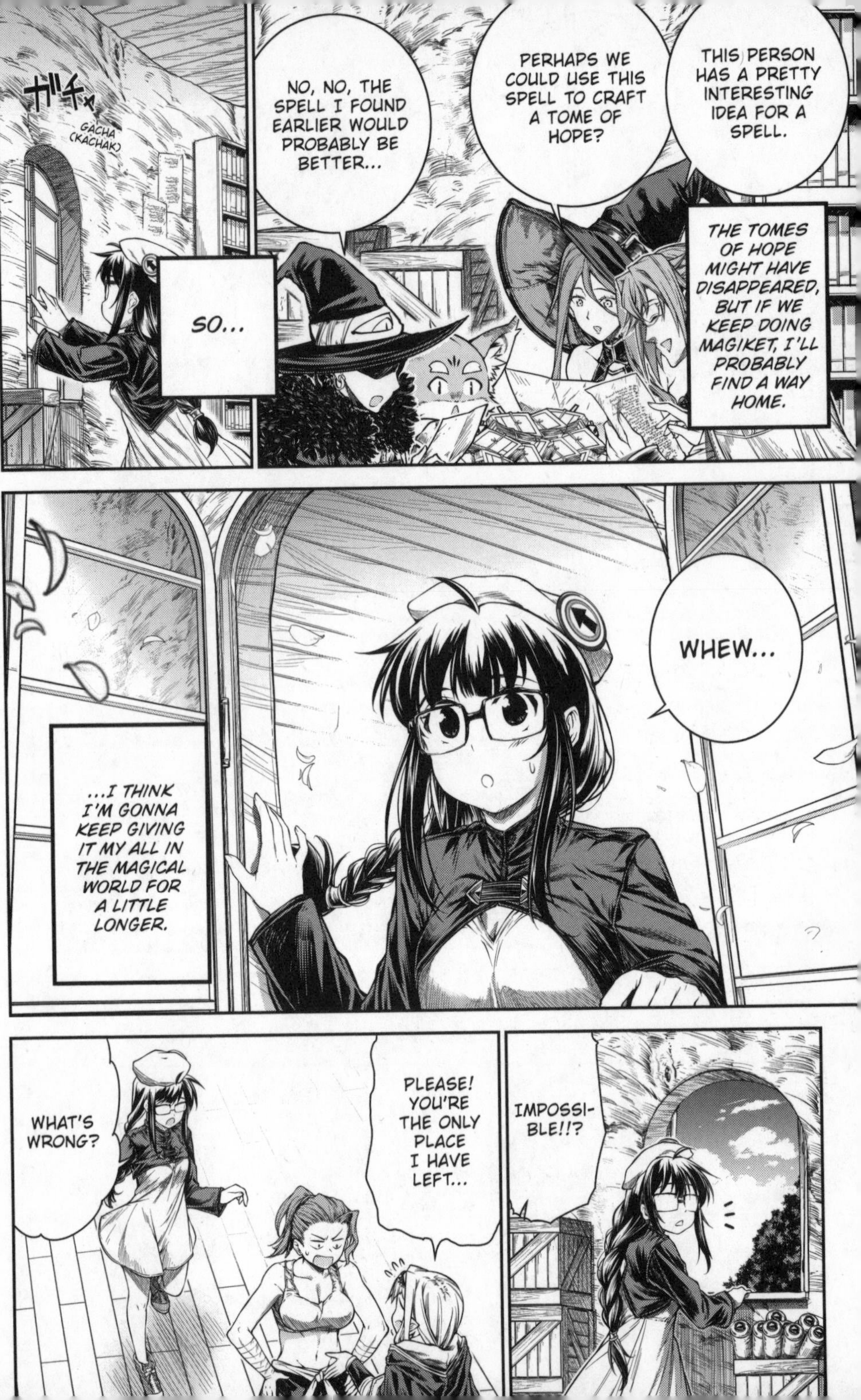
THIS PERSON HAS A PRETTY INTERESTING IDEA FOR A SPELL.
PERHAPS WE COULD USE THIS SPELL TO CRAFT A TOME OF HOPE?
NO, NO, THE SPELL I FOUND EARLIER WOULD PROBABLY BE BETTER...
THE TOMES OF HOPE MIGHT HAVE DISAPPEARED, BUT IF WE KEEP DOING MAGIKET, I'LL PROBABLY FIND A WAY HOME.
SO...
ガチャ
GACHA (KACHAK)
WHEW...
...I THINK I'M GONNA KEEP GIVING IT MY ALL IN THE MAGICAL WORLD FOR A LITTLE LONGER.
IMPOSSI-BLE!!?
PLEASE! YOU'RE THE ONLY PLACE I HAVE LEFT...
WHAT'S WRONG?

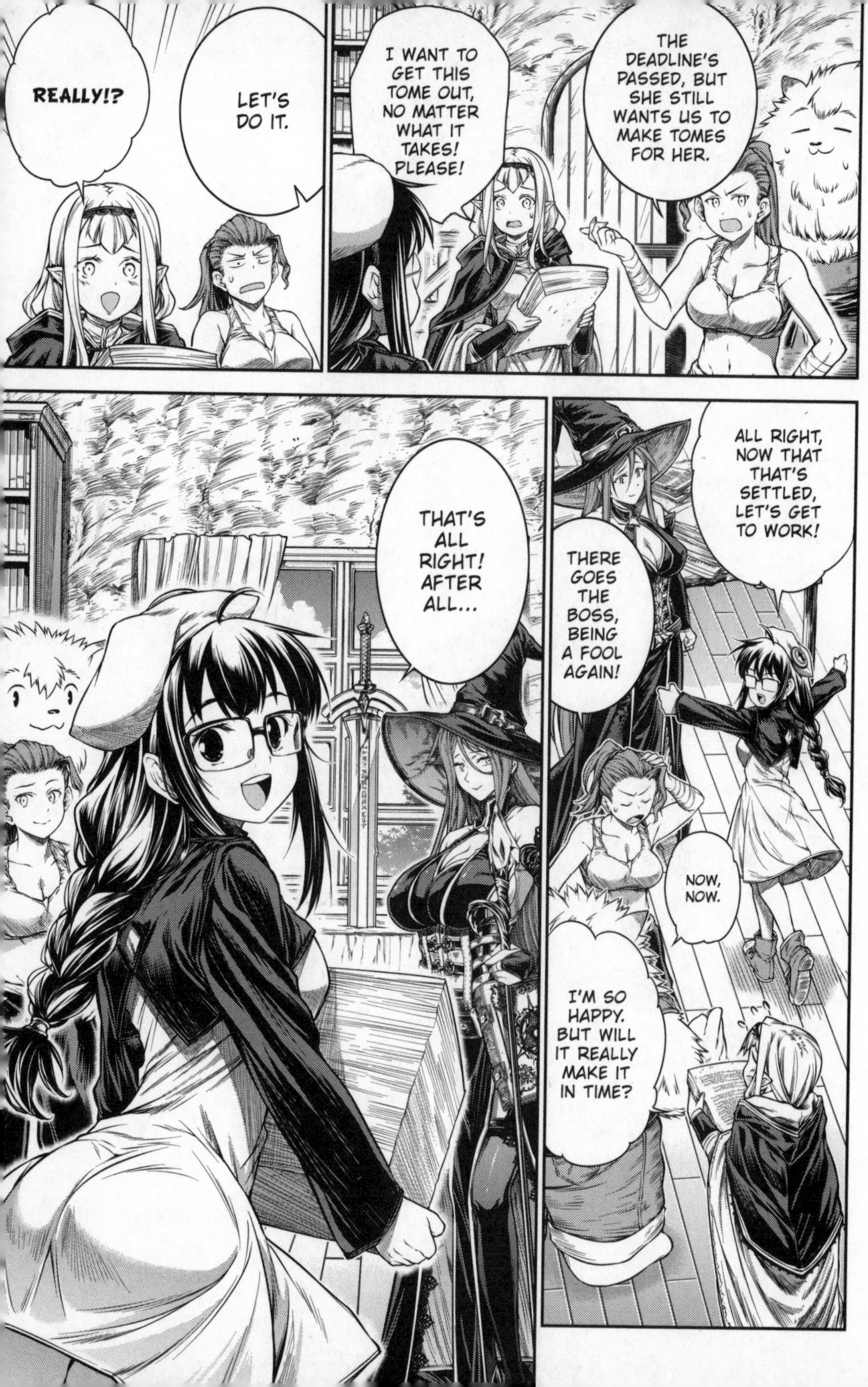
THE DEADLINE'S PASSED, BUT SHE STILL WANTS US TO MAKE TOMES FOR HER.
I WANT TO GET THIS TOME OUT, NO MATTER WHAT IT TAKES! PLEASE!
LET'S DO IT.
REALLY!?
ALL RIGHT, NOW THAT THAT'S SETTLED, LET'S GET TO WORK!
THERE GOES THE BOSS, BEING A FOOL AGAIN!
NOW, NOW.
I'M SO HAPPY. BUT WILL IT REALLY MAKE IT IN TIME?
THAT'S ALL RIGHT! AFTER ALL...

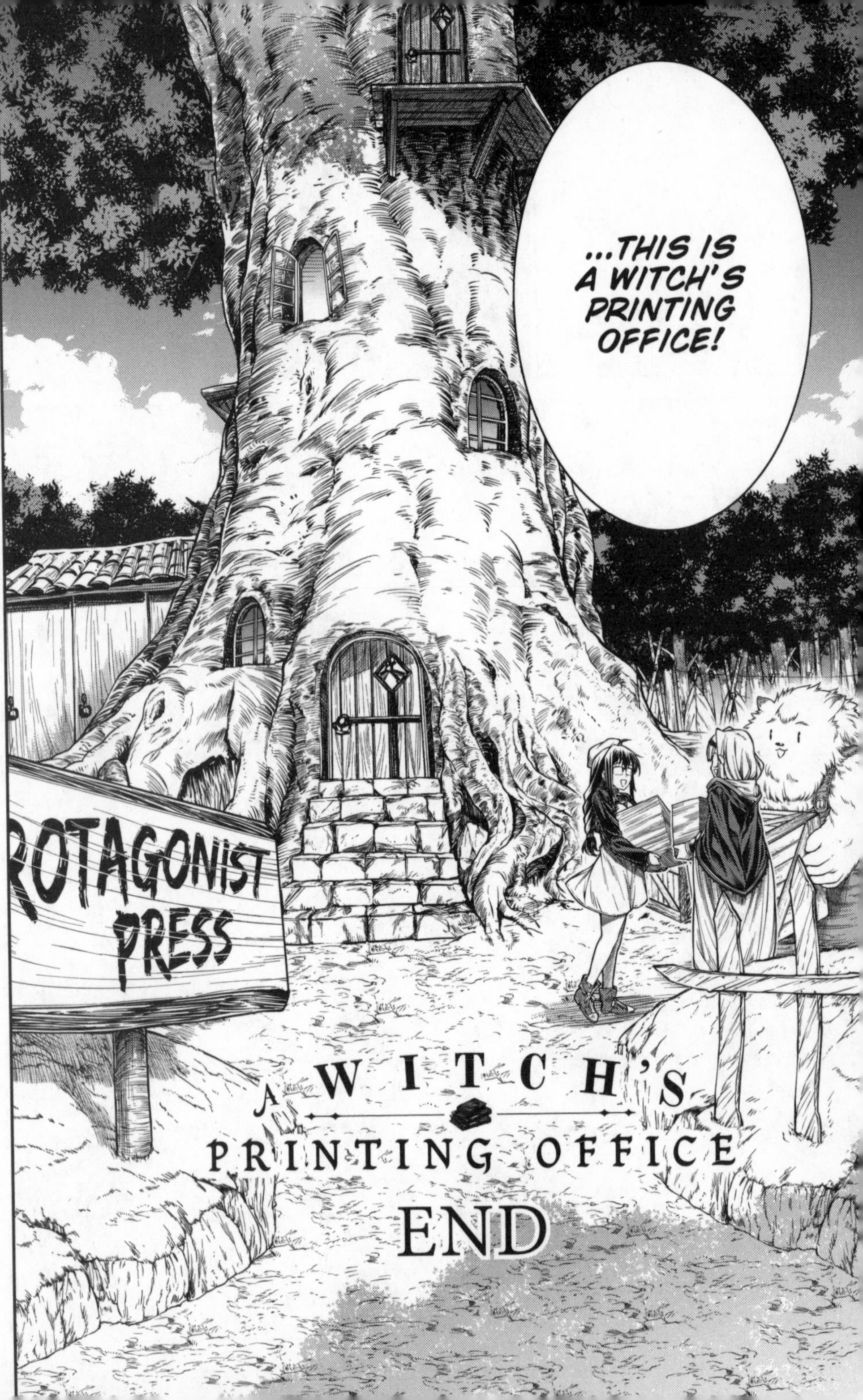
...THIS IS A WITCH'S PRINTING OFFICE!
ROTAGONIST PRESS
A WITCH'S PRINTING OFFICE
END

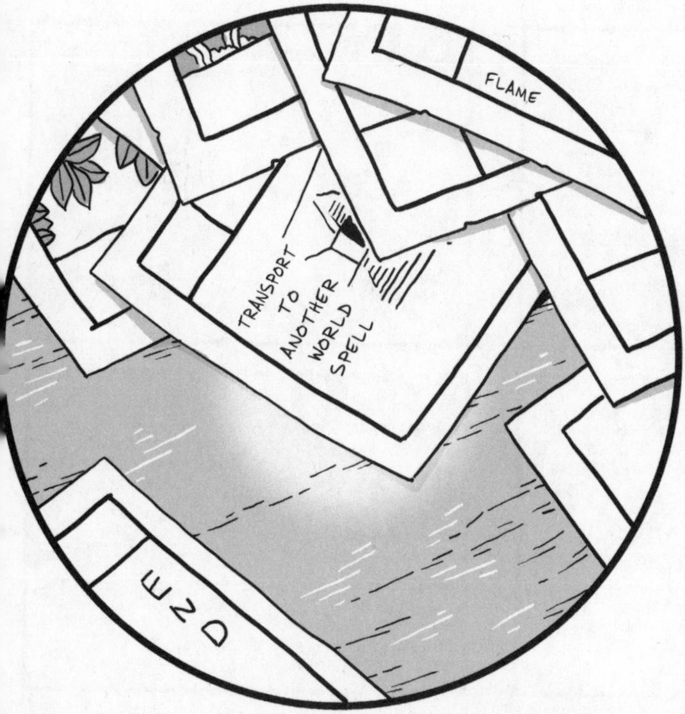
FLAME
TRANSPORT TO ANOTHER WORLD SPELL
END

IT'S THE FINAL VOLUME, BUT LET'S TAKE SOME QUESTIONS

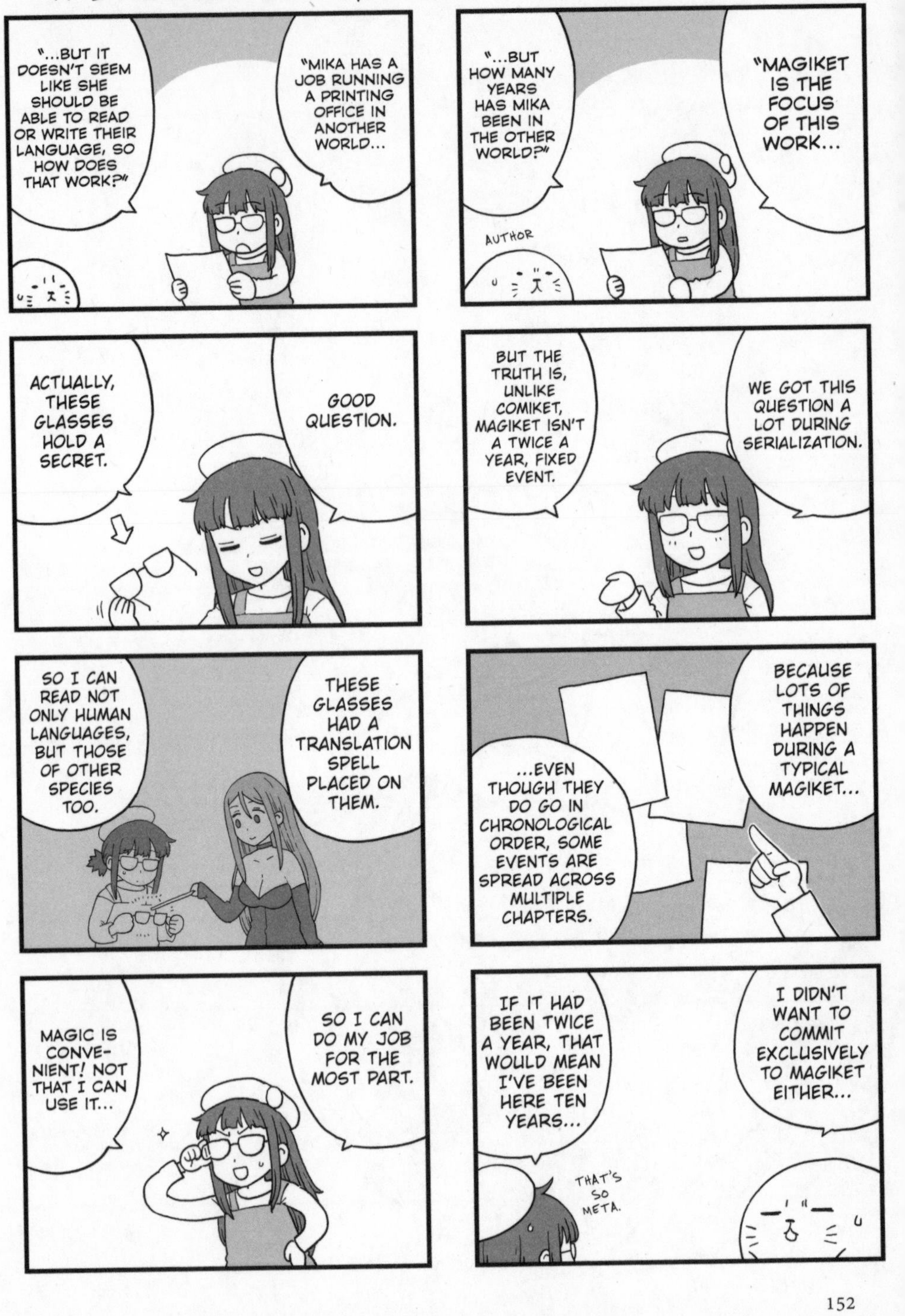
"MAGIKET IS THE FOCUS OF THIS WORK...
"...BUT HOW MANY YEARS HAS MIKA BEEN IN THE OTHER WORLD?"
AUTHOR
WE GOT THIS QUESTION A LOT DURING SERIALIZATION.
BUT THE TRUTH IS, UNLIKE COMIKET, MAGIKET ISN'T A TWICE A YEAR, FIXED EVENT.
BECAUSE LOTS OF THINGS HAPPEN DURING A TYPICAL MAGIKET...
...EVEN THOUGH THEY DO GO IN CHRONOLOGICAL ORDER, SOME EVENTS ARE SPREAD ACROSS MULTIPLE CHAPTERS.
I DIDN'T WANT TO COMMIT EXCLUSIVELY TO MAGIKET EITHER...
IF IT HAD BEEN TWICE A YEAR, THAT WOULD MEAN I'VE BEEN HERE TEN YEARS...
THAT'S SO META.
"MIKA HAS A JOB RUNNING A PRINTING OFFICE IN ANOTHER WORLD...
"...BUT IT DOESN'T SEEM LIKE SHE SHOULD BE ABLE TO READ OR WRITE THEIR LANGUAGE, SO HOW DOES THAT WORK?"
GOOD QUESTION.
ACTUALLY, THESE GLASSES HOLD A SECRET.
THESE GLASSES HAD A TRANSLATION SPELL PLACED ON THEM.
SO I CAN READ NOT ONLY HUMAN LANGUAGES, BUT THOSE OF OTHER SPECIES TOO.
SO I CAN DO MY JOB FOR THE MOST PART.
MAGIC IS CONVE-NIENT! NOT THAT I CAN USE IT...

CULPRIT

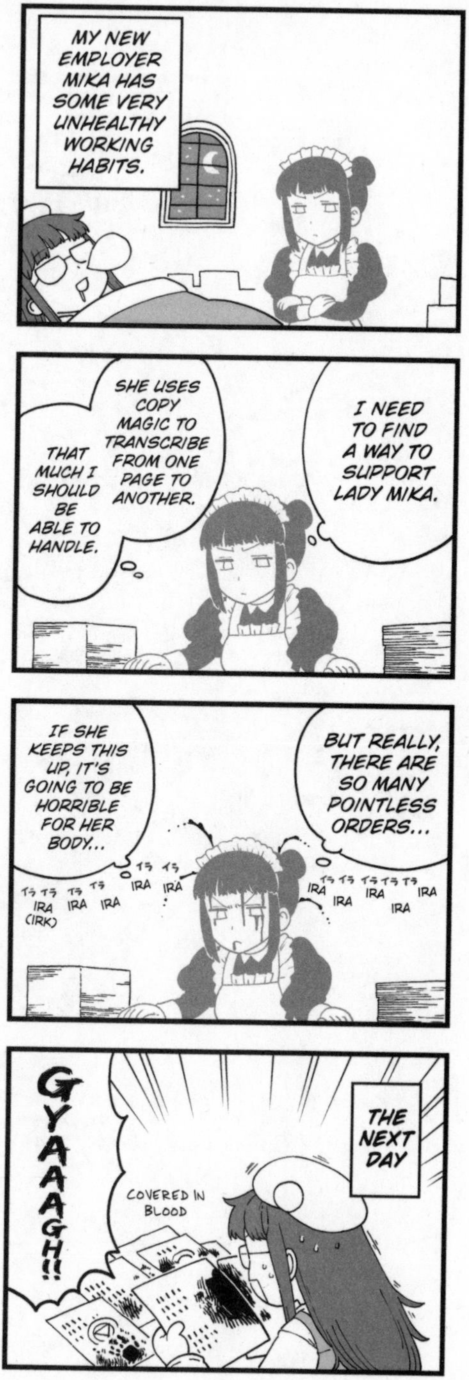
MY NEW EMPLOYER MIKA HAS SOME VERY UNHEALTHY WORKING HABITS.
I NEED TO FIND A WAY TO SUPPORT LADY MIKA.
SHE USES COPY MAGIC TO TRANSCRIBE FROM ONE PAGE TO ANOTHER.
THAT MUCH I SHOULD BE ABLE TO HANDLE.
BUT REALLY, THERE ARE SO MANY POINTLESS ORDERS...
IF SHE KEEPS THIS UP, IT'S GOING TO BE HORRIBLE FOR HER BODY...
イライライライライラ IRA IRA IRA IRA IRA
イラ イラ IRA IRA
イライライラ IRA IRA IRA (IRK)
THE NEXT DAY
GYAAAGH!!
COVERED IN BLOOD

FRUSTRATION AND CUSTOMERS

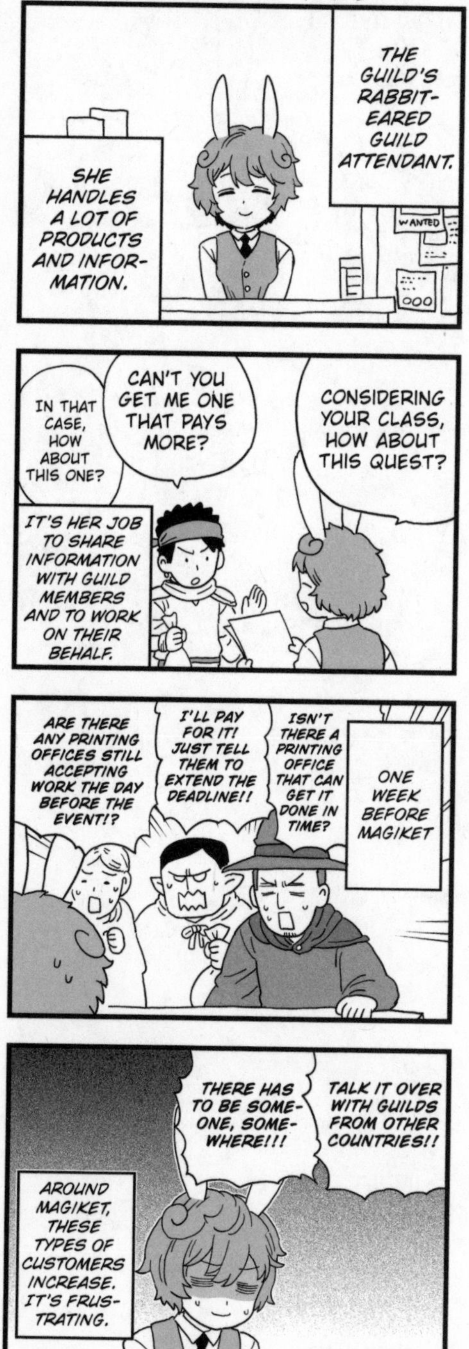
THE GUILD'S RABBIT-EARED GUILD ATTENDANT.
SHE HANDLES A LOT OF PRODUCTS AND INFORMATION.
WANTED
CONSIDERING YOUR CLASS, HOW ABOUT THIS QUEST?
CAN'T YOU GET ME ONE THAT PAYS MORE?
IN THAT CASE, HOW ABOUT THIS ONE?
IT'S HER JOB TO SHARE INFORMATION WITH GUILD MEMBERS AND TO WORK ON THEIR BEHALF.
ONE WEEK BEFORE MAGIKET
ISN'T THERE A PRINTING OFFICE THAT CAN GET IT DONE IN TIME?
I'LL PAY FOR IT! JUST TELL THEM TO EXTEND THE DEADLINE!!
ARE THERE ANY PRINTING OFFICES STILL ACCEPTING WORK THE DAY BEFORE THE EVENT!?
TALK IT OVER WITH GUILDS FROM OTHER COUNTRIES!!
THERE HAS TO BE SOME-ONE, SOME-WHERE!!!
AROUND MAGIKET, THESE TYPES OF CUSTOMERS INCREASE. IT'S FRUS-TRATING.

SAGE DUTY

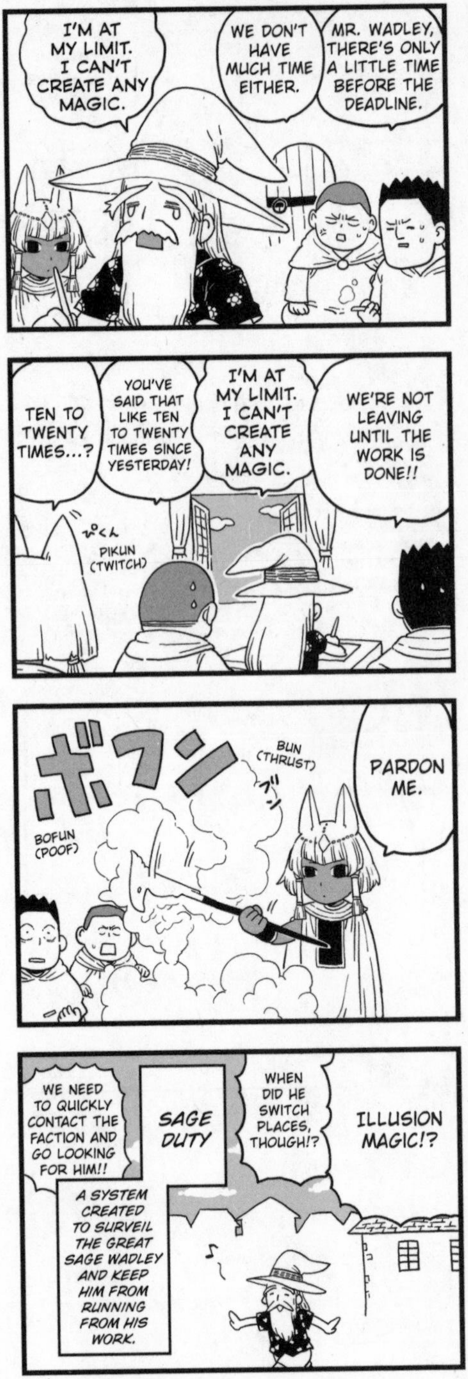
MR. WADLEY, THERE'S ONLY A LITTLE TIME BEFORE THE DEADLINE.
WE DON'T HAVE MUCH TIME EITHER.
I'M AT MY LIMIT. I CAN'T CREATE ANY MAGIC.
WE'RE NOT LEAVING UNTIL THE WORK IS DONE!!
I'M AT MY LIMIT. I CAN'T CREATE ANY MAGIC.
YOU'VE SAID THAT LIKE TEN TO TWENTY TIMES SINCE YESTERDAY!
TEN TO TWENTY TIMES...?
ぴくん
PIKUN (TWITCH)
PARDON ME.
BUN (THRUST)
ブン
ボフン
BOFUN (POOF)
ILLUSION MAGIC!?
WHEN DID HE SWITCH PLACES, THOUGH!?
SAGE DUTY
WE NEED TO QUICKLY CONTACT THE FACTION AND GO LOOKING FOR HIM!!
A SYSTEM CREATED TO SURVEIL THE GREAT SAGE WADLEY AND KEEP HIM FROM RUNNING FROM HIS WORK.

YOU CAN DO IT, BEHJI

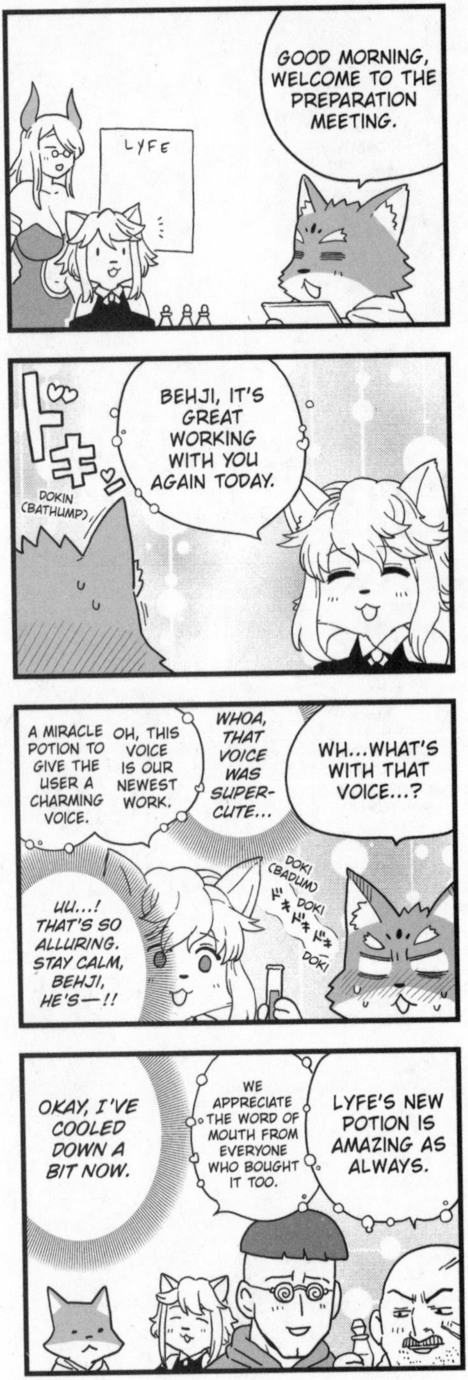
GOOD MORNING, WELCOME TO THE PREPARATION MEETING.
LYFE
BEHJI, IT'S GREAT WORKING WITH YOU AGAIN TODAY.
ドキ
DOKIN (BATHUMP)
WH...WHAT'S WITH THAT VOICE...?
WHOA, THAT VOICE WAS SUPER-CUTE...
OH, THIS VOICE IS OUR NEWEST WORK.
A MIRACLE POTION TO GIVE THE USER A CHARMING VOICE.
DOKI (BADUMP) DOKI DOKI
ドキドキドキ
UU...! THAT'S SO ALLURING. STAY CALM, BEHJI, HE'S—!!
LYFE'S NEW POTION IS AMAZING AS ALWAYS.
WE APPRECIATE THE WORD OF MOUTH FROM EVERYONE WHO BOUGHT IT TOO.
OKAY, I'VE COOLED DOWN A BIT NOW.

HOLY BLADE

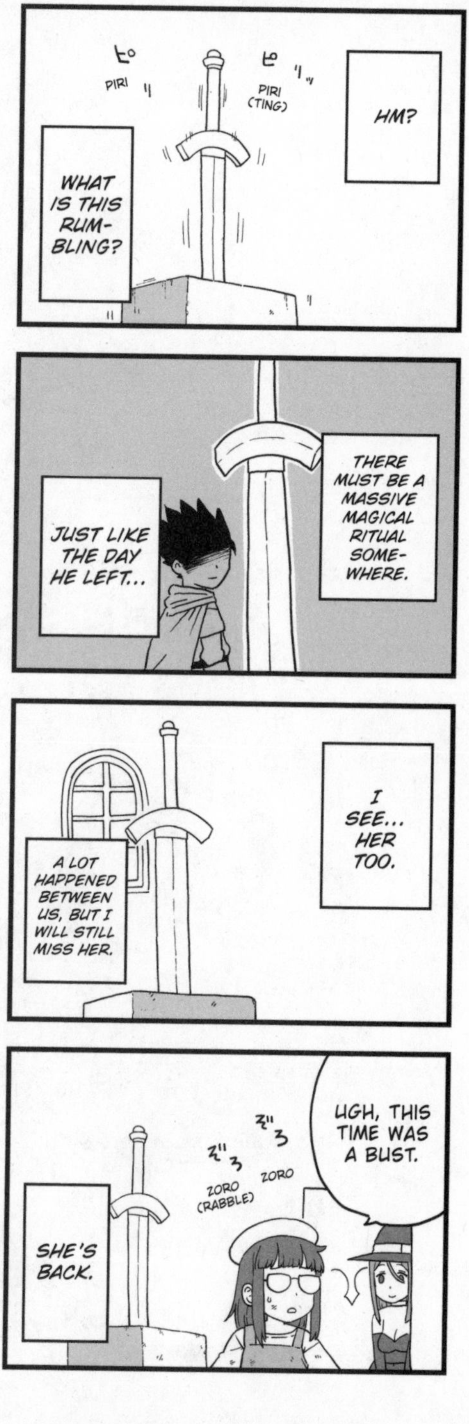
HM?
ピリッ
PIRI (TING)
ピリ
PIRI
WHAT IS THIS RUM-BLING?
THERE MUST BE A MASSIVE MAGICAL RITUAL SOME-WHERE.
JUST LIKE THE DAY HE LEFT...
I SEE... HER TOO.
A LOT HAPPENED BETWEEN US, BUT I WILL STILL MISS HER.
UGH, THIS TIME WAS A BUST.
ぞろ
ZORO
ぞろ
ZORO (RABBLE)
SHE'S BACK.

AFTERWORD

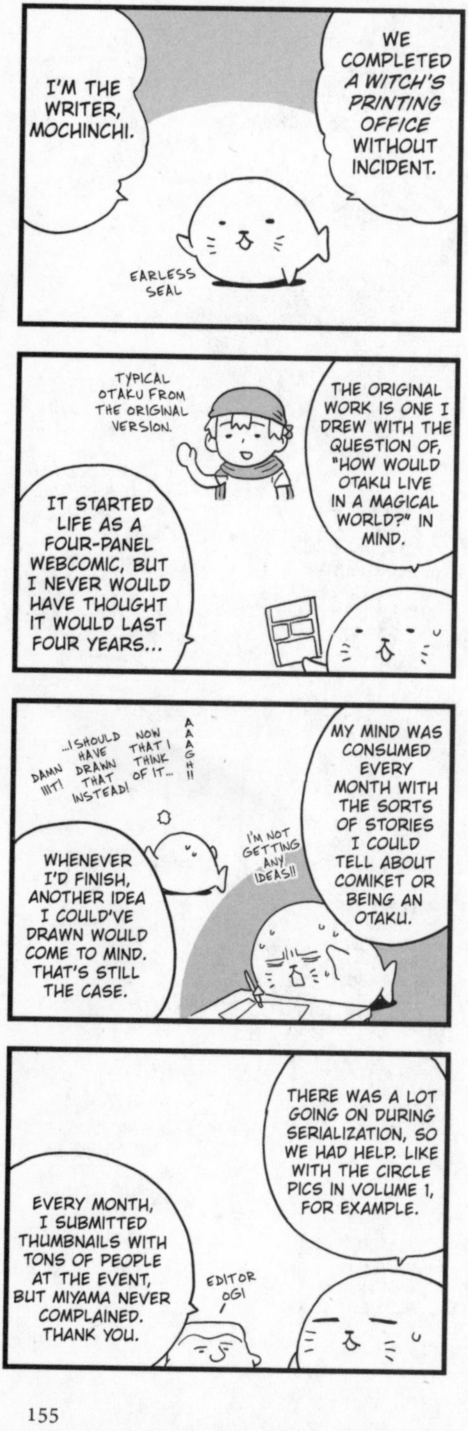
WE COMPLETED A WITCH'S PRINTING OFFICE WITHOUT INCIDENT.
I'M THE WRITER, MOCHINCHI.
EARLESS SEAL
THE ORIGINAL WORK IS ONE I DREW WITH THE QUESTION OF, "HOW WOULD OTAKU LIVE IN A MAGICAL WORLD?" IN MIND.
TYPICAL OTAKU FROM THE ORIGINAL VERSION.
IT STARTED LIFE AS A FOUR-PANEL WEBCOMIC, BUT I NEVER WOULD HAVE THOUGHT IT WOULD LAST FOUR YEARS...
MY MIND WAS CONSUMED EVERY MONTH WITH THE SORTS OF STORIES I COULD TELL ABOUT COMIKET OR BEING AN OTAKU.
AAAGH!!
NOW THAT I THINK OF IT...
...I SHOULD HAVE DRAWN THAT INSTEAD!
DAMN IIIT!
I'M NOT GETTING ANY IDEAS!!
WHENEVER I'D FINISH, ANOTHER IDEA I COULD'VE DRAWN WOULD COME TO MIND. THAT'S STILL THE CASE.
THERE WAS A LOT GOING ON DURING SERIALIZATION, SO WE HAD HELP. LIKE WITH THE CIRCLE PICS IN VOLUME 1, FOR EXAMPLE.
EVERY MONTH, I SUBMITTED THUMBNAILS WITH TONS OF PEOPLE AT THE EVENT, BUT MIYAMA NEVER COMPLAINED. THANK YOU.
EDITOR OGI

TO ALL OUR READERS

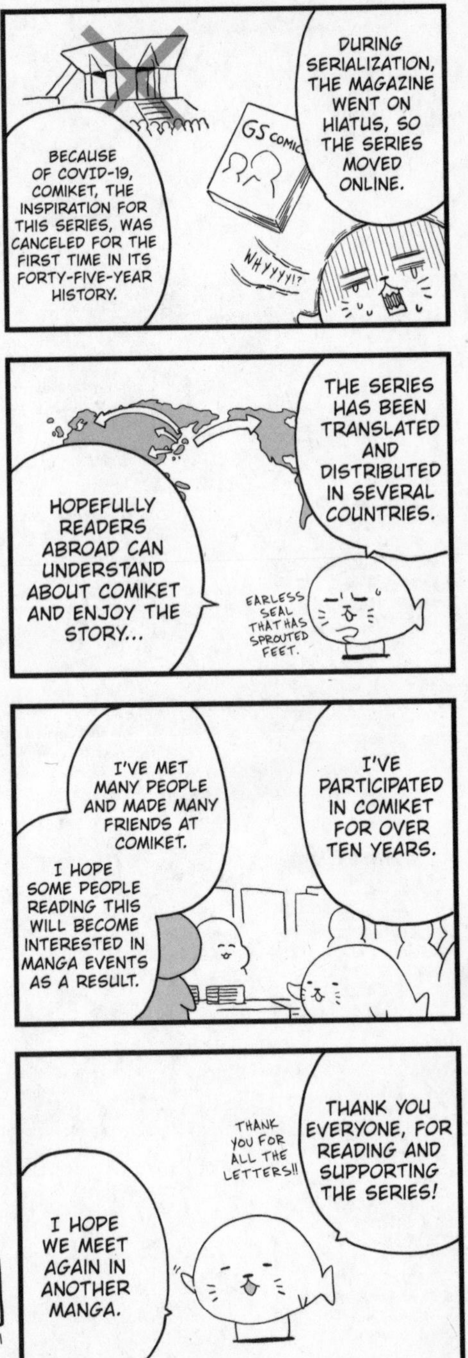

DURING SERIALIZATION, THE MAGAZINE WENT ON HIATUS, SO THE SERIES MOVED ONLINE.
GS COMIC
WHYYYY!?
BECAUSE OF COVID-19, COMIKET, THE INSPIRATION FOR THIS SERIES, WAS CANCELED FOR THE FIRST TIME IN ITS FORTY-FIVE-YEAR HISTORY.
THE SERIES HAS BEEN TRANSLATED AND DISTRIBUTED IN SEVERAL COUNTRIES.
HOPEFULLY READERS ABROAD CAN UNDERSTAND ABOUT COMIKET AND ENJOY THE STORY...
EARLESS SEAL THAT HAS SPROUTED FEET.
I'VE PARTICIPATED IN COMIKET FOR OVER TEN YEARS.
I'VE MET MANY PEOPLE AND MADE MANY FRIENDS AT COMIKET.
I HOPE SOME PEOPLE READING THIS WILL BECOME INTERESTED IN MANGA EVENTS AS A RESULT.
THANK YOU EVERYONE, FOR READING AND SUPPORTING THE SERIES!
THANK YOU FOR ALL THE LETTERS!!
I HOPE WE MEET AGAIN IN ANOTHER MANGA.

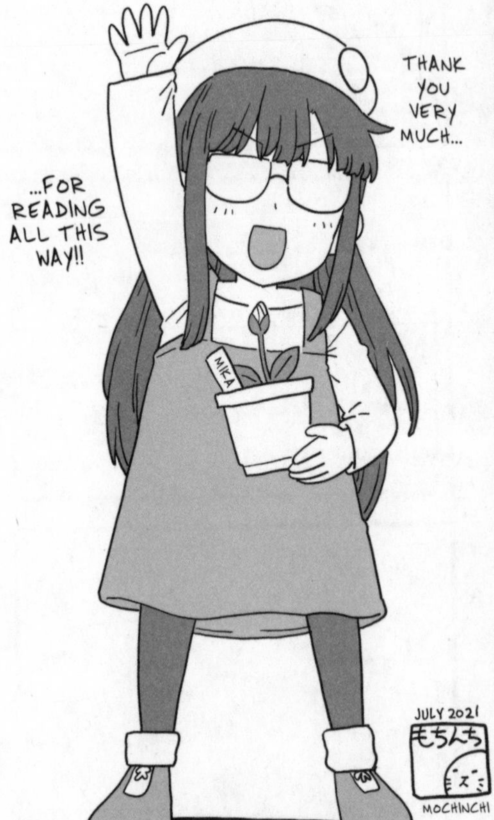

THANK YOU VERY MUCH...
...FOR READING ALL THIS WAY!!
MIKA
JULY 2021
もちんち
MOCHINCHI

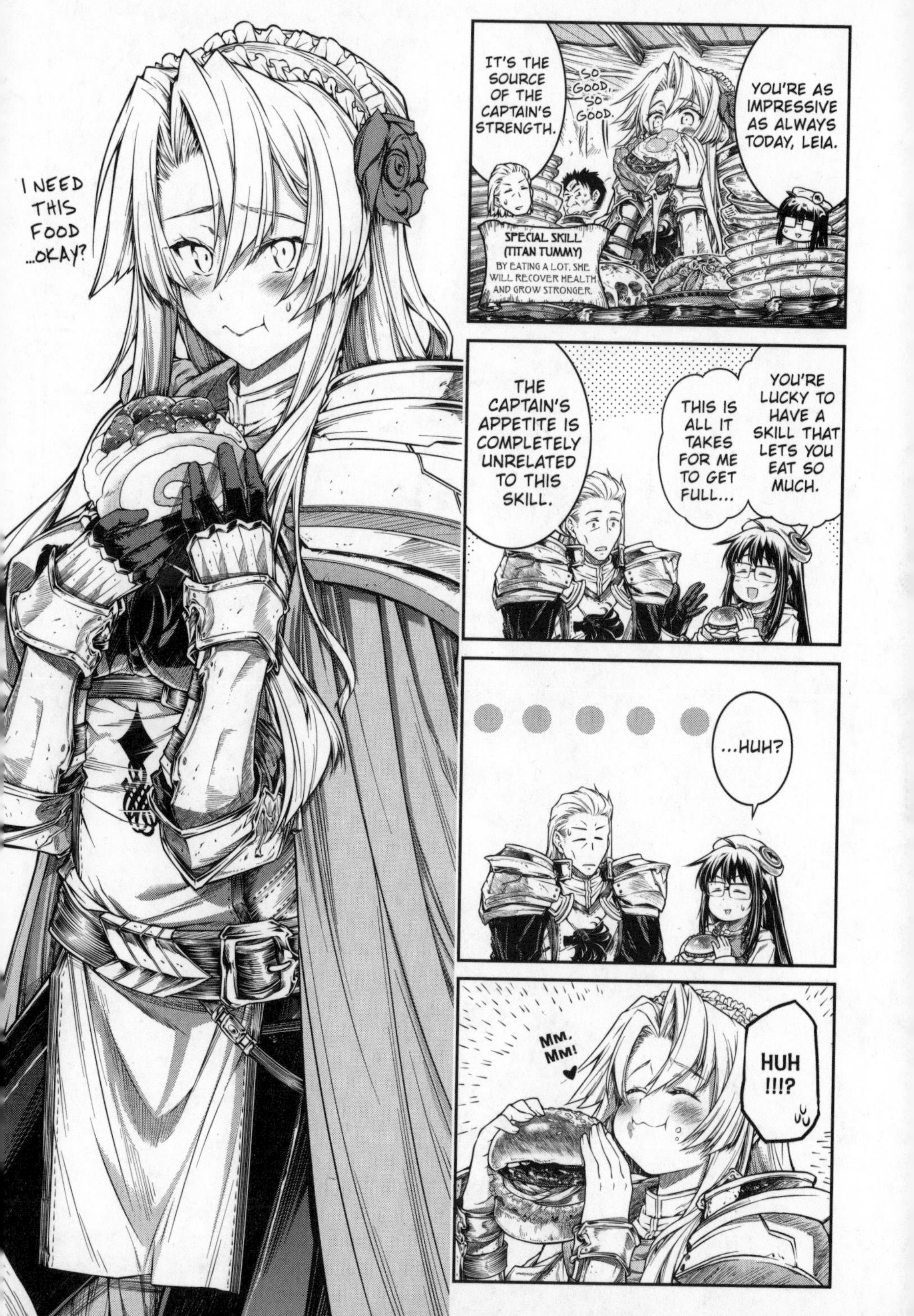
YOU'RE AS IMPRESSIVE AS ALWAYS TODAY, LEIA.
SO GOOD, SO GOOD.
IT'S THE SOURCE OF THE CAPTAIN'S STRENGTH.
SPECIAL SKILL (TITAN TUMMY) BY EATING A LOT, SHE WILL RECOVER HEALTH AND GROW STRONGER.
YOU'RE LUCKY TO HAVE A SKILL THAT LETS YOU EAT SO MUCH.
THIS IS ALL IT TAKES FOR ME TO GET FULL...
THE CAPTAIN'S APPETITE IS COMPLETELY UNRELATED TO THIS SKILL.
...HUH?
HUH !!!?
MM, MM! ♥
I NEED THIS FOOD ...OKAY?

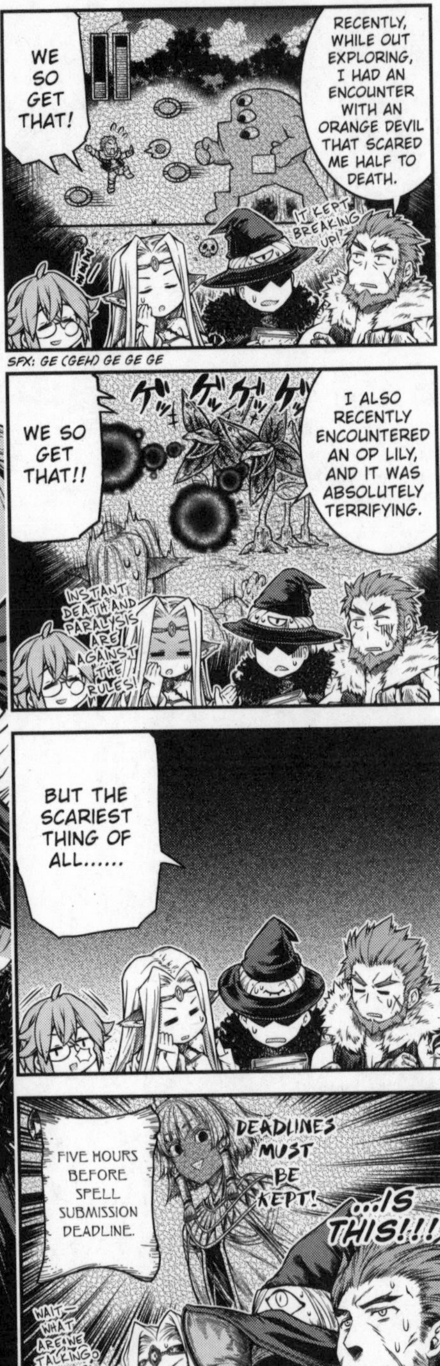
RECENTLY, WHILE OUT EXPLORING, I HAD AN ENCOUNTER WITH AN ORANGE DEVIL THAT SCARED ME HALF TO DEATH.
IT KEPT BREAKING UP!?
WE SO GET THAT!
SFX: GE (GEH) GE GE GE
I ALSO RECENTLY ENCOUNTERED AN OP LILY, AND IT WAS ABSOLUTELY TERRIFYING.
WE SO GET THAT!!
INSTANT DEATH AND PARALYSIS ARE AGAINST THE RULES!
BUT THE SCARIEST THING OF ALL......
...IS THIS!!!
DEADLINES MUST BE KEPT!
FIVE HOURS BEFORE SPELL SUBMISSION DEADLINE.
WAIT—WHAT ARE WE TALKING ABOUT?
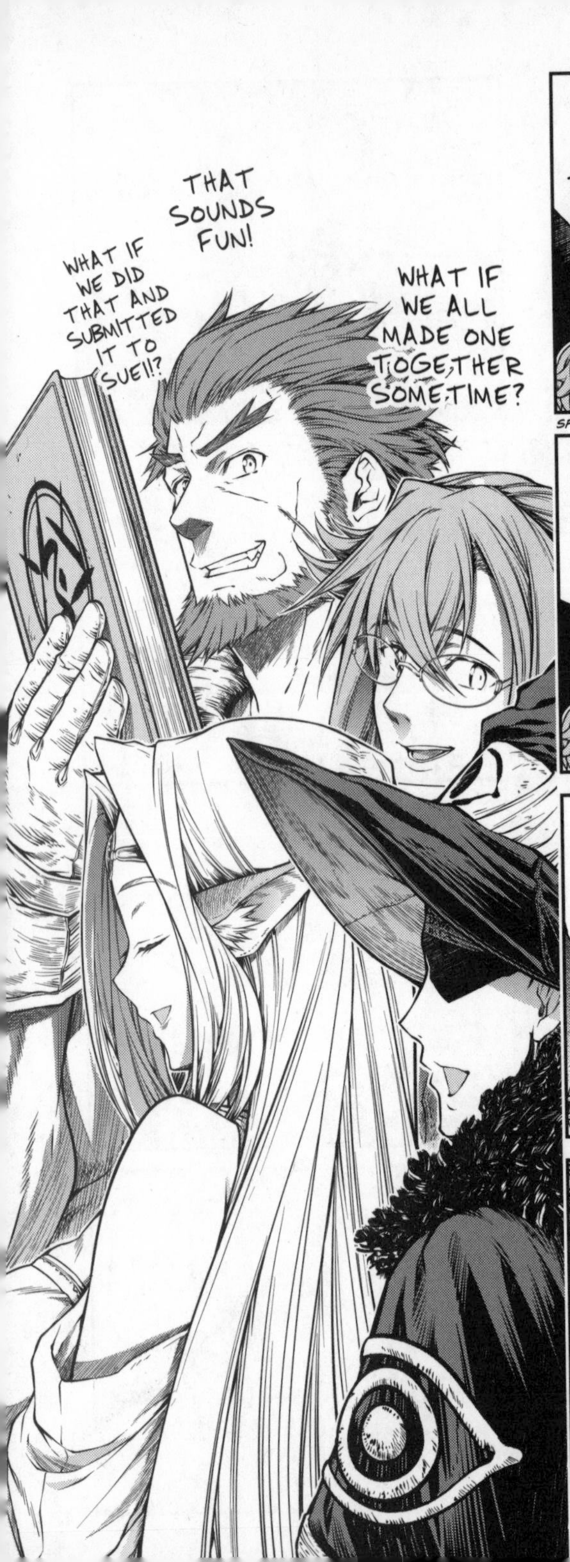
WHAT IF WE ALL MADE ONE TOGETHER SOMETIME?
THAT SOUNDS FUN!
WHAT IF WE DID THAT AND SUBMITTED IT TO SUE!!?

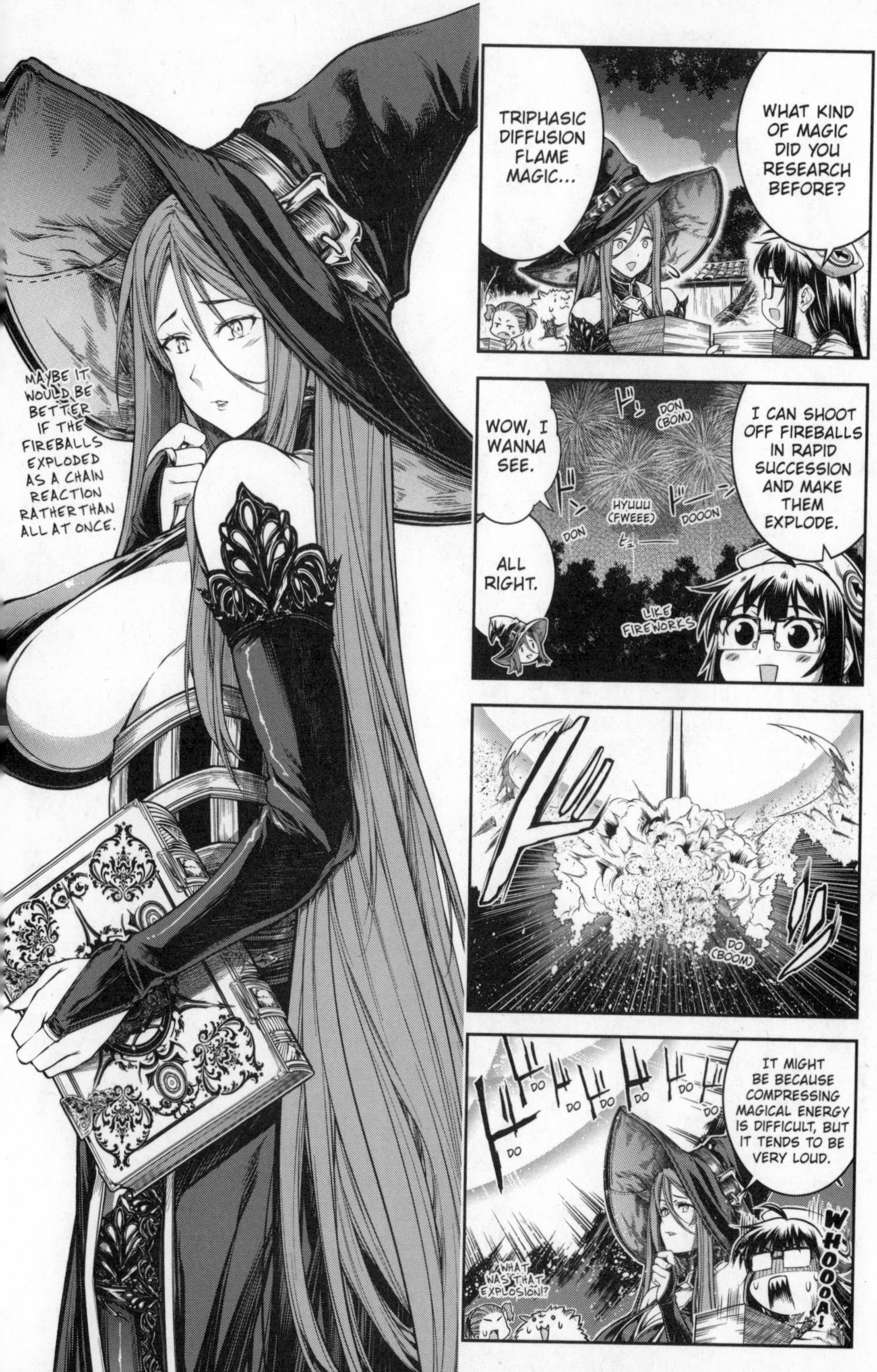
WHAT KIND OF MAGIC DID YOU RESEARCH BEFORE?
TRIPHASIC DIFFUSION FLAME MAGIC...
I CAN SHOOT OFF FIREBALLS IN RAPID SUCCESSION AND MAKE THEM EXPLODE.
DON (BOM)
DOOON
HYUUU (FWEEE)
DON
WOW, I WANNA SEE.
ALL RIGHT.
LIKE FIREWORKS
DO (BOOM)
IT MIGHT BE BECAUSE COMPRESSING MAGICAL ENERGY IS DIFFICULT, BUT IT TENDS TO BE VERY LOUD.
WHOOOA!
DO DO DO DO DO DO DO
WHAT WAS THAT EXPLOSION!?
MAYBE IT WOULD BE BETTER IF THE FIREBALLS EXPLODED AS A CHAIN REACTION RATHER THAN ALL AT ONCE.

BACK PAGE

▉ HELLO. MIYAMA HERE.

THANK YOU VERY MUCH FOR PICKING UP VOLUME 6 OF A WITCH'S PRINTING OFFICE!

EVEN THOUGH I WORKED ON THE MANUSCRIPT, ONCE I WENT BACK AND REREAD THIS BOOK AS A FINISHED PRODUCT, I BURST INTO LAUGHTER AT THE CHARACTERS' FOOLISHNESS AND HIJINKS.

THANK YOU, MOCHINCHI-SAN, FOR SUCH AN UNBELIEVABLY ENTERTAINING MANGA.

I HOPE YOU READERS WERE ABLE TO ENJOY IT AS WELL.

FOR ONE LAST TIME, YOU HAVE THE DEEPEST GRATITUDE FROM THE BOTTOM OF MY HEART.

HANKYUVEYMUH!!